0-36 Months

W9-AOB-201

Growing Child®

Contributors:

Phil Bach, O.D., Ph.D.

Miriam Bender, Ph.D.

Joseph Braga, Ed.D.

Laurie Braga, Ph.D.

George Early, Ph.D.

Carol R. Gestwicki, M.S.

Liam Grimley, Ph.D.

Robert Hannemann, M.D., F.A.A.P.

Sylvia Kottler, M.S.

Bill Peterson, Ph.D.

© 1971-2021 Growing Child, Inc.

P.O. Box 2505

W. Lafayette, IN 47996

ISBN: 0-9729649-0-8

800-927-7289

www.growingchild.com

Preface

Don't be in a hurry to make your children into adults and rob them of the joy of mud and dandelions. The time to put away teddy bears and dolls will come all too soon.

In 1971 a group of people sat around a lunch table at Purdue University to discuss the beginning of Growing Child. This group of developmental professionals—who became our first contributors—helped my son overcome learning disabilities which could have been addressed much earlier had my wife and I been better-informed parents.

The purpose of Growing Child was then and still is to provide parents with a child development newsletter that is timed to the age of their child. We wanted to help parents provide the right kind of stimulation at the right time in the child's development; to alert parents to the typical pattern of development; and to encourage parents to consult with their physician when they had questions about their child's development.

As parents, we hope that each of our children will grow up to be a good citizen, a loving spouse, a cherished friend, a friendly neighbor. Most importantly, when the time comes, we hope our children will be ready for school. But parents don't always know what they can do to help achieve these goals, and many times, no one tells them.

Having a child is one of life's most special events, and this occurs with greater ease, comfort and joy when parents assume their roles with knowledge. No one is at their best when they are living in a state of fear or uncertainty, when they are apprehensive about the well being of their child. When parents know what to expect and have reasonable expectations about their child's development, they can enjoy being a parent.

The chapters of this book are the same as the monthly newsletter issues that our subscribers receive. The best way to use this book is to mark your calendar to read the issue that is appropriate for your child's age each month.

Not every child will follow the same development exactly, but they will be close. While it will be tempting to read ahead and to try and accelerate a child's rate of development, this is not always in the best interests of the child and can lead to frustration for both child and parent.

As grandparents, one of our bits of advice to parents is to enjoy being a parent. Don't be in a hurry to make your children into adults and rob them of the joy of mud and dandelions. The time to put away teddy bears and dolls will come all too soon.

There are many ways to raise a child but the key ingredient is your unconditional love. Children need to feel that they are safe and loved. Hannah Kahn said, "Child, give me your hand that I may walk in the light of your faith in me."

We hope you will learn from Growing Child articles the importance of unstoppable curiosity, enthusiasm for learning, and realistic goals for your child. Enjoy the light.

Dennis Dunn, Publisher

Nancy Kleckner, Editor

Healthy Children Are Ready to Learn

Now is the time to prepare your child for school. Yes, right now, even though it may seem that your work consists mostly of feeding and diapering.

Research studies consistently find that the first three years of life are critical to the emotional and intellectual development of a child.

The effects of this emotional and intellectual development will not be seen, in many cases, until your child reaches the third or fourth grade.

But what you do now will greatly affect whether your child is ready to learn when he or she enters school.

Consider this:

- A child who is held and nurtured in a time of stress is less likely to respond with violence later.
- A child who is read to has a much better chance of becoming a reader.
- A child whose curiosity is encouraged has a better chance to become a lifetime learner.

If you bungle your children, I don't think whatever you do well matters very much.

Jacqueline Kennedy Onassis

The most important period of life is not the age of university studies, but the first one, the period from birth to the age of six.

Maria Montessori

How Development Works

Even before your child is born, all the nerve cells he will ever possess have been formed. These nerve cells are like a mass of unconnected electrical wires. From the time your child is born, his brain will constantly strive to connect the wires.

But what makes the wires connect and what does the connection mean to a growing child?

Every time an infant is held, read to, or plays with a toy, these nerves make a connection.

During the early years of life, these wires are connecting at an amazing pace, and once-in-a-lifetime windows of opportunity are opening to learn certain tasks.

The wiring for sight, for example, is developed during the third and fourth month of life. If the visual system is not stimulated during this time, the ability to form the connections for sight are lost. The same concept is true of intellectual connections in the developing brain.

Until about eight months of age, many things a child can do will be initiated by his own interest. First, he becomes a looker. He shows his curiosity in many ways—interest in your face, in his hands, in feeling his clothing and blankets.

During the period after eight months and until the age of two, every one of the four educational foundations—language, curiosity, intelligence and sociability—is developing.

Introduction

It is important to establish the basic brain wiring during this very early age.

We are not suggesting a program to develop genius, rather, we advocate activities you can initiate to help your child be ready for school and excited to learn. The following list includes some basic ideas.

- Hold your baby.
- Rock your baby.
- Talk to your baby.
- Sing to your baby.
- Most especially, enjoy and respect your child as an individual.

The brain feeds on stimulation. For example:

VISION • In the 1960's Dr. David Hubel and Dr. Torsten Wiesel found that vision does not develop normally in cats if the eye and brain fail to make connections during a critical window of time in early life.

In the test, one eye of the kittens was held closed after birth. After several weeks the restraint was removed and none of the kittens could see out of the eye that had been closed, even though it was perfectly normal.

There are several ways to stimulate vision. Try a mobile over the baby's bed, or black and white picture patterns. Your baby likes to look at objects held about 8 to 15 inches in front of him.

LANGUAGE • Children whose parents talk to them frequently have better language skills than do children of parents who seldom talk to them.

Research studies have shown that babies whose parent talked to them more had a more extensive vocabulary. At 20 months, babies of talkative parents knew 131 more words than infants of less talkative parents. At 24 months, the difference was 295.

BRAIN POWER • Mice and rats raised in enriched environments, with toys and playmates, have billions more connections between brain cells and are better learners than mice and rats raised alone in empty cages.

PLAY IS A GOOD INFANT STIMULATION • Toys do not have to be expensive, and can include pots, pans, and boxes. Toys and books are the tools of childhood.

Dr. Stanley Greenspan's "The Challenging Child," coined the phrase "floor time." It means getting down on the floor and playing with your child. This starts at a very young age and progresses into "Candyland" and kick ball. Raising a child is not a spectator sport. Be involved in play with your child in the lead.

AGGRESSION • Exposure to violence can hinder a child's ability to learn. "Children living with some chronic threat, domestic or community violence or physical abuse, continue to act fearful even when they are in school," said Dr. Bruce D. Perry, director of the Child Trauma Program at Baylor College of Medicine in Houston.

Constant exposure to an unpredictable, threatening environment causes the brain to repeatedly activate the brain systems that respond to threat or stress. Over time, fear becomes so ingrained that it becomes the child's normal state. The result is disastrous for children trying to learn.

A child held and nurtured in a time of stress is less likely to respond with violence later. There is great medicine in a hug.

TOUCH • Touching is the way babies learn. Premature infants whose sensory systems are activated by being held and cuddled are more mentally alert and physically stronger than those who are isolated in incubators.

There are many activities you can play with your child as he grows. The aim can be fun, but many such activities will also help him develop and use his brain.

A Positive Circle

A premise in education is that we learn what matters to us. During these early years, an enriched curiosity and good language skills will lay the foundation for a child. It is a positive circle. The more a child explores and is exposed to new situations, the more that will matter to him, and the more he will want to learn.

A wonderful tradition as your child grows older can begin at your family's dinner table by asking your child, "What did you learn today?" As your child grows, it will be a routine part of the meal. A friend I knew would send her child to the encyclopedia for a morsel of information if she did not come to the table prepared for a discussion.

"A torn jacket is soon mended, but harsh words bruise the heart of a child."

Longfellow

Unique and Special Qualities

It has taken hundreds of thousands of years to arrive at the birth of this very special child. Just think of parents, grandparents and greatgrandparents whose decisions and genes contributed to your child. If just one had moved to another city or country, the entire pattern would have been changed.

In this child, a new individual has been created, born with her own unique set of special qualities.

Your child is now beginning a journey which could span 100 years. The time you spend or don't spend with your child during the first few years can dramatically affect his or her entire life. Make the commitment to know your child. There is no greater gift a parent can give.

It is also important to help all children because many of them will be your child's future friend, fellow employee, neighbor, wife or husband. Every child is our child.

Until you start understanding that everybody's child is yours, the world won't be good for any of our children.

Susan Sarandon

If you could say just one thing to parents, it would be simply that every child needs someone who believes in him no matter what he does.

Alice Keliher

Written by Dennis Dunn, Publisher, and Nancy Kleckner, Editor

Kindergarten Readiness Test

A child who listens:
• To directions without interrupting;
• To stories and poems for five to ten minutes without restlessness.

A child who hears:
• Words that rhyme;
• Words that begin with the same sound or different sounds.

A child who sees:
• Likenesses and differences in pictures and designs;
• Letters and words that match.

A child who understands:
• The relationship inherent in such words as up and down, top and bottom, over and under, little and big;
• The classification of words that represent people, places, and things.

A child who speaks clearly and can:
• Stay on the topic in class discussions;
• Retell a story or poem in correct sequence;
• Tell a story or relate an experience of his/her own.

A child who thinks and can:
• Give the main idea of a story;
• Give unique ideas and important details;
• Give reasons for his/her opinions.

A child who adjusts:
• To changes in routine and to new situations without becoming fearful;
• To opposition or defeat without crying or sulking;
• To the necessity of asking for help when needed.

A child who obeys:
• Classroom rules as established by the teacher;
• Safety rules on playground and school bus;
• Fire drill rules quickly and quietly.

A child who plays:
• Cooperatively with other children;
• Shares, takes turns, and assumes a share of group responsibility;
• Can run, jump, skip, and bounce a ball with comparative dexterity.

A child who works:
• Without being easily distracted;
• And follows directions;
• And completes each task;
• And takes pride in his/her work.

Since 1971 serving millions of families
in the United States and around the

Grandma Says

THANK YOU FOR YOUR CHILDHOOD

In The Giver, the Newberry-award-winning book for older children, as the oldest children are moved on to their assignments for their adult lives, the elder says, "Thank you for your childhood." This little phrase is meant to signify that childhood is now over.

The phrase resonated in my thinking long after I read it. It spoke to me of the often unspoken joy involved in being a parent, and reminded me that it is important to acknowledge what our children's childhoods have done to enrich and expand our own lives.

We hear a lot about the challenges, anxieties, and just plain exhausting work of parenthood. We use words like sacrifice and loss to signify the disadvantages of taking on the responsibility for nurturing a small human. We focus on the time we don't have for ourselves, and the money that is unavailable for exotic purchases, directed as it is for more prosaic things like small sneakers and pediatric dentists.

But I urge you to sit back with me and reflect on all the things for which to be grateful, for which we can genuinely say, "Thank you for your childhood."

- For those first gummy smiles, that pierced right to your heart in the early months, when your child showed how vital you are to his/her sense of well-being.
- For the chance to jump in the waves or roll in the grass and giggle with him, over nothing at all.
- For the occasion to read again your very favorite children books, and watch the delight on her face as she savors the words.
- For the joy of playing Santa Claus, and feeling the vibrating excitement of a young child's anticipation and wonder.
- For the privilege of watching the determination with which your child approached the task of learning to ride that first bike.

Without that childhood you have witnessed, you might not have remembered again

- how humans need friends, and are willing to work hard to acquire the skills of being a friend.
- how we all struggle with our own self-interest and our desire to care for others.
- how the desire to grow and develop is strong within us all
- how we all need comfort when we are feeling afraid and alone.
- how mastering a new accomplishment gives us all a rush of pride and pleasure.

Sit back for a moment and recall some of your favorite memories of that childhood. Think of the times you could see the results of your teaching and training, and how that gave you a secret smile. Remember the times when you were blown away by the uniqueness of your child, surprised by new words or behaviors, wondering where that came from.

Dredge up long ago memories and experiences, and realize how none of that would have been in your mind without this amazing childhood that you have shared. And consider how you have grown as a person, having had the opportunity to be a parent to this child. Sometime today, find a way to say and show that you are indeed thankful for their childhood.

Growing Child Index: Birth to 36 Months

FREE BONUS

Here's how to make this book work for you:

1. Go to www.GrowingChild.com/bonus

2. Complete the subscription form.

3. On your child's monthly birth date, as a reminder, you will receive the Growing Child newsletter, timed to his/her age. (It will be the same or updated copy of the issue in your book.)

4. This Free Bonus goes from the current age of your child until he or she is a senior in high school. You may also add other children to this subscription at no cost.

5. Plus: You will also receive each month the Growing Parent newsletter and essays about "Grandma Says" (twice a month). These publications are brief and easy to read. See samples at www.GrowingChild.com/bonus.

GUARANTEE: All of our newsletters are free of commercial bias with our no-advertisement policy; all addresses are used only to administer subscriptions, and are not disclosed to other individuals or organizations. You may cancel any subscription at any time if it does not meet your needs.

To purchase other books or send a Growing Child gift, go to: www.GrowingChild.com

NOTE: To make certain you continue to receive our e-mail, please add: service@GrowingChild.com and GrandmaSays@GrowingChild.com to your address book or safe sender list.

Growing Child®

If you want children to improve, let them overhear the nice things you say about them to others.

Haim Ginott

Here You Are!

Something new and wonderful has happened to you: You're probably feeling happy, excited, elated, and yes, just a little frightened at the thought of caring for the brand new baby in your home and the responsibility of being a parent.

Don't feel alone. We've just described what is probably a universal reaction to parenthood.

During this first month you're going to be concerned with many things. Most of them will be new situations for you, such as adjusting to Baby's schedules.

But after some of the excitement has died down, you're going to have a lot of questions about the proper growth and development of your child.

Today there's a great deal of research being done on infant development and how to help stimulate it.

The most important period of life is not the age of university studies, but the first one, the period from birth to the age of six.

Maria Montessori

Most research suggests there are lots of things parents can do to help their child develop mentally, physically, and emotionally.

This is the purpose of *Growing Child:* To emphasize the importance of development and to provide you with information to help you learn about your baby and about yourselves as parents.

Growing Child will also help you learn what you can provide for your child so that he or she might develop mentally,

Baby Likes to:
• Suck, sleep and enjoy basic comfort.
• Listen to repeated soft sounds.
• Stare at movement and light.
• Be held and rocked.
• Lift head when lying on her stomach.

Give Your Baby:
• Head support when lifting or holding her.
• The sound of your voice talking and singing.
• Light patterns from a lamp.
• Your arms.

physically and emotionally to his or her fullest potential.

A special note for those of you who have other children: Learning about development is not restricted to a first child. This information is just as important for your second or third child. ∎

The Newborn

Magazines for parents-to-be should publish pictures of newborns more often to better prepare new parents for the shock of seeing their baby for the first time.

One mother told her husband in the delivery room, "Oh, honey, he's beautiful, but we'll really have to love him hard because he's so homely!"

She was right. A new life is beautiful, but newborns are not always the round, perfectly formed babies smiling from the magazine pages.

A newborn's skin is often red and scaling and her little nose is often misshapen or flat. It also may be difficult to see her eyes as they're often tightly closed.

Baby's head accounts for about one quarter of her size. Although this makes her look a little odd, it's a result of normal head and brain development.

It is important during the first few months to provide support for the baby's head while holding or feeding

her, since the muscles which perform this function have not yet fully developed.

Learning head control will be one of the major tasks that Baby will accomplish during the next few months.

From now on the brain will continue to develop, and the rest of the body will catch up.

The typical pattern of development is from the head downward to the rest of

continued on page 6

Baby's Birth Certificate

Be sure to get a birth certificate for your baby. It is legal proof of the date of your child's birth and citizenship.

Throughout life, she will need this proof of identity. It may be required when a child enters school, requests a driver's license, or goes to work.

It may be needed to prove her right to vote, to marry, to draw Social Security benefits, to hold office, inherit property, or obtain a passport to travel in foreign countries.

If the baby is born in a hospital, the staff will see that the necessary information is sent to the local health department or registrar of births.

It's important to select a name for your baby as a name is required for a Social Security card.

If the baby is born at home, the midwife or doctor (or the parent if no one assists at the birth) is required by law to report the birth to the local authorities.

You will be officially notified when the record of your baby's birth is on file. Some states send a copy of the registration.

If any of the information is wrong, be sure to get it corrected immediately.

In some states, the birth certificate is sent only on request and for a fee. There is almost always a charge for a second copy,

so keep your baby's certificate in a safe place.

A birth certificate is legal proof of the date of your child's birth and citizenship.

If you don't receive notice of the proper registration in a few weeks, check on it.

Call the hospital or local health department. Or write to your state health department, which is usually located in the state capital. ∎

The Old-Fashioned Rocking Chair

Was there a rocking chair in your childhood?

Do you remember one of the old-fashioned kind with comfortable arms and a high back to rest your head against?

Rocking chairs are good for anyone, but they seem to have been made especially for parents and babies.

By holding your baby, rocking and talking gently to her, you communicate love, warmth and security in ways that even a newborn baby understands.

Rocking chairs are wonderfully comfortable and relaxing for parent and child, and doctors tell us that gentle rocking

Rocking chairs are good for anyone, but they seem to have been made especially for parents and babies.

improves circulation in the legs. As you rock, the easy to and fro movement stimulates the balance and position sensors deep in Baby's inner ears.

As she lies in the curve of her parent's arm, she feels the movement.

When she is lifted and held upright with her head on your shoulder, she feels movement in a different direction.

If you lay her across your knees on her tummy, she becomes aware of still a different kind of movement.

With each change of position, Baby experiences the rocking motion in slightly different ways. But always her nearness to her parent provides warmth and security as a background for her growing awareness of changing positions and of movement in different directions.

From these experiences, an infant learns how to interpret and to use the sensations produced in her balance centers.

Later the ability to interpret these sensations will help her develop and maintain the balance she will need as she learns to stand and walk.

So, we say ..."long live the old-fashioned rocking chair, symbol of love and learning." ∎

Your Baby's Intelligence

Experts in child development know that the right kind of experiences in infancy and the early childhood years can increase a child's intelligence, and there are many scientific studies which support this idea.

There also are many studies of identical twins reared in different homes. In general, these studies showed that the twin who had the best kind of early experiences had a higher intelligence than the twin who had poor early experiences.

These tests are important, since identical twins come from the same cell, which means their heredity is identical—they have the same genes.

Heredity therefore is not the only factor which determines intelligence. Experience in early life also plays an important part.

In 1939 there was what experts call a "classic study." The results are rather startling, and further support the idea of early experiences.

The study, by H.M. Skeels and H.B. Dye, tells about 13 infants and young children between the ages of 7 months and 30 months who were transferred from an orphanage to a school for children with cognitive delays.

After the transfer, these children were placed in a ward with some older and brighter girls, who started playing with them during most of the time they were awake. Just by playing with these babies, the older girls provided many more experiences and much more stimulation than was provided for the children left behind in the orphanage.

After the new arrivals had been in the ward for some time, the people making the study gave a second intelligence test. All 13 children showed gains in IQ ranging from 7 to 58 points.

As a check on these results, 12 children who stayed behind at the orphanage were given intelligence tests. The differences were amazing: all the children at the orphanage showed a decrease in IQ ranging from 8 to 45 points.

Twenty-one years later, all the children in both groups were located and the differences in their life situations were startling. Of the 13 transferred to the school for children with cognitive delays, all were self-supporting. Of the group that remained in the orphanage, one died in an institution for children with cognitive delays; five were still in institutions.

Heredity is not the only factor which determines intelligence. Experience in early life also plays an important part.

The differences in education between the two groups is just as startling. For the transfer group, the median grade completed (midway between highest and lowest) was the 12th grade, or graduation. Four completed one or more years of college, with one boy receiving a bachelor's degree from a large state university. For the group of 12 who remained at the orphanage, half did not complete the third grade, and none of them went to high school.

Clearly, this study shows the importance of early learning experiences for development of intelligence and for general independent functioning in the world.

Stimulation doesn't have to be packaged or expensive programs, CDs or DVDs. The average home provides activities and an environment that offers stimulation and interest to babies. Most important stimulation comes via language, physical, and eye contact.

A school for children living with cognitive delays is not the best place for giving these early learning experiences, but even in this setting, the older girls who played with the children seem to have given the kind of stimulation that made tremendous differences in the children's later abilities.

This is what **Growing Child** is all about—to help you give your infant the early experiences that can have an important influence on intelligence and independent functioning. ■

Baby Seating

It's now the law in all 50 states that children must be properly restrained while riding in automobiles.

It isn't a pleasant fact, but 1,500 babies and children under the age of five are killed every year in auto accidents, and another 60,000 are injured.

In addition to fatalities, a major concern is permanent brain damage which could have been prevented by a proper child restraint seat.

There are many excellent car seats for children that meet or exceed federal specifications. To obtain up-to-date information, contact the National Highway Traffic Safety Administration hotline at (800-424-9393) or **www.nhta.gov.**

You can write to the American Academy of Pediatrics, Division of Public Education, 141 Northwest Point Boulevard, P.O. Box 927, Elk Grove Village, Illinois, 60007, and ask for an updated list of infant/child safety seats or go to: **www.aap.org/family/carseatguide.htm.**

In many communities, hospitals or civic organizations also have a rental program for car seats.

Watch for free safety checks for proper installation of a car seat. These checks are often offered by fire departments or hospitals. Many seats are improperly installed and therefore not effective.

A car seat can be a real lifesaver, so be sure to buckle up your baby and yourself too. Make every ride a safe ride for you and your child. ■

Baby's Amazing Reflexes

Reflex	Description	Disappearance*
Walking/stepping	When Baby is held upright under his arms, with his head supported, he will lift one foot after another in a walking/stepping motion, provided his feet are barely touching a flat surface.	2 months
Moro/startle reflex	While lying on his back, if Baby is startled by a loud noise, or if his head suddenly drops slightly, he will arch his back, hold back his head, extend his arms and legs and then draw them in toward his body.	2-3 months
Rooting	When Baby's cheek is stroked near the corner of his mouth, he will turn his head toward the touch, open his mouth and make sucking movements. This reflex helps new mothers get Baby started nursing.	4 months
Palmar grasp	When Baby's palm is stroked with a finger, he will immediately grasp the finger tightly.	4-6 months
Tonic neck reflex	When Baby's head is turned to one side while lying on his back, his body will assume a fencing posture, with one arm flexed and the other arm extended on the side toward which his head is facing.	5-7 months
Babinsky reflex	When the sole of Baby's foot is stroked, his toes will first fan out, then curl inward.	8-12 months
Eye blink	Baby immediately closes his eyelids whenever a bright light or a puff of air comes near his eyes. He may blink more often when he is tired or when his sensory system is overloaded.	Permanent

*Not all infants lose these reflexes at exactly the same time, but this table provides general indicators for a "typical" baby.

Baby's Reflexes

Babies are born with an amazing repertoire of over 70 reflexes. Many of these reflexes are needed for survival or are related to later development of the central nervous system.

For example, if you put your finger in Baby's mouth, he will instinctively begin to suck, without having to learn what to do. Even before birth, a baby can be seen, by means of ultrasound, sucking his thumb in his mother's womb.

There are reflexes that remain with us for life, such as swallowing, yawning, coughing, eye blinking and elimination. As Baby's central nervous system develops, some reflexes will simply disappear while others develop into voluntary behaviors. For example, the rooting reflex, (see table above) whereby a newborn will turn his head toward your hand if you stroke his cheek near the corner of his mouth—usually disappears by about four months of age. By then, Baby is able to turn his head voluntarily to a position for

his mouth to begin sucking. So a voluntary behavior now replaces an automatic one.

Although many of Baby's reflexes will have disappeared by the end of the first year, reflexes are more than merely passing curiosities. Tests for abnormality in reflexes form an important part of a baby's diagnostic neurological examination.

Failure of an expected reflex to appear is usually an indicator of some underlying problem. Likewise, when a reflex persists beyond normal expectation, it may be the first indicator of some neurological damage or dysfunction. But the most common reason for doctors to check a baby's reflexes is to make sure that all is well, since reflexes are good indicators of later healthy development of physical skills, such as walking, grasping and feeding.

Although the walking/stepping reflex described in the table usually disappears

around two months of age, a similar behavior re-emerges toward the end of the first year—when leg muscles are able to support the weight of the body—in the form of voluntary efforts to walk.

Observation of a baby's reflex behaviors can also serve as a predictor of future learning. For example, although sucking, swallowing and breathing are each an automatic reflex behavior, it takes time for some babies to coordinate these three reflexes, in order to suck, swallow and breathe at the same time. Not surprisingly, the complex coordination of these three reflex behaviors has received much attention in research studies as a possible predictor of a child's later learning and adaptive abilities.

Although diagnosis of any abnormality in a baby's reflexes should be left to a medical doctor, the awareness and observation of a newborn's amazing repertoire of reflexes can greatly enhance the joys of parenting. ■

How to Communicate With Your Child's Doctor

Communication is not a one-way street. The doctor needs your help to better serve your needs.

When your child becomes ill, the doctor is aware that you are worried and nervous, but to help you, she must have some idea what you are thinking, and she must have facts so she can determine how quickly she must see the child.

The first place to start is with the doctor's receptionist. Get to know her. She knows the doctor's routine and can guide the message. Ask if the doctor has regular telephone hours for questions.

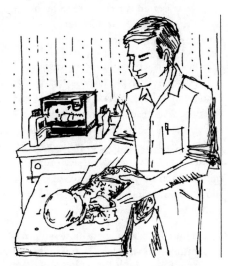

One of the keys to saving yourself and the doctor much time and stress is to clearly state your child's needs. Many times your questions can be answered quickly by the receptionist or a nurse.

Second, when you describe your child's problem over the telephone, be prepared to answer questions.

A checklist follows which gives you an idea of the information needed.

You should come to the telephone prepared with this information.

When talking to the doctor, make your concern very clear. If you're upset, don't be afraid to tell her. ■

Checklist for Calling the Doctor

Check the following situations which are present:

___ Fever which rises or returns after the second day.

___ Unusual physical behavior (Does he appear sick?).

___ Cold associated with earache, hoarseness of voice, shortness of breath.

___ Stomachache with vomiting and /or diarrhea.

___ Severe headache.

___ Sprain with swelling.

___ Head injuries.

___ Swallowed something thought to be poisonous.

___ Deep cuts that might need stitches.

___ Broken bones.

In the case of swallowing poison:

___ Call your local Poison Control Center or the National Poison Control Hotline (1-800-222-1222) immediately. (Keep the address and telephone number of the poison center near your telephone.)

___ Locate the poison container, plant specimen or substance the child swallowed.

___ **DO NOT USE SYRUP OF IPECAC.** It is no longer used to treat poisonings. Some swallowed poisons will cause more damage if you try to cause vomiting.

DO NOT follow directions on the container label until confirmed by the poison center. Antidote instructions may be inaccurate.

Be prepared before calling your doctor:

___ Take child's temperature.
___ Know the specific symptoms.

Examples are:

    ___ Fever
    ___ Runny nose
    ___ Headache
    ___ Nasal congestion
    ___ Cough
    ___ Earache or ear drainage
    ___ Sore throat
    ___ Abdominal or other pain
    ___ Swollen glands
    ___ Rash
    ___ Sore eyes
    ___ Vomiting
    ___ Diarrhea
    ___ Constipation
    ___ Changes in urination
    ___ Changes in sleep pattern

___ Know the name, address and telephone number of your pharmacy.

When calling the doctor:

___ State your name and your child's name and age.

___ Give your telephone number in case you're cut off.

State reason for calling:

___ This is an emergency (leg broken, deep cut, swallowed poison).

___ My child has the following symptoms (list them). I'd like to see the doctor as soon as possible.

___ I would like to make an appointment for a physical examination of my child. ■

Thoughts about Curiosity

the body, and from the center of the body to the extremities (the fingers, for example). As an illustration, in a very short time Baby will learn to watch things.

Her eyes do see from the beginning, but she is attracted by sharply contrasted or colored objects that are close to her.

When you lean over the crib or hold Baby close to you, she does see your features. And she will continue to use her eyes to explore the world long before she can use her entire body to investigate her surroundings.

Right now, Baby may move her arms a little but the fists are usually clenched tightly and the movement is jerky. Later she will develop better control of her arms and bat at things. Still later she will be able to use her fingers to try to grasp objects.

This is another example of development from the center of the body outward (from the whole arm to the fingers). If you allow Baby to grip your finger, you'll be surprised at the strength of the grasp.

Undoubtedly someone has provided a new rattle for Baby to play with. Don't be surprised that Baby won't take it in her hand. Her fists are usually clenched tight during the first few weeks.

If you unlock her clenched fist by unfolding the little fingers, Baby will grasp the rattle placed high in her hand—but only for a moment. Then she'll drop it and show no more awareness of its existence.

Don't be surprised if you see Baby startle at a loud noise, an abrupt change in position or a jolt to the crib. It's perfectly normal for her to startle at any sudden change in environment—this is a reflex babies are born with. They prefer slow movements rather than sudden ones.

You may need to hold her for a minute or two after she startles and cries to reassure her that everything is okay now. ∎

Every baby is born into this world with enormous curiosity and a drive to make sense of the world. You can see this happening when an infant grasps a new object and examines it thoroughly as if this single object will reveal all the secrets of the universe. But, sadly, we know that a few short years later, first grade teachers worry about how to motivate children to learn.

What happens to that innate desire to learn in the few years between? What can parents do to ensure that young children remain inquisitive?

One of the first hazards to curiosity is boredom. Once all the possibilities in a plaything have been explored, babies get bored. Researchers document that after spending long periods of time using every available sense to explore a new toy, babies spend less and less time at each successive encounter.

This reaction shows that the initial curiosity has been satisfied, especially if the toy reacts in the same way each time—-the dog always barks when the baby's hand presses the dog's picture. Baby's decreasing attention span is a sure indication of when novelty is needed.

How do parents keep up with the need to find a supply of new items for explora-

Growing Child®

P. O. Box 2505 • W Lafayette, IN 47996
(800) 927-7289
©Growing Child, Inc.
www.GrowingChild.com

Contributing Authors

Phil Bach, O.D., Ph.D.
Miriam Bender, Ph.D.
Joseph Braga, Ed.D.
Laurie Braga, Ph.D.
George Early, Ph.D.
Carol R. Gestwicki, M.S.
Liam Grimley, Ph.D.
Robert Hannemann, M.D., F.A.A.P.
Sylvia Kottler, M.S.
Bill Peterson, Ph.D.

tion? One suggestion is to find playthings that have lots of open-ended possibilities for exploration, with resulting variable outcomes for the curious child.

The common joke that the child would rather play with the box and wrapping paper than the toy it packaged illustrates the multiple possibilities of these and other objects commonly found in most households.

Kitchen drawers and cabinets, bedroom drawers, and the recycling bin all provide interesting items for exploration, once parents have scrutinized each for size, durability and safety.

Rotating toys is also helpful; when something has been in the closet for a month or two, the child will have additional skills to use in exploring it anew.

Another enemy to curiosity is constant restrictions from exploration. Once babies become mobile, they have new scope for what they can reach and investigate. Since everything in the house is now fair game, parents are challenged both to keep their children safe and protect others' property rights. Often they find themselves saying "no" and removing things from children all day long.

While initially this may encourage more exploration—"I wonder if Mom will take this away from me again"—soon toddlers will settle into a resigned awareness that exploring gets you into trouble.

Rather than thwart curiosity, parents would do well to create areas that are free from verbal restriction. When children are young, it is important to baby-proof all areas of the house so that babies and toddlers can explore freely. In order to protect others' property and have one room that satisfies a family's need for entertaining, one room can be gated off for grownups.

Recently experts have emphasized again the importance of the first years for learning. It is vital that we remember that helping children keep their innate curiosity is a prerequisite for later learning. ∎

Growing Child®

There is more to life than increasing its speed.

Mohandas K. Gandhi

How Can I Tell If My Baby Is Okay?

At one time or another most new parents ask themselves, "How can I tell if my baby is okay?"

Your new baby is important to you—you want the best for her, so naturally you want to be certain she's growing, developing and behaving according to a normal pattern. But unless you've had lots of experience with other very young babies, you have no way to judge what is normal.

Briefly, this is the purpose of *Growing Child*—to guide you in the evaluation of your child in these areas. Because you are vitally interested in how well your baby is getting along, each month *Growing Child* will describe the progress of a typical baby, whom we will simply call "Baby."

Careful study of a large number of infants has given us a great deal of information about the average baby at certain key ages.

Of course, there is really no such thing as an "average" baby since each infant is an individual, but all babies follow a general pattern of behavior and development. Therefore, we can compare any individual baby with this general pattern.

Our discussion begins at the end of Baby's first month. By this time you're more used to having Baby around. She's not so "tiny" and you're handling her more easily.

How does Baby look and act? When you place her on her back, her head may turn far to one side and the arm toward which

she's looking may be outstretched about shoulder level.

The other arm is usually bent with the hand close to her shoulder or the back of her head. Her hands are tightly closed with the thumbs lying inside her curled fingers. Sometimes one fist goes to her mouth.

If you gently turn Baby's head to midposition (looking directly ahead) she will turn it back to the side again when you release it. But if you turn her head to the opposite side and hold it there, she frequently will reverse her arm position by straightening the arm toward which her face is turned and bending the other arm close to her shoulder.

This consistent position of the arms and head in relation to each other is due to a special type of reflex, called the asymmetric tonic reflex, or tonic neck reflex. This response varies in strength from baby to baby and may be difficult to elicit in the very active, alert or fussy child. It disappears at five to seven months of age.

What about Baby's feet and legs? Still on her back, Baby holds her hips and knees bent with her feet turned up at the ankles. Sometimes her heels rest on the bed but more often her thighs are drawn up close to her abdomen with her knees slightly apart. Her feet are close together—sometimes they are crossed.

If you gently press Baby's knees outward, you will feel resistance from

her muscles. If you gently straighten one leg she may resist the pull or kick out vigorously and then return to her usual position.

Sometimes when Baby is awake but quiet (it does happen!) she will move her arms in and out and kick her legs, sometimes both together, sometimes alternately. These movements have some rhythm but are aimless.

At other times if you put her on her stomach when she is awake and active, she alternately bends and straightens her legs in a crawling movement and sometimes pushes her toes against the bed hard enough to move her body.

If you place Baby facedown on her bed, she will turn her head to one side to rest on her cheek. Her elbows are bent and close to her body with her hands near her head. Her legs are drawn up under her into almost a kneeling position with her little bottom humped up.

If you gently turn her head facedown, Baby will lift it enough to clear the surface of the bed, turn it to the side

continued on page 8

At One Month Baby Likes to:
- Listen to your voice.
- Stare intently at faces, especially eyes.
- Be cradled and fed by parent or caregiver.
- Sleep.

Give Your Baby:
- Warm, loving response to his physical needs when he cries.
- Your embraces, cuddling, and your voice.

Ask Your Doctor About:
- Hepatitis B vaccine (Hep B).

The Reasons for Growing Child

Why is it that some bright children don't learn in school even when they try hard? There are bound to be many different reasons, but often it is not possible to know the specific causes for a particular child's problem.

Perhaps an example will make the point clearer. One of the school learning problems frequently seen is the child who gets certain letters or even words "turned around." He may not be able to tell the difference between "b" and "d," or the difference between words such as "was" and "saw."

The problem here is one of knowing the simple directions of "left" and "right." Typically, when a child has this type reading problem, tests imply that he doesn't "feel" the difference between left and right inside his own body.

Children need the proper developmental experiences for good early childhood learning to take place.

Most children have gotten the feel of left and right sorted out inside themselves by the time they go to school. But some have not, and these children are in trouble when they try to learn reading, writing, and math.

Knowing about left and right is something a child begins learning in the very first year of his life, and he refines that learning for several more years. But why do some children learn this while others do not?

The answer, we believe, is that **children need the proper developmental experiences for good infant and early childhood learning to take place.**

Good experiences generally assure that a child will do well in school and in other life situations where he must make judgments and decisions. The example of learning about left and right

is only one instance. There are countless other experiences which a child must have if he is to develop to his maximum potential. And this is what *Growing Child* is all about.

How can *Growing Child* play a role in guiding and assisting parents in that all-important job of child rearing? Here are some ideas:

• **Good developmental experiences do not just happen.** We will spell out for you some of those early experiences which are so essential for your child.

Parents can do things—and fairly simple things—to make sure that their child has the right developmental experiences at the right time. A vast amount of information is available to parents so that they may learn to know, encourage and appreciate the skills, characteristics, and personality of their child. *Growing Child* is one of those resources.

• **Parents need support as they enter the world of parenting and undertake what is probably the most challenging and important job they will ever do: raising a child.** The more you know about a task, the easier it becomes and the more competently you perform.

The same thing is true of raising children. When parents are confident that they are doing the right things to encourage their child, they project a positive, can-do attitude.

Listening, watching and reading information about children and how they develop is an excellent way for parents and other adults to understand what children are capable of doing as they grow and develop.

Knowing what is going on and what to look for can give parents the confidence they need to play an active role in their child's life. Information gives power and it helps build parents' self-confidence.

• **Often parents receive conflicting advice and information about their child's growth and development, and**

it isn't necessarily based on knowledge or practices. In the next few months and years you will be laying the developmental foundations for the whole life of your child.

As his parents, you will control the experiences of infancy and early childhood. Make sure you are reading and keeping up with your baby. When it comes to your particular child, you are the expert! Over time and with experience, no one else can match your knowledge of your child.

• **Today's parents are often pressured to push their child, to compare the child with other children, and then to compete with other children and their families.** Information about your child's development can help you relax and focus on your child's abilities and interests.

You need to know what to do and when to do it so that you can give your child the best possible start on his or her grand journey into life itself. *Growing Child* is here to help. ■

continued from page 7

again and drop it. Does Baby see you or know you are there? Sometimes she seems to stare at a far wall or window without really focusing her eyes. But if you lean over her closely, talking to her and smiling, she usually will stop staring and watch your face. More later about what she does "see."

Just a couple more points—if you take Baby's hands and gently pull her up by her arms as if you were going to pull her up to a sitting position, her shoulders lift but her head lags completely behind.

And what about those little hands? If you open her fingers (if you can!) and place the rattle against her palm, she'll grasp it for a moment but then drop it. ■

Vision: Order or Disorder?

What does your new baby see when he turns that puckered little face to you and the world? We used to think the infant's world was a jumbled blur of lights and noises, a "great blooming buzzing confusion," as one famous thinker called it.

Thanks to some careful experiments we know that even very young infants can make some order out of the confusion around them. For instance, they will spend much time looking at face-like drawings, and they prefer to look at certain kinds of designs (such as stripes rather than solids) as though some forms have greater meaning or interest for them than others.

From this we might determine there are ways to give your baby some pleasant experiences, ways to make his surroundings more interesting and enjoyable.

The research findings go even further. They show that the right kind of "enrichment," including special experiences for looking, can make a big difference later on in the mental and social growth of your child.

The trick is in knowing what your baby's basic abilities are at each stage of his development and then giving him the opportunity to use and expand these abilities fully.

But we are about to get ahead of our story. Let's go back and look at the baby who is less than one month old—your baby.

Right now he is very nearsighted. Like a camera which is focused for close-ups, his eyes see clearly only those things about 8-12 inches from his nose.

It is very important to note that eight inches is about the distance from Baby's eyes to your eyes when he is being held in your arms during feeding. That eye-to-eye contact is an important part of the development of the social relationship between parent and child. As we

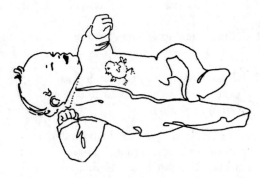

shall see, there is also another important object he sees.

His farsightedness is caused by the same automatic focusing mechanism that lets you see clearly at close range or in the distance. But whenever the baby's eyes are open, his focus adjusts itself to about eight inches. This means that anything closer or farther away than eight inches will be blurred and indistinct.

All of this may seem strange to an adult who is used to seeing many things clearly at many different distances; but for the newborn, it is nature's plan to give his vision a good start in its vital early development, because it happens that eight inches is also the distance of the infant's outstretched hand! This is the second important object he sees which we just mentioned.

It works like this: In a world where most objects are far away and out of reach, the infant's hand, first of all, provides a stable and dependable object which he can look at.

Secondly, one eye and then both eyes must learn to stabilize upon a point or object, and this is the hand. This is important because control of eye movement and two-eyed vision with depth perception are necessary later on for the learning process and the management of objects.

These are things which distinguish humans from animals.

You might now be eager to help this process with objects of your own for the baby to look at. But notice how completely nature is ahead of you, even at this early stage: even the matching of hand with eye has been done by inborn reflexes.

You will remember the asymmetric tonic reflex we mentioned earlier? This reflex (also called the tonic neck reflex) is very handy for putting the hand into position for the eyes to see.

Remember how Baby will turn his head to the outstretched arm? It may not be a coincidence that the reflex disappears about the time the nearsightedness disappears.

The first month, then, is a time for watching and waiting. Your baby's activities are guided by his reflexes, and he has few unoccupied moments for you to capture his attention. Next month he will sleep noticeably less, and you can begin to bring the outside world a bit closer to him.

In the meantime, here is one simple way to exercise his vision and the reflexes that go with it. Place Baby with his head at one end of the crib one day, then the next day turn him around so that his head is at the other end, and so on, back and forth. This will cause light from the window to fall upon him from opposite sides on alternate days.

Baby will get practice in turning his head both ways toward the light source, and this will in turn exercise his tonic neck reflex equally on both sides.

In addition, it is a first step toward developing the sense of two different sides of the body, an appreciation of external direction, and even a primitive sense of time.

All of these will be important to later learning. ∎

Your Emotional Well-Being: Understanding the Blues

The "baby blues" is a mild depression that many women experience soon after their babies are born. These blues can be caused by hormone changes as well as by the personal challenges that a woman goes through after childbirth. They are sometimes called the "third-day blues" because they happen most often from the third or fourth day to the first or second week after delivery.

Understanding postpartum depression

The baby blues can be a normal part of the postpartum process. But you should be aware that some women experience a deeper, more serious depression. How is this depression different from the "blues"?

• **It lasts longer.** Any depression that lasts beyond 2 to 3 weeks could be post-partum depression.

• **It starts later.** The baby blues tend to start soon after delivery. A depression that begins in the third week or later (even up to several months after birth) could be a cause for concern.

• **The depression is stronger.** In addition to experiencing anxiety or doubt, a depressed mother may feel very alone, vulnerable, or completely overwhelmed by the experience of parenthood. She may believe that there is something truly wrong with her abilities as a mother. She may start to distance herself from her partner, family, and friends.

• **The symptoms are more varied.** The mother may experience headaches or bowel problems as well as the insomnia, confusion, sadness or fear of the "blues." She may even have trouble producing breast milk.

It is very important that you pay attention to your moods and emotions after you've had your baby. The earlier you catch postpartum depression, the easier it can be to recover.

It is very important that you don't try to take care of everything on your own. If your family or friends can't help, your health care provider should be able to recommend resources.

You can get help with your physical needs—yours and your baby's health, child care, housework, or financial help.

Help is available, too, for your emotional needs—discussion or support groups, for example, or a personal counselor and/or psychiatrist who will pay attention to your distress, listen to your needs, and who may prescribe antidepressant medication if you agree. ∎

You May Have The Baby Blues If:

• **You cry often,** and not always for a reason you can understand.

• **You feel tired,** or you don't have the energy you need to get through the day.

• **You have insomnia,** which can mean that you have trouble falling asleep or trouble sleeping through the night (even when you are not awakened by someone) or that you wake up too early in the morning and can't fall back asleep.

• **You have trouble concentrating**, or you often feel confused or distracted.

• **You often feel irritable or angry,** sometimes for no reason.

• **You don't feel hungry** and are losing weight too fast, or you are often hungry and are gaining weight you don't want or don't need.

Don't let these blues get you down. They may last from several days to a week or more, but they almost always go away by themselves.

Be open with your partner, family, and friends about your concerns. Ask them to help you with housework or child care until you feel better. And most important, be realistic about motherhood: about how fast you will recover or learn mothering skills, about how much rest you need, about the support you need and deserve from others, to name a few.

If the blues last more than two or three weeks and start to seriously interfere with your life, speak with your health care provider. ∎

Test Yourself

Am I Blue?

Many new mothers feel anxious, sad or angry about the changes in their lives after the birth of their new baby.

It is perfectly normal to feel this way, but sometimes the feelings grow so strong that they make life difficult.

This quiz lists many feelings and experiences of "blue" or depressed mothers. Mark how strong each of these feelings or experiences is for you, compared to what is normal for you.

For example: do you feel no anger [0]; mild (very little) anger [1]; moderate (some) anger [2]; or severe (very strong) anger [3] compared to the way you usually feel?

Add up your total score when you're finished and discuss the results with your health care provider.

Score:

0—31 = MILD BLUES
This will probably pass, but pay attention to your feelings and needs.

32—64 = MODERATE BLUES
You may want to ask for help from a close friend or family member, or ask the advice of your health care provider.

65—98 = SEVERE BLUES
You could be depressed; see your health care provider for a checkup and advice as soon as possible.

0 = Not there at all 1 = Mild 2 = Moderate 3 = Severe	0	1	2	3
Anger				
Anxiety attacks: periods of very strong fear, shortness of breath, rapid heartbeat				
Increased or decreased appetite and/or weight gain or loss that doesn't seem normal				
Strong feeling that you need to get away, need more time for your own interests				
Problems in a relationship with a family member, lover, close friend, etc.				
Crying spells				
Less interest in your personal appearance				
Less motivation—less energy or interest in accomplishing goals				
Depression				
Fatigue—feeling tired or exhausted				
Fear of harming yourself or your baby				
Loss of your sense of humor				
Nervousness, feeling tense or edgy				
Feelings of guilt				
Feelings of panic				
Feeling alone or lonely; without the support of others				
Feeling no love, or not enough love, for your baby				
Feeling forgetful, distracted, absent-minded—having trouble concentrating				
Frustration				
Hopelessness				
Insomnia				
Feeling irritable, bad-tempered				
Loss of sexual desire and/or pleasure in sex				
Loss of self-respect or confidence—feeling like you don't count or can't do anything right				
Feeling confused, uncertain				
Mood swings—your moods and emotions change all the time				
Obsessive thoughts—ideas or feelings you can't stop from repeating in your mind				
Odd or frightening thoughts—thoughts or images that scare you or that you can't control				
Thoughts of suicide, feeling like you want to die				
Feeling sad, unhappy				
TOTAL				

Talk To Your Baby

Today many scientists tell us that a baby is born with all the equipment needed to understand speech and learn to talk. What happens after he is born depends upon what his parents and family—his first community—do to enrich his life and his verbal experiences.

The first sounds he makes are cries, his response to body feelings such as hunger, pain or other discomfort.

At first, when Baby is content, he sleeps much of the time. Soon, however, he will begin to make sounds of contentment.

When you attend to the different sounds of contentment or discomfort, you are helping to establish a communication system which works like this: One person makes sounds and another person does things in response to those sounds.

The infant's inborn gifts also include a tendency toward listening and responding to the sounds he hears. Newborns are known to respond to sudden, loud noises by moving their entire bodies at once; or their breathing or heart rate increases.

Biologists think the infant, like the very young animal, is born to respond to a wide range of sounds which aren't specific. However, very quickly his response becomes more specific to the sounds he hears from his parents. He learns to associate a soothing voice with a smiling face, caresses, and loving words.

Parents and other caregivers continuously talk to their babies during bathing, feeding, dressing and playing. This talk is definitely important in shaping the child's future communication skills, and language is one of the most important of those skills.

Much research deals with infants who are raised in hospitals and institutions. This research shows that these babies are delayed in some areas of development, but they are especially delayed in their listening habits. While they listen to all the sounds around them, they do not learn to choose between important and not-so-important sounds.

While they may receive good medical and nutritional care, they do not receive the tender, loving talk from a parent or other loved ones, and this in turn affects the way they respond to the people and sounds about them.

So, even in infancy, there are two groups of factors that will continue throughout the child's growth: (1) the child utters sounds and responds to the human voice; (2) his parents and other adults respond to his sounds and talk to him.

If either of these conditions is impaired, the child's language development will be affected.

Parents can learn to differentiate the different sounds of Baby's cries and to interpret the message as they and their child interact.

We can understand how a hearing defect will seriously interfere with a child's language and speech development, but we should also realize that the absence of tender loving talk will be almost as serious a handicap.

Parents—talk to your baby! ■

Growing Child®

P. O. Box 2505 • W Lafayette, IN 47996
(800) 927-7289
©Growing Child, Inc.
www.GrowingChild.com

Contributing Authors

Phil Bach, O.D., Ph.D.
Miriam Bender, Ph.D.
Joseph Braga, Ed.D.
Laurie Braga, Ph.D.
George Early, Ph.D.
Carol R. Gestwicki, M.S.
Liam Grimley, Ph.D.
Robert Hannemann, M.D., F.A.A.P.
Sylvia Kottler, M.S.
Bill Peterson, Ph.D.

Baby Tales

Dave went in to look at his sleeping newborn daughter ... and she just about scared him witless. A person has got to be pretty hard boiled not to be moved by the sight of a sleeping baby, especially if she is his own.

Dave found this to be such a nice experience that after tiptoeing in to look at his four-week-old daughter, he quietly moved the chair to the side of the crib, sat down and just watched.

All was quiet. He watched the gentle rise and fall of the baby's chest, and he studied her features.

Then wham, suddenly there was a violent spasm in which both arms flew out, the legs flexed and the baby's head went back on the mattress. The spasm was in such utter contrast to the bliss of the moment before that Dave nearly jumped out of the chair himself, but in a second all was peaceful again. Just as though nothing has happened.

Dave watched for a while and sure enough, it happened again just as surprising as the first time. It was as almost as though the baby was going to fly up from the crib.

This time, Dave was definitely shaken. He got up and did a quick and quiet retreat and rushed out to consult with the expert, the wise one, the keeper of infant secrets. His wife.

The wise one was wise enough not to laugh, but she smiled rather broadly. "It's called startling," she said. "All babies do it during the first few months of life. Scares the pants off of you, doesn't it?"

Now Dave smiled, and said he was going to watch for it again. What he did not say was that he had been convinced for a terrible moment that his daughter had some serious nervous affliction.

But all babies do it, his wife had said. Huh. Dave was sure nobody's baby ever did it the way his kid did. ■

12

Growing Child®

The most precious thing a parent can give
a child is a lifetime of happy memories.
Frank Tyger

Two Months Old

Your baby still seems very small and helpless at two months old, but you can begin to feel a difference as you hold him.

He seems to be more compact and somehow more of a person.

Actually, during the past month, your baby has been occupied full time in getting used to his new, open-air world.

Most of this adjustment has involved his newly functioning organs, such as lungs and digestive system, which have developed and strengthened as he ate, cried and slept.

When you think about it, Baby has been awfully busy for such a little person.

A month ago your baby seemed always to be "half awake" or "half asleep." Now the difference between sleeping and waking is more defined; he is much more active and alert.

He looks at things and really seems to be studying them. When you lean over him closely, he really looks at you. He has more time to absorb the sights, sounds and feelings of his new world.

At two months, when Baby is lying on his back, he may still keep his head turned to one side, but not as much as before.

The arm toward which his face is turned may still be stretched out and his other arm bent at the elbow with the hand held near his shoulder.

His hands are still closed but he is gaining control of his eyes and head. Instead of fixing his eyes on a large mass such as a window or wall, Baby now looks at his outstretched hand or your moving hand, following it briefly.

When you dangle a bright-colored object over him, his eyes pick up the movement and he turns his eyes and head toward the midline of his body to focus on the object better. More about this later.

Baby shows this improved head control in other ways. When you hold him up to your shoulder, his head no longer rests limply against you. He lifts it from time to time in a bobbing motion.

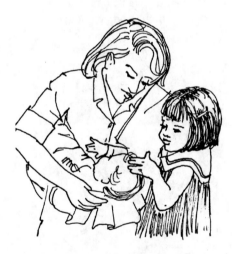

When he is lying on his tummy, Baby's arms and legs are still usually drawn up to his body but not as tightly as a month ago. He lifts his head further off the bed and holds it up briefly.

As yet this lifting is limited to the head. His upper chest still remains on the bed. But with this improved head and eye control, Baby's range of vision widens.

These changes may seem rather slight when put in words, but during the first two months of life, Baby has been very busy.

At Two Months, Baby Likes To:
- Listen to sounds.
- Look at her hands.
- Hold her head up and follow moving objects with her eyes.
- Smile and be smiled at.

Give Your Baby:
- Soft, safe toys to feel and scratch.
- An opportunity to develop head control by frequently placing her on her stomach.
- Your voice.
- Your smiles.

Ask Your Doctor About:
- DTaP vaccine (diphtheria, tetanus, acellular pertussis).
- IPV (inactivated polio vaccine).
- H influenza type b (Hib) vaccine.
- Hepatitis B vaccine (Hep B).
- PCV (pneumococcal conjugate vaccine).
- Rotavirus vaccine (Rota).

He suddenly entered a brand new world and has been occupied full-time in learning to live in it.

Breathing, sucking, and swallowing had to be stabilized.

His brain and nervous system have been receiving and recording countless new sensations, all of which will serve as the foundation for his later learning experiences.

Everything Baby does is pointed toward greater accomplishments to come. ■

Settling into a Schedule

What is an infant's life? It's a bundling in blankets, a blurring of faces, sleeping, awakening, crying, being fed. And then the same thing all over again. And parents know well that as the events in an infant's life begin to happen at the same times each day, everything gets easier. But the settling of a baby into a schedule may mean even more to the baby's development than it does to the adult's convenience.

Between our parent's generation and our children's generation there has been a confusing swing of opinion about schedules for infants. Thirty years ago the attitude was that babies had nothing to say in the daily matters of their early lives. The four-hour feeding schedule was only the beginning of years of training a child to "good habits." It was thought that a baby getting what she wanted, when she wanted it, was a bad habit. Giving in to a baby was spoiling her.

Then, suddenly, the attitude changed and the baby had everything to say. It was demand feeding—and if the demands weren't met, it was thought the baby's emotional development could be damaged for life.

These two opinions and the rules that go with them are still in the air. Probably no one follows either religiously anymore, but we have reaped a crop of guilt from both. If we feed a baby every two hours, we do worry about spoiling her. If we make her wait, we do worry about damaging her.

Perhaps parents could worry less—and choose their way more easily—if they understood more about what is really happening as a newborn baby and her parents settle into a routine. Forget

The settling of a baby into a schedule may mean even more to the baby's development than it does to the adult's convenience.

whether babies should call the rules. This is done by both parents and child.

At first a baby needs to eat as often at night as during the day. A mother adjusts to tough nights. Then her attitude changes. She is tired of getting up at 2:00 a.m. She is less pleased to see her baby then. She doesn't talk much to her; she is too sleepy. Not wanting to wake up herself, and not wanting to stimulate her baby, she keeps only a small light on for the feeding; she doesn't play with her baby; she diapers her without elaborateness; she puts her back to bed. Subtly, her movements, her voice, her manner, tell her baby the dark time is the calm time, the sleep time.

But the baby is telling her mother things too. She may go five hours between feedings one night, and even longer the

next. She may drink only half her bottle, or fall asleep at the breast. She may wake and fuss at 2:00 a.m., but by the time her mother gets there, be fast asleep again. The mother and the baby are playing into each other's hands, telling each other what to do. The early routine established between mother and infant is their first mutuality, or sharing.

More is happening too. During the day a sequence of events is repeated. She wakes, cries. Her mother comes, she's fed. After milk comes bath; after bath, wakefulness; then diapering, sleep. With

repetition, a pattern is formed in Baby's mind: there are things she can expect; things she knows will happen next. Once she cried and cried and cried until the nipple was in her mouth. Now when her mother picks her up, she stops crying. She knows food comes next. She can wait for it.

We can even imagine that with this expectation comes the baby's ability to think about the breast or bottle, to hold off her need for a few minutes. In time, she may cry when she wakes up, only to quiet again if her mother calls to her. The voice will be followed by mother, mother will be followed by food.

These expectations that grow with the infant's daily routine lead to more complicated kinds of learning. A child comes to understand her earliest time concepts, like "after lunch," because she has understood that events occur in sequence, one after another.

As events are repeated, she understands they will happen again. And when an infant can trust that what has happened in the past will happen again, she also becomes able to wait.

Routine is the beginning of other kinds of trust; trust in people that they can be relied upon to do for her what needs to be done, and trust in herself, that she can express what it is she needs from other people. She is starting to make sense of herself in the world.

Let's deliberately distort a schedule that is mutually agreeable to parent and child. Let's assume we go back to the old way of scheduling a baby by the clock.

If Baby gets hungry when it isn't time, she can just scream. A baby can make sense of that. It seems to her that her expressive cry of hunger has no value. It isn't followed by satisfaction. It doesn't work. The adults in her life can tell her what to do, but she can't tell them what she needs. Or so it appears.

continued on page 15

Feeding Your Baby

Baby Coos

Many doctors now recommend feeding young babies according to Baby's own schedule. True, it's good for your sake and for Baby to have some sort of schedule, but keep it flexible.

If Baby wakes up because he's hungry, all the comforting in the world will not relieve his hunger. Letting a baby cry merely because he is "ahead of schedule" does not make good sense.

On the other hand, if you have just finished feeding Baby his "regular" bottle, then his crying is not likely to be due to hunger. So, look for some other cause for his discomfort, such as a need to be burped or a change of diaper.

If Baby wakes up in the middle of what is usually a sleeping period for him, giving him a pacifier may help him catch up on the sleep that he needs at this age. But if hunger is clearly the reason for his crying, then he should be fed, irrespective of the time of day or night.

Most young babies require a feeding in the middle of the night. Within a few months you will find that this feeding time will be the first to drop out of the schedule as Baby develops the need for a longer period of sleep during the night.

As the number of feedings decreases you will need to increase the amount of each feeding so that Baby has an adequate supply of nutrition during a 24-hour period.

Some babies get their days and nights "mixed up." They sleep more during the day and are more wakeful during the night. As this places an added burden on parents, you will probably want to change your baby's sleeping and eating patterns.

Here are some suggestions. Make sure that your baby receives enough food during the day. This may mean spending a little more time with each daytime feeding.

After you think Baby has finished feeding, let him rest for a while and then try feeding him again but don't try to force him to feed.

Another suggestion is to keep Baby at evening time in a place where other members of the family are. If Baby is left in a crib in his bedroom during the daytime, it is not too surprising if he sleeps all day since there is little to stimulate his interest.

But if you bring him to the family room in the evening he will enjoy listening to the sounds of the voices and even with his limited vision his eyes will be exploring this new world around him.

By the time the night arrives he will be ready for a good long rest. ■

Around six to eight weeks of age, and usually not before, Baby begins to coo. You will hear her when she is contented and it will sound like she is repeating a string of the same sound.

This sound is different from comfort-making sounds. Baby is playing with sounds because they please her. She is playing with and exercising her speech organs just as she plays with and exercises her fingers and toes.

As a result of the oral exercises, Baby learns to repeat the noises that please her, and she finds pleasure in the rhythm created by regularly repeating a pattern. With this experience, she is making a first step in the prespeech-listening match. She becomes aware of the fact that the sounds she hears and the sounds she makes have a relationship!

From the beginning, adults play an important role in helping the child master the skills of language and speech. Whenever a child does something which satisfies and pleases us, we express our satisfaction with affection and approval.

In the case of the infant, the adult often reinforces the babbling by babbling back or by using words to encourage further sound production. Together they play dialogue games. Soon the child's response is automatic—she produces an expressive response to the expression of others! ■

continued from page 14

Let's look at this the opposite way, too: The second a baby shows signs of discomfort, the food, already warmed, is ready to relieve her. A baby could make sense of that, too.

Next time she is uncomfortable or hungry, she must be relieved—right now! Waiting does not happen. And neither does the trusting expectation that comes of a routine mutually agreed upon in the give and take of both a parent's and a baby's needs.

Luckily for most babies, born thirty years ago or born tomorrow, parents soon discover that other people's rulebooks don't fit their own real lives. Whether they think it right or wrong, parents will give in to a screaming baby, and feed her early—and their baby will be soothed by that answer to her cry.

And then again, whether they intend to or not, parents will frustrate a hungry baby to answer the door or grab the telephone or sleep a few more minutes—and their baby will soothe her own waiting with the image of what she knows will happen next.

As the adjustment continues over the first months of a baby's life, a mother is learning a talent that is more important than any other. To listen, to guess, to try: to find a way to satisfy her baby's developing needs within the frame of her own necessities. The key to settling into a schedule is the responsiveness between parent and infant which is related to secure attachment and trust.

Parents will take clues from Baby, and the baby will take clues from her parents—because, whether it's basic trust, or team concepts, or the ability to wait, we just can't help communicating with each other. ■

A Spectator Looks Around

Your baby is a spectator right now and will stare at objects for surprisingly long periods. He will lock his eyes onto anything that moves and during this "staring period," important things are happening. Your child's eyes are learning to point together at the same thing.

This fine coordination of his eyes is necessary not only for good depth perception but also for keeping him from seeing double. Single vision is one of the first things on the program since it must be achieved before more complicated maneuvers, like reaching, can be learned.

The focusing action of his eyes is becoming a little more flexible, although clear vision at all distances will not be possible until the fourth month. Baby is becoming more accurate at following a moving target with his eyes—one of his basic abilities.

While focusing ability can't be speeded up, experiments have shown that movements, like controlled reaching and using both eyes together, will develop more quickly if the right experiences are provided at the right time.

What are these useful experiences? One of them involves a simple addition to the crib.

It is a device used by one group of researchers in an experiment that caused controlled reaching and grasp to occur in the third month for most of their subjects instead of the fifth month as would otherwise have happened.

It also made the experimental infants more visually attentive to their surroundings.

Here's how you make this device: Paint some bright red polka dots on the white shield of a pacifier, then tie it by the ring to an upright crib rail about 8 inches above your baby's shoulder.

Let the string go through the center of an 8 inch diameter circle of white cardboard so that a uniform light background is provided. (See the picture.) Ideally, there should be two of these devices, one on each side of the crib. This gives the baby a

stationary object to look at just above his hand. Its shape and color are intriguing and invite more complete investigation.

Sometime during the month, probably toward the end, he will take a swipe at the object, first with his fist, then (next month) with partly opened hand.

Finally, in a couple of months, with his hand opening in anticipation of contact, he will reach for the pacifier, coordinating his arm movement with vision as he does so.

The achievement of his coordination has enormous significance, as we shall see. We want him to discover his hands and their use at the earliest possible time.

In addition to alternating his position in the crib as we discussed last month, there is more early visual training you can expose your child to.

Once or twice a day take a small rattle and move it in front of his eyes (about 10-12 inches away) until you catch his attention. It may be necessary to make little shaking movements as you go.

If the rattle has dull colors, tape some bright colored ribbons to it, leaving bows or ends free to flutter.

At two months old, Baby is becoming more accurate at following a moving target with his eyes —one of his basic abilities.

When he looks at your target, move it slowly to the side of his field of vision and see if his eyes follow it. If Baby is in his tonic neck reflex position (eyes turned toward outstretched arm) start with the rattle on the mattress in front of his eyes and try to lead him up toward his body midline.

At first you will see large jerks of his eyes as the target gets away from him and his fixation reflex moves to recenter it. Later, he will follow more accurately and actually anticipate the continued movement of the target.

Let him follow the rattle for a few passes, then reward him by placing the handle of the rattle in his little curled hand.

Don't worry if he holds the rattle without looking at it; the different channels of experience still act separately and they need a little exercise separately before getting together. In other words, he'll learn. ∎

Observation Skills

It's never too early to learn how to observe your baby. During the next twelve months your baby will go through more developmental changes than at any other time during her life.

The changes are usually gradual and each month will bring new ones to watch for. In addition to helping your child progress through these developmental stages, it will increase your thrill as a parent if you have developed the observational skills needed to detect your child's growth and development.

To help sharpen your observational skills, each month *Growing Child* will tell you about the most important developments that will normally be taking place. Every baby is different and each one will progress at a different rate. The more you are able to develop your own powers of observation, the more you'll know about the individuality of your child. ■

Know What to Look For

The most important thing about observing is knowing what to look for. Sometimes when a mother brings her baby to the clinic, the doctor asks questions to which the mother may not know the answers: Does the baby respond to the mother's voice? Does Baby make cooing or babbling noises?

The reason the mother doesn't know the answers is not due to incompetence. She simply didn't know what behaviors to look for. Leave her with her baby for an hour and she'll be able to tell anybody exactly how her baby responds. As you read *Growing Child,* you will learn what to look for to learn more about your child's growth and development.

If you want to learn more about your child's individuality, you may want to develop some additional questions of your own that will focus on specific behaviors. For example, does your child constantly wiggle when awake or asleep, or does she lie quietly? Does she have a regular schedule for eating and sleeping or does this vary from day to day? Does she appear happy most of the time or is she a "cranky" baby? The questions are endless, but by considering these questions, you have taken the first step in understanding your child's individuality, demonstrated by temperament. The most important part of caregiving is to make a good match between adult responses and the baby's temperament. ■

Learn to Observe

Observation is simply consciously attending to what you're looking for. For example, the parent of a coughing baby can consciously attend to the number of times the child coughs in a given period of time.

Most of the observations about your child will not be that specific. In fact, if you were to observe your child methodically for sixty minutes, chances are that nothing would happen during that hour. This type of observation is more appropriate for the research laboratory than the home.

The type of observation we're talking about here is mainly incidental. For example, when did you first notice that Baby found her mouth with her fist? When did you first notice Baby staring at her hands? When did she first join her two hands together?

There are various important milestones in Baby's development that you won't want to miss and that's our job at *Growing Child*—to make you aware of these exciting developments in your child, so that you may learn to observe and be aware of them. ■

Keep A Record

Just watching your baby's development is quite an experience, and how precious the memories will be years from now.

So, record what you see. Buy a diary, one with spaces for each day. Or you can use an ordinary notebook.

Each day, or every few days, write some little thing about Baby. How does she look? What did she do? How do you feel about her?

Some parents keep a diary for each child until they're grown up. If you miss a few days, don't give up; everyone has busy days. Instead just skip a few pages and continue.

In addition to providing a lot of fun for you as you read it over, a diary may be of value to a doctor if your child later develops some medical problem.

And don't forget pictures! You'll never regret even one picture that was taken.

There are some things you can do to develop a good photographic record of Baby's growth. Decide to take a weekly picture for a few months. Later you'll want to change to monthly pictures.

Try to remember to note on the photo the Baby's age. When an important news event occurs, like a presidential election, take a picture of Baby that includes the front page or headlines of a newspaper.

Keeping a photo album for an adopted child provides an excellent way to talk to him or her in later years about adoption.

Many parents of adopted children have found that having a photo album encourages children to seek information in a very natural way about things they might otherwise be afraid to ask.

With today's cameras, it's also easy to keep friends and relatives updated with e-mail photos. Whatever pictures you take, just remember to keep your camera handy! ■

Crying and Contentment

What a thrill it will be the first time your baby responds to your patient coaching by saying his first recognizable word! Will it be "dada"—or maybe "mama"?

In the meantime Baby is making small talk of a sort. His first sound-making is related to how his body feels—his comfort and discomfort. These first sounds are universal—babies all over the world make the same sounds at about the same time. They include all the possible sounds for all languages in the world. Babies are born with the potential to learn any language, not pre-programmed to speak Spanish or English, for example.

Most mothers soon recognize their child's sounds of contentment or calls of distress and can distinguish between them because of the differences in pitch and tone. Almost from the beginning, Baby has an awareness of the relationship between the sounds he makes and how his body feels.

Let's look at the steps in Baby's sound-making which begin immediately at birth and continue beyond the first few months. The discomfort sounds appear earliest and they emerge in three stages. The first noises sound to us like shrill nasalized vowels; we hear a lot of e's (teeny), eh's (pen), and a's (Annie). Very shortly the consonant-like sounds emerge. They include friction noises, clicks and trills. And finally we hear what sounds like "m" and "n".

In acquiring comfort sounds, Baby also progresses through three steps. The first sounds of comfort are vowels also but they are very different from the crying sounds. They are cooing sounds which come from an open, relaxed mouth, are lower in pitch and rarely nasal. They sound like "ah," "oh," and "oo."

Next the consonant-like/g/and/k/ sounds appear. And finally, sounds resembling those made in the front of the mouth /p/b/t/d are produced.

Two points can be made. First, these sounds are physiological reactions. Secondly, at this stage these sounds are primarily noises, probably not features of the sound system that the child will eventually develop.

It is no accident that the sounds Baby makes follow such an order. The development of these sounds coincides with physical state and his abilities to respond to how his body feels.

You will notice the vowels come first and then the consonants. An abundance of consonant sounds occurs when Baby is content and relaxed and here's why: The act of sucking brings the lips together—and remember Baby doesn't suck only when he's feeding—he sucks for pleasure during sleep and wakefulness. Therefore, when he's relaxed he brings the lips together to suck and makes a variety of lip sounds—p/b/m/w.

Now, during this early period, the infant begins to make primitive relationships—he learns that his mother comes and relieves his discomfort when he cries. She soothes him with her fondling hands, loving words and pleasant voice. These characteristics of Mother's voice affect the baby's response and this certainly has an influence on his later listening attitudes. ∎

Growing Child®

P. O. Box 2505 • W Lafayette, IN 47996
(800) 927-7289
©Growing Child, Inc.
www.GrowingChild.com

Contributing Authors

Phil Bach, O.D., Ph.D.
Miriam Bender, Ph.D.
Joseph Braga, Ed.D.
Laurie Braga, Ph.D.
George Early, Ph.D.
Carol R. Gestwicki, M.S.
Liam Grimley, Ph.D.
Robert Hannemann, M.D., F.A.A.P.
Sylvia Kottler, M.S.
Bill Peterson, Ph.D.

Toys?

New parents usually receive lots of gifts when their new baby is born — clothing, blankets, diapers, keepsakes — and toys.

It isn't too soon to begin thinking about toys for your new baby.

Toys and playthings are just as important for your baby's growth as food and cuddling. Toys are more than trivial fun or rewards for good behavior, or presents for special occasions.

Toys are what children use to discover what they are capable of doing and how things work in the world.

The right toys will help your baby develop both physically and mentally.

Here's how this happens. During the first couple of months, your baby is just emerging from a nearly continuous half-sleep.

If you will give him things that are interesting enough to look at and listen to, he will want to remain alert and to use his eyes and ears. And the more he looks and listens, the more skillfully he will use his developing senses.

A toy suggestion for this age:

An unbreakable, long-lasting mirror with reflective surfaces of safe plastic.

Since Baby's head is turned to one side or the other, the best visual stimulus is not a mobile that hangs out of his view above the crib, but rather something placed at the side of the crib at mattress level.

A few months from now, when Baby becomes fascinated with faces, he'll use this mirror to study the one face that's hardest to get to know — his own!

Remember, safety first. As with any object that comes in contact with your baby, make sure there are no sharp edges or corners, strings or cords that he may reach or become entangled in.
∎

Growing Child

The most important period of life is not the age of university studies, but the first one, the period from birth to the age of six.

Maria Montessori

Three Months Old

By the time Baby is three months old she has become quite social. She coos and smiles at you as you approach her.

When you lean over her playfully and talk to her, she responds by smiling, gurgling and even chuckling.

She may still prefer to turn her head part way to the side, but more and more often brings it to mid-position.

She promptly looks at a dangling toy, and if you move it slowly from one side to the other, she turns her head and follows it with her eyes.

Baby's hands are no longer tightly closed. Her fingers have started to relax, and if you place a rattle in her hand, she will hold it and glance at it.

If supported in a sitting position, she shows a good deal of head control. Her head no longer sags but is held fairly erect, bobbing only occasionally.

When an object is within reach, she looks at it and waves her arms, some-times managing to make contact with it with her fist. She cannot yet reach for and grasp it.

When placed on her tummy, she lifts her head, holds it strongly, and props her chest up with her forearms.

Her knees are no longer pulled up under her, and her hips now rest on the bed; her feet wave above her bent knees.

Baby has a definite personality of her own. Although most of her movements are still random, she is learning to control her arms and legs.

Her improved head and eye control let her follow you with her eyes. Her sleeping and waking patterns are well-established.

She has learned to communicate with you.

Her cries tell you when she is hungry, wet, distressed, frightened—or just lonely. It is a joy to watch her grow! ∎

At Three Months Baby Likes to:
- Wave and watch his hands.
- Bring objects to his mouth to explore them.
- Listen to the sound of his voice.

Give Your Baby:
- A view of himself in a mirror.
- Bells on booties.
- A patterned sheet on his bed.
- Music.
- Mobile (as described in this issue of **Growing Child**).
- The great outdoors.
- Play time with you.

Reminder:
During waking hours, have Baby spend as much time on his stomach as on his back so that he will be stimulated to lift his head and chest.

Fathers Are Different

A baby's world is a world of feeling, smelling, tasting, and touching.

He's been busy the past few months exploring the world around him which is made up of comfort or discomfort, dryness or wetness, hunger or fullness, and he is learning from all these things.

Baby has also learned that Father and Mother are different. As he is held and carried, comforted and played with by Mother and Father, a baby learns that Fathers feel hard and solid but Mothers feel soft and warm. Father's hands are gentle but they are larger and hold him differently from Mother's hands.

Father's face feels prickly while Mother's face feels smooth. Father's chest rumbles and vibrates as he talks.

Fathers play differently and that's okay. Father-play may be a bit more rough and tumble. All of these differences increase Baby's knowledge and awareness of the fact that there are two different kinds of people in his world.

Both of them mean love and security.

As Baby learns about these differences, he is laying the foundation of a loving relationship which hopefully will last his whole life long. ∎

Moving Parts in Action

When a baby is born, she experiences the effects of gravity for the first time. Her body, head, arms and legs have weight and she must learn to live in a world where everything she does is affected by her own weight and the weight of objects she handles.

To learn to live in this new world, Baby begins by moving first her arms and legs. Her head weighs about one-fourth of her whole body, so she doesn't move it much at first.

The early fist-clenching, arm-waving and leg-kicking a baby does are mostly reflex-responses to hunger or discomfort.

When she has been fed, she usually goes back to sleep. But there are a few periods each day which the very young baby spends in just moving.

As she develops from week to week, these periods become longer and her movements become stronger and more frequent.

Baby's kicks and waves may seem aimless to you, but she is busy learning about herself and her new world.

She learns how her legs feel when she kicks or stiffens or stretches them. She learns how her arms feel as they change

position. She learns that when she moves against gravity, she must work harder than when she moves with it.

She begins to learn that there is a difference between herself and everything else in the world that is not herself.

As she kicks her legs or waves her arms, a constant stream of sensations is fed back into her brain from her muscles, joints, tendons and skin.

These are sorted out, matched with similar sensations and filed in Baby's "memory bank."

With this "feedback" of sensations from her moving body, Baby learns about her world and about herself.

She is developing patterns of movement on which she will later build such important coordination skills as purposeful reaching and grasping, crawling on her stomach, creeping on her hands and knees, walking, and running.

"Exercise periods" for the young baby should be encouraged. Loose clothing should allow Baby free movement of arms and legs.

At least once during the day, she should have some time in a warm, draft-free place where she can play in just her diaper.

Baby Talks Back

An infant responds to sound almost from birth. His earliest responses, however, are not vocal. Hearing his mother's voice he may stop moving his arms and legs, or cry.

A bit later, he will smile. But between the third and fourth month he responds to sound and speech by using his voice.

For example, when someone talks to him, he will answer with noises. If he is already babbling, the speaker's voice will stimulate and increase the amount of sounds he makes.

We cannot say that Baby is imitating what he hears because his responses sound so different from the speaker's.

But the fact is, there is something new in his behavior. He now "speaks" when spoken to! And the speaker will encourage the baby to continue by his expressions of pleasure—smiles, hugs, and words.

Researchers agree that how well a baby "imitates" or responds to speech will depend to a large extent upon the responses his speech gets from his listeners.

Well, what are the adults in his life saying to Baby? All adults are different but

most of them use "baby language" in speaking to their infants, and this is very important to the child.

Mother helps to bridge the difference between Baby's own speech and the adult speech in the home.

She chooses the repetitive sounds common to his own vocabulary: "mama," "dada," "bye bye." And she uses them meaningfully: "mama coming," "dada bye bye."

So-called "baby talk"—higher pitch, exaggerated pronunciation, repeated words, simple words— is not really baby talk but ways of talking with babies matched to a baby's abilities to hear and comprehend. ■

Gentle roughhousing will encourage activity. Roll her gently from side to side. Gently hold one foot, then the other, then both feet so she must pull or push to free herself.

Don't restrict her movement to the point of frustration and anger. When she pushes or pulls, resist her gently then let her move. Talk to her all the while and make a happy game of it.

Moving is learning for the baby. Not only does she learn from movement itself, she also learns that when she moves purposefully, she can make something happen. This is a giant step toward gaining confidence in her ability to change. ■

Don't Push the Panic Button!

Don't push the panic button! In other words, don't be scared. There is a difference between being concerned and being scared.

If you are concerned about your baby's development, you will still be able to look at her honestly and tell your pediatrician clearly about what she is doing (or not doing).

If you are scared, you will not be able to tell anyone clearly just what the problem is or come up with a solution.

One thing you can do which will help a lot is to make good observations of your baby's activities.

Good observations are something you learn to do, but most people need a lot of practice. Learn to really look at what Baby is doing. Clear reports to a pediatrician about what you actually saw can help make the difference between fright and proper concern.

The important thing about a good observation is to keep the activity you saw or heard separate and distinct from what you think the activity means.

For example, a mother may notice that her baby usually cries while taking her bottle. However, when she tells the pediatrician (or grandmother or a friend), she says, "Her formula doesn't agree with her."

Now, what Mother observed was the crying during feeding, but what she reported was her interpretation of what she saw.

The problem may be too much or too little flow from the nipple or air in the tummy, or any one of several other problems.

So, be sure to separate what you observe from what you think your observations mean. This simple practice can spare you a lot of wasted energy and frustration.

This doesn't mean you should never try to interpret what you observe.

It does mean that you should first be clear about what you actually observed, and then make your interpretations.

Or, when seeking advice, report your observations separately from your interpretations. ∎

What To Do About Problems

What if your baby does have serious problems? Then it is even more important that you not panic.

Our advice about making good observations and clear reports is of primary importance.

If your baby has problems, he needs you even more. And he needs you to be functioning at your peak, getting the best help for him you can.

If anxiety drags you down, your energy gets drained. Save your energy for helping and getting help for your baby.

You will find it much easier to get the right help if you have learned to make good observations and to report them clearly to those professionals who can bring aid to your particular situation.

Many parents have no idea about the different kinds of professional help actually available in the local community, but it is probably not far away—possibly closer than you think.

Your pediatrician or family doctor usually is the professional who can best advise you where to go and whom to see if your baby needs services beyond those the doctor can provide.

Above all, enjoy your baby as much as you possibly can.

Of course, there are many things about caring for Baby which simply are not fun at all.

But when the diaper has been changed, the laundry folded, and all other emergencies under control (for the moment) take some time every day just to enjoy this very special bundle of life who is doing so many fascinating things.

Moments of pure enjoyment with your baby are sometimes rare, but they are some of the best times you will ever have. And they can help keep you away from that panic button. ∎

Moments of pure enjoyment with your baby are some of the best times you will ever have. And they can help keep you away from that panic button!

A Learning Mobile

It is now time to put together an object for your baby to look at that will serve a variety of purposes. It is a simple mobile which has an object hanging from each end of a single "see-saw" crosspiece.

The mobile should be designed to be attached from beneath, from the baby's viewpoint.

For support you can tie a dowel rod or yardstick across the top of the crib above Baby's chest. From this a stout piece of twine holds the cross-piece at its middle. The cross-piece should be a length of rubber hose or a cardboard tube like the one that comes on clothes hangers—but no sharp rods or sticks in case the mobile breaks.

From each end dangle another length of string to which is tied an object small enough for Baby to grasp. For instance, on one side might be a small square or round block and on the other side a short rubber bone to balance it.

Other objects you can use are a teething ring, squeaky toys, a bootie, rattle, or small plastic bottle. Make sure the objects are large enough that they cannot be swallowed by Baby. The strings used to attach the objects should be less than 6" long.

These objects should be at the distance of Baby's outstretched palm. The swing of the crosspiece should be enough so that when Baby grasps the object, he can get it near his mouth.

Baby will be more interested if the objects have bright colors and contrasts of light and dark. For instance, if the block is solid colored, paint a bull's eye on the bottom with a black non-toxic marker. Infants at this age find such a design more interesting than simple lines and corners. If the bootie is white, lace and hang it with a black shoelace.

With the mobile in place, you should soon see Baby batting it with his newly opened hand. Later this month he should show his first grasp—a clumsy one—with fingers closing only after they touch the object.

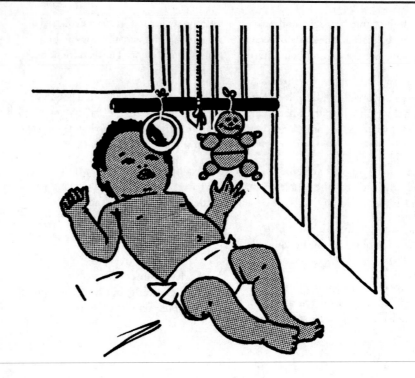

When he finally has a grip on the elusive object, he will reflexively bring it to his mouth to explore it with his tongue and lips.

He cannot let go voluntarily, but he will relax his grip when something else catches his attention—at which time the object will pop neatly up into the air to entice him again later.

This, then, is the first major educational objective: to get several systems—seeing, reaching, feeling, tasting—to work together on a single object. At this point, an object begins to be something real and permanent to Baby, apart from his own self.

This perception is necessary before he can begin his next intellectual task: finding out what objects are for and what he can do to them. We'll have more to say about this next month.

There are commercial hanging devices available and perhaps you have received one or two as gifts. They usually have several objects hanging on cords or springs from a fixed bar. These are fine as far as they go, but the mobile we've described seems to have several advantages.

First, it allows you to change objects. They should be changed once a week or more often if Baby loses interest. By using fewer objects at a time and changing them more often, you will avoid overstimulating him.

This is important because loading your baby up with too many things can kill his curiosity just as too limited an environment can.

Another advantage of the mobile is that when Baby bats the object, it moves more slowly and over a greater range. It is easier for his eyes to follow, and it will widen his field of visual attention. Also, the mobile allows him to bring the object to his mouth where he can feel the texture and shape of what he sees and holds.

Finally, it poses a fine challenge to a careful grasp and will encourage the early use of his two hands together. When the baby loses interest, parents will see less attention or looking away from the object quickly.

For safety's sake, the child should not be left alone when this mobile is in place. No strings should be tied across the crib. All mobiles should be removed when Baby can pull himself up. ∎

Nature or Nurture?

Is human nature determined by heredity or environment? It's an age-old question, and the best answer is that it is a combination of the two.

As your baby grows and develops, nature and nurture work together in interesting ways.

Before your baby can learn to do something, her muscles and nervous system must grow to a certain level of development.

This growth follows a timetable that is set by her inherited genes. After the right amount of development, her system is ready for particular activities.

Now environment comes in. Once she's ready, the child must have an opportunity to use her new capacity.

If the opportunity is present, she will learn the activity easily and well and she will be ready to learn other skills which depend on learning the earlier skill.

But if the opportunity is missing or delayed, she will learn the skill much later, less well, and with greater effort—or maybe not at all.

Compared with animals, human beings have longer periods during which they can efficiently learn certain skills.

While your baby is growing rapidly, she learns many basic skills in movement, speech and perception. So, you will want to be on your toes in order to "strike while the iron is hot."

Growing Child will help you evaluate your infant's progress and will describe when the typical child is ready to do certain things.

Then you can give your child the needed opportunities when the ideal time approaches. ■

Loving Is Learning

An article in Parent's Magazine entitled "New Ways to Measure Intelligence in Infants" by Suzanne S. Fremon, makes some important comments about the mental growth of babies.

Psychological studies provide strong evidence that the mental growth of a baby is directly affected by the way his parents and family respond to him.

That is, the baby learns more and learns it faster when his mother, father or whoever takes care of him answers when he cries, smiles at him when he smiles, talks to him and plays with him.

It seems clear that a loving atmosphere helps a child grow and develop. This does not mean that parents should immediately begin to grant all the demands of their children in the hope of making them brighter!

However, every individual, even if he is only a few months old, needs to have someone pay attention to him and to understand and respond to his needs.

It follows then that when an infant feels uncomfortable and cries, his parent comes to investigate, picks him up, holds and cuddles him, talking softly. If he's hungry, he is fed. The baby is content.

If the parent responds in this manner whenever he is uncomfortable, he soon learns the relationship of discomfort, crying, parent, comfort.

Two kinds of learning are taking place. First, the child has learned that specific action on his part results in specific action on the part of his parent.

The second kind of learning is more general. After the baby has learned to expect a specific response to his needs, he is then able to move on to other kinds of behavior, to act in ways that are new to him.

It is as though the baby reasoned: "When I do something, something happens, so I'll try something else."

When a child learns this, he has begun to learn about cause and effect. As he learns that what he does has an effect on what happens to him, he is encouraged toward further exploration—to learn what effects will follow new kinds of activity on his part.

The child whose needs are neglected does not learn as early or as easily that he can affect what happens to him.

The child whose every need is anticipated is equally deprived of this learning experience, which may seem difficult for a protective parent to accept.

Baby's basic belief: "When I do something, something happens," is the foundation of self-confidence and a willingness to work to achieve a goal.

On the other hand, the belief "When I do something, nothing happens," leads only to despair and defeat.

You can give your child no greater gift than the loving, responsive care which teaches him that what he does is important and will affect what happens to him and to those in his environment. ■

A Baby Book Is More Than a Keepsake

Almost every first-born child receives a baby book from some relative or friend.

New parents are delighted to enter all the important information about their child's birth, christening, gifts, etc. But a baby book can be more than a sentimental keepsake—it can serve as a written record of your baby's developmental progress.

At three months Baby has already shown many changes.

Now is the time to resolve that you will faithfully keep a record of her important developmental achievements if you have not been doing so already.

We suggest that you plan to record the approximate age at which Baby reaches the milestones which we have listed here.

At three months of age many normal babies will not have reached even the first of these. However, you can look forward to her reaching most of them within the next two or three months.

Just remember that each baby develops at her own rate. Don't fret and worry if her rate is not as fast as you think it should be.

In a later issue we will discuss the ages at which developmental delays should be investigated. For now, enjoy your baby.

Look for these behaviors and record the approximate date:

• On back: Brings hands together in front of face and watches them.

• On back: Waves arms together.

• On back: Kicks vigorously, legs can alternate and move together.

• Rolls completely over from back to stomach.

• On stomach: Lifts head strongly and holds it up and steady, face forward.

• On stomach: Raises head and chest, supporting self on forearms.

• Sitting, supported at the ribs, holds head erect and steady. ■

Dance With Your Baby?

Why not? A baby learns through movement.

She learns from the movement she experiences as she is being lifted, held, carried and cared for as well as from the movements of her own body.

The baby's nervous system is not yet completely developed and she startles easily. A loud noise, a sudden movement or loss of support is very frightening to her.

However, gentle rhythmic motion is soothing. This is why she responds to being rocked or walked when she is uncomfortable or wakeful.

But dancing? Yes, dancing! Remember, Baby learns from being moved as well as from moving. She cannot yet learn from rapid or jerky movements but she can learn from smooth, rhythmic changes of position.

So, if you enjoy moving to music, if you like to dance—your baby will enjoy it, too. Find some music that is soft and

P. O. Box 2505 • W Lafayette, IN 47996
(800) 927-7289
©Growing Child, Inc.
www.GrowingChild.com

Contributing Authors

Phil Bach, O.D., Ph.D.
Miriam Bender, Ph.D.
Joseph Braga, Ed.D.
Laurie Braga, Ph.D.
George Early, Ph.D.
Carol R. Gestwicki, M.S.
Liam Grimley, Ph.D.
Robert Hannemann, M.D., F.A.A.P.
Sylvia Kottler, M.S.
Bill Peterson, Ph.D.

rhythmic—a waltz or ballad. Hold your baby gently but firmly so that she feels secure. Then sway from side to side, move forward and backward, turn and twist in time to the music.

Your movements will stimulate the sense organs deep within Baby's ears. The sensations she experiences will help her develop the position sense and balance she will need when she tries to sit, stand and walk.

If you hum along with the music, your baby will get additional stimulation from the vibration of your chest.

If you enjoy moving to music, your happiness will communicate itself to your baby as you hold her.

Sweet music and gentle movements while holding Baby securely are the ingredients for happy moments for both of you. ■

Growing Child®

> If you bungle your children, I don't think whatever else you do well matters very much.
>
> Jacqueline Kennedy

Four Months Old

Baby is four months old. And what a big difference there is between the tiny, sleepy newborn who came to live with you and the bright-eyed, alert individual who now smiles and makes noises at you.

As you look back over the past four months, you begin to realize what a tremendous amount of development has taken place.

Baby has developed many motor and sensory skills involving hearing, vision, and touch, as well as muscle control. But many of these skills have been developing somewhat independently, almost like a person learning the separate components of a golf swing.

At four months Baby starts bringing together these fragmented skills for purposeful behavior—like the golfer who now hits the ball two hundred yards.

Vision, hearing and muscle control all begin to function in conjunction with one another as Baby turns his head in order to see the person when he hears a familiar voice.

Even the most complex computer is simple compared to the intricate network that is coordinating all these messages and activities.

As you watch those little hands gradually develop mastery under the guidance of his eyes and ears, you begin to realize that they are not just individual players in a game any more. They are now part of a team with the brain—an impeccable coach—directing the action. ∎

At Four Months Baby Likes to:
• Raise herself up by her arms.
• Turn her torso from one side to the other.
• Hold her feet in the air and kick when lying on her back.
• Chew on things she can bring to her mouth.
• Splash with hands and feet in the tub.

Give Your Baby:
• A variety of objects to examine and explore (a cube, ball, rattle, bell).
• More dangling toys to watch and swipe at with hands or feet.
• Music and nursery rhyme music.

Ask Your Doctor About:
• 2nd DTaP vaccine (diphtheria, tetanus, acellular pertussis).
• IPV (inactivated polio vaccine).
• H. Influenzae type b (Hib) vaccine.
• PCV (pneumococcal conjugate vaccine).
• Rotavirus vaccine (Rota).

Fragile–Do Not Shake!

We're all familiar with warnings on packages of fragile objects that warn us not to drop, shake, or handle them roughly. It might be wise if similar warning labels were applied to the heads of infants.

According to current injury statistics, there has been an increase in the number of injuries to the brains and spinal cords of children, particularly those under six months of age.

In reviewing these cases, investigators have found that the injury is caused by a whiplash-type motion which frequently occurs when the infant is held under the arms and shaken.

There have been so many of these cases that a special name has been applied to the signs and symptoms: the "shaken baby syndrome."

An even more severe injury results if the infant's head strikes an object like a mattress, wall, or crib edge. The damaging results in these cases are called the "shaken impact syndrome."

Regardless of the name applied, these are serious events and can result in permanent brain damage or even death.

These injuries most often occur when a parent or caretaker becomes angry at a young child's behavior and shakes him to make him "stop" or "pay attention."

Injuries also can occur when a child is jiggled too vigorously or playfully thrown high into the air and then caught. The sudden stop of the fall may causes the whiplash-type injury.

So, when you look at your baby, imagine a sign on his or her forehead that says "Fragile: Do not shake, jiggle, or throw into the air."

If you feel yourself becoming angry and frustrated, take time out to count to ten and calm yourself before handling the baby.

Although most infants are quite sturdy, they can be severely injured by excessively vigorous play or handling. ∎

Encouraging Physical Development

In the fourth through the sixth month, it is important to give a baby every opportunity to develop the strength and coordination she needs to progress to independent sitting, standing, and walking. This means Baby must be free to move. Too many clothes may keep Baby from experiencing the variety of movements by which she learns.

A baby's room should be free from drafts and warm enough to allow light clothing—preferably only a diaper and perhaps a light, loose shirt.

From time to time change the location of the crib in the room. Place it against one wall, then against another. Sometimes have the crib in the middle of the floor.

If you must place the crib against one wall, change the baby's position often, placing her head first at one end and then at the other. This will encourage Baby to turn her head from side to side.

When Baby is awake, she can spend time on the floor or occasionally in an infant seat.

A toy or mobile hung directly overhead within reach will encourage her to look straight ahead and to reach for it.

When Baby is able to sit or stand, it is best to remove mobiles from the crib. Serious accidents have occurred when infants have become entangled in low-hanging playthings.

Upon waking, Baby will tend to turn her head toward the direction from which she receives care and social stimulation. If she spends much of her waking time with her head turned in only one direction, she may not develop equal strength and flexibility on both sides of her body. She will also probably be slower in bringing her hands to the midline in front of her face—an important developmental step.

To promote equal development, feed her alternately from one side and then from the other. This will happen automatically if you breastfeed your baby. However, it is equally important for the formula-fed baby.

During waking hours, it is a good idea to have Baby spend at least as much time on her stomach as her back.

While she is awake and on her stomach, she is stimulated to lift her head and chest, to push up on her elbows and finally straighten her arms. Only while she is on her stomach will she be able to arch her back.

This straight-arm, arched-back posture is important because the child (1) gains information by visual exploration—raising the head and looking about, and (2) develops readiness for rocking, crawling and creeping. ∎

Safe Sleeping for Babies

The cause of sudden infant death syndrome (SIDS) is not known. SIDS is the unexplained death of a healthy baby less than a year old, usually during sleep.

A combination of physical and environmental factors can make an infant more vulnerable to SIDS, such as (1) placing babies on their stomach or side for sleep (2) sleeping on a soft surface and (3) sleeping with parents.

On the positioning of young infants during sleep, the American Academy of Pediatrics (AAP) as well as other authorities now agree with findings that indicate that **the back is a safer position during sleep, particularly as it relates to the Sudden Infant Death Syndrome.**

This recommendation applies to infants from birth until the time they roll over on their own, usually between four and seven

months of age. Some doctors recommend placing babies on their back for sleeping until they are one year old.

Somewhere between seven months and one year, babies will usually roll into the position most comfortable for them. In some cases, this might be the stomach.

It is also best to make sure there are no soft objects, blankets, toys, bumper pads, pillows or other objects in the crib.

This reduces the risk of entrapment, suffocation or strangulation in the crib and keeps the baby's airway clear.

In the same way, a baby sleeping in the parents' room but in the baby's crib, reduces the risk of impaired breathing.

Plainly said, healthy babies should sleep on their backs day or night and for naps.

If you have any questions about your baby's sleep position, consult your child's physician.

Some Myths about Baby's Crying

Many parents feel helpless and frustrated when they are unable to comfort a crying baby.

Babies generally have a reason for crying. It is their way of communicating when they are hungry, or in pain, or tired or experiencing some other kind of discomfort.

Before considering the reasons why babies cry and what parents can do to soothe them, it is important to discuss some myths related to crying.

Myth #1: Crying isn't normal. When adults cry, it's an indicator that something is wrong.

For babies, on the other hand, crying is their primary way of communicating with those around them. Even periodic fussy crying is not abnormal. About four out of every five babies have fussy periods at one time or another.

This doesn't mean, however, that a baby's cries should be ignored. On the contrary, if a baby is hungry or experiencing discomfort, the sooner his needs are met, the sooner the crying will cease.

Sometimes a baby will cry inconsolably for no apparent reason. Crying is often a baby's way to relieve stress which parents might not otherwise detect. Not only is crying perfectly normal in babies, it also serves an important developmental purpose.

By crying, babies exercise their vocal cords and become aware of their mouth, tongue and lips, and the different sounds that are produced—all of which are related to the development of later communication skills.

Myth #2: Babies who cry a lot will have personality problems later in life. It should be consoling for parents to know that no relationship has been found between fussy crying in infants and later personality problems.

If parents are unable to detect the reason for their baby's persistent crying, it would be wise to discuss the matter with their pediatrician or family physician.

Since the baby is unlikely to exhibit the fussy behavior in the doctor's office, it is important that the parents be able to report accurately:

(a) the frequency of the crying (how many times a week does baby have fussy periods?);

(b) its duration (it's wise to measure with a watch how long baby cries, because two minutes of a baby's shrieking cry may seem like an eternity to an anxious parent); and

(c) its intensity (is it usually a low wail or a high-pitched shriek?).

The doctor will help parents decide if the crying is normal or if it is related to a specific problem. The doctor may also recommend some soothing techniques that might relieve baby's crying.

Myth #3: If I repeatedly attend to my baby's cries, I may create a spoiled child. According to child development experts, at this age, babies won't be spoiled when parents or other adults attend to their needs.

It has been found in research studies that babies whose parents ignored their cries actually cried more at one year of age than babies who had been consoled promptly.

In other words, parents who respond to their baby's cries will later more likely have infants who cry less rather than more.

Myth #4: When a baby cries, it always and invariably means something is wrong. While a baby's cries will, most times, communicate some specific need ("I'm hungry," "wet," "tired"), there are times when some babies will cry for no apparent reason.

No one knows for sure the cause of these fussy periods when a well-fed, well-rested, dry, good-natured baby will cry inconsolably for several hours. If the parents become anxious, or if they pick up an already over-stimulated baby, it may only result in the baby crying louder and longer.

Some babies have a routine of crying immediately before going to sleep.

If all possible causes of such crying have been explored with a pediatrician or physician, it may be necessary to leave the baby alone for several minutes.

Myth #5: My baby's crying proclaims loudly to the world that I'm not a good parent. It's unfortunate that many parents take their baby's crying personally, as though it were somehow an indicator of poor parenting skills. What could be more humbling and embarrassing for you, as a parent, than for your previously inconsolable baby suddenly to stop crying when held by some visitor in your home!

Far from being a reflection of poor parenting skills, child development experts recommend that sometimes one of the most effective ways to stop a fussy baby's crying is for the parent to hand over their baby to a friend or neighbor. Somehow the change involved—the stranger, for example, doesn't have a familiar smell—may be just what causes the baby to stop crying.

No parent, no matter how expert, is able to soothe and console a baby every time he cries. So don't be too hard on yourself if you are sometimes unable to calm your crying baby. In fact, the more upset you become with yourself, the more you may cause Baby to cry.

So, if your baby sometimes won't stop crying, in spite of all your best efforts, it doesn't indicate that you are a bad parent. Just try to relax and remain calm.

Remind yourself that if you have made sure that Baby isn't hungry, tired, wet, or otherwise uncomfortable for a reason, it's normal for babies to have occasional fussy periods at this age.

The more you are able to relax, in spite of your baby's crying, the better it will ultimately be, both for you and for your baby. ∎

Soothing a Fussy Baby

Most babies sometimes have fussy periods in the day. You will find, for example, that although your baby is dry, comfortable, well-rested and well fed, he may still cry for no obvious reason.

At such times it is helpful for parents to be aware of a variety of soothing techniques. No one technique will soothe every baby. Nor will the same baby always respond positively to a particular soothing technique.

It simply becomes a matter of trial and error to find out what will work for an individual baby in a given situation.

Here are some soothing techniques which many parents have found helpful:

• Give your baby a pacifier. The sucking reflex isn't just related to feeding. Sucking also helps to soothe and comfort Baby.

• Give Baby a favorite teddy bear or doll to hold. A stuffed animal can become Baby's most consoling "friend" in time of stress.

• If Baby has a special soft blanket, he may reach for it whenever he needs to be comforted.

• Distractors can often be effective in helping a baby to stop crying. The distractor might be a new toy, for example, or letting Baby see his face in a mirror.

• Dimming the lights and playing music softly can also be an effective way to calm a fussy baby.

• The sound of a vacuum sweeper or turning on an electric fan are effective ways to soothe some babies.

If you find these sounds are effective with your child, you can tape record them so that they will be readily available whenever and wherever they are needed.

• Wrapping Baby snugly in a soft swaddling blanket will sometimes be effective.

• Try holding Baby in your arms to see if he will stop crying.

• Place your baby on his tummy and gently massage his back.

• Give Baby a nice warm bath if he usually enjoys his bath time.

• Put baby in a front-pack carrier and take him with you as you go about the house.

• Take Baby with you for a car ride to the grocery store, making sure he is safely strapped in a baby seat.

• Hold Baby in your arms in a rocking chair or put him in a baby swing. Most babies find rocking motion to be soothing.

• Find someone, such as a friend, neighbor, or family member, to give you a break from child care, even for 15 or 20 minutes.

The change will not only be refreshing for you, but the novelty of having someone else care for him will often end his crying.
∎

Joining the Senses Together

Baby is now looking closely at everything his hands touch. No longer do each of his senses react separately in seeing one thing while feeling another and hearing a third: he can now use all his senses together on the same object. Some examples will illustrate the importance of this ability.

Let's say that while blindfolded, you are asked to identify an object resting on a table. It appears to be an electric clock, but it ticks.

As you touch the object, you can feel only a flat surface. Is it a wind-up clock in an electric clock case? Or is it an illusion produced by optical tricks and a hidden speaker?

Without coordinating your senses—using hearing, touch and vision, with the blindfold removed—you won't be able to say for sure just what the nature of the object is.

There is a more realistic experience that shows us what this process of combining senses involves. Once in a while a baby is born with a condition called congenital cataract. This means that the lenses of the eyes are clouded so that only hazy light gets through. For all practical purposes he is blind—no shapes or forms can be seen. (Don't worry, the doctor checked your baby for this just after he was born.)

In the past, some babies with this problem grew to adulthood before their lenses were surgically removed and glasses substituted so they could see normally. But all their lives they had learned to get along without vision and had formed impressions of things with their other senses.

Now, with sight given to them, they were pleased and fascinated with what they saw. But they could not identify the simplest thing by sight alone. They had to explore objects with their hands, feeling the texture and the shape as they had always done, before they could say what the objects were.

In fact, it usually took several days of combining seeing with feeling before they could even distinguish with certainty between a block and a ball. As the weeks and months went by, they gradually learned to identify objects just by looking.

Your baby has been in a haze for most of his first three months. He has been seeing, hearing, and feeling many things—but these senses have operated mainly independently of each other.

How many times in the past did you place something in his hand and watch him hold it for some time without ever looking at it? Or see him turn his head toward

ontinued on page 29

Growing and Learning At Four Months

By now you may have seen Baby hold up one hand and look at it for long periods of time.

You have probably noticed with delight that she now reaches for things that are within range of her hands, and rather than merely grasping at them in a reflex action, she now accepts small objects that you give her.

She can hold a toy ring or rattle between her fingers and her palms and often brings it to her mouth to explore it further.

If she has not done so already, she will soon bring her two hands together and begin exploring the fingers of one hand with those of the other. This joining of hands is an important event in Baby's life because it gives her an opportunity to learn an important thing about herself.

As she grasps one hand with the other, she feels the squeezing. This feeling, in response to her grasp, tells Baby that what she has seen and grasped are both part of her.

Discovering herself as something distinct from the other objects around her is very interesting and exciting to her, and she will spend hours exploring her two hands and finding out what they can do.

Now begins an earnest effort to find out what is Self and what is Not-Self. Baby must pay careful attention to everything she touches to see if feelings come from the touched object as well as the hand that does the touching.

In this way, after many touchings and graspings, she will begin to distinguish more fully between herself and the outside world.

This concept of Self and Not-self will continue for many months until it is fully formed around 18 months.

By the end of the fourth month, Baby should have longer waking periods.

The difference between waking and sleeping periods will be more marked.

She may begin to demand social attention by fussing. This fussing is quite different from her cry of hunger or discomfort.

When Baby is lying on her back, she no longer lies with her face turned toward one side; now she turns her head freely from side to side, leaving it centered for most of the time.

If you take Baby by the arms and draw her gently toward a sitting position, instead of letting her head fall back, she begins to lift her head to assist in the movement. But she is still unable to keep her head in line with her body.

Baby now enjoys sitting on your lap while supported at the chest, and can balance her head with only an occasional wobble.

Propped with pillows in a sitting position, she looks happily at her world from this new point of view. She may sit for a time in a high chair when pillows are used to give her additional support.

When a toy is placed on her high chair tray she will corral it with her arms and hands and rake it closer to her.

Of course, she is just as apt to knock it off the tray as she tries to encircle it.

When Baby is placed on her stomach, she shows the effects of growing strength in her neck and back muscles.

She now lifts her head and chest off the bed or playpad (often pushing herself up onto her elbow in an attempt to arch higher) until her face is pointing straight ahead. In this position she can easily turn her head from side to side.

At four months Baby has begun to recognize her mother and other family members who help care for her.

She smiles when a familiar person approaches and shows that she expects her needs to be met. Smiling may cease at the sight of a stranger.

The end of the fourth month marks a turning point. The next three months will bring important changes in behavior as Baby becomes more of a sitter and graduates from crib to chair. ■

continued from page 28

something making noise that could only appear as a hazy blur to his nearsighted eyes?

Not only has Baby lacked the experience to make educated guesses about the nature of an object from one sense alone, but it is doubtful that the object can even be real to him in the way that we know it until several senses can be trained together on the object.

Coordination of vision and touch gives an object an "out there" feeling and after repeated encounters in the next months, Baby develops the idea that the object is there permanently, even when he is not looking at it.

As he begins his fourth month, your baby is working toward the idea of object permanence which is demonstrated around nine months. This is one of Baby's first real concepts and it must be present before more advanced ones like cause and effect can be developed. ■

Quality Child Care

With more and more of today's mothers returning to work within the first year of their babies' lives, it becomes ever more important for parents to make good choices about the childcare they find.

This is such a difficult thing; there are often many choices that could involve care in your home, care in someone else's home, or care in a childcare center. There are the considerations of costs involved, as well as the psychological issues of leaving ones' beloved baby with someone else.

In the following discussion, recognize that the considerations mentioned are based on the primary developmental needs of your little one.

The most important developmental task of the first year of life is forming a sense of attachment to the primary caregivers. Obviously the baby's parents are primary caregivers, but so is the individual in the care arrangement you select.

Forming a sense of mutual attachment lies at the foundation of all other development—healthy personality, social and emotional development, as well as the language and cognitive development in early years.

This means that you are looking for an individual who understands that quality care of infants relies on forming a close relationship with the baby, as well as supporting the strong attachment between infant and parents. Such relationships should continue over time, rather than subjecting the infant to the disruption of multiple caregivers with whom it is difficult to form attachments and trust.

This is one of the reasons that many parents choose a care situation in their home, where one individual can become part of the family over an important period in the young child's life. Another appealing arrangement is a small, family childcare home that can function as a sort of extended family during those critical early months and years.

Continuity of care—repeated experiences with the same people over time—is something that you should look for, whether in a home arrangement or in a childcare center. It is important to assess whether the caregivers have been there for a while, and are likely to remain.

Many quality child center programs now also institute patterns of primary care giving, meaning that one adult is primarily responsible for the care and communication with a small group of infants and their families.

Primary care giving arrangements allow caregivers to tune in to individual needs, facilitating attachment and relationships. A good recommendation is to put continuity of care and primary care giving arrangements at the top of the list of your requirements. Babies thrive on responsive care—having their individual needs recognized and met by their caregivers in a prompt, predictable way.

Questions about feeding and sleeping schedules should elicit responses that indicate that your child's individual needs will be the driving force behind a personal schedule in the early months, and later individualized planning will support children's and family needs.

Caregivers who are knowledgeable about child development will understand how their care giving interactions not only support a sense of trust, but also embed the stimulation needed for early brain development. It takes very special people to become involved in warm, nurturing relationships with babies and their parents, and to provide the interesting environments that support healthy foundations for early learning.

Take the time to assess the emotional climate and relationships in the places you consider for your baby's care. ■

Growing Child®

P. O. Box 2505 • W Lafayette, IN 47996
(800) 927-7289
©Growing Child, Inc.
www.GrowingChild.com

Contributing Authors

Phil Bach, O.D., Ph.D.
Miriam Bender, Ph.D.
Joseph Braga, Ed.D.
Laurie Braga, Ph.D.
George Early, Ph.D.
Carol R. Gestwicki, M.S.
Liam Grimley, Ph.D.
Robert Hannemann, M.D., F.A.A.P.
Sylvia Kottler, M.S.
Bill Peterson, Ph.D.

Erica Listens

Michelle is reading stories to her baby. Right now, she's reading, "Pride and Prejudice."

Baby Erica is four months old. She doesn't move around much yet but she can be made content by sitting in an infant seat or lying on a pad, trying to grab or swipe at any playthings near her.

In the afternoons, if Michelle is lucky, she will have a chance to sit down near Erica and read for a time. She's noticed, however, that after she has been absorbed in her book for a few minutes, Erica will begin to fuss a little. Michelle will say a few words to her and Erica will quiet down.

Now, instead of interrupting her reading, Michelle just starts to read out loud. It works just as well. Erica apparently accepts that the sound of Michelle's voice is intended for her and so she is comforted, but is she understanding any of it? Most experts would say Erica is not getting any of the message from a complicated adult book. But, there is an important message going the other way.

Michelle is aware that Erica is a listener. Later, from about eight months onward, Erica will benefit more directly from the live language that Michelle speaks to her. And perhaps, when Erica begins to deal with language seriously, it will be a bit easier from having listened to her mother reading from, "Pride and Prejudice." ■

Growing Child®

Parents must make room in their hearts and then in their houses and then in their schedules for their children. No poor parent is too poor to do that, and no middle-class parent is too busy.

Jesse Jackson

5 MONTHS

Five Months Old

At five months Baby is pushing ahead rapidly and learning new skills. Some time during the past two months he has learned to hold his head in the middle and to bring his hands together in front of his face.

His eyes have discovered his hands and he has spent a lot of time playing with his hands and fingers.

His head control is good now and body control is better also so that he can observe and reach out to objects and people.

Where earlier Baby's head fell back when he was lifted or pulled toward sitting, now he braces himself and holds his head in the middle throughout the whole movement.

Baby's head and upper trunk are quite stable now and he loves to be held or propped in a sitting position.

He follows moving objects and people with his head and eyes and focuses on those within his range of vision.

By now Baby has learned to lift his head and chest strongly when lying on his tummy and pushes up onto his forearms to support this position.

He may already have begun to move himself about on the floor or bed when placed on his stomach.

He will continue to attempt these purposeful movements until he eventually moves to creeping on his hands and knees.

For the present, though, he may move himself over short distances by rocking on his belly while kicking with his legs

and "swimming" with his arms. He also may push himself backward with his arms or pivot around on his stomach. Most babies will be attempting to do at least one of these things by age five months.

At this age Baby's reach and grasp have improved. He has learned to grasp an object by holding it against the palm of his hand with his fingers and thumb.

Certainly he is moving toward that skill. With repeated efforts he somehow manages to get what he wants.

Although Baby still frequently corrals an object by gathering it in with both arms and hands, he also is beginning to reach for things with one hand.

Once he has grasped an object, he will usually bring his prize to his mouth for further exploration of its qualities.

Before long he will be transferring the object from hand to hand.

At Five Months Baby Likes to:
• Feel, shake, and bang things.
• Roll over.
• Sit with support.
• When awake, lie on tummy, lift head and chest high off mattress and look around.
• Bite on things he can get to his mouth.

Give Your Baby:
• A toy to kick.
• Rattles to play with.
• A spoon or teether to hold in his mouth.
• Sounds to listen to. Put bells on his booties.

A baby learns to grasp and hold an object securely quite some time before he learns to release it on purpose.

At first he releases the object because his grasp relaxes gradually or because his interest is attracted to something else.

He first learns to release his grasp on purpose by throwing the object—something you can look forward to!

While he is learning and perfecting the skills of reach and grasp-release, Baby will use either hand equally well.

He will need lots of practice with either hand before he is ready to establish a preferred hand. You can help give him this practice by always presenting an object directly in front of him so that he can reach for it easily with either hand.

This early use of both hands is necessary if Baby is to establish a complete body image of himself as a person with two different sides. ■

Fascination With Faces

You have probably noticed that your baby is taking a great deal of interest in people's faces. In fact, he is a delightful little person to be around right now!

He smiles and gurgles whenever he sees a parent's face, and he finds it great fun to play peek-a-boo.

He may smile a little less for a strange face, but he will still watch it with interest.

Why is Baby so fascinated with people's faces? Scientific studies of what infants perceive have shed some light on this question.

When infants as young as two and three months old were shown a variety of visual images, they paid more attention to the picture of a human face than to any of the others.

They appear to be fascinated with faces, not because they immediately recognize them as faces—since they have not yet formed an intellectual concept of face—but because certain aspects of the human face intrigue them.

For example, one-month-olds were found to concentrate on the outer edges of the face, such as the hairline and the chin. But older infants focused more on central features of the face such as the eyes, nose, lips and teeth.

Between three and six months, infants become better able to focus with both eyes together which greatly helps their development of face perception. It is during this period that infants first develop some rudimentary concept of what a face is.

What seems to be happening is that the baby is working to build up a concept—in this case, the concept of what we call a face. A concept or idea is a kind of picture in his mind about what a thing is like.

Baby starts out with an impression of his mother's face, which has certain features in certain places. When a new face

comes along, it has the same general form but with little changes here and there that make it look different.

Is the new thing a face? Baby must study the pattern to make sure. He probably looks at the main landmarks—eyes, nose, and mouth—to see if they conform to the pattern that he has seen before.

If they do, he may give a little smile. It seems to be his wordless way of saying to himself: "I know what that is—it's a face."

Needless to say, a face has great significance for him. If you look at the pattern of objects in the illustration below, you automatically see a face. In fact, it is hard to see anything but a face.

The quality, "faceness," that comes through to you is more than the sum of

the parts. It is a concept that was developed in your infancy, not through the repetitious exposure to one face but from experience with a large variety of faces.

Baby's looking preferences suggest that he actively seeks variety so that he can try out his new concepts on the world.

If there is the right amount of discrepancy between the old and the new, he will carefully study and absorb the new into the old, thereby broadening and enriching his concept.

If there is too much discrepancy, he may have to form a new concept or at least

When two- and three-month-old infants were shown a variety of visual images, they paid more attention to the picture of a human face than to any of the others.

make subdivisions of the old. More about this in later months.

So that is why Baby is so interested in different people and their faces right now. He is digesting variations on the theme of his parents' faces so as to build one of his first permanent conceptions of an object in the world.

This idea of theme and variations is an important principle in learning, and we shall return to it often in the future.

How long will Baby's present social period last? We are sorry to say it will soon come to an end, at least temporarily. In another month or two, he is likely to develop grave reservations about strangers so that he will cling to his caregiver apprehensively when they come near.

This means that the time for friends and relatives to get better acquainted with Baby is right now while he needs and accepts them as interesting subjects in his learning laboratory.

While Baby is still in this happy, genial, extroverted period it is wise to encourage others, such as grandparents, neighbors or babysitter, to interact with him. This helps him to learn that other people besides his parents are warm and loving.

The more parents isolate their baby from other caregivers, the more he is likely to be apprehensive about strangers in later months.

So don't think you are neglecting Baby at this stage if you occasionally get a babysitter in order to take an evening off—you are probably doing him a great favor by helping him expand his social world of friends, not to mention the good you may be doing yourselves. ■

The Home Where You Live

Baby is beginning to move, and soon she will be highly mobile. Not only will she be moving, she will be exploring—and her movements and her explorations at this point are extremely important for her future development and learning. The "home where you live" is the place where nearly all this moving, exploring, and learning will take place.

Your home is, in one sense, a laboratory of child development where one very special baby—your baby—is going to get acquainted with the world while she also gets acquainted with herself as one person in that world.

It is the place where your baby will conduct thousands of experiments, discovering the world about her.

We urge you, right now, to take a careful look at your home. Try to see it as a laboratory where your baby will conduct her own special experiments—and then try to make it the best possible laboratory you can.

A picture-perfect home straight out of a magazine may be gratifying to its adult occupants, but such precise and rigid arrangements, which put restrictions on baby's movements and explorations, are seldom best for her. Make your home liveable. From the baby's point of view, perhaps the best place to start is at the bottom—the floor.

The floor is one of the most important parts of the place where you live—for Baby, that is. As soon as she becomes mobile, she should spend a lot of time on the floor. It's her school now, the place where she will do her moving and have some of her most important early learning.

Try this experiment: lie down on the floor yourself and see how your rooms look from your baby's point of view. Lie on your back and look around.

You'll be surprised at the different things you see and feel. Is the floor nice and warm or are there drafts? Roll over on your stomach and take another look. Is there room to move and crawl about without tripping over wires and furniture legs—and are there things to look at?

Raise your head, from this lying down position, and look at the objects within reach. Everything down there is fair game for an exploring baby—any object you do not want her to grab, taste, bang, drop, throw, or otherwise explore is best put away—or at least put up high—for now.

That's called "baby-proofing"—and it's as necessary for her own safety as for the safety of your prized china doll collection.

After you have taken away all the breakable, dangerous, or non-touchable items from Baby's reach, turn your thoughts to the kind of common household things you do want her to be able to touch and explore like accessible plastic bowls, or pots and wooden spoons.

Early exploration of common objects is extremely important for future learning. Provide many different opportunities for Baby to see, handle, taste, smell, and hear. Do not "hem her in" by keeping her in the playpen too long. Let her move on the floor as she will. Help her get acquainted with the fascinating world about her. ■

Touch Is Important To Your Baby

One of Baby's earliest ways of learning is through her sense of touch. Long after she has gained control of her eyes and has begun to learn through them, she will continue to learn by the sense of touch—holding, handling and mouthing objects.

The world is full of so many things which have different "feels" when Baby comes in contact with them.

The idea that some things are the "same" and other things are "different" is one of the most basic of all early learning. One way to help her learn more about "same and different" is to give her many opportunities to experience all those interesting "feels."

The active, even the fussy baby, never lacks for the stimulation of lifting and handling.

However, the placid, "very good" baby may be deprived of stimulation that she needs simply because she makes no demands on her parents.

All babies can benefit from gentle stimulation of their sense of touch. If Baby is placed on her stomach without clothing for a short time before her bath, she experiences sensations over her body's skin which she may otherwise miss.

Gently stroke and rub her back, arms and legs with your hands. Pat her gently all over or tap her with your fingertips. Sometimes rub her gently with something soft and velvety. A piece of soft corduroy is an excellent source of stimulation.

After her bath, don't just pat her dry. Rub her arms, legs, tummy and back with a soft terry cloth towel. Kiss her head, her hands, her feet. Play with her toes as you talk to her. Pat her feet together. Pat her hands together. Make a bubbling noise against the skin in the hollow of her neck or against her soft tummy.

A "ticklish" baby is often very sensitive to touch because she has not had enough stimulation of this sense.

If your baby is ticklish, begin by using her own hands to rub and pat her body. As she learns to trust her own touch, you can gradually begin using your own hand.

Remember that a light touch feels more "tickly" than a firmer one. A gentle but firm touch with the palm of your hand is less apt to "tickle" than feather-like stroking with fingertips. ■

The Perfect Family and Other Fairy Tales

Most likely as a child you read those fairy tales that ended with the prince and princess getting married and "living happily ever after."

Or you've seen some of the old family television shows where all problems are worked out, and everyone and everything is perfect—mother, father, the whole family. It is this fantasy-family we want to talk about.

The mother, is almost perfect. She is wise and understanding, loving and concerned, and almost everything else a mother is supposed to be.

Little dark clouds appear occasionally and cast a brief gloom over the family landscape; but these are always small clouds, and one or the other of the television/movie parents has a way of pushing them away with a Smile of Wisdom, or Understanding, or Whatever.

This is all well and good so long as we recognize one important fact: a perfect-type family is a fairy tale.

The thing about a fairy tale is that what happens isn't real. The people may seem quite warm and wonderful, but they are characters in a fairy tale; unreal people in an unreal world.

Very few real families can keep all this warm, wonderful business going for long. People worry. The new baby yells in the middle of the night, and the first thing you know, the weary parents are yelling at each other.

The scene is not warm and wonderful, but it definitely is real.

Sure, there are warm and wonderful times in families—times when things really go right, times when you can almost touch the stars. But no family is like that all the time.

A family has its ups and downs. Tempers flare and people say and do hurtful things to each other.

In real, honest-to-goodness families you find a mixture of good times and times that are not so good.

Families come in all kinds of combinations—some have one parent, others have grandparents or other extended family members.

No one can give you a nice, neat formula for creative family living. Perhaps it is enough to say a thing or two about the not-so-good times which come to all families.

The first thing we want to emphasize is that you should not take the fairy-tale-perfect family too seriously.

If you can come to know that real families must come to grips with the nitty-gritty of life, then you will not find yourself in deep shock when things occasionally get completely out of hand.

There is much to be said for not letting yourself be overcome by the shock of one human personality banging up against another —because this is inevitable in the closeness of family life.

The second point is this: Creative marriages happen when the partners learn how to pick up the pieces and put the whole thing together again.

Creative marriages do not happen by aiming for fairy tale goals, such as having a perpetually warm and wonderful family like the TV family.

There is no formula for picking up the pieces and getting the whole thing started again. Every family has to work this out for itself.

Whatever your family situation may be, it is important for each member to recognize that reconciliation is a very large part of family living. Trying to make it happen is well worth the effort.

We wish you all the best as you build your own very special family. ■

Talking and Listening

Baby is now sitting up with props and paying attention to everything in the world about him.

He turns his head to seek out sounds he hears; both his eyes and ears appear to search for the source of the sound, particularly if he drops something and it makes noise.

This is a good time to check for a hearing impairment if Baby is not responding in this way to the noises in the world around him.

You can assess Baby's hearing by observing how he responds when you deliberately make sounds yourself or make sounds with objects which are within his hearing world (five to six feet) but not visible.

Does he turn his head to look when someone talks to him? Does he look toward loud, unexpected or unfamiliar noises?

If the answer if yes, you can be pretty sure that his hearing is adequate.

On the other hand, if he fails to respond, or if his responses aren't regular, you must not automatically assume a hearing impairment.

For example, the time schedule for premature infants or those with delayed development will not be the same as for the "typical" infant.

If you are concerned, consult your pediatrician. He may do a hearing test himself, or refer you to a specialist or clinic.

To obtain information about the closest hearing center, we recommend that you contact the American Speech-Language-Hearing Association, 10801 Rockville Pike, Rockville, MD 20852, online at: www.asha.org. You can also contact the speech, language and hearing program at your local university or hospital.

Research hospitals administer hearing tests to newborns but the practice is not common to many hospitals in this country. About one in every 1000 infants is born with a hearing defect. It is vital that such babies are identified by five months of age so that they can be helped to develop normal speech. Unless he can hear his own voice and the voices of other people, a baby will experience problems with both language and learning.

During this period of babbling, Baby produces an enormous variety of sounds. It is even hard to describe them without using medical terms, but you can listen to the great variety of hisses and throat clicks.

Babbling is very important and here's why: As he babbles, Baby is building memories of what happens when he makes sounds with his voice. These early memories are necessary when he begins to make words later on, and babbling is the way the early memories get "wired in."

When Baby babbles, two things happen at the same time: He "feels" something and he hears something. What he feels is his own activity: movements of lips, tongue, jaws, vocal cords, etc. What he hears are the sounds which his own activity produces. Different sounds "feel" differently.

In babbling, he is beginning to develop an automatic memory for what kind of "feel" makes a particular kind of sound. When he begins to make words, the memories are all there, wired in so that when he wants to make a word he knows automatically how to make the sounds.

Babbling helps get this whole complicated process going.

If you want a verbal youngster, this is the time to encourage his vocal skills. Imitate what he says. You will find that within a short time your imitation will cause him to "say" more.

Incidentally, what he says may not sound like what you said, but it doesn't matter. Continue the dialogue, especially during bathing, dressing and playtime. Although he is far from talking, Baby is listening and learning.

Melody, or the music of our speech, plays an important role in language development. At this time Baby responds to the rhythm and melody of your voice rather than to the meaning of the words.

In fact, throughout life we depend on the rhythm of speech to obtain meaning.

For example, when you listen to a foreigner talk, although he may use all of the English words correctly, if he retains the melodic pattern of his native tongue, understanding may be difficult. ■

Mouthing

In the past Baby, has come to enjoy her hand sucking. There is coordination between mouth and hand. But now if an object is placed in her hands, she will attempt to bring it to her lips and mouth it vigorously. Often the mouth opens and closes in anticipation of the object.

This exploration with her mouth is a vital part of learning. Baby has more nerve endings in the mouth than anywhere else, and this activity helps her make important discoveries.

Make sure that her playthings and available objects are washed frequently, so that you do not feel it is necessary to discourage mouthing. It will not develop bad habits nor make the child a confirmed thumb sucker; it is too important to her development to prohibit.

In a few months mouthing will focus on feeding. Right now the infant is learning to interact with objects. And by means of mouthing she is learning much about their properties. ■

Why Your Baby Should Not Have a Walker

Human babies follow a certain developmental pattern whereby head control leads to sitting balance; learning to sit alone prepares the child for creeping, and learning to creep prepares him for walking.

A number of factors contribute to walking readiness. For example, Baby's back muscles must be strong enough to keep him upright and balanced over his legs and feet.

Baby must have developed certain balancing and protective responses which will protect him from serious injury during the many falls he will experience as he learns to walk.

Through creeping, Baby must learn to use his arms and legs rhythmically and alternately while holding his head up to see where he is going.

The many small bones of Baby's feet are not hard like an adult's but are cartilage which is firm but flexible like hard rubber. The muscles which support the bones and which eventually hold the arches in place must be strong enough to hold the bones in good position when Baby stands on his feet.

Left to himself, Baby will creep and pull to a standing position. During this period he just stands with his feet fairly far apart and turned out for better balance. Later he will begin to sidestep while holding onto a support.

Baby needs lots of practice in all of the activities—creeping, balancing, standing—which strengthen his muscles, improve his balance, and lead to strong standing and walking positions. Walkers steal time from these essential readiness activities.

In a walker, Baby gets no stable standing practice. Any random leg movements push the walker from place to place. Rhythmic patterns of leg movement are not established and coordinated arm and leg movements fail to develop as they should.

Most manufacturers now design baby walkers with wide, opaque plastic trays and relatively small leg openings to decrease the likelihood of tipping accidents.

Growing Child

P. O. Box 2505 • W Lafayette, IN 47996
(800) 927-7289
©Growing Child, Inc.
www.GrowingChild.com

Contributing Authors

Phil Bach, O.D., Ph.D.
Miriam Bender, Ph.D.
Joseph Braga, Ed.D.
Laurie Braga, Ph.D.
George Early, Ph.D.
Carol R. Gestwicki, M.S.
Liam Grimley, Ph.D.
Robert Hannemann, M.D., F.A.A.P.
Sylvia Kottler, M.S.
Bill Peterson, Ph.D.

However, this design prevents the infant from seeing his moving legs. Such visual feedback about body position and limb movement is necessary for coordination, and depriving infants of it can delay normal muscle control and mental development.

Studies show that walkers either do not influence walking at all, or may even delay time of walking, with those infants scoring lower on Bayley scales of mental and motor development.

A child who can move in a walker before he has balance, control, and judgment can have dangerous misadventures. Common accidents include rolling down the stairs, causing serious injury; rolling into pools and water sources with a risk of drowning; and being able to reach higher objects with the risk of burning or poisoning.

Such accidents can occur even with adult supervision as baby walkers can move as fast as three feet in one second.

The American Academy of Pediatrics states that walkers are never safe to use, recommending that adults in home and child care centers never place babies in walkers with wheels. The Academy has even gone so far as to lobby for the ban of manufacture and sale of all baby walkers.

Baby will walk when his body is ready. A fat, placid baby usually walks later than an active, wiry baby.

Some children walk at nine or ten months. Others do not walk until 12 to 14 months.

One thing you can be sure of—given plenty of opportunities to crawl, creep, to pull to a standing position and to cruise along supporting furniture, your baby will walk when his body and nervous system are developmentally ready for walking. ■

Growing Child®

Until you start understanding that everybody's child is yours, the world won't be good for any of our children.

Susan Sarandon

Six Months Old

As Baby continues to develop, he must build each new achievement on those which have gone before. Now when you pull him from a lying to a sitting position, he lifts his head strongly and actively cooperates by pulling with his arms. He sits well in a high chair with little or no additional support, although if the high chair is a large one, he may still need a pillow at his back to fill up the extra space.

If you sit him on the floor, the six-month-old baby usually can sit alone for 5-10 seconds by leaning forward and using his hands and arms for support. His back is rounded and he sags forward unless he props himself on his arms.

About half of all six-month-old babies can roll over from back to stomach easily in either direction. Once on his stomach, Baby continues to improve his way of

pulling and kicking himself along the floor or bed and turning himself around. He may roll over and over to reach his goal, or roll onto his back and push himself along with his feet. Generally, however, he will prefer lying on his stomach.

Baby has improved his reaching coordination and purposefully reaches for things when he sees them. Sitting in his high chair, he is now usually able to reach for and grasp a dangling toy. This kind of reach and grasp requires much more control than taking an object from the tray or someone's hand. He probably will grasp the object in his palm, but soon will start to use his thumb as well as his fingers to hold it. During this month he may begin to reach for a toy with one hand instead of two. ∎

At Six Months Baby Likes to:
- Roll over.
- Mouth a teether or spoon.
- Smile at familiar faces.
- Drop, throw or bang things.

Give Your Baby:
- Household objects such as plastic cups, spoons and small pot lids.
- A ball to roll and clutch.
- Mouthing toys.

Ask Your Doctor About:
- 3rd DTaP vaccine.
- H. Influenzae type b (Hib) vaccine.
- Hepatitis B vaccine (Hep B).
- IPV (inactive polio vaccine).
- PCV (pneumococcal conjugate vaccine).
- Rotavirus (Rota) vaccine.

New View, New Interests

Now that Baby is sitting alone, his view of the world is full of many new things. For the first time there is a dimension of up and down, as well as a to-and-fro direction.

No more will he be content to just sit and watch the scene or grasp nearby objects. Soon, something new and dramatic will happen: Baby will hold an object in his hand and hit it against something else.

Here we see how separate processes of development begin to work together. In order to be able to sit upright, even with

support, he needs to have developed the necessary muscles and sense of balance.

As soon as he can sit with support in an upright position, his arms will be free. Over the next few months those arms will be moving up and down.

With this newly developed ability, he will be able to lift an object and bring it down on a flat surface like the floor or a table top.

Reaching for, grasping, and moving the object involves the development of eye-hand coordination skills.

The entire activity requires a remarkable combination of interconnected abilities and skills that enable Baby to strive toward and reach new levels of learning.

Right now what Baby does with an object is mostly a matter of what he himself has learned which, of course, builds on the potential with which he was born.

For instance, when Baby could first pick up an object, he may have shaken it by chance. This gave him a different feeling

continued on page 42

Six Month Milestones

At six months, Baby is already halfway through her first year ... and it's time to take inventory of just what a "typical" baby is doing now.

Our description uses the Descriptive Scale of Developmental Progress by Mary D. Sheridan, with cross-references to the Denver Developmental Screening Scale and a more recent Developmental Assessment published by Haskins and Squires.

Posture and Large Movements
When lying on her back, the typical six-month-old raises her head from the pillow to look at her feet. She also will lift her legs straight up in the air and grasp one foot, perhaps bringing it to her mouth. She moves her arms strongly and purposefully, holding them up to be lifted. When her hands are held, she braces her shoulders and pulls herself to a sitting position. She kicks strongly, alternating legs, and can roll over from front to back and often from back to front.

When lying prone, our typical six-month-old lifts her head and chest strongly, supporting herself on flattened palms and straight arms. She sits easily with support in a chair, and turns her head from side to side to look around. When held sitting (held by the arms) on a firm surface, she holds her head firmly erect and sits with a straight back. She may sit alone momentarily.

When held standing with feet touching a hard surface, she will bear weight on her feet and actively bounce up and down.

Vision and Fine Movement
The typical six-month-old never stops visually examining her surroundings. Everything that moves, everything that is new or different, and everything that is within reach attracts her eager attention.

She follows an adult's activities from across the room. Her eyes move in unison—as a team. Any deviation from this, such as a wandering eye or one that is even slightly crossed, is considered abnormal.

Interesting small objects—toys, small blocks, etc.—six to twelve inches away are focused on immediately, and she reaches out with both hands to grasp and examine them.

She still uses her whole hand to grasp, but now passes a toy back and forth from one hand to the other. She may even transfer one toy to the other hand, and reach for or accept a second toy. When a toy falls from her hand, she usually watches where it lands—if it lands where she can see it. If it falls where she can't see it, she will just forget it, or may search for it vaguely with eyes and patting hands. As yet she has not established a concept of "object permanence." Most objects still cease to exist for her when she can no longer see them.

Hearing and Speech
Her parent's voice from across the room gets immediate turning response from the typical six-month-old. She also shows evidence of selective response to different emotional tones of her parent's voice.

She is now making a wide variety of pre-speech sounds. She laughs, chuckles and squeals aloud in play. She vocalizes tunefully to herself and others using sing-song vowel sounds in single or double combinations. She babbles this way as much for her own amusement as in response to others. She also screams in annoyance or anger. She may initiate speech sounds or other play sounds, although these still are not words.

Social Behavior and Play
Six-month-old hands reach for and grasp any small object within reach. Everything is taken to the mouth for further exploration.

The typical six-month-old finds feet just as interesting as hands, and often uses one foot and one hand to hold objects for observation. She will work hard to get an object that is out of reach. She attends somewhat doubtfully to peek-a-boo, but is learning to enjoy it.

When offered a rattle or a similar sound-maker, she will reach for it at once and shake it deliberately to make the sound. Often she will watch it closely as she shakes it.

Much solitary playtime is spent in manipulating objects, passing them from hand to hand, to mouth, to hand while watching attentively as she turns them over and over.

While usually still friendly with everyone, in another month she may become reserved with strangers.

All in all, the typical six-month-old is quite a person. The first half-year of life has been a busy one, and some major developmental steps have been achieved. ∎

Developmental Checklist—Six Months

Social/Emotional

- Exhibits friendliness toward strangers, but slightly uneasy yet when parents are not present.
- Puts hand on breast or bottle while drinking, and may pat gently.
- Responds selectively to the emotional tones of parents' voices.
- Smiles, laughs and squeals.
- Explores with head and eyes.

Communication

- Turns head to parent's voice, even if across the room.
- Babbles using single and repetitive syllables.
- Locates a sound by looking (produced at a distance of 18" to the side of each ear).

Vision

- Eyes follow activities from one side to the other.
- Both eyes move in unison.

Motor (Fine)

- Uses whole hand (palmar grasp) to obtain objects.
- Reaches with two hands for objects up to one foot away.
- Transfers objects from one hand to the other.

Motor (Gross)

- Kicks strongly.
- Kicks alternately with both legs.
- Pulls self up from back-lying when hands are grasped.
- When lying prone on stomach, supports self on extended arms and lifts head and chest strongly.
- Rolls over front to back.
- Sits alone briefly.
- Keeps head and back straight when held in a sitting position.
- When lying on back, brings legs up and over chest, and can grasp and bring one foot to mouth. ∎

These milestones are guidelines only. All babies do not develop at the same speed, nor do they spend the same amount of time at each stage of their development. Usually a baby is ahead in some areas, behind in others and "typical" in still other areas. The concept of the "typical" child describes the general characteristics of children at a given age.

One Language Or Two?

We hear from many parents who either speak more than one language in the home, or who want their child to learn a second language.

The questions they ask most often are when is the best time to start a second language, and won't the child be confused by trying to learn two languages at the same time?

There is some experimental evidence that a child who is exposed to the influence of two languages before she arrives at a fair degree of understanding and proficiency in one language is sometimes delayed in language development.

This delay is not permanent but may be observed particularly when the child starts to talk around the second year. There are differences in bilingualism based on the time and circumstances under which two languages are acquired.

Some children may regularly hear two different languages spoken at home, depending, perhaps, on the mood of the parent.

This is known as compound bilingualism, when a child is exposed to both languages interchangeably.

Obviously such children have to learn two different words for every object. As a result of their initial confusion, their development of each language may be delayed, especially in the early stages.

Coordinate bilingualism means the child learns two languages but the experiences are quite distinct.

The child's parents speak essentially one language at home while the second language is heard from peers and learned at school.

The consequence is often deficiency in the use of the second language. This does not mean, however, that children cannot learn two languages at the same time.

Parents who wish their child to learn a second language, or bilingual parents who speak two languages in the home should consider a workable strategy to simplify the introduction of two languages in early childhood.

One idea is to designate specific times or places where each language is to be spoken regularly. For example, one language can be spoken in the home during the daytime hours, while the second is spoken in the evening. This avoids the confusion of switching from one language to another during a given time period.

Learning a second language can continue and extend the rich cultural heritage from one's family as well as span the generations. ∎

Who is the "Typical" Baby?

From time to time in your reading you may find statements such as this: "The typical baby, when lying on her tummy, can lift her head and hold it up by the time she is six weeks old."

If your child could lift her head and hold it up before she was six weeks old, you might think she is much smarter than most babies.

Or, if your child is six weeks old and is not yet able to lift her head and hold it up, you might begin to wonder if she could be "slow" or "cognitively delayed."

Neither of these conclusions may be appropriate. So, we need to explain what we mean by the "typical" baby.

We use the word "typical" to describe the characteristics normally exhibited at a particular stage of development. As you look at your own six-month-old baby, think of all the other six-month-old babies in the world.

By examining large numbers of babies of the same age, researchers are able to identify the characteristics of this age group. And if your child shows these characteristics in one given area of development (for example, recognizes familiar faces), then we can say that your child is "typical" in that given area.

It is important to realize that it is most unlikely that there will ever be a baby who is truly "typical" in every aspect of development.

Usually a baby may be somewhat ahead in some areas, somewhat behind in others, and "typical" in still others.

So, in a very real sense, the "typical" child (that is, "typical" in every single aspect of development) doesn't really exist. Yet the concept of the "typical" child is a useful one to describe the characteristics one would expect to find at a certain age.

For example, when we say that "the typical six-week-old child can lift her head and hold it up," we mean simply that if we looked at a large number of six-week-old babies, we would find that a majority of them had mastered this skill while some others had not.

Conscientious parents want to know what is reasonable to expect in terms of their child's behavior or development.

For that purpose, the concept of the "typical" child is useful, since it provides a research-based means of comparison. However, our efforts to identify the characteristics typically found in children at a given age in no way implies that the child who is "slightly ahead" or "slightly behind" is either a "genius" or "cognitively delayed."

Human growth and development is not a process that takes place with clockwork regularity. Children simply do not grow and develop by the calendar.

Although children generally progress through the same stages, each child develops in her own way and at different rates at different times in her life.

For instance, no two children grow in height at the same rate. Nor does any child

grow at a constant steady rate. She may grow two inches one year, four inches the next year, and only one inch the year after. Yet her growth might still be "typical" for a child of her age.

So, "typical" or "normal" covers a wide range of differences—in the age at which a baby lifts her head and holds it up, as well as the rate at which she grows in height.

The "typical" baby's rate of development is described somewhat roughly in terms of certain developmental milestones. These milestones help us to identify specific abilities which mark important stages of learning: Lifting and holding the head up, sitting unsupported, creeping, standing alone, walking alone, first word, first sentence.

There is a normal range of time within which 60 to 70 percent of all children reach each of these milestones. This normal range of time will vary from one ability to another. That is, for some abilities, the range of time will be shorter; for others it will be longer.

The normal range includes a period of time both before and after the age at which our "typical" child reaches a milestone. If a child reaches a given milestone earlier than or within this normal rate, there is no cause for concern.

But a child's failure to reach one of these milestones by the time 75 to 80 percent of all babies her age have passed it is still no reason for the parents to panic.

They should, however, observe her carefully, and call the delay to the attention of her physician. Many problems can be remedied more effectively if they are detected early.

Delay in development is more likely to be cause for concern. Should the child not have reached a milestone which 90 to 95 percent of babies her age have already passed, parents should seek medical help.

Whatever the difficulty, there are many sources of help available. Usually the first of these is your child's physician. ■

Understanding Language

Most professionals believe that children who are spoken to a great deal in early infancy talk better than children of less verbal parents.

One long-term investigation analyzed tape recordings of verbal interactions between parents and infants in their home. Although all the children started to speak at about the same time, their vocabulary as measured by the number of different words used varied significantly, based on the number of words individual children heard in one hour. Later the study found positive correlations between verbal abilities and intellectual development as the children were followed to age nine or ten.

This study matches findings that toddlers and preschoolers who are read to a great deal read more easily and better than those having less experience with language.

A baby's receptive language depends upon his good listening and looking habits in his relationship with parents or other familiar people. Receptive language—that which he understands—always precedes expressive language—that which he can say—by several months. That is, he will understand the word "ball" several months before he tries to say it.

At this age he doesn't understand the exact meanings of words, but he does understand something of what the person using them means since the words are delivered along with feelings, facial expression, gestures and body movement.

For example, when Father says, "Come here," he holds his hands out to receive Baby.

When Mother says, "Give it to me," she reaches out for the object, and when she says, "Here, I'll give it back to you," she hands it back.

Another example is the game where an adult pretends he can't see Baby and says, "Where's Baby, where's Baby?" as he dramatically pantomimes the search for Baby, and finally exclaims, "Here he is!"

Activities like this contribute to the baby's developing capacity to understand language. If you're not already playing such games of language development, try some.

When you play games, talk to Baby, be a ham—put lots of drama into your voice. Make it rise and fall, change from soft to loud, alternate from slow to fast.

Baby is learning to match words with actions, and soon he'll be understanding a lot of these games well. Consider the game of peek-a-boo. To play, cover your face with a towel and encourage Baby to push or pull it off. If he doesn't, peek through the towel to be sure he is looking at you. Remove the cover yourself as you say, "Peek-a-boo."

Remember that while Baby is becoming used to noises, he is still frightened when they are too loud or too sudden, so don't make your "peek-a-boo" explode like a bomb.

There's a bonus from this game which is important for Baby's intellectual development. From peek-a-boo, he'll discover that you are present even though he may not be able to see you. Soon he'll learn that people and objects exist even when they're not immediately visible. ■

What is Baby Saying?

Early sound production is largely a motor function, and like other motor abilities, its development follows a definite order. For example, most of the first sounds are formed in the back of the mouth. Once Baby starts to use his tongue and lips (and later his teeth), he is able to expand his vocabulary by using the front of his mouth.

By six months, Baby has a good many sound combinations, the result of his ability to blend about twelve consonants with a variety of vowels. He can also vary their loudness, duration and pitch.

There is experimental evidence to indicate that rewarding an infant for sound-making—by smiling, hugging, kissing or stroking his stomach—produces an increase in the amount of babbling.

In one comparison between infants under six months living in an orphanage and those living with a family, it was observed that the orphanage infants were slower in the number and types of sounds they produced and the variety of pitch.

Now is the time to use dialog activities regularly. After a pause in his babbling, imitate what he has "said." Continue to repeat what he's said each time he pauses.

Baby may also be talking for the pleasure of hearing his own voice and will smile politely when you respond but won't engage in dialogue.

Remember that while Baby's responses may not exactly resemble what he heard, he is stimulated to make his own sounds. Have you tried tongue clicking, making raspberries with your lips, winking, or saying "buzz?" When he exhibits amusement, be sure to laugh and smile in turn. And pause long enough to permit a vocal response. With practice, you will observe how much the length of the dialogue increases, and how serious baby can become.

On the other hand, don't be disappointed if the imitation or dialogue game doesn't always succeed. There are many occasions when Baby cannot do too many things at one time.

If you catch him babbling while he is playing with a toy, or if you choose to engage him in play with an object, he will be too absorbed in you and the toy to initiate any "back talk." For imitation to contribute to Baby's language learning, you must imitate him. Then he will imitate you. ■

continued from page 37

in his arm and a larger sense of movement than just the action of his hand could provide.

This pleasant new experience was rewarding enough to cause him to continue the shaking, repeating the movements until he was tired, or something distracted him. Thus, what he learned about the sight and feel of an object and the movements of shaking it stayed with him until he was given a new object.

Then, when he felt this new object in his hand, he automatically shook it. Shaking thus became a kind of standard action when Baby had an object in his hand.

The same thing probably happened with banging. The object he was shaking happened to strike a surface, and Baby heard the sound and felt the bump. So, once he made the contact and heard the noise, he would repeat the action again and again.

The point is that at first there is no clear idea in Baby's mind about what he really wants to do with an object. There is no real intention of doing something (like banging it) before it gets into his hand, and there is only a fuzzy connection between his efforts and the effect they produce.

If you try picking Baby up while he is banging something on the high chair tray, chances are his movements will stop completely once he has lost contact with the tray.

There was not really a thought-out strategy for making a sound. When you broke the cycle he was repeating, he stopped. He did not try to reach down to continue making contact with the tray.

Soon Baby's experience with objects will show him that he cannot use the same action on everything.

Table legs, for instance, can be grasped but they cannot be shaken or banged. Therefore, he will develop a wider variety of activities with different objects. This will help him learn to tell the difference between them.

Along with improved control of his movements, his different responses to different objects may include patting the furniture, turning up the corner of the throw rug, or carefully grasping carpet pile. You may find it interesting to keep track of the number of ways Baby can manipulate objects.

Does he use his thumb and fingers to pick up a toy without using his palm? How many fingers? Does he turn his wrist back and forth as he explores a toy? Has he found his feet yet? If he hasn't, he will find them soon. Don't be surprised when he grasps a foot and tries to put it in his mouth.

You will be amazed at how quickly new actions appear. He is indeed learning many things in a short time. During the early stages of exploration, the ordinary household things such as plastic cups or jar lids will provide plenty of experience and stimulation.

Later it will be appropriate to give Baby some additional objects to increase the number of building blocks of experience that will be his stock in trade when it comes to thinking and solving problems. ∎

Growing Child

P. O. Box 2505 • W Lafayette, IN 47996
(800) 927-7289
©Growing Child, Inc.
www.GrowingChild.com

Contributing Authors
Phil Bach, O.D., Ph.D.
Miriam Bender, Ph.D.
Joseph Braga, Ed.D.
Laurie Braga, Ph.D.
George Early, Ph.D.
Carol R. Gestwicki, M.S.
Liam Grimley, Ph.D.
Robert Hannemann, M.D., F.A.A.P.
Sylvia Kottler, M.S.
Bill Peterson, Ph.D.

Starting Baby on the Road to Discovery

What an exciting time for Baby! Each day is filled with fascinating new discoveries.

She's becoming more alert and aware of her surroundings and anxious to become an active participant in your world.

Because the right experiences at this formative age will help enhance a child's development, toys and books take on a new importance during the upcoming months.

Baby seems to be grabbing the world with her eyes, and her hands. Toys and playthings she can touch, squeeze, grasp, pull, push and handle will help stimulate learning and satisfy her need to manipulate.

Books should play an important role in a child's life, right from the start. Reading to Baby helps foster a bond between you and your child.

An introduction to books at an early age helps language development and encourages a sense of communication, inspiring your growing child to want to learn.

Board books are ideal first books for Baby. They're sturdy, safe and offer simple first stories perfect for introducing children to the pleasures of reading.

You can make good use of your local library's children's section to see what books are available and those that are most attractive to your child. Children's libraries provide an interesting variety and selection.

You can build your youngster's personal library with a book or two at a time—and create a library to be added to as she grows, with books that will be treasured for a lifetime. ∎

Be ever gentle with the children
God has given you.

Burritt

Baby Power

At seven months Baby is in the habit of making noises and "babbling." Babbling is a repetition of sounds such as "papapa" which continues when the adults in his life reward him with smiles, affection, and other demonstrations of their satisfaction.

He is also in the habit of listening to sounds when the adults in his life talk to him and cause him to pay attention.

In addition, at seven months, we have something new: Baby power! He knows that he can attract attention by expressing his interests and needs. He knows that when he cries, someone will come and feed or relieve him. Also he is aware that when he babbles, someone nice shows delight with him.

Gradually these pleasant experiences will become strong incentives to babble more and more. However, if no one responds, the drive to continue babbling will weaken.

Likewise, if Baby is allowed to cry for long periods without any attention, then he will not associate his cries with the satisfaction of his needs and his crying will be aimless.

On the other hand, a child's communicative development may be slow if the adults in his life anticipate all of his needs. For example, if the family routine is so exact that everything is on schedule or if the instant he starts to cry someone always responds quickly, the incentive to cry may be weakened. Likewise, the incentive to babble may be weakened if there is always someone ready and waiting to entertain and play with him.

What Baby needs is a good balance between too much and not enough help—between over-indulgence and indifference.

What is different about the babbling of a seven-month-old? Until now, sound-making has been associated with the body states of comfort and discomfort. Now he not only babbles to express contentment but he produces sounds at will, just for the pleasure of making them.

He enjoys the results of feeling and listening to the sounds themselves, their

At Seven Months Baby Likes to:
- Sit without support.
- Use fingers and thumb together for a purpose, such as to pick up a block.
- Bite on his first tooth.
- Listen to sounds.

Give Your Baby:
- Toys in the bath.
- The sounds of music and nursery rhymes.
- Objects for making noise like utensils and squeaky toys.
- A splashing good time in the bath.

pattern, rhythms, and tunes. He repeats their pitch, combines and inter-weaves them to make new tunes.

How does this babbling also affect speech development? It gives his tongue, lips and throat muscles plenty of practice and increases their efficiency. As he plays with sounds, he learns how it feels when he makes the movements necessary to produce them, just as he is learning about the other movements of his body and limbs. ■

Listening

By the time she is six to seven months old, Baby can distinguish "friendly" from "unfriendly" speech.

She is beginning (and it is a very modest beginning) to make some sense out of what she hears and sees.

She doesn't understand actual words, but she responds to the intonation of the voice, gestures, body movement and facial expression, particularly the

eyes. In other words, she responds not to what we say but how we say it.

Generally when adults talk to babies, they tend to exaggerate the differences in intonation. Baby knows that a friendly tone is a pleasant sound, and an unfriendly tone is an unpleasant sound.

These characteristics are strengthened by the infant's experiences, pleasant

or unpleasant, which coincide with the tones. For example, we use different tones when we say "Hello, Baby!" and "Time for bed."

In other words, babies learn to derive meaning from the total context of what we say—facial expression, intonation of voice, for example—long before they understand the actual words we use. ■

Eyes and Hands Together

One of Baby's strongest urges at this age is to explore objects with her hands and eyes together. She wants to know how objects feel.

Her eyes naturally turn to what her hands are exploring. She will pick up a block, plastic cup or toy and feel it, finger it, twist it, all the while looking at it.

This urge to explore with hands and eyes is so strong that she is quite happy by herself for brief periods. When she is playing alone like this, let her be.

Exploring with both eyes and hands together is extremely important. Whenever a baby feels an object and looks at it at the same time, she is getting some very basic information about that object.

She is getting that information through two different channels at the same time: Her hands tell her how the object "feels" and her eyes tell her how the object "looks."

Such looking and feeling activities are actually scientific experiments which Baby is making whereby she is learning some fundamental realities about her world.

At the same time she is learning something about herself: She has eyes and she can use them to get information about what's going on around her.

In time what Baby's eyes see "matches up" with what her hands feel. It is through such repeated "matching" of looking and feeling that she learns how to use only her eyes to acquire organized information.

Some very interesting research has been done with people who were born blind, but who as adults regained their sight when cataracts were removed. Before their surgery, these people knew only by "feel" about the shape and form of different objects.

After they could see, it was extremely difficult for them to learn how to recognize simple shapes and forms (triangles, squares, and rectangles) simply by looking at them.

Even after they had painstakingly learned to recognize some simple shapes by looking, they would be quite confused if some minor visual detail in the form was changed.

For instance, if they learned to recognize a white triangle, they could not immediately recognize a yellow triangle; it looked new and they had to start all over to learn about this unfamiliar yellow shape.

This example illustrates the importance of activities that combine feeling and looking. These activities help to improve visual learning which is a very important tool for later learning.

A baby is still learning about her eyes and how to get them organized so that they tell her the shapes of things by looking. At first, her hands tell her about shapes, but when she looks and feels at the same time, her hands teach her eyes how to look and see and know.

When she is no longer a baby but a child in school, she will need well-organized eyes to learn to read. She must use her eyes to recognize all those squiggly little lines, with different shapes and forms, which we call letters and words.

We see many school children who have difficulty using their eyes to get organized information. They have trouble recognizing shapes of many letters and words, and so reading is very difficult for them.

In helping these children learn better, we often have them do many things with their hands while their eyes watch what their hands are doing. In other words, we help them learn years later what most children learned as babies: how to develop their visual learning.

"Looking" and "feeling" activities are actually scientific experiments which Baby is making whereby she is learning some fundamental realities about her world.

You can help your baby now by giving her objects to explore. Give her different objects with different "feels" to them: curved and straight, rough and smooth, heavy and light, big and little, solid like blocks and open like cups, all in a variety of colors.

Give her only a few at a time, but give her different ones from time to time. When she no longer is interested in a particular object, replace it with a new one.

Pots and pans are excellent, and an old-fashioned coffee pot is one of the best. If you don't want her playing with your good utensils, get her some inexpensive ones of her own.

Give her balls, blocks, simple wood or plastic toys (not the tiny sizes which she could swallow) and anything else around the house which is safe for her to explore.

You can be sure of one thing: Every time you see her using her eyes and hands together, she is improving her visual learning . . . and she is getting ready for reading. ∎

Little Ears Are Listening

If you have ever tried to learn a foreign language, you know how difficult it can be! Even using the most modern technological resources available, it is very difficult to develop the fluency of a native speaker. How then does your child learn to speak English, while a child in Tokyo will learn to master the very different sounds of Japanese?

Research studies provide some insight into young children's language development. These studies help to underline the importance of talking to and reading to a child long before he develops the ability to speak.

For many years linguists, who study language development, focused most of their attention on what happens after a child uses his first words. In recent years, however, much important research has been done on the pre-linguistic period, which is the time before a child develops the ability to communicate by using words.

These research findings have important implications for what parents can do to stimulate a child's language development. One of these implications is the realization that little ears are listening. An infant's learning of sounds begins even before birth.

Studies indicate that newborn babies show a preference for their mother's voice—even when the father spends as much time with the baby after birth—presumably because they have been accustomed to hearing the sound of their mother's voice while in the womb. Likewise, babies show more interest in hearing melodies and stories that they heard while they were in the womb.

Not surprisingly, therefore, newborns come into the world with a fairly well developed hearing ability—much better developed, for example, than their seeing ability. It has been found that, within the pitch and range of the human voice, an infant's hearing ability is about as good as that of an adult. There is an important difference, however, between an adult's or older child's listening and that of an infant.

Older children and adults will focus on the meaning of the words they hear, whereas infants will focus on the sound patterns.

Thus, if you are reading the same story to an infant and to an older child, the infant's attention will focus on the sounds of the words while the older child will attend to the meaning of those words.

It has also been found that very young infants, in some ways, have better sound discrimination than adults. In other words, they recognize and react differently to differences in sounds that adults would not even notice.

How can researchers test sound discrimination in infants? In one fascinating study infants were given a special nipple that activated a recording of the sound "ba." It was found that, at first, each infant sucked more vigorously on the nipple, thus indicating interest in the sound produced. Eventually the infants sucked less vigorously on the nipples, indicating they became bored and lost interest in hearing the same sound over and over again.

When the researchers changed the sound from "ba" to "pa," infants even as young as one month old immediately showed renewed interest and began sucking vigorously to activate the new recorded sound. The conclusion from this study is that infants as young as one month old are capable of quite sophisticated sound discrimination.

In studying the different sounds that infants make, it has been found that very young infants are capable of making the sounds found in all known languages—even if they have never previously heard those sounds in their own environment.

Infants appear to be born with the ability to process the sounds of any language. Thus, for example, infants with English-speaking parents were found to be capable of discriminating between two sounds found only in the Czech language—even though they were never exposed to anyone who spoke that language. By contrast, English-speaking adults were not able to detect these fine sound discriminations.

This ability for sound discrimination is one which infants eventually lose—which helps to explain the difficulty adults experience later in trying to learn and speak a foreign language.

As infants experiment with the various sounds they themselves can produce, they eventually limit the range of those sounds. By five months of age they begin to focus more attention on the sounds they most commonly hear in their own environment. It appears that the brain ceases to process those other sounds that are not part of the infant's language environment.

Parents who frequently talk to and read to their child are thus helping his language development by exposing him frequently to the sounds he needs to learn. There is now evidence that indicates that as an infant grows older, he not only learns sound patterns but he may also be able to store words in memory which would account for a dramatic spurt in vocabulary several months later.

In one study, tape-recorded stories were played to eight-month-olds once a day for 10 days. Two weeks later the infants were tested to determine if they remembered any words from the stories.

Earlier studies had shown that infants tend to turn toward the source of sounds that they recognized. The researchers therefore used two lists with 36 words each: one list with words from the stories, the other list with similar words that were not in the stories.

It was found that even though two weeks had elapsed, the eight-month-olds paid considerably more attention to the words from the stories than those which were unfamiliar. In other words, infants as young as eight months of age were capable of remembering the sounds of words they had not heard for two weeks—words that they cannot yet reproduce or fully understand their meaning.

Even though, as a parent, you may not notice any learning taking place as you talk to and read to your infant, be aware that little ears are listening—and that this listening is directly related to the development of your child's memory and language abilities. ∎

Reading Baby's Signals

Even though seven-month-old babies can't talk, they are constantly sending communication signals. Many of these signals have to do with their desire to develop new skills.

Most babies have a natural, built-in drive to want to do more and more things on their own.

Mastering one challenge leads them on to a new, more difficult challenge. But they generally can't accomplish this on their own. They need the help and support of a loving, caring adult.

To help stimulate this developmental process, parents need to develop the ability to accurately "read" a baby's signals.

At the same time they must maintain a delicate balance: helping to stimulate Baby's development without inappropriately "pushing" her.

Baby must be the one who ultimately sets the pace of development. The parents' role is to help her move to a new developmental level when, and only when, she gives a signal that she is ready to move ahead.

Let's focus, for example, on a baby's signals with regard to feeding.

At first a newborn infant is fed solely by means of liquid foods. But around four to six months of age, Baby starts looking at and reaching for the solid foods that she sees other people eating.

Her signals indicate that she is probably ready to be introduced to some solid foods.

If she is not ready, she will definitely send a quite different signal, usually by pushing the food away either with her hand or even with her tongue.

When baby demonstrates that she can sit without support, that's a signal that she is probably ready to sit in a high chair.

If her body seems too small, you can pad the high chair with a blanket so that she can more comfortably sit straight.

Sometime between seven and eight months of age most babies send a new signal: They want to try to feed themselves.

One sign of readiness for self-feeding is when your baby wants to help guide the spoon into her mouth.

At first she will be content to hold the spoon with you. Eventually she will want to try to do the feeding by herself.

Most babies won't fully master self-feeding with a spoon until past their first birthday. In the meantime, they send strong signals that they want to try.

It's sometimes difficult for parents to let go of the pleasure of feeding the baby. It can also be very trying on the parent's patience to observe the mess that Baby makes.

She can't even get the food on the spoon without making a mess! Then as the spoon is brought toward her face, the food is as likely to land on her nose or chin as it is to end up in her mouth!

In this scenario Baby is sending an important signal: "I want to be able to do this for myself." Parents who accurately

Baby must be the one who ultimately sets the pace of development. The parents' role is to help her move to a new developmental level when, and only when, she gives a signal that she is ready to move ahead.

read that signal won't be bothered too much by the mess, in the interest of helping Baby develop new competence.

On the other hand, parents who—in the interest of cleanliness—insist on feeding her themselves, deprive her of an important developmental experience.

One way to enable a baby to experience the competence of self-feeding without creating a great big mess is to provide carefully selected finger foods on her high chair tray.

In this way she will experience the satisfaction of feeding herself without the parents being burdened with a major clean-up. Soft foods, such as small pieces of bread, are ideal.

Don't give Baby solid pieces of food, such as a slice of carrot on which she could choke.

The principles that apply to reading Baby's signals with regard to feeding also apply to other areas of her behavior.

When parents are sensitive to their child's signals—such as wanting to crawl to explore her world—she is enabled to move to a new development level by means of these new learning experiences.

Healthy parent-child interactions occur when parents accurately read Baby's signals and react in a manner that fosters growth and development. ■

The Permanence of Objects

In the past months we've talked about Baby's understanding of objects. We've noted how important it is for her to be able to concentrate all of her senses upon an object. This will begin to stabilize her world.

We described how Baby seems to form ideas (some psychologists call them "schemas") about common objects like faces, and then to test out her ideas on similar objects.

Experiments have indicated that at seven months a baby can recognize an object from one time to the next because she will often pay more attention to a new object than to one which she has seen a lot.

But what about objects that she can't see at the moment? Does she ever wish for a face she can't see that brings her a smile and love? Does she imagine a favorite toy she would like to play with?

It is important for us to know what she thinks about unseen objects, or if she thinks about them, because most of the knowledge and ideas which will influence her behavior when she is older are based on objects and experiences that are not present at a particular time.

For imagining and problem solving, she will need to recall ideas, to visualize them in her mind's eye.

While we cannot get inside Baby's head to see what her thoughts and memories are, we can observe her actions.

Try this experiment: While you and your baby are playing with some object that interests her, like a ribbon bow or a squeaky toy, place the object in front of her and then cover it with an empty can or small cardboard box.

After it is covered, she may look at you questioningly or find something else to occupy her (perhaps the cover itself) but she is not likely to remove the cover just to get the object.

She appears to forget about the object as soon as it is out of sight. It is as if any-thing that is out of sight is out of mind, with no further thought or attention given to it until it reappears.

This kind of behavior led the famous theorist Jean Piaget to suggest that for a child of this age, an object does not exist if she cannot see it.

Her memory operates only when it is stimulated by something she sees. She recognizes things when she sees them but does not call up their likeness in her memory.

So the next step in Baby's understanding of the world is to realize that objects exist even when they are out of sight.

We can help this process along by giving her experiences with things that disappear and reappear frequently, without long periods of absence.

You've probably already started this process by playing peek-a-boo. When your head repeatedly bobs in and out of sight, she develops an expectation to see you again, even when you are temporarily hidden.

You can also make voice sounds while you are hidden, then see if she can later anticipate where your face will appear by listening to the sound and associating it with your hidden face.

You might tie a toy on a string and pull it slowly behind a barrier. Or put the toy behind a piece of cardboard that has holes in it so she can partially see it.

A good toy for this purpose is an open-ended container that hides an object when it is turned in some direction.

For instance, you can suspend a block inside a can like the clapper of a bell by tying a string securely around the block, then running the string through a hole punched in the top of the can.

The free end can be anchored by a Lincoln log or a large button. The block will have weight and will make a sound against the can but can only be seen when the open end of the can is looked into.

When your baby continues to show interest in an object even when that object is out of her sight, you will know that she has reached an important stage of development which psychologists refer to as "object permanence."

In the months ahead, as she becomes more familiar with the permanence of objects, you will even see her purposefully removing everything that stands in her way to seek out a desired object that is temporarily hidden from her view. ■

Learning is Watching, Tasting, Throwing

Has Baby become a "watcher" this month? Is he sitting up by himself and looking around?

This is something new and different for him. He now has a different view of the world which he enjoys and which makes him feel important.

He's probably pulling himself up in his bed and playing with his toes, rolling around on the floor and reaching for his toys, making new noises and trying to "talk" to you.

He shows likes and dislikes for the things he eats and toward the people he sees and hears.

Baby is now using his hands, mouth and tongue to touch and explore things.

If you give him a plastic cup, he will probably look at it, feel it, mouth it, and end up banging it against something.

In this manner, he learns about the size, texture, taste and weight of the objects within his reach.

You can encourage his natural curiosity by exposing him to a variety of carefully selected objects. Allow him to reach for and feel such natural things as snow, leaves, rocks, etc.

Talk to him about what he's doing and about the shape, feel and texture of the objects.

At mealtime, give him a small unbreakable juice glass and a spoon. Continue to feed him as before, but let him try to feed himself.

At this age, Baby has learned to grasp quite well, although precise thumb/ forefinger pick-up has not yet fully developed.

He is also beginning to learn how to "let go."

At first, he lets go simply by relaxing the hand completely when attention is distracted from the object he is holding.

Growing Child®

P. O. Box 2505 • W Lafayette, IN 47996
(800) 927-7289
©Growing Child, Inc.
www.GrowingChild.com

Contributing Authors

Phil Bach, O.D., Ph.D.
Miriam Bender, Ph.D.
Joseph Braga, Ed.D.
Laurie Braga, Ph.D.
George Early, Ph.D.
Carol R. Gestwicki, M.S.
Liam Grimley, Ph.D.
Robert Hannemann, M.D., F.A.A.P.
Sylvia Kottler, M.S.
Bill Peterson, Ph.D.

Voluntary release—letting go when he wants to—is a more difficult skill and is learned in several stages:

Casting (throwing), exaggerated letting go after putting the object down, and controlled letting go.

As Baby begins to develop voluntary release, he finds it necessary to straighten his whole arm in order to straighten his fingers and open his hand.

In other words, he throws the object in order to release his grasp on it. This usually begins at about seven months.

At first Baby throws just to let go of whatever he is holding. He needs this practice.

Soon he begins watching to see where the object goes and listening to the sound it makes when it strikes something. Eventually he begins to throw things just to see what happens.

These are all learning behaviors. They may be hard on Baby's caregivers for a time, but throwing is an important part of learning.

Baby is not just doing it to be "bad" or to get attention. He is learning how to let go of objects when he wants to.

He is learning a lot about cause and effect and about gravity which makes every object go down and out of reach.

But what can you do to let Baby learn these essential lessons without being completely at his beck and call to retrieve things thrown on the floor?

Some objects or toys can be fastened to the high chair with a short cord or piece of elastic.

Now Baby has a new experience to learn about. Some things he throws fall to the floor—but others don't!

He will learn that the ones on cord or elastic can be pulled back up and he will begin to retrieve them himself. ■

Growing Child®

In every task the most important thing is the beginning, and especially when you have to deal with anything young and tender.

Plato

Eight Months Old

Baby's eighth month is truly an exciting one in many ways. During her first seven months she has grown in strength and coordination so that by the eighth month she is ready to develop some really new and different skills.

By this time her hips have straightened. The muscles of her back, neck and hips have grown much stronger.

She can lift her head high and push up onto her straight arms so that her back is arched with her hips and legs flat on the floor. Further, she can rock on her stomach, back arched, arms and legs moving, as if she were swimming.

As she rocks on her stomach in this position, we marvel at her strength and flexibility and find ourselves thinking, "I couldn't do that!" But this strength and flexibility are the necessary qualities Baby must develop if she is to progress to sitting alone, standing alone and finally to walking alone.

Baby has also grown stronger and more flexible in other ways. When lying on her back, she has found her feet and toes. She plays with them, lifting her legs straight up, with knees almost straight, and reaches for her feet with both hands.

Rolling from back to stomach is now very easy for Baby. She is no longer content to lie on her back, and when placed there soon rolls over onto her stomach.

There she pushes up on her arms to see better and can support her weight on one hand as she reaches for a toy with the other.

By now she can sit alone without support for as long as a minute at a time.

She is unsteady, but is learning to use her arms to catch herself when she loses her balance to one side. However, much as she wants to sit now, your baby has not yet learned to move from lying to sitting by herself, and still must depend upon your help.

Her sitting balance is much better when she sits on the floor or in her crib where her legs are out in front of her. She needs back support when sitting with her legs dangling.

Baby is using her hands more efficiently to grasp and hold objects. She now approaches them from the side with a "raking" kind of movement of one hand.

The little finger side of Baby's hand rakes the object in, her fingers curl around it from the side and her thumb holds it against the side of her index finger.

She uses a grasp much like that of a monkey because she has not yet learned to use her thumb efficiently.

Usually everything goes to Baby's mouth. She transfers a toy from one hand to the other, mouths it, bites it, chews it, bangs

At Eight Months Baby Likes to:
• Pivot around on her stomach.
• Look for toys she has dropped.
• Transfer toys from hand to hand.
• Creep or pull herself along on the floor.

Give Your Baby:
• Several toys to bang together.
• Nested plastic cups.
• Spoon and cup at mealtimes. (Continue to feed her but encourage her to feed herself.)
• Washable cloth or plastic books.
• A mirror in which to see herself.
• Washable or plastic books.

it, shakes it, and does all of these things over and over.

If she drops the object, she picks it up again.

All of this activity involves learning. Baby is finding out everything she can about an object: its shape, texture, size, hardness or softness, taste, smell, and sound.

She repeats her experiments with the object until she is sure that these qualities are unchangeable.

For Baby, these qualities and the pattern they make help identify the object for her.

Although Baby now reaches and grasps with one hand, she is not yet ready to establish "handedness." For a long time to come, she will use either her left hand or her right hand indiscriminately, sometimes seeming to prefer one hand, sometimes the other. ∎

Moving On

All of Baby's achievements up to now have prepared her for the exciting discovery which babies usually make during the eighth month: She can go someplace to get something! This is an important milestone in Baby's life—she has taken the first step toward having some control over the world around her.

This discovery seems to come almost by accident, but it cannot happen unless Baby is developmentally ready for it.

Usually Baby sees a desirable object which is just out of reach. She rolls and stretches but it remains beyond her grasp. In her excitement, Baby rocks on her stomach, moving her arms and kicking her legs. In the process, she pulls and/or pushes against the surface she is lying on, and suddenly she finds she can reach the object she desires.

What an exciting discovery: "If I move, I can go somewhere and get something!" Now Baby has found a way to get what she wants all by herself.

This new discovery is so exciting that Baby begins to pull herself around just for the sake of moving from one place to another.

She learns better ways of moving herself by pulling with her arms and pushing with her legs.

She pivots around and around on her stomach. She pushes herself backwards. She pulls herself forward. Her "reachable" world enlarges and she can explore objects and places previously out of reach.

But dragging herself along on her stomach is not a very efficient way of getting from place to place. So Baby continues to search for a better way—which leads to creeping.

By the last part of the eighth month many babies have found this better way or at least have shown evidence of progress toward it. They have been helped by an important developmental reflex which has been getting stronger over the past couple of months.

Here's what happens: When Baby tilts her head up and back, a reflex tends to strengthen the muscles which straighten her elbows, as well as those which bend her hips and knees. So, when she lifts her head and chest, her arms stiffen to support her weight and her hips and knees bend to pull her knees up under her.

Now, the same reflex which helped Baby get into this crouching position tends to keep her crouched. When she tries to push forward, her arms give, her head goes down, and she collapses on the floor again.

To continue her progress toward the upright position, Baby must learn how to inhibit this reflex and hasten its normal weakening. She does this by rocking forward and back, forward and back, until one day her arms continue to support her and she does not collapse. Instead, she moves forward and begins her first attempt at creeping.

By the end of their eighth month, a third to one half of all infants have progressed to creeping.

Still later this reflex helps her pull to a standing position while holding on to the sides of her playpen or on to a convenient piece of furniture.

It will be some time before Baby will walk alone since she has much learning still to do. But in this exciting period, she has progressed a long way toward the day she will take her first independent step. ∎

Separation Anxiety

Around seven or eight months, babies may show separation anxiety where they display great distress when a beloved care-giver leaves their sight. This is related to a change in the baby's relationship to his parents. No longer content to just have his needs satisfied, he has become enormously attached to those individuals who have met those needs.

This indication of true attachment is as intense as a first love affair, and even though expressed with loud cries and distress, is really a sign to be celebrated. All the hard work of parenting a young infant has resulted in this strong feeling of love. At this stage of attachment, the baby experiences the parent's disappearance or

absence as a loss. With a shaky new sense of object permanence, he may fear that when his mother or father go away, they're never coming back.

This clinginess may be upsetting to some parents unless they understand its origin in attachment and limited understanding. Over time, with repeated parting and return, the baby comes to understand the process of being apart, and becomes calmer about parents' leave-takings.

Parents need to be gentle in their understanding of the baby's strong feelings, and unhesitating in their clear leaving and return. If possible, adjusting to new experiences such as childcare are best either

before or after this time of acute separation anxiety.

A related anxiety may occur in some infants at about the same time. This is stranger anxiety, protesting when less familiar faces come too close. Not to be interpreted as sudden shyness that must be combated, instead evidently by this age the baby has learned to distinguish his own people, and feels less comfortable with others.

Again, gentle understanding and not forcing the issue at this point are the appropriate responses. With time, both separation and stranger anxiety lessen, occasionally reappearing in toddlerhood. ∎

What Motivates My Child To Learn?

It appears that infants, like all human beings, want to control their environment. It is this inborn desire that accounts for an infant's motivation to learn how to explore and control what happens in his environment.

Why then are some infants more highly motivated to gain this important sense of competence? Why do others behave in a more lethargic and helpless manner?

Although eight-month-old infants cannot tell us what they are thinking or feeling, it is possible, from careful study of their behavior, to draw some inferences about what motivates them.

There appear to be three important factors that help stimulate an infant's motivation to learn:

(1) Having a secure, loving relationship with parents;

(2) Being provided with adequate and appropriate learning experiences, and

(3) Developing a sense of personal control over his own life.

Parental warmth and affection provide the atmosphere of trust and security in which an infant's sense of self-reliance and self-confidence can develop.

Infants who have a secure, loving relationship with their parents have been found to be more interested in exploring and to demonstrate a strong sense of curiosity about the world around them. As a result, they are more courageous in seeking out new experiences.

The second important factor is the need for adequate and appropriate learning experiences.

In each issue of *Growing Child* we try to identify various activities which will provide an infant with exposure to a wide variety of learning experiences. Parents can select those activities that appear to be most interesting and challenging to their own child.

Infants have been found to demonstrate more fascination with new challenges than with success that comes too easily. Likewise they have been found to show little interest in tasks that are too difficult.

The secret is to select activities within an infant's range of capability and which will stretch his learning abilities.

The third important factor that helps motivate an infant to learn is a more complicated one, namely, the infant's development of a sense of personal control over events in his life.

In a fascinating study of eight-month-olds, researchers sought to find out if an infant's motivation to learn would be enhanced by the expectancy that his own behavior affects events in his environment.

The infants were placed in front of a screen on which pictures appeared with musical accompaniment. Half of the infants had to learn to pull on a string attached to their wrist in order to produce the pictures and music. The others just saw and heard the pictures and music without having to do anything to produce it.

In later tests the infants who had learned to control their environment by pulling the string were able to produce the pictures/music whenever they wanted but the other infants were not able to do so.

In the second part of this research study both groups of infants were provided the opportunity to produce the pictures/music by a different means, namely, by making vocal sounds.

The first group (who had earlier learned to pull on a string to produce the pictures and music) quickly learned to produce the outcome by making vocal sounds. The group who had not learned earlier how to produce the event failed to learn this new way of producing the audio-visual outcome.

One of the most important implications of this study is that when an eight-month-old infant learns that his behavior can influence events in the world around him, it enhances his motivation to learn. He also more readily learns new ways to help him gain even more control over his environment.

It has been found, on the other hand, that if an infant develops an expectancy that he does not have any impact on his environment—for example, if his crying is repeatedly ignored—his incentive to learn is reduced.

When infants find themselves repeatedly in situations where they have no impact on the events in their lives, they become passive observers of life rather than active learning participants.

Eight-month-old infants, therefore, need to become aware that they can exercise some control over events in the world around them. This measure of control helps to stimulate their motivation to learn. But this sense of personal control must be counter-balanced by an equally important need, namely, the need to accept some measure of external control over their lives.

Otherwise, parents can be faced with the opposite extreme, namely, a spoiled child who wishes to rule his environment as a young tyrant. ■

The Spoiled Child

Is my eight-month-old baby spoiled? This is a very difficult question to answer for the following reasons:

(1) Parents who spoil their child are generally the ones least likely to be aware of it;

(2) There is much opinion, but little general agreement, about what constitutes spoiled child behavior;

(3) Even if a definition was agreed upon, it could not be applied equally to the behaviors of an eight-month-old, for example, and a two-year-old child.

Despite the controversies, we believe there are certain patterns of behavior observable at about eight months which, if left unchecked, could be indicative of greater problems in later weeks, months and years.

If parents learn to be watchful for these patterns, they can help prevent these problems from occurring.

Why does spoiling a child sometimes begin to be a problem around eight months of age?

It is because an eight-month-old infant has developed new social and intellectual interests but doesn't yet have the kind of physical mobility that will later enable her to pursue these interests on her own.

If she wants someone to interact with her, for example, she must somehow get that person to come to her. By now she has probably learned that the louder she screams, the quicker someone will appear.

She also likes to be picked up and cuddled. She has probably learned that crying is a very effective way to get Mom or Dad to do just that—on demand.

All of this behavior is a very normal part of growing up. In the process, an eight-month-old infant learns that she can have some control over events in her life. But if this exercise of control shows signs of becoming unreasonable and tyrannical, we must confront the problem of spoiled child behavior.

A good way to begin is to consider how to respond to an infant's crying, since unreasonable crying is one of the most common ways in which an infant exhibits spoiled child behavior.

Infants cry for different reasons such as hunger, the discomfort of a wet diaper, or to get attention. It is the inappropriate craving for attention, combined with the parent's catering to an infant's every whim, that constitutes spoiled child behavior.

Since an infant's crying is sometimes an ambiguous signal, how should a parent respond?

Let's consider three different ways in which we have seen parents respond to their infant's crying.

The Ignoring Parents. These are the parents who are so afraid of spoiling their child that they decide to ignore all but the most obvious cries of distress.

In this case, crying is likely to become more frequent at first, until the baby becomes withdrawn and loses all desire to get attention. Such a child will have little motivation to interact with the world around her.

The Overly-Protective Parents. In this home there are a number of misguided beliefs:

(1) A belief that if baby is crying, the parents must be doing something wrong;

(2) A belief that a crying baby should always be held and hugged;

(3) A strong belief that other parents who don't always pick up and cuddle a crying baby are unfit to be parents.

It is in this setting—with overly-protective, overly-conscientious, overly-loving parents—that one is most likely to witness spoiled child behavior.

The Loving, Realistic Parents. These are the parents who try to be firm, consistent and loving in establishing and applying standards of appropriate behavior. When their baby cries, these parents are likely to do the following:

(1) Attend as promptly as possible to their infant's cries since research studies indicate that parents who responded quickly had infants who cried relatively little;

(2) Determine as soon as possible if there is a physical cause—such as hunger or discomfort—for the crying, in which case they attend to their infant's immediate physical need;

(3) Decide if the crying was merely to get attention, in which case they try to deal with the situation in a rather business-like manner—for example, by talking for a few moments or introducing the child to something interesting to do or explore—without over-indulging the child with hugs and caresses. ■

Crying in the Night

Many parents face the problem of what to do with a child who repeatedly cries in the middle of the night.

If you haven't yet faced that problem, it is well to consider even now how you will handle it if and when it arises.

Parental attitudes about this problem vary considerably. Even child development experts are not completely in agreement.

In the final analysis parents will decide for themselves how they want to handle this problem in their own home. We hope we can bring some clarity to the decision by discussing some of the issues involved.

The ignoring parents would always let their child cry through the whole night.

Children need to learn that they can have some impact—by crying, for example, when they need help—on the people in the world around them.

Eventually the child might not cry even in the case of hunger or discomfort. Such a child of "ignoring parents" is likely to grow up emotionally deprived and intellectually disadvantaged.

We can also surmise how **overly-protective parents** would react. They are likely to feel that their infant's crying is somehow their fault.

To alleviate their guilt, they would pick up their child every time she cries. They will do just about anything—hug her, caress her, entertain her—just to get her to stop crying.

The problem with this method is that, even though she may stop crying temporarily, as soon as the parents put her down or leave her, the crying routine begins all over again.

There appear to be no limits to what over-protective parents will do to accommodate their spoiled child's crying.

In one of his excellent books, on infants and toddlers, Dr. Burton White, the noted psychologist, reports the case of a dentist and his wife in Georgia who began taking their ten-month-old child for auto rides in the middle of the night as their way of dealing with nighttime crying.

By the time they were taking two or more auto rides every night between midnight and 6:00 a.m., they decided there must be a better way to deal with the situation!

How would **loving, realistic parents** deal with this problem?

Their behavior would most likely be guided by some reasonable principles such as the following:

(1) Never totally ignore an infant's crying. There may be a physical cause for the crying.

It is better to err on the side of loving and caring than on the side of neglect.

(2) If the inappropriate behavior—in this case, crying in the middle of the night—only occurs infrequently, don't worry about it unduly.

(3) If the inappropriate behavior occurs more frequently—such as crying every night at 3:00 a.m.—give thoughtful consideration to your actions.

For example, take a long-term rather than a short-term view of the situation.

Be aware that expectations are quickly established in an infant's mind, whether it be a trip to Mom's and Dad's bed, or a car ride in the middle of the night.

(4) If you do something once to stop an infant's habit of crying at night, you'd better be prepared to do it every night.

Spoiled children have a way of becoming more and more demanding.

So, the middle of the night is not the time for warm hugs, kisses and playful games, unless you are prepared to be awakened for the same routine, on demand, every night.

Would that be good for the child? Would that be good for the parents?

In summary, all children need to learn that they are loved and cherished.

They also need to learn that they can have some impact—by crying, for example, when they need help—on the people in the world around them.

They also must learn, sooner or later, that they cannot always have their own way. They must learn to accept some measure of external control over their lives.

If children learn from an early age to maintain this balance in their living—neither totally controlling nor being totally controlled by others—their own lives will be much happier.

The task of parenting will also be made easier and more enjoyable. ∎

Still Babbling

At eight months Baby is still in the babbling stage. We have given considerable attention to the subject of babbling in past issues and have encouraged you to stimulate the frequency and richness of this activity.

One research study of 9-12-month-olds has shown that the variety of sounds in babbling and the length of the utterances increases after periods of adult stimulation.

Of course, babies babble when they are alone. Remember that the process of babbling itself is one that develops naturally.

Deaf children babble initially even though they cannot hear their own sounds. However, they do not initiate advanced babbling, so by eight months deaf children would probably have stopped babbling.

This early development of babbling is the combined result of the natural maturation of the child and his responses to his environment.

Even at eight months it is not too late to play "dialogue" games if you haven't already started. If Baby says "mmpah," for instance, you enthusiastically repeat it, and he'll say some more.

After he has had plenty of practice, he'll move on to imitation of what he hears you say. What he says may still not resemble what he hears but don't be discouraged from continuing the dialogue.

The more you talk and make dialogue, the closer Baby's imitations will eventually resemble your speech.

It is very difficult to know when Baby's first word is spoken, but it generally occurs sometime between the eighth and fifteenth months.

The age when the first word comes is not necessarily correlated with intelligence.

Generally the first child speaks sooner and more maturely than the second or third child.

The only child often is an earlier and more fluent speaker than twins or triplets. The explanation may simply be that parents have more time, with fewer distractions, to talk to their first child.

There are some very interesting characteristics connected with a baby's speech acquisition:

(1) He shows an understanding of words before he himself begins to use them.

(2) The stages of speech development are basically the same for every child. One child may be faster or slower than another but both follow the same developmental pattern. ∎

Growing Child

P. O. Box 2505 • W Lafayette, IN 47996
(800) 927-7289
©Growing Child, Inc.
www.GrowingChild.com

Contributing Authors

Phil Bach, O.D., Ph.D.
Miriam Bender, Ph.D.
Joseph Braga, Ed.D.
Laurie Braga, Ph.D.
George Early, Ph.D.
Carol R. Gestwicki, M.S.
Liam Grimley, Ph.D.
Robert Hannemann, M.D., F.A.A.P.
Sylvia Kottler, M.S.
Bill Peterson, Ph.D.

Learning

Phillip's mother thinks he is a genius. Perhaps he is. Here's what he did. At 8.5 months of age, with only three weeks of crawling experience behind him, Phillip decided he wanted to cruise. (Cruising is pulling himself up to a standing position, holding on to some solid object, then moving around wherever there is something to hang onto.)

So, Phillip was cruising along the front of the sofa with both hands busy. He has a little wicker basket in his left hand and a toy radio in the other.

The family dog was following along closely at his heels. His older sister was pulling at the front end of his undershirt, and Phillip was trying to get the radio into the basket or the basket into the radio. He didn't care which, because he didn't know which was which.

Remember, both hands are busy, he's leaning at a wicked angle against the sofa, his sister is giving him a very hard time, and the dog is very busy around his feet and ankles.

Well, Phil didn't mind that all this action was going on around him at the same time. He just kept stabbing away with the two objects in his hands—the radio and the basket—waiting for something to happen.

Finally, it did! The radio went into the basket and stayed there. Phillip looked at it with enormous satisfaction. Then he made a loud squealing noise—and promptly fell down.

To judge from his mother, you'd think he just solved the energy crisis! But, you could tell that Phillip just ate up her praise.

Think about it. Here's a kid who never saw a basket before nor a radio, but he somehow managed to get one object inside the other.

He learned something about bigger and smaller, in spite of his sister and the dog. All in all, a great learning experience, one of maybe 60 big ones Phillip had that day. Remember, he's just not playing. He's learning. ∎

The important thing is not so much that every child should be taught, as that every child should be given the wish to learn.
John Lubbock

Nine Months Old

During the first three months, Baby began to gain control of her eyes and mouth. From three to six months, she gained control of her head, neck and shoulders.

By the ninth month she has progressed to having better control of her trunk, arms and hands.

Baby now sits on the floor with good balance for 10 to 15 minutes at a time. She can lean forward to pick up a toy without losing her balance.

She can also turn her body and look sideways while stretching out to grasp a dangling toy or to pick up an object from the floor.

She may not yet be able to move herself from a lying to a sitting position but will probably master this skill very soon.

A dedicated wriggler and squirmer, Baby's arms, legs and body are active whether she's in her bath, stroller or sitting on your lap.

On the floor, she pulls herself along on her belly or rolls over and over to get where she's going. Some babies have started creeping on hands and knees or hitching along in a sitting position.

Baby is moving toward the erect position and pulls herself up to a standing position for a few moments at the side of her crib or any other object that will support her.

Unfortunately, she cannot lower herself yet so she simply lets go or loses her balance and falls backward with a bump.

When held in a standing position, she will step purposefully from one foot to

the other. However, there's still a lot Baby can learn about the world by creeping on hands and knees before progressing to independent walking.

In the meantime, she is busy watching and paying attention to people, objects and happenings around her. She immediately reaches for an offered toy, usually with one hand leading the other.

Baby has also achieved midline competence, meaning she can now bring her hands together in the midline, to pass objects from one hand to the other and use both hands to explore an object.

This is important because this ability extends the possibilities for exploration, and the kinds of toys that can be manipulated.

She manipulates objects with sustained interest, turning them over, examin-

At Nine Months Baby Likes to:
• Pull himself up.
• Creep on the floor.
• Play interaction games like pat-a-cake.
• Stare at his image in a mirror.
• Study the different shapes, forms and textures of objects.

Give Your Baby:
• Opportunities to feed himself.
• Safe places to explore.
• Your praise and approval for vocal and motor abilities.
• Safe toys and teething objects to bite and chew on.

ing them from all angles, banging them against the floor or her high chair.

She has learned to poke at small things with her index finger and may have begun using that finger to point at more distant objects.

While she may still grasp small items—a string or a crumb—between her thumb and forefinger, she is developing a finer feel. Soon she will be picking up small objects between the tips of her thumb and index finger in a precise pincer grasp.

Baby can now release a toy by dropping it or pressing it against a firm surface. But she lacks the coordination and muscle control at present to deliberately place an item and release it.

Now she looks in the correct direction for falling toys, including those that have toppled over the side of her high chair or crib. She may still drop or throw a toy just to watch it fall.

continued on next page

Time to Eat

While this can sometimes be aggravating to a busy parent, please be patient. Baby is learning a lot in the dropping-looking-retrieving process. This repetition is necessary for her to truly assimilate a concept, such as "dropped objects fall down," in this case.

She will watch the activities of nearby adults, children and animals with sustained interest for minutes at a time and is eagerly attentive to everyday sounds, particularly human voices.

She now vocalizes deliberately as a means of communicating. She shouts to attract attention, listens, then shouts again. She screams in anger or frustration.

She babbles loudly and tunefully in long strings of syllables (dadada, mamam, agaga, ababa.). This babbling is practiced mainly for self-amusement but also as a form of communication.

Baby has also begun to imitate the playful sounds of adults—coughing, smacking lips, making "the raspberries," and the like.

By this time Baby, is reaching for independence in feeding. She will hold, bite and chew a cracker and put her hands around her bottle or cup. She will try to grasp the spoon when being fed.

Peek-a-boo is now an active game with Baby a participant as well as a watcher. Pat-a-cake is imitated briefly but not sustained, although she enjoys being taken through the whole game.

Baby now clearly distinguishes strangers from familiar persons and may cling to a known adult, hiding her face. After reassurance she will usually accept the newcomer.

She expresses annoyance, resistance and frustration in no uncertain terms by throwing her head back, stiffening her body and crying or vocalizing her protests.

The concept of object permanence is gradually developing. If a toy is partially hidden under a cover or cushion while she watches, she will find it promptly. She may find it even if it is completely hidden under a cup or cushion while she watches.

At nine months Baby is busy watching everything that is going on in her world. Soon she will be an even more active explorer of that world as the last quarter of her first year brings even more dramatic changes in her development. ■

At nine months, feeding time is a time to learn. Since Baby is interested in the spoon and cup, give her extra ones to bang with while you feed her with another spoon.

When she is more independent and less interested in your feeding her, give her some bits of food to pick up and put in her mouth herself. While she is occupied with that, you can spoon the messier foods into her mouth.

Those bits of food she's holding aren't just to keep Baby happy. A baby of nine months or so really can feed herself if you make her a meal or a snack of bits of food—finger foods. (Be careful that they are soft and not likely to break off into large chunks that could cause choking.)

In the beginning Baby will have some trouble holding onto the food in order to get it into her mouth.

When she finally grasps it, she will clench it in her fist, raise it to her mouth, then open her fingers against her lips and push the food with her palm.

It's messy but allowing her this experience encourages her ability to feed herself and keeps alive her interest in food.

Finger foods also give a baby a kind of contentment. Her fingers succeed in holding onto food and her fingers bring the food to her mouth. That's achievement.

And she can choose all by herself what she wants to put into her mouth. That's independence.

From about nine months, a baby is starting to discover that she is an individual and separate from her parents. This is a good feeling, and necessary. It happens to every baby. But separation is a real struggle, with much anxiety, a struggle your child has to resolve for herself.

How well she does so has a lot to do with developing initiative and making decisions of her own.

Finger foods offer a baby a choice, and a chance to do things for herself. ■

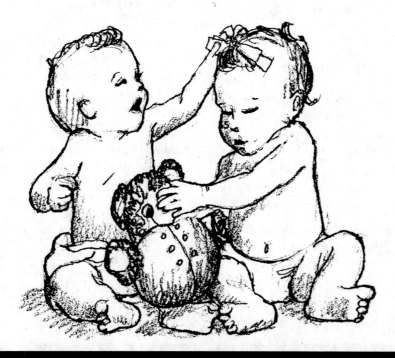

Baby Equipment— Uses and Abuses

Probably you received a playpen, or an exersaucer, or baby jumper among your baby gifts. Such devices can be a real blessing to a busy parent whose baby has begun to get around under his own power.

They provide a safe place for Baby to play while parents are busy cleaning the house or fixing meals.

They keep Baby out of trouble and occupied with things to explore.

They allow him to strengthen leg muscles while he jumps or stretches his legs out.

But a playpen also restricts the range of Baby's activities.

Stationary activity centers or jumping devices also restrict the range of Baby's activities and limit the space he has to move around in.

Too much time in a playpen, activity center or crib limits his experiences—and thus his opportunities for learning.

Baby should have several hours a day of freedom to move about in all directions and to explore the larger world around him.

A child learns about himself and his relationship with objects by discovering that some spaces are too small for him to crawl through and some pieces of furniture are too low to wriggle under.

He learns how to move backwards by finding himself in a dead-end with no place to go but backward.

He discovers the differences in feel between carpet, tile or wood floor. He learns that one object is farther away than another by finding that he must work harder to get there by creeping.

He sees "another baby" in the mirror. He discovers that some objects are solid. He can pull up to and hold on to them for support, but other things come down on top of him when he pulls on them.

Baby learns by moving, creeping and exploring. All that baby equipment restricts this learning, even when toys are provided.

Used wisely, playpens and activity centers can be a great help to parents. They provide protected play areas for Baby. Misused, those same things limit Baby's learning experiences and may delay his development.

A common-sense balance of freedom and restriction will be best for both Baby and parents. ■

Making Your Home 'Child-proof'

Baby is creeping on all fours now and before too long, he'll be crawling and walking.

Some babies creep for a long time, others walk without doing much creeping first. In either case, your baby will be moving like lightning and exploring with zeal once he senses his new powers.

If not watched very carefully, he's going to get into mischief. Telling him "no" or "don't touch" or even smacking his hands won't do much good at this age.

Why not?

Baby is just beginning to understand words. While he may not understand what you say, he does understand from the tone of your voice and your gestures that "no" and "don't touch" mean he is not pleasing you.

He does not understand DANGER. His memory is too short—he can't remember your warning for more than a few minutes.

So, the next time he encounters a "no-no," he doesn't recall your warning or recognize the danger and plunges right in.

Your punishment (at this age) is not effective. Training in "touching" and "not touching" will be much more effective in a few more months.

Right now make your life—and Baby's— easier and more relaxed by making your home "child-proof."

Place all dangerous objects, as well as valued treasures, out of his reach. Cover unused electric outlets with plastic inserts purchased from a hardware store.

Keep medicines and vitamins in child-proof containers, on a very high shelf.

Remove all household cleaning fluids, such as furniture polish, ammonia and window cleaner, from beneath the sink and put them well out of reach.

The same caution must also be carried to the outdoors, especially if the yard is not fenced. Baby is no longer a passive watcher. He will creep like an athlete when his curiosity is stimulated by the sight of traffic or some other exciting enticement.

Once the yard and house are "child-proof," make sure you provide plenty of objects, even safe household objects like pots and pans with which Baby can play, because for him, play is learning.

Often leaving a low, accessible cupboard or shelf stocked with such items satisfies Baby's need to explore while staying near the adult who is busy working.

Baby is highly curious right now to learn about new objects so this may be a trying period for you.

Remember that every new thing is raw material for his knowledge factory.

This direct experience will provide the basis for his intellectual curiosity, creativity and language development in the future. ■

Games Baby Will Love to Play

With a little care and caution, your child can have a lot of fun playing even the simplest games. Parents can enjoy them, too!

Imitation games are important for two reasons. First, Baby is learning to imitate what you are doing (sounds, actions, etc.).

Second, these games are a social experience (eye contact, smiling, etc.) because of the interaction between adult and child.

Here are some simple imitation games you can play:

- Clapping hands.
- Waving bye-bye.
- Nodding head.
- Touching nose.
- Thrusting tongue.
- Smacking lips.

Peek-a-boo is still a favorite game. Toss a thin scarf or light cloth over your head and say, "Where's Mama (Dada)?" "Where did she (he) go?"

Then when she (or you) has pulled the scarf away, you can exclaim, "There she is!"

When Baby is familiar with this game, introduce some variations. Try placing the scarf over her head, provided this does not frighten her unduly.

If she doesn't remove the scarf when you say, "Where's Baby?", you can gently lift the scarf as you exclaim, "There she is!"

This game helps to teach Baby the concept of "object permanence," namely, that objects continue to exist even when we don't see them.

Another game which teaches this same concept is "The Vanishing Object."

While Baby is watching you, pick up "the vanishing object," something non-breakable that she admires greatly, and slip it behind a pillow.

Then stand back and watch her pounce on the pillow and grab the object.

A more challenging exploit is to put your keycase in a box and partially close it while Baby is observing you. Now, encourage her to find the case.

If she finds it, she has learned that an object can be hidden from sight and yet can still exist.

This is a tremendous development in her learning and a wonderful experience.

The baby under nine months old has no awareness that an object exists whether she sees it or not. This applies also to human objects—such as parents—as well as pets, toys and a bottle.

When an object disappears from view, she can't imagine that it is someplace else.

Ah, but when she is nine months old, she becomes a "pocket-size detective." She is beginning to know that things are permanent, even when she can't see them.

Baby will enjoy other simple games like pat-a-cake or "How big is Baby? S-o-o big!" as you stretch both of her arms wide apart or high over her head.

"This little piggy went to market" will also continue to be a great favorite.

Another game Baby will enjoy is to loosely wrap a piece of brightly colored ribbon around her arm or leg for her to pull off.

She will love "escaping" from such "restraints." Naturally, you will greet her achievement with great surprise and much excitement.

Baby also will love tumbling on the floor. An adult's legs and stomach make exciting hills to climb, obstacles to overcome or high places on which to sit.

A laugh or a cough causes a parent's chest and abdomen to sink and rise in ways that are thrilling to Baby. And when Mom or Dad talks, Baby feels the vibrations through her whole body.

Toys that can be taken apart and put together again will also provide much fun.

In general, toys with which Baby can do something are preferable to those she can only watch. Cause-and-effect toys are popular such as simple busy boxes—and bath busy boxes.

Toys with which Baby can make a noise are fun. Soft toys are comfortable to hug and make good pillows when Baby is tired.

See-through toys whose insides can be seen to move when the toys are shaken are very exciting, too.

Put floating and squeezy sponge toys in her bathtub. Make bath time an opportunity to splash and play.

Play safe and never leave Baby alone in the tub for even a moment. Her sitting balance may still be uncertain. Should she lose her balance, she might bump her head and be unable to get her face out of the water.

Whatever the toy or household object used as a toy, be sure to consider the effects of banging or chewing.

Plastics that can break and result in a sharp, projecting edge should be avoided.

And remember, because Baby puts everything in the mouth, be certain that lead-based paint has not been used on toys or furniture. Even small amounts of lead, swallowed over a period of time, can cause serious illness.

A final word of caution: While parents often enjoy throwing Baby high into the air and catching her, health professionals warn that this is a dangerous practice.

Never toss the baby into the air, even in fun. Likewise, even though some babies enjoy being swung in circles while someone holds them by their wrists, this practice can also be dangerous. ∎

The Sick Child

Although illness is always undesirable, it is as normal a part of a young child's life as teething, learning to walk, and "growing up." In fact, it is part of growing up.

Without the illnesses of infancy and childhood, there would be no normal build-up of your child's resistance to the diseases he will have to face and ward off for the rest of his life. It is only when the illnesses get out of hand that they need be a cause of concern.

The most common of all diseases are those caused by viruses—namely colds and flu. They strike all age groups, including infants.

Mothers pass along some protection against contagious diseases to their newborn babies, particularly the childhood illnesses such as measles, three-day measles and mumps.

However, this protection or immunity lasts only for nine months to a year—which, incidentally, is the reason why the immunizations for these diseases are delayed until the child passes that age.

The immunity to colds, flu and other viruses is much less complete. Immunity to chicken pox is nearly completely absent.

Because of this, the baby can and will get viral illnesses frequently. How frequently depends upon two factors—his exposure and his resistance.

Exposure occurs naturally every day of a child's life. It is through such natural exposure that he builds his resistance. However, because the extent of this resistance is unknown, it is unwise to deliberately expose a child to any disease.

This precaution includes diseases to which the child has been immunized since such immunization, although very effective, is not 100 percent perfect.

When your child does get a cold or mild flu-like illness, it will usually include one or more of the following symptoms: fever, running nose, cough, vomiting, or diarrhea.

Remember, it is important to give all medications in proper dosage according to the age and/or weight of the child. Follow directions on the label or those given by your physician.

These symptoms, particularly the fever, are usually worst during the first 24 hours. Temperatures up to 104°F or 105°F are a scary but normal response of children to infectious diseases.

Cooling off methods, such as sponging with cool (not cold) water and the use of acetaminophen drops or liquid, are usually successful.

Because of its relationship to Reye's syndrome (a form of severe liver and brain disease, associated with viral illnesses such as chicken pox and flu) aspirin is not recommended for fever treatment in children and adolescents.

Remember, it is important to give all medications in proper dosage according to the age and/or weight of the child. Follow directions on the label or those given by your physician.

The other symptoms can be handled by similar simple "home remedy" methods prescribed by your physician or well-recognized child care guides.

However, if the symptoms are unusually severe or get progressively worse in the second 24 hours, your doctor should be consulted.

Colds usually precede more serious illnesses, such as ear infections, tonsillitis, bronchitis and pneumonia. These are heralded by earache, sore throat, increasing cough or chest pain. It is these complications, not the cold or flu, that require and respond to antibiotics.

So, when your child becomes ill, watch him carefully for signs of complications. But look upon the experience as nature's preparation to combat any disease exposure that lies ahead. ■

Beginning to Understand

We have no way of knowing what words mean to a child. We can only observe what happens when he hears a particular word.

We know that a baby understands when he consistently responds with a definite reaction to our word.

For example, when the parent raises his voice and says "No!" in disapproval, the child stops the movement he is about to make. But is he reacting to the word "no" itself, or to the pitch and rhythm of our voice?

Parents and caregivers tend to repeat the same words and sentences each time they talk to Baby.

Before long he will borrow the tone and even the rhythm of your voice and use it in his imitations of you.

The demonstration of your pleasure will encourage him to say more and say it better. Even if his repetitions are imperfect, his pitch will resemble yours.

In a study made of vocalizations of infants between six and eight months of age, it was possible to identify a Chinese infant because of his distinct speech patterns.

Another study demonstrated how quickly children learn to mimic intonation. The researcher recorded the babbling and crying of two babies, 10 and 13 months old, under three conditions: when they were alone, in the presence of the mother, and in the presence of the father.

The results indicated that the pitch of their crying did not vary with any of the three situations.

However, the pitch of their babbling did vary. For Father, the infants' pitch was much lower than was the pitch used for Mother.

Clearly the infants imitated the pitch associated with the adult's voice—high for female, lower for male. ■

New Speaker in the House

A child is born to be a speaker in a world of speakers. Her first words usually occur between the eighth and fifteenth months.

It is very difficult to pinpoint the time of the first word because Baby has been babbling for several months and imitating what she hears, however imperfectly, for about two months.

More important than the date of the first word is the quantity of the vocalizations. Baby is heard to repeat patterns of different sounds, as well as long strings of the same sounds. She plays dialogue games with gusto.

At nine months, you can prepare your future speaker by talking, singing and reading to her a lot, continuing the dialogue games and emphasizing early literacy aspects.

You will observe two things. First, as a result of the past month's experience, Baby's imitations in the game have improved enormously.

For example, it used to be that when you would say "goo,"—one of Baby's old vocabulary words—she would respond with "wee." And when you repeated "goo," she would again say "wee." Sometimes she could even be heard privately practicing the pattern "goo...wee ...goo...wee."

Now, however, she has a better understanding of the game. When you say "goo," her imitation is very close in sound, something like "guh" or even "goo."

The second observation you will make is Baby's vocalization of "mama" and "papa."

At this early age the words have different meanings for the parents and for the child, who is just imitating a sound. Nevertheless, we respond enthusiastically because we want to believe that she is addressing us, her mama and her papa!

In effect, the power of reinforcing speech attempts with our response makes it likelier that those sounds will be repeated.

She has taken a step closer to us. She is becoming more of an individual than she was. ■

P. O. Box 2505 • W Lafayette, IN 47996
(800) 927-7289
©Growing Child, Inc.
www.GrowingChild.com

Contributing Authors

Phil Bach, O.D., Ph.D.
Miriam Bender, Ph.D.
Joseph Braga, Ed.D.
Laurie Braga, Ph.D.
George Early, Ph.D.
Carol R. Gestwicki, M.S.
Liam Grimley, Ph.D.
Robert Hannemann, M.D., F.A.A.P.
Sylvia Kottler, M.S.
Bill Peterson, Ph.D.

Safety First

Clare had never had tension headaches in her life, but then, she never had a baby before either.

Clare's tension headaches usually struck in the afternoon when her nine-month-old Greg was taking his nap. She suspected they were caused by motherhood or her inadequacy at it.

She also suspected that feeling inadequate as a mother made the headaches worse. It was a self-compounding mess. So, she didn't tell anyone about it, not even her husband.

She was saved by a good friend who came to the house with her own baby who was about the same age as Greg. Her friend started to put her baby down to crawl.

Then she scanned Clare's living room and said, "This place is a nightmare. Let's go out on the porch or I'll be hopping up and down like a yoyo."

Well, Clare demanded details, and the friend gave them. Four flower pots for her child to get into; a lamp that the baby can pull off the table in two minutes; two electrical outlets unprotected; an open fireplace full of ashes, and a three-legged end table to be knocked over.

The friend said, "You must be a wreck, trying to keep Greg out of trouble."

Well, you could almost see a light bulb blink on over Clare's head. She suddenly remembered the constant near misses as she had snatched Greg from one peril after another. It had never occurred to her that she was constantly trying to out-guess her infant explorer and failing.

So, she and her friend did radical alterations, moving anything that babies might wreck and eliminating anything that might hurt them.

Clare didn't get her house child-safe and baby-proof in one day, but by the end of the week, she had him pretty well out-guessed. And she hasn't had to go for that child-safe aspirin bottle since. ■

Children are our most valuable natural resource.

Herbert Hoover

Baby is 10 Months Old

Baby has been developing more and more rapidly over the past few months. When you hold him upright around the ribs, he may support a lot of weight on his own legs, pushing strongly against your lap or the floor.

Some babies have started to pull to a stand by grasping a heavy piece of furniture or the side of the playpen.

Be sure to check that all items available to pull up on are sturdy and solid enough to not fall over on Baby.

By the tenth month, about 65 percent of all babies have begun to creep on their hands and knees, or to use some other method of deliberate movement to change location.

Baby's first creeping may not be very organized or skillful, but he uses it purposefully to move from place to place. Very soon he will become an expert creeper—moving like a "streak of greased lightning!"

Baby no longer tolerates lying on his back except when he is asleep. He escapes by quickly rolling over and sitting up. This can make diapering a challenge, as well as raise safety issues for possible falls.

Once sitting, he can turn to one side or the other, lean at almost any angle to reach a toy, and sit up straight again.

When he has explored all the things he can reach from one spot, he rolls over on hands and knees and looks for fresh fields to conquer.

Baby's hands are looking less like little fat starfish. His tiny fingers are becoming more skillful at grasping things.

His index finger and thumb have learned to work together to pinch and hold. He can even pick up a crumb of toast or cookie.

He has learned to use his pointer finger to poke and pry. If he finds a hole, in goes his finger to find out what is "inside" or to enlarge the hole for a better view.

By poking and prying into the insides of objects, he is learning about the three dimensions—length, width and depth.

When Baby sees something that attracts him, he may point with his index finger and vocalize demandingly.

By holding objects, transferring them from hand to hand, putting them to his mouth, banging them on the floor and all the other methods of handling that he can manage, Baby is learning about forms and textures.

Although he still frequently brings objects to his mouth and explores them with his lips and tongue,

Baby is becoming more and more interested in using his hands and eyes to learn about the objects around him.

A single detail may come in for Baby's close attention, but he can also now react to two details together, or one after the other.

Baby is taking more and more interest in the persons and things around him.

He drinks from a cup with less dripping around the edges, and has begun to put his hands to the cup to help steer it toward his mouth.

At Ten Months Baby Likes to:
- Poke her finger into tiny openings.
- Play pat-a-cake.
- Pull herself to a standing position.
- Explore her physical environment.

Give Your Baby:
- Cloth or stiff cardboard books of her own.
- Plastic discs on a chain.
- Some stacking blocks, toys or empty boxes.
- Motion toys.

DENTAL NOTE: It is generally recommended that a child be seen by a dentist by the age of one year or within six months after the first tooth comes in.

Pat-a-cake and peek-a-boo are exciting games, and Baby responds to them gleefully.

He is beginning to make himself a part of the family, responding to the words, tones, and emotions of those around him. ■

The Beginning of Active Discipline

It's hard to believe that this bundle of energy who is scurrying all over the place, getting into everything, reaching, grabbing, looking, listening and in general trying to soak up the whole world at once is the same "helpless bundle" who was born just ten months ago.

She has taken giant strides, growing and developing. She's getting to be her own person, and more and more she's becoming independent.

For one thing, ten months ago she stayed just where you put her. But this isn't true any more.

Now she can get around under her own power. She can go where her curiosity leads her. She can do, or try to do, many things by herself.

This means there is now something else to consider: How can you allow her to learn about all those exciting objects in the world and at the same time teach her that some things (for example, electrical outlets) are not safe for her?

There are some things you want her to do and have—and others that are "no-no's." What we're talking about is the beginning of active discipline.

The foundations for discipline really begin at birth as parents respond respectfully to their child and form the relationship that is the biggest motivator for correct behavior.

Discipline has many meanings. From the point of view of child-rearing, some are helpful and others are unhelpful.

Helpful meanings:

1. "Instruction." The dictionary tells us that this is an old-fashioned definition and that "discipline" doesn't mean this any more.

That's a pity because we think good discipline should instruct the child.

2. "Training which corrects, molds, strengthens or perfects." We really like this description of discipline. We hope you'll read it over and over until it becomes your meaning of the word.

The heart of the matter is this: How can you best use discipline to help Baby grow?

Unhelpful meanings:

1. "Punishment, chastisement." Many people think of discipline as punishment. They try to decide if certain kinds of punishment are better or worse.

Instead if you think of discipline as something positive that helps your baby learn, grow and develop, then you begin to think about it in an entirely different manner.

2. "Control gained by enforcing obedience or order, as in a school or army." This definition of discipline does not focus on strengthening Baby's desire to learn by instructing or training him.

Let's take a concrete example to illustrate the difference between unhelpful and helpful discipline.

At the very beginning of discipline, sometimes the answer to a problem is not to insist that the child adhere to a set of adult rules but to find some means of temporarily changing the situation.

Suppose you own a lovely vase which has been in your family for years and was passed on to you by your Great-Aunt Mehitabel. Because you want to enjoy this vase, you have put it on a low table in your living room.

Now, here comes Baby into the living room, and her eyes light on Great-Aunt Mehitabel's vase.

Immediately she wants to get at the vase, but naturally you don't want her to have it. So, every time she reaches for the vase, you slap her hands.

If you are consistent, this kind of discipline will be very effective in preserving your vase. In time, Baby will not even

reach for the vase. But she won't have learned anything positive by the experience. Why?

Because at 10 months, a child is still too young to fully grasp why a particular object is off-limits. And you have spent a lot of time punishing her for her natural curiosity. Remember, a baby learn by imitation—if you slap, she learns to slap.

A more helpful form of discipline would be to put the vase out of sight for the time being, or in full view but out of Baby's reach.

Instead of the vase, put some objects on the table that she can play with and which will help her grow and learn.

The point is that you can create a positive experience by substituting something your daughter can play with for something she can't. You are helping her to learn from her exploration.

Remember, right now we're talking about a ten-month-old child. As you may have already experienced, most children this age will continue to do exactly what they want to do rather than what you want them to do.

Their curiosity is enormous. Their physical drive propels them from one situation into another. Presented with fascinating new objects and places, they do not have the necessary knowledge—or experience—to determine what things are "yes" and what things are "no."

In short, ten months old is just too young to fully understand why some things are acceptable for exploration and others are not.

By wisely selecting what you will leave within Baby's exploring reach, you will not only create a better learning environment for her but you will also save yourself many moments of anxiety or grief.

We can just hear you saying, "But I want my child to learn respect for my valuable

continued on next page

things as well as other people's. How will she learn this if I don't start correcting her now?"

We're not advocating that you allow your child to run wild, pulling and grabbing at everything in sight. Children can learn the difference between yes and no, and we're certainly in favor of that. (More about this in later months.)

What we're suggesting is that a distinction can be made between situations where something is to be learned and situations where "no" is the only choice.

Evaluating each situation will lead to fewer "no's." Those "no's" can be taught and enforced with more success as your child grows older and is more capable of understanding what's going on.

Let's consider another example. You want to visit a friend who collects lovely "knick-knacks" that are placed around the house within easy reach of your active daughter.

You can't expect your friend always to put away every single piece just because you and your daughter have come to call.

What to do? There are several ways you can deal with this situation:

1. You may leave your child at home. There are times, however, when this is not possible nor desirable.

2. You may slap your daughter's hands every time she attempts to pick up or touch one of the items, telling her repeatedly "no-no."

Remember that Baby learns by imitation, so you can expect her to slap at you if you slap at her.

Or you can take the items from her as she attempts to pick them up.

We don't think either of these choices will be a pleasant experience for you or your daughter.

3. You may allow your daughter to look at the items while you hold her securely in your arms.

At least this way the objects won't be broken. Baby will probably enjoy sitting in your lap, although you won't get much visiting done.

4. Bring some favorite toys from home that will attract her attention more than the forbidden "knick-knacks."

This solution is probably the best in that the discipline here is "helpful" because she gets to explore her own things undisturbed.

In any case, the visit will probably be a strain on you.

There may be no simple solution to this situation. You will likely find your conversation disrupted and your attention wandering as you attempt to monitor your daughter's behavior.

The only consolation you have is that in a few months your daughter will be old enough to learn "no-no." You can then return to your friend's home knowing the visit will be different.

What we're talking about is just the beginning of discipline. Sometimes the answer to a problem is not to insist the child adhere to a set of adult rules but to find some means of temporarily changing the situation.

In that way your child has room to explore, look, feel, learn, and at the same time, stay out of trouble or harm's way.

In babyhood almost all situations are "temporary." Today's "big" problem quickly gives way to another as your child grows and develops.

In the months to come we'll have more to say about the important subject of discipline, but we want you to get off to a good start.

The best way we know is to ask the question this way: Does my discipline help Baby to learn or does my discipline restrict her learning explorations? ∎

Baby's Amazing Memory

As you observe your baby's reactions to the world around her, you have probably wondered what's going on inside her little head!

Is she able to store in memory whatever she is learning about her environment? If so, will she be able to retrieve those memories at a later time?

The findings from several fascinating studies of memory in infants clearly demonstrate that (a) an infant's memory abilities are much better than what was previously realized; (b) infants can use their memories in practical ways; and (c) there is much that parents can do to stimulate the development of an infant's memory skills.

One of the reasons why child development experts underestimated the memory abilities of infants is because it had long been considered that language—which helps us to label and categorize our experiences—had to be developed before memories could be formed.

We now know that this is not the case.

How much then do infants really remember? To be sure, infants can't yet recollect as accurately as adults. But even newborn babies demonstrate some ability to remember.

One of the most fascinating ways in which memory of infants has been studied is by means of "habituation" tests.

Habituation occurs when an infant, after being repeatedly exposed to the same stimulus, eventually loses interest in that stimulus.

For example, if a baby is placed in a room where there is occasional loud noise—such as the sound of traffic—the baby will at first become startled every time loud noises occur until she eventually becomes "habituated" to those noises and therefore won't pay any attention to them.

She will only exhibit a startle response when she is exposed to a new, unfamiliar noise, such as an ambulance siren.

Clearly, habituation would not occur unless the infant had some memory of the original stimulus. Otherwise it would not be possible for her to recognize that a new stimulus differed from an earlier one.

An interesting way to observe habituation in your own infant is to show her a large picture of a face. Let her look at it for as long as it holds her attention.

After you have shown her the same picture a number of times in the same way, you will find that she will become "habituated," that is, she will show little or no interest in the picture any more.

Your child's later language development is related to her present learning experiences— thanks to the memory skills she is now developing and the amount of talking to her that you do.

Now hold up a same-size picture of a different face alongside the picture with which she is already familiar. You will likely note that she will show far more interest in the new picture.

One of the implications for parenting is that while babies need routine and stability in their lives, they also need variety at times.

Researchers have been able to determine a baby's reaction to a new stimulus by measuring respiration and heart rates. They have also been able to pinpoint when habituation occurs.

The speed with which habituation takes place has been found to be related to later IQ scores. When the habituation rate of four-month-old babies was tested, for example, it was found that those who habituated the soonest had higher IQ scores and better language development when tested again at three and four years of age.

Several studies also provide us with a clearer understanding of what attracts the attention of infants. They also give us

insight into how infants store and record information in memory, how they can later retrieve from memory what they have already learned, and how their memory skills develop during the first year of life.

In one study, for example, children were shown an animal puppet wearing a felt mitten. When the mitten was removed, it revealed a bell that the baby could ring.

It was found that when one-year-olds were shown only once how to do this, they could still remember the next day how to remove the mitten and ring the bell.

Six-month-old infants, on the other hand, needed to be shown what to do at least three times before they remembered where the bell was hidden.

Another interesting study of the development of memory in infants involved attaching a string from the baby's foot to an attractive mobile. The babies were taught that by kicking with one foot, they could get the mobile to move.

The researchers later tested a baby's memory by hanging the mobile over the crib, then watching to see if the baby remembered to kick with the foot to which the string had been attached.

There were a number of important findings from these studies: (1) The age of the baby was found to be an important factor. For example, two-month-olds remembered to kick provided the experiment was repeated within a 24-hour period; three-month-olds could remember what to do as long as one week later; and six-month-olds remembered beyond one week.

(2) For all infants, not only age, but also the length of delay between the first experience and the subsequent test of memory was an important factor.

(3) It was found that context and routine were also important. When babies were trained in one particular setting to move the mobile by kicking a foot—always using the same foot, the same mobile, and the

continued on next page

continued from previous page

same crib—they did not remember to kick with their foot if they were placed in a different setting with either a different mobile or if placed in a different crib.

(4) Both non-verbal and verbal prompts helped to reactivate an infant's memory. For example, when an adult shook the mobile, it helped to remind the infant to kick her foot.

All of these findings have important implications for helping an infant develop better memory skills. Here are some recommendations:

1. Play memory games. If you have played "peek-a-boo" with your child, just saying the word will probably prompt her to remember to raise a blanket in front of her face.

At ten months of age, a child is capable of playing a more advanced form of this game, namely, searching for a hidden toy if she sees where you put it.

As she gets better at this game, you can make it more challenging for her by letting longer periods of time elapse—for example, by distracting her with another toy— before she goes to look for it.

After she has mastered that challenge, you can stretch her memory by hiding two or three toys at the same time and then letting her find each one of them.

2. Talk to your baby while playing these games. As you talk, Baby is becoming more familiar with the sounds used to communicate and is storing those sounds in her memory.

Linguists now hold that the reason that there are often dramatic spurts in language development between 18 and 24 months is because children at that age learn to access the sounds that they have been storing in their memories for several months.

In other words, your child's later language development is related to her present learning experiences—thanks to the memory skills she is now developing and the amount of talking to her that you do.

3. Provide stability and routine in Baby's world. Stability and routine provide a context in which learning occurs. (Even college students like to sit in the same seats in the classroom when they are daily exposed to new learning experiences!)

Remember that in the research study it was found that babies didn't remember to kick with their foot to make a mobile move if they were placed in a different setting or if a different mobile was used. So, stability and routine are important for memory to function well.

4. Repeat activities and learning experiences. Repetition helps memory to hold on to what is learned.

Young children have a much higher tolerance for repetition than adults. They want you to sing that song again and again or read that story to them one more time. They enjoy recognizing, through the power of memory, their own previous learning experiences.

5. Sequencing helps memory. Putting activities in a sequential context (for example, first you'll take your bath, then we'll dress you for bed, then I'll read you a story ...) helps develop a child's memory skills. As a child gets older, she will remember longer and longer sequences.

6. Provide variety. While infants enjoy the security of routine, they eventually habituate, that is, become bored with what becomes over-familiar. That's when they need variety for new learning to occur.

A good way to provide variety, for example, is to remove most of the toys from Baby's crib, leaving only two or three. When she shows signs of losing interest in those toys, remove them and replace them with two or three other toys.

As you rotate the toys in this way, Baby's interest will be stimulated as she encounters "new" toys that are really like "old friends." Each time she encounters a favorite toy, her memory helps her to recognize it while at the same time she re-discovers it in a new way. ■

Basic Baby Language

What do we mean by basic baby language? At this early age, we mean the sense a baby makes from what he sees and hears about him.

For example, we know he can follow some simple commands, ("No"). He can respond to gestures of pat-a-cake, bye-bye, and similar words. We know he understands them, even though he doesn't say them.

Language can also include the sounds that Baby makes as well as what he does with his hands, eyes, and other parts of his body.

How does Baby acquire language? Actually he has been developing language for most of his young life.

Baby has been listening to the variety of sounds about him. He has been attending to the speech of the important people in his life—those who take care of his physical and emotional needs.

You, in turn, have been tailoring your speech to his development and to particular situations. For example, when you kissed or hugged him you also told him in a special tone of voice, "I love you."

The books you've read to him and the nursery rhymes you've repeated have added another dimension to his basic language learning.

Playing dialogue games, you have attracted his attention and made him attentive to your voice. With your encouragement he has gotten the idea of using his own hands and body to move, to get what he wants, to manipulate and explore objects to learn about his world. And you have been interpreting his experiences by telling him in words what he is doing.

What is important to understand is that even though Baby is not yet saying words, all of his experiences are contributing to his acquisition of language. ■

Explorer in Diapers

Now that Baby is creeping, a whole new world of space exploration is open to her. To a baby on the floor, an ordinary-size room must seem to be an enormous space with posts scattered here and there—the legs of various pieces of furniture.

Baby is increasingly curious about everything she sees, hears or touches. Sometimes it seems that she is driven to learn. It is almost as if she realizes the great amount of learning she has to do and is rushing to do it as quickly as she can.

This curiosity in Baby is a precious thing. It leads her on exciting trips of discovery across the broad floor, behind chairs, under tables. Sometimes it leads her into the dead end of a corner, or behind a door.

What to do now?

Perhaps Baby has never crept backward before except by accident. Now she must shift into reverse to solve this problem.

If she has not been creeping long, she may not be able to do this easily. She may just keep trying to push her way ahead until, in frustration, she begins to cry.

If this should happen, of course you will go to her rescue. But—careful now!

Growing Child

P. O. Box 2505 • W Lafayette, IN 47996
(800) 927-7289
©Growing Child, Inc.
www.GrowingChild.com

Contributing Authors

Phil Bach, O.D., Ph.D.
Miriam Bender, Ph.D.
Joseph Braga, Ed.D.
Laurie Braga, Ph.D.
George Early, Ph.D.
Carol R. Gestwicki, M.S.
Liam Grimley, Ph.D.
Robert Hannemann, M.D., F.A.A.P.
Sylvia Kottler, M.S.
Bill Peterson, Ph.D.

Make this a learning experience for Baby. Comfort her with your voice and hand. Gently coax her backward until she is free. Then praise her for her bravery and her learning.

Had you just snatched her up and fussed over her, Baby would have learned nothing from her experience—except, perhaps, to be afraid of corners and strange places.

A playpen makes a fine protected area for play. But if a baby is frequently confined to her playpen, she will soon lose some of her wonderful curiosity.

The restricted space will not give her enough room to perfect her creeping and to learn the many things about herself that creeping will teach her.

Unless Baby can experience the various distances between objects, she will be slower to learn about judging distance and time.

These early lessons form part of the solid foundation for later learning at school.

If Baby is to explore safely, you must take a good look around your house, at low cabinets and drawers, at the tops of low tables, and at any containers which may be standing on the floor.

Remove all cleaning materials from lower and under-counter kitchen cabinets.

That means soaps, detergents, window or oven cleaner, cleansers, furniture polish, disinfectants, floor wax, floor cleaner, insect or ant sprays or liquids—anything that Baby might break, pour over herself, put in her mouth or swallow.

Replace these with safe, unbreakable objects such as pots, pans, pie tins, lids, plastic bowls and the like.

Now if Baby pulls open a cabinet door, she can explore and learn in safety with her own special collection of favorite toys and objects. ■

Give me the first six years of my life
and you can keep the rest.

Rudyard Kipling

Eleven Months, Going On One Year

By now Baby is so much a part of the family that it is hard to remember what things were like without him.

He creeps rapidly and effectively, sometimes with a purpose, sometimes just for the fun of moving around.

He spends much of his time practicing and perfecting skills already learned.

Many babies at this age progress to standing alone, and some have even started to walk. But although walking is a new and exciting way of getting about, Baby continues to prefer creeping as he plays.

He moves from sitting to creeping and back to sitting with practiced ease.

His sitting balance is now very secure. He leans in all directions and easily comes back to sitting erect.

When he does lean too far, he quickly catches himself on one outstretched arm.

Now that Baby sits so securely, bath time has become great fun time.

Washcloths are for sucking, water is for splashing. Floating toys are fascinating but sometimes a little frightening when they move out from under Baby's reaching hands.

Baby seems to get busier by the day—creeping, standing, balancing with "no hands," cruising along the sides of furniture or playpen, touching and grabbing everything within reach.

Baby must still pull himself to a stand either with your assistance or by grasping the side of his playpen or a piece of furniture.

Once standing, Baby will side-step along, usually holding on with at least one hand.

Although Baby's standing balance is getting better all the time, he has not yet found a way to sit down easily.

He pulls to a stand, then reverses the process by just letting his legs collapse under him.

Sometimes he lands with quite a thud. Since he is still well-padded with a diaper, this doesn't seem to bother him.

He may pull himself up in the crib in the middle of the night and cry to get help in getting settled back down again.

Baby is beginning to cooperate with dressing, ducking his head, sometimes putting one arm through a sleeve, or putting out both feet for one shoe.

He waves bye-bye. He may even indicate his desire to leave by reaching for the door and vocalizing his message in some way.

Toys are now transferred from one hand to the other, to the mouth, back again to be turned over and over under close inspection. His eyes are watching what his hands are doing.

Some babies have begun to show a preference for reaching with one hand rather than the other.

This is not true handedness, though, and Baby will probably use both hands or either hand interchangeably for about another year before he eventually becomes right-handed or left-handed.

Let him come to this choice by himself. Don't try to force it one way or the other.

At 11 Months Baby Likes to:

- Handle and examine toys and objects carefully.
- Be danced with and sung to.
- Play alongside, but not yet with other children.
- Show affection toward primary caretakers, especially parents.

Give Your Baby:

- A ball and other rolling toys.
- A set of plastic mixing bowls.
- Lots of conversation about himself and the world around him.
- Opportunity to develop mastery of new motor abilities creeping, standing, and walking.
- Board books

Some babies are beginning to try to use a spoon in feeding. These attempts frequently end with more food outside than inside.

Still, it is true that more finger foods now find their way into Baby's mouth. The drive for independence continues. Give him a chance. Let him try.

Baby is learning, learning, learning! Each day brings new accomplishments. Only a daily diary can keep up with the changes your baby is making. We recommend that you keep one.

It isn't necessary to make entries daily. You will still have a lasting record if you can make notations several times a week. ∎

Another Step Forward

By eleven months, Baby has made great strides in her perception of the world. She can recognize familiar objects, even when they are in unusual positions.

Try handing Baby her bottle backwards—with the nipple pointing away from her. She will not even pause before turning the bottle around the right way.

By now she is routinely removing any covering you might place between her and some object she wants. Thus she now knows that objects are both permanent and that they look different in different settings.

A sense of cause and effect is also developing. Earlier there was only one kind of cause—her own actions. She could "make" something disappear by looking away from it. She could call forth faces by babbling or crying.

But now she will sometimes wait for you to do things for her which suggests her awareness of other people besides herself.

The act of pushing aside a barrier or removing a cover means that she perceives the barrier or cover as being a cause of her inability to see the desired object. This is also a step toward a less self-centered view of reality.

But now an interesting thing happens. While Baby has learned to see other objects as things distinct from herself, the associations she makes between objects are made in an inflexible way. Let's consider an example.

Sit down with Baby and hide her toy two or three times beneath the same cover—let's say a hat—letting her take away the hat each time to get the toy.

Now find another possible cover, like a pillow, and place it beside the hat. This time, with the toy in her full view, place the toy under the pillow instead of the hat. As soon as the toy has disappeared, she will attempt to find the object—under the hat! Try it again; she will still look

under the hat, the place where the toy first disappeared or where she is used to seeing it disappear.

Thus, while the object is permanent, the permanence is associated rather rigidly with a particular covering. She expects the object to appear under the familiar cover.

Before you smile at the simplicity of this notion, consider that this kind of rigidity of association persists to some extent even into adulthood. Think of the times when you repeatedly searched the same location for a missing object because it **had** to be there.

So perhaps we can forgive Baby at this stage for missing what to us seems obvious. At the same time our next play-teaching task is cut out for us: to teach Baby to associate an object with its current cover, not just the original one.

You can play this second cover game with her by starting with covers that are very similar. That way it will be harder to know the difference between them. The associations to the original cover will more easily connect up to the new one.

Be sure to alternate the right and left positions of the original cover so that she does not develop a position habit of reaching to one side consistently. Gradually you can make the two covers more and more

different as Baby learns to follow her eyes' information rather than the original connections between object and covering.

There is another activity that is useful in strengthening Baby's sense of cause and effect.

Place a desired object out of reach at the end of a strip of cloth or paper. The other end of the strip should be just in front of her. Restrain Baby so that she can't crawl over to the object. See if she will pull on the strip to bring the object within reach. If not, show her how it works; then see if she can do it for herself.

This, of course, requires her to see the connection between the object and the strip and recognize that the strip can be used as a means to an end.

There are really two causes in a series here: she causes the strip to move and the strip causes the object to move.

As a variation use a string tied to the object.

These games will sharpen Baby's intellect and help her take some giant steps forward in thinking logically about the world.

If you and your baby don't accomplish these games right now, don't be alarmed. These and other activities may be carried on during the next few months. ∎

Fascination With Containers

With control of her hands and fingers getting better all the time, and with a growing appreciation for the shapes of objects, Baby is now fascinated with holes and openings.

She's beginning to get the idea that some objects have both an inside and an outside. She pokes her finger into all available cracks and crevices to confirm visually what the hand exploration suggests.

She turns small objects all around to search for irregularities that would have gone unnoticed not long ago.

At playtime, show Baby how you can drop toys one by one into a shoe box, then take them out again. She will be fascinated by this game.

Present the box of toys to her and invite her to reach in and take one out. Then teach her by example to pick a toy from the floor, and drop it into the box.

Dropping is an exciting new skill for her. Combined with her interest in contain-ers, this should cause her to fill and empty the box over and over again once she has learned how.

You can also make your own containers with coffee cans and lids with holes cut in.

A little more difficult variation is to drop a spoon into a cup. She will have to be more careful of the position of her hand before letting go.

The satisfying jingle of the spoon in the cup, and your smile of approval will be reward enough to keep her trying.

An old coffee pot makes an excellent container for several small toys and poses a greater challenge in getting the objects out, for they cannot all be removed by a simple tipping or dumping of the pot.

Another way to stimulate Baby's curiosity about containers is to leave a small paper bag containing a toy at some spot where she will be able to see it. Notice how soon she comes to investigate the bag and how quickly she looks inside. ∎

Feeding a Baby

You can usually tell when Baby is hungry and when she's not hungry any longer. When her body needs food, Baby cries or bangs her spoon on the highchair tray. You know she wants to eat. When she sweeps her arm across the tray, neatly disposing of what's on it, you know she's had enough.

It sounds simple, but it's true; she'll eat enough to fulfill her needs and no more. Sometimes you worry because she's eating hardly anything at all.

Or you think, oh no, she's going to be a finicky eater. Or you're sure she's being defiant and obstinate. Or, you think, as her parent, you know best. But she's following her biological instincts: She's going by her body's wants, not her will. And her body knows best.

There are foods she may not like. She's entitled to dislike some things. It doesn't mean she'll never like them.

Relax about feeding Baby. She won't overeat. She'll tell you when she's had enough so that you won't feed her too much. And her body won't let you feed her too little. ∎

A Treasure Box

Giving Baby his own "treasure box" is an excellent idea.

Start with a cardboard box about 16 inches high, or tall enough so that he can just reach over the side when he is sitting or kneeling beside it.

Fill it half full with folded newspapers so he cannot tip the box over by pulling on one side.

Then put four or five toys or small ob-jects on top of the papers in the box. At least some of the objects should be new to him.

Before long, Baby will find the box and look over its side to discover the contents. If he has to stretch to reach the objects, they will be a more valued prize.

This container will be his own fun box, a magic source of new things to play with. When you get new toys, put them in the box so that he will "discover" them.

Just as we suggested with the learning mobile several months ago, it is better to use fewer objects at a time and change them more often than to load him up with a confusing variety of things all at once.

With fewer objects you will increase his attention span and get more mileage out of a toy.

After Baby is used to creeping over to the box to find new sources of entertainment, move the box to a new location when he is gone. See if he goes to the accustomed place to find the box.

After he learns the use of that box, you might change its appearance by painting it, or substituting another container.

If you think we're teaching Baby to get into things, you're right. We want him to be curious and to have his curiosity rewarded. It is your job now to see that things within his reach contain nothing that might be harmful. ∎

More Language Games

These language games are designed to help children increase listening attention, follow simple directions, and recognize objects.

They foster an understanding of the relationship of objects to their names.

1. Cup 'n Block.

Place a coffee can and a small block on the table in front of Baby. Tell her to put the block into the can.
If she doesn't understand, point to the block and then to the can as you give the instructions, "Put the block into the can."

Should she still not understand, show her, but don't forget to describe what you're doing as you're doing it. "I'm putting the block in the can."

Then give her a chance. Once she has the idea, increase the challenge.

Give her a lot of blocks and tell her to "put them all in the can."

2. Squeeze the Baby.

The "baby" can be a small rubber doll which, when squeezed, makes a noise.

Place the doll on the table in front of Baby and gently squeeze it.

\Then give her a turn by instructing her to "squeeze the baby." Repeat your lesson until she understands it.

Just like our other games, don't forget to describe what you're doing when you demonstrate, "I'm squeezing the baby."

3. Be a Winner.

The objects for this event may be a toy, a familiar household item or a piece of clothing. Baby should be on her hands and knees with three objects lined up across the room. Tell her, "Go get the shoe."

When she obtains the desired object, reward her with a championship hug. After all, she's learned to link the object with its name!

Perhaps three objects are too many at first and you may have to reduce them to two.

4. Which Hand Is It In?

The object may be a favorite small toy, or piece of fruit. Show Baby the object and transfer it several times back and forth between your hands.
Next offer her both hands which are closed, and ask, "Which hand is it in?"

If she is correct, reward her with the object as well as praise—"Yes, you found the (object or fruit)!"

If she makes a wrong choice, open that hand and allow her to look while you tell her, "It's not here. Where is it?" Obviously this time she will choose the correct hand.

This game is also good practice for the concept of object permanence described earlier as well as teaching the child to observe and to concentrate. ■

Developing Independence

It's not too soon to be thinking about cutting the emotional umbilical cord which connects Baby to parents. Although Baby is a separate person, she is still in a sense linked to her parents by emotional ties.

She will travel the road from total dependence to total independence in a series of stages. It is important that you, her parents, help her through each stage. Decide right now that you want her to become independent, and that you will start doing those things which make for independence.

You can develop independence by letting a child do things for herself. Even now, you can help by letting her struggle a little.

Whatever she's trying to do, if she has a reasonable chance of doing it herself, let her try. You may see her try to get to a ball while she's on the floor. You can tell she wants it, but as she struggles to get it her efforts are not too efficient. So you, trying to be helpful, may get the ball.

Please don't! She needs to work for that ball because as she does, she inches forward in her development of independence.

If you do it for her, she won't have to struggle. If she doesn't struggle a little, she won't learn to do it for herself. If she doesn't learn to do it for herself, she won't develop independence. It's as simple as that.

There will be many times—now and later—when your child will try to do something for herself. It may be reaching for something just beyond her grasp. Or getting from where she is now to some other place she wants to be.

Other times, she will fix her attention on some object and try to either bring it to her, or get herself to it.

In all these situations she will have a chance to interact, to struggle a little with the world. As she works, she learns and develops. If you step in too soon, you take away the effort and the learning and development.

The older your child becomes, the more she will be able to do for herself. Always praise the child for trying—it makes the struggle worth the effort. You will encourage dependence if you do too much for her.

One of the most important gifts you can offer your baby is the opportunity to become a person in her own right. Of course, you will do for her all the things she cannot do for herself now.

At the same time, let her do for herself whenever possible. It's not too soon to start helping her to develop independence. ■

A Safe Home

Baby has entered a new period of development where he can get around either on his feet or on all fours. With this stage Baby begins to explore actively.

While Baby is learning to investigate and explore the house, parents are learning about all the things he can get into and out of!

A long period of quiet is generally a signal that Baby is into something. He may be pulling out clothes from drawers and hampers, or coloring the walls with lipstick, or playing with water in the toilet bowl.

Since this is the "Age of Exploration," the family should decide how it views the function of a home in relation to the young explorer's development.

If this is to be a house primarily for the adults, then parents will find themselves spending much of their time restraining Baby—actively saying "no-no" very often, or redirecting his attention and interest so that he'll forget about his present discovery or exploration.

What can happen to a Baby whose curiosity is constantly interfered with? For one thing, it will affect his motivation to learn. The curiosity he exhibits today is the same curiosity which later on will help him be successful in school.

If his curiosity is consistently discouraged, he will begin to repress the desire to discover as much as he can about his world.

What can parents do to encourage exploration without threatening valuable property?

As we have said before, remove those things which are fragile or dangerous. Then Baby will be free to move about without risk to himself or to your possessions. You will feel more relaxed because you won't have to play police officer.

Try to look at your home through the eyes of your baby. We suggest only that you be protective, not overprotective.

Checklist for Making Your Home Safe

Common items that can be dangerous. What is in the home, yard, basement, garage, that Baby could get at and put into his mouth and injure himself or choke on? Are there coins, buttons, pins or needles, paper clips, rubber bands, beads, bottle tops, razor blades, glass, nails?

Use gates and barriers to protect Baby from areas you don't want him to get into.

Lethal toys. If there is a workshop, is it safely out-of-bounds for Baby? Can he get to such lethal "toys" as power tools? Kerosene, knives, paint, putty?

Physical safety. Are floor coverings fastened down? Can Baby get at electric cords and pull them? Are electrical appliances disconnected when not in use? Do pan handles protrude from the stove tops? Are drawers and cupboard doors kept closed? Are there doors on discarded iceboxes or refrigerators? (If there are, take them off.)

First aid. Do you know the location of your nearest hospital? Do you, or the older children, know how to phone the fire or police departments? Do you own a first aid kit? Do you know the location of the nearest "Poison Center?" ■

Be a Patient Listener

How well is Baby communicating at 11 months?

1. He can recognize and respond to his own name.

2. He understands a lot of what is said to him and around him.

3. He has established a large repertoire of sounds; he "talks" at length with babbling that has intonations resembling our speech. He may even have one meaningful word in his vocabulary.

4. He imitates an assortment of sounds combined with movements such as grunting, coughing, lip smacking.

For several months we have talked about babbling. At last Baby is on the threshold of talking. We've given him the necessary experiences—hearing interesting sounds around him and people talking to him. He has explored and manipulated with his hands and eyes. Within the next three months he will start to speak. His wealth of experiences will give him something to talk about.

Don't be upset if Baby's speech is not precise. He may make a variety of sound substitutions and omissions—"ta" for "cat," or a little later, "yiyon" for "lion" or "wed" for "red." He will require another two years— until he is around three years of age— before most of his sounds are clear and distinct.

What is involved in sound production? Dozens of small muscles in the throat, tongue and lips must work together in perfect time. Lots of practice helps to coordinate these muscles with sound which comes from the larynx or voice box.

The different ways in which the tongue and lips move make the distinction between sounds. For example, the tongue tip is important in the "t" sound. It scrunches up flat and curves carefully up to touch the gum behind the front teeth. What about "th?" The tongue shoots out between the front teeth while we blow air across it.

If you examine your own speech as you talk, you will recognize how complex the task is. Remember, speech is learned, it is not automatic. So be patient with Baby's first attempts at speech—another two years of practice will make a big difference. ■

Is Your Baby Ahead of Schedule?

We received a letter from a mother who liked our newsletter but said that her baby was several months ahead of our schedule. Many of the things we said a "typical" baby should be doing at a certain age her child had already done a month or so before.

The mother asked us to keep sending *Growing Child* on the regular schedule but at the same time to send advance issues several months ahead so she could know what to expect for her baby.

We've mentioned many times that babies develop at their own pace. Their growth and development takes place in spurts. This month the child may appear to be ahead in some areas and behind in others; next month the reverse may be true.

Because of this, it is important for parents to encourage consistent development in all areas, not just in areas where a child appears to excel.

We believe children who are pushed to achieve ahead of schedule may miss important developmental experiences that would normally occur along the way.

The results sometimes show up in school. Education professionals often see children who are intelligent but who cannot cope with ordinary tasks of reading, writing, and arithmetic.

The problem is not that the children lack intelligence, but that as babies they did not have the right developmental experiences at the right time.

These experiences are the kinds of things we tell you about each month in such areas as cognitive, emotional, physical and social development. In fact, this is the reason we started publishing our monthly newsletter in the first place.

We believe if children get all the developmental experiences they need, and if they get them at the proper time, they will most likely not have problems later in learning to read, write, and do arithmetic.

Babies need to have the opportunity to go through all the developmental experiences appropriate for their age. If we send advance issues, there is a danger the parents may start trying to get their baby to do things typical of older babies.

Every baby needs time—not just to perform a given task—but to gain mastery of the skills involved. That mastery is only accomplished with time and much repetition.

It is important to consider the concept of the whole child and to focus on all aspects of development, not just school or readiness tasks, so that a child can cope with frustrations with others or taking turns as well as doing math or reciting the whole alphabet.

You know your baby better than anyone else, and the decisions about child rearing belong to you. We hope you'll think about the points we've raised. ■

Growing Child

P. O. Box 2505 • W Lafayette, IN 47996
(800) 927-7289
©Growing Child, Inc.
www.GrowingChild.com

Contributing Authors

Phil Bach, O.D., Ph.D.
Miriam Bender, Ph.D.
Joseph Braga, Ed.D.
Laurie Braga, Ph.D.
George Early, Ph.D.
Carol R. Gestwicki, M.S.
Liam Grimley, Ph.D.
Robert Hannemann, M.D., F.A.A.P.
Sylvia Kottler, M.S.
Bill Peterson, Ph.D.

Walking Is Tricky

Harold is 11 months old and he fell down today. Harold is learning how to walk.

He began crawling quite early at little more than six months of age. He hadn't been crawling for long before he learned to cruise. That's pulling himself up on a solid object and moving along on his feet, if there is something solid to hang onto. Then at slightly before 11 months, he discovered balance! He could get up on his feet, let go and not fall over.

Now he is into the extremely tricky business of moving a foot while not holding on, regaining balance, then moving the other foot. It's a skill called walking.

Harold's mother is worried. People who don't know how to walk, can fall. Could Harold get hurt? She said this about Harold's daring experiments: "Suppose he is leaning against the sofa and looking at the coffee table. It takes only eight of his steps to get there, and he's only good for about four.

"Suppose he falls then; he's just close enough to whack his head on the table. Should I let him try or should I stop him?"

Well, she let him try with a cushion padding the table. Sure enough, daring Harold took off, and just as surely, he only went four steps, but he didn't fall, he collapsed. And when he hit the floor, there was a pad under him: his own behind.

If you watch babies who are experimenting with walking, they don't fall forward, unless they stumble. They aren't dummies! When balance leaves them, they quit and take a bump on the bottom.

It's a smart system, which is probably why there are so many adults able to walk around on two feet without black eyes.

Must you always be present when your baby is learning to walk? Don't worry about it, because if there is one thing a baby learns well it is how to take a sudden sit-down. ■

Children are full of curiosity about the gift of life. Parents need only nurture this natural sense of wonder.

Robert Coles

First Birthday

Baby's first birthday is a great occasion. Since the end of the first year is a major milestone in her development, this seems to be a good time to look at what the "typical" baby has achieved.

We've talked before about the concept of "typical" development. Usually a baby may be somewhat ahead in some areas of development, somewhat behind in others, and "typical" in still other areas.

We use the concept of the "typical" child in describing the general developmental characteristics at a certain age.

A "typical" one-year-old is very busy, moving about independently. She may creep on hands and knees, bear-walk on hands and feet or scoot over the floor in a sitting position. And she can be fast!

She pulls to a stand against furniture and cruises around it by stepping sideways. She walks forward when one or both of her hands are held—and demands this help from anyone available.

She may stand alone for a few moments or in some cases will be walking alone.

Wiry, active infants often walk several months before the stocky, heavier ones whose feet and ankles are not yet ready to support that extra weight while navigating around the room.

For some time now ONE has been able to sit securely on the floor for extended periods—leaning forward or sideways, even rotating her body to reach for something behind her.

She can move quickly from lying to sitting, to creeping. Then she can pull to a stand, let herself down, repeating the process again and again as she explores her surroundings.

ONE is also quick to pick up a crumb, a small piece of string or a tiny piece of cheese. She uses a neat and precise pincer grasp between her thumb and the tip of her index finger.

Remember that she can now spy, pick up and examine needles, straight pins, a small piece of glass, and may even want to put them in her mouth. (Keep close watch so you can find these tiny dangers before she does.)

A one-year-old is very interested in what happens to toys or other objects when they are dropped or thrown. She has also learned to follow a rolling toy until it goes out of her sight Then she retrieves it.

ONE has learned to point at objects she wants or things that interest her.

At 12 Months Baby Likes to:
- Master new motor abilities.
- Put lids on containers and take them off again.
- Climb modest heights (six inches or less).

Give Your Baby:
- The affection she seeks and needs.
- Praise for her accomplishments.
- Loving but firm discipline.
- Objects to play with and explore such as board books, pots and pans, pull toys on a string.

Ask Your Doctor About:
- Varicella (Var).
- PCV (pneumococcal conjugate vaccine.)
- MMR

She watches a small toy pulled along the floor even if she is across the room.

Out of doors she watches moving people, animals, cars, and trucks, with fascinated attention.

She recognizes familiar people or animals approaching from 20 feet or more.

ONE uses both hands freely but she may show some preference for the left or the right. However, permanent hand preference is usually not established for another year or more.

Pictures have begun to catch her interest but only briefly. She wants the

continued on next page

Developmental Milestones—12 Months

Social/Emotional
- Gives objects on request.
- Imitates hand and face gestures such as waving bye-bye, clapping hands, closing eyes.
- Helps with dressing by putting arms out for sleeves and feet for shoes.
- Seeks and finds hidden toys easily.
- Is affectionate toward familiar people.

Motor (Fine)
- Holds spoon but needs help with its use.
- Moves blocks in and out of small box.
- Uses pincer grasp (thumb and index finger) to pick up small objects or pieces of food.
- Points with index finger toward a desired object.
- Uses both hands freely but may demonstrate a preference for one.

Motor (Gross)
- Pulls to standing position and lets self down by holding on to furniture.
- May stand alone for a few seconds.
- Sits well for an indefinite period of time.
- May creep on all fours.
- May walk independently.

Communication
- Imitates adult's playful sound-making.
- Recognizes own name and turns to speaker when hearing it.
- Follows simple directions: "Give it to Mommy," "Come to Daddy," "Clap hands."
- Babbles a lot with rhythm and variations in pitch.

Vision
- Recognizes familiar people at a distance of 20 feet or more.
- Intently watches small toys that are pulled across the floor at a distance of 10 feet. ∎

These milestones are guidelines only. All babies do not develop at the same speed, nor do they spend the same amount of time at each stage of their development. Usually a baby is ahead in some areas, behind in others and "typical" in still other areas. The concept of the "typical" child describes the general characteristics of children at a given age.

continued from front page

pages in books and magazines to keep turning and wants to help turn them.

Receptive language is developing. Our "typical" ONE knows her own name and immediately turns in response to it.

She shows by her behavior and response that she understands several common words in context such as cup, spoon, ball, car, dinner, and kitty.

She understands simple instructions associated with gestures, such as "Come to Mommy," "Give it to Daddy," "Where are your shoes?" "Wave bye-bye."

Upon request she may hand an adult a familiar object such as a cup, ball or shoe.

At one year, a child occupied in quiet play will generally hear the sound of crumpling paper or of a rattle three to four feet away, outside of her field of vision. She will generally respond by turning her head toward the sound. However, once she has located it, she will ignore further sounds from the same side.

If the same sound is produced from her other side, she may turn her eyes toward it, then lose interest. If you suspect that your child does not respond normally to these kinds of sounds, consult your physician or pediatrician.

At this age, normal hearing is essential if language development is to continue without interruption.

ONE has also come a long way socially. She is affectionately demonstrative with familiar persons.

She likes to be constantly within sight and hearing of a familiar adult.

In fact, your one-year-old is now a socially responsive individual, building herself into your family structure as an active participant.

She drinks from a cup with little assistance. She chews solid foods. She holds a spoon but usually cannot use it by herself.

She has learned a lot about objects and takes them to her mouth less often. Drooling is now minimal.

ONE will put wooden cubes or small toys in a cup, bowl or box when shown how it is done.

She may take them out again and put them back again.

She will listen with pleasure to toys that make sounds.

She may even repeat the actions necessary to reproduce the sounds.

When a toy is hidden while she's watching, ONE will find it quickly. She has learned the basic concept of object permanence. ∎

More Careful Observation

At 12 months, there is increasing evidence that Baby is looking very carefully at objects and visualizing what will happen if he does something with them.

His many weeks of scrambling around the floor and latching onto everything in sight have allowed him to begin the process in which his eyes now communicate important information to his brain.

In one interesting experiment, six-month-old babies were presented with a strange object, a plastic form shaped like an ice cream cone. The babies made a grab for the object as soon as they saw it.

When the object was shown to one-year-olds, the older children looked at the item for a second or two before reaching for it. It was as if they were recalling everything they knew about such a shape.

While One-Year-Old still gets into everything, he doesn't wade into things quite as recklessly as before. He is selective; he goes for the challenging stuff. He uses his eyes to guide his movements more than ever before.

Before becoming a walker, an infant relies on the contact method—which means that by the time his feet feel an object, it is usually too late to save himself from stumbling.

However, as One-Year-Old gains more and more walking experience, he reaches out with his eyes instead of his hands to guide his feet safely around or over any obstructions on the floor.

You can use ONE's improved visual attention in little games that will sharpen his observation and further improve his logical thinking.

Some of the activities suggested last time, like hiding objects under new covers or using a cloth as a "conveyor belt" between your child and his toy also involve observation and thinking about logical consequences.

You are probably still working on the harder activities and that is fine. Don't worry if you don't get everything done before the next issue of *Growing Child* comes along.

The following lesson game may be more demanding still, but if you do it in the spirit of fun, One-Year-Old will enjoy it.

First, tie an interesting toy or object on the end of a string and show him how to pull on the string to bring the object within reach.

He will like the challenge of picking up the small string in his fingers.

When he can do this well, lay a second string of the same length parallel to the first and about an inch away so that it just misses the object on one side.

See if Baby can visually judge which string is the right one to pull.

You can vary the difficulty of this game by adjusting the closeness of the free string to the object. Start with a great enough separation that he will have no trouble choosing the string that is connected. Then gradually move the loose string closer to the object.

ONE also is ready to begin judging size relationships. Get two pans of different sizes so that one will fit within the other.

Take the smaller pan and slowly place it in the larger, while saying, "The little pan goes in the big pan."

If you smile and show delight at your accomplishment, ONE will understand that such a placement is a "great feat" and he will try it when you give him a chance.

Conversely, you can show him that the big pan won't go in the little pan.

The addition of a third pan of the same general shape (so that size alone is the cue) may seem only a little harder to you, but it will provide him with a challenge for some time to come. ∎

Roseola, Rubella, Rubeola, Varicella and Others

Roseola, Rubella, Rubeola, Varicella—sounds like the beginning of a Latin poem!

Actually these are the medical names of the four most common "childhood diseases" every parent should know about. They are contagious by direct contact with the sick person but cannot be "carried" by someone who has already had the disease.

Roseola is a puzzling illness that usually occurs during the first two years of a child's life.

It has only two symptoms, fever and rash. The fever is usually high (103°-105°F) for three or four days. After the fever has been gone for almost 24 hours, a faint rash will appear on the body—only to disappear in another 24 hours.

Although the fever may be frightening, it usually causes no harm. Since this illness often occurs around the time of teething, the fever is often blamed upon that event.

Rubella is the medical name for German or 3-day measles. This is an illness that can cause damage to an unborn baby if the mother becomes infected during the first three months of her pregnancy. However, it is a preventable disease.

The vaccine is usually given at 12-15 months of age with a booster between the ages of 4 and 12 years.

The disease itself is not serious. After a two-to-three week incubation period, there is a low-grade fever for about three days, accompanied by a rash that appears on the face, spreads to the rest of the body and is gone within three days. There are also painful "knots" or nodes on the back of the neck and skull.

Rubeola is the "old fashioned," "two week," or "hard" measles. After a 10-to-12 day incubation period there is a fever, cough, and eye irritation for four or five days. Then there is a very high fever, increasing cough, and a rash that starts on the face and spreads over the entire body.

This illness may have many complications such as pneumonia and ear infections, and can affect the brain with what is called encephalitis.

Although there may be a great deal of eye irritation and sensitivity to light, there is usually no permanent eye damage from the measles. A darkened room for the measles patient is not a necessity, although it does help make light-sensitive eyes less painful. This disease is also preventable by a vaccine that can be given as early as 12 months of age.

Varicella or chicken pox is a childhood disease for which there is also a preventive vaccine which can be given as early as one year. The incubation period is 11-21 days.

Although he may be contagious, the patient may have very little illness before the rash breaks out. It usually starts with small blisters that appear in daily crops starting on the trunk and then spreading to the face, scalp, and other body areas.

Sometimes even the palms of the hands and soles of the feet are involved. For this illness the only treatment is for the itching of the rash. Various kinds of lotions and anti-itch preparations are used.

Aspirin should not be given because its use in the patient with chicken pox is related to the development of a life-threatening disease called Reye syndrome.

There are two other common diseases of childhood—scarlet fever and mumps. **Scarlet fever** is often called Scarlatina. It is not a viral illness like the other childhood diseases. Instead, it is caused by a bacteria called streptococcus—"strep" for short, and as the name implies, the rash is very red.

The incubation period for this illness is very short—two to seven days. Once a child gets the rash, he becomes immune to that part of the disease. However, he can get strep throat more than once. This type of infection can be serious because it is related to two complications: rheumatic fever and nephritis.

Rheumatic fever causes painful, swollen and red joints. Sometimes there can also be involvement of the valves of the heart causing "rheumatic heart disease." This does not happen very often because the strep bacteria can now be destroyed by antibiotics such as penicillin.

Nephritis is an inflammation of the kidneys that can be quite serious. There can be blood in the urine and a high blood pressure. Permanent kidney damage may occur but that does not happen very often.

Mumps is a childhood disease that causes swelling of the glands on the side of the jaw in front of and below the ear lobe. Sometimes there is also swelling of the glands under the jaw. This disease has a long incubation period of 17-21 days.

It is usually very mild in young children. However, in older children and adults it can have serious complications such as inflammation of the brain (encephalitis), pancreas gland (pancreatitis), and the sex glands.

Treatment of mumps consists of bed rest or at least very quiet activity during the first few days of the illness.

Sour and spicy foods need to be avoided during the acute phase of the illness since they stimulate the flow of saliva and cause pain in the inflamed gland. Severe headache, stomachache or persistent vomiting are danger signals for some of the complications already mentioned.

This disease can be prevented by mumps vaccine (given as MMR) which can be given to children or to adults who have not had the disease. ■

The Naming Game

Baby's intellectual and language development strongly influence each other at this age.

The more Baby is stimulated to listen and to look, the better she will understand what she hears and sees and the more rapidly her intellect will develop.

We know that the spoken word aids a child in comprehension and perception. A well-known experiment demonstrates this point.

Two groups of children, aged 13 to 31 months, were introduced to the same task—to identify which of two boxes, red or green, contained a piece of candy.

In Group A the children were left alone to learn by means of trial and error which box—actually the red one—contained the candy. This learning took considerable time and the children forgot from one day to the next.

In Group B, however, the experimenters said the word "red" every time the children made a correct choice. This group needed only 15 trials to make the connection consistently between the red box and the candy.

One week later, both groups were invited back to find the box which contained the candy. The children in Group B remembered which box without any practice or help.

Those in Group A could not remember and had to have the task re-taught. In this experiment, saying the word "red" focused the children's attention. This focused attention helped them to remember one week later.

If you haven't begun already, start now to help Baby label her world. You can do this with the Naming Game in which you point out and identify objects and events in Baby's world. For example:

1. Dressing. As you dress Baby, talk about what you are doing, identifying parts of her body and pieces of clothing she wears. "Put the hat on your head."

2. Bathing. When you have Baby in the tub, gently splash water on her and say, "The water splashes your tummy."

3. Feeding. Name the food on her spoon. "Put this ice cream in your mouth."

4. Play. Play means anything Baby enjoys doing. It can be banging or making other noises, putting objects into containers and taking them out again, or pulling objects from place to place on the floor.

In any event, name the objects and events. "You can make noise with a pan and a spoon."

In these examples, you'll notice: (1) The talk is short and simple; (2) You talk about things that interest Baby as well as things you think she should know.

Studies of babies tell us that they learn best from activities in which they are interested and involved. If you take Baby to the supermarket, use the opportunity to advantage. Talk to her as you selectively shop.

Tell her what you need, show her the pictures of the object on the label and describe to her your choices. "Here's some lettuce. It's wet. Feel the water?" Or "We need oranges. Let's put them in the basket."

Shopping will continue to be a great educational experience for a very long time. Actually this is an extension of the Naming Game except that now your objects and events are in a new surrounding.

How else can you play the Naming Game? Through books. At first Baby may put them in her mouth—remember it's her earliest means of exploration.

So, you may choose books with pages of cloth or heavy card board with one object on each page.

As you turn the pages, name the objects for Baby. She will "read" on her own, stroking and patting the pictures and sometimes even jabbering. ∎

Toilet Learning

Even though you may have heard success stories about your friends and their babies, it's too early to begin toilet training.

Toilet training is a learning process and some basic skills are necessary before you begin.

1. Muscle control. The sphincter muscles work to control the opening and closing of the bladder and bowel outlets. At the same time, the child must be able to squeeze with the larger abdominal muscles. To be toilet trained, children must be able to make these muscles work when they want them to. This generally takes about two years.

2. Communication. Children can't always maneuver their clothing or use the toilet unassisted. So, they need to be old enough to be able to tell you in some way that they want to go to the bathroom.

3. Desire. While a child may not necessarily want to be done with diapers, he does want to please his parents, or to be like his friends or older siblings who are trained. Whatever the reason, willingness on the child's part is essential.

As in many other areas of child development, the age to start training is highly individual. Around the latter part of the second year is a good time to start watching for signs that your child is achieving the skills required. ∎

Busy Hands and Prying Fingers

By now you have discovered just how many things Baby's hands can get into! For a while she used her hands as though she was wearing mittens without thumbs.

Then she discovered that thumbs could be useful and from about her eighth month on she began to use her thumb and fingers with greater and greater skill.

Our one-year-old no longer reaches for objects just for the satisfaction of grasping them. She tries to secure a hold which allows her to manipulate them or to use them in some way.

Her reach is quite accurate at close range; but, if she has to lean very far to reach something, her balance becomes unsteady and she grabs at the object any old way she can.

When she wants an object, she must rake it toward her. She can then pick it up between her thumb and forefinger with considerable accuracy.

Once the object is in her hand our one-year-old explores it thoroughly. She takes the top off a box and pulls everything out to find out what is inside.

She pokes, pries, turns, twists, bangs and pulls at everything she gets hold of, just to see what will happen.

Beginning about now her parents are going to become very conscious of that peculiar sort of silence which signals that something fascinating is being examined—and that fascinating something is usually a great big "no-no!"

By the end of her first year there are few containers Baby can't open, given enough time.

Although she is not yet able to twist off screw caps or tops, somehow in the process of pushing, pulling, and banging she manages to get them off anyway.

Because the one-year-old is now so handy with her hands, and because she can reach so much higher from a standing position, she manages to get herself into an amazing amount of trouble.

Small bottles or containers, pill bottles, lipsticks, tubes of toothpaste, hand lotion or a tube of anything, small packages and bottles of nail polish are all made-to-order for her busy little fingers.

You name it and the one-year-old will find it if it is within her reach. (Check again to make sure she can't reach bottles, jars or containers of any substance harmful to her.)

If it is any consolation to you, the reason your one-year-old is so busy exploring is because she is busy learning.

As she learns what various objects are used for she will begin to use them appropriately, but right now she just plays with them in all the ways she can think of. ■

Growing Child

P. O. Box 2505 • W Lafayette, IN 47996
(800) 927-7289
©Growing Child, Inc.
www.GrowingChild.com

Contributing Authors

Phil Bach, O.D., Ph.D.
Miriam Bender, Ph.D.
Joseph Braga, Ed.D.
Laurie Braga, Ph.D.
George Early, Ph.D.
Carol R. Gestwicki, M.S.
Liam Grimley, Ph.D.
Robert Hannemann, M.D., F.A.A.P.
Sylvia Kottler, M.S.
Bill Peterson, Ph.D.

Listening to Sounds

We had a letter recently from the mother of a 12-month-old. She told us that the TV is turned on in her home most of the time. Her baby seems to pay very little attention to what is going on while the "program" is in progress. However, when the commercial is on, her baby seems to pay very close attention. This is an important observation.

Why does this baby pay attention to the TV only when the commercials come on? For one thing, the commercial usually brings a definite change in sound. TV broadcasters say they do not increase the volume for commercials but commercials seem to have a greater intensity nonetheless.

Incidentally, having the television on all the time creates background sound which makes discriminating sounds difficult for new listeners. Playing music occasionally is good background.

This baby is noticing that something is different about the sounds he is hearing. It may be in volume, rhythm or pacing.

There are many interesting sounds for Baby to learn about. Each is different and has its own special quality; the swish of water, the hum of the refrigerator, the rattle of dishes, the buzz of conversation, and even the sounds which Baby makes with his own voice or movements.

It is very important that babies learn that there are differences in sound. Professionals call this type of learning auditory discrimination. This is the ability to tell one sound from another or to pick out one particular sound from many and it is a very important skill which starts at a very early age.

The baby we are talking about shows definite indications that already he is aware of differences in sounds. When the commercial comes on, the sound is different.

Since Baby pays attention to the difference in sounds, we might say that he is beginning to develop auditory discrimination. ■

Words of praise, indeed, are almost as necessary to warm a child into congenial life as acts of kindness and affection. Judicious praise is to a child what sun is to flowers.

William L. Howse

Security Blankets and Other Favorite Cuddlies

Sometime between one and three years of age, your child may develop a special attachment to a blanket, teddy bear, or other cuddly object.

About 60 percent of toddlers in Western societies develop such an attachment. The custom is not as common in non-Western cultures for various reasons related to different child-rearing practices.

Although many children begin to exhibit some signs of attachment as early as three months, attachment to a specific object, such as a teddy bear, becomes more noticeable by about 12 months, and peaks between 15 and 36 months.

By one year, a child's sense of self is beginning to develop. He is now old enough to go get or ask for an object that he wants. At this stage in his life, he is dealing with the transition from infancy to toddlerhood.

Because a child's favorite cuddly object can help to make this transition smoother, these "cuddlies" are sometimes referred to by psychologists as "transition objects."

During this transition period, children want to become more independent, yet they experience anxiety and insecurity related to their new-found autonomy.

By choosing his own specific cuddly object, a young child is able to express his unique individuality and autonomy.

At the same time, that cuddly object provides feelings of comfort and security when needed.

The bond between the child and his self-chosen object of attachment is unique. Don't be surprised, therefore, if your child doesn't show any attachment toward a stuffed animal that you want him to cherish.

By choosing his own cuddly object he can exercise more control during his emotional experiences.

Children will use a cuddly object in a variety of situations. It provides comfort when they are tired or frustrated. It helps to make a dark room less frightening.

It can also provide the security of companionship in new situations—much like an adult who says, "I won't go into that room by myself, but I will go if you come with me."

A young child may also bring a cuddly object when enjoying a pleasurable experience such as listening to a favorite story or nursery rhyme. But most of all, the

At 13 Months Baby Likes to:
- Investigate and discover.
- Turn pages of a book.
- Communicate.
- Walk holding your hand (or independently).

Give Your Baby:
- Push/pull toys.
- Soft drum.
- First set of blocks.
- Toys with removable parts that he can take apart and put together again.

cuddly object will be used and appreciated in times of stress and anxiety.

In general, children who possess a favorite object of attachment have been found to be well adjusted. The exception is the child who sits alone with his "blankey" in the corner of a room, using the object as a way to avoid social contact with other children.

Parents or other caregivers sometimes think that taking the blanket from the child will force him to interact with other children.

But such a child—rather than being merely over-attached to his blanket—is likely to be experiencing other problems as well, such as poorly developed social skills. So merely taking the blanket from him will not likely be a satisfactory solution.

continued on next page

13

79

continued from front page

Self-concept

Most child psychologists seem to agree that a blanket, teddy bear, or other cuddly object can serve many useful purposes for a young child.

Research studies indicate that children who use a favorite comforting object like to be cuddled themselves and show a preference for quiet activities.

These children also have strong emotional reactions in both pleasurable and stressful situations. Many of them are highly sensitive.

Some parents become concerned about what to do if a child's favorite attachment object is lost or damaged.

In the case of a favorite stuffed animal, one solution would be to have an identical backup—although you may find, to your surprise, that your child was attached to the smell of the old one!

In the case of a favorite blanket, some parents have cut the blanket in half in order to keep one part hidden for possible later use.

Another solution used by parents when a blanket is worn beyond repair is to sew a piece of the original blanket onto a new one in order to provide an element of continuity.

Even if you are sometimes embarrassed at the sight of your child clutching an old blanket, just rejoice that he has found a most effective and appropriate way to handle his life's problems and experiences. ■

There is no cause for alarm, however, if your child doesn't have a specific object to which he is attached. After all, about two out of every five children find other ways to deal with anxiety and stressful situations.

For those children who develop an attachment to a favorite cuddly object, it can help them both to express their own individuality and to deal with their emotional experiences. ■

Self-concept is the way we think about ourselves and the feelings we have about ourselves. These thoughts and feelings can be positive or negative. The person who has positive thoughts and feelings is said to have a healthy self-concept.

As adults, we can control and influence our feelings about ourselves. We can accept or reject others' opinions. We can monitor the events in our lives that cause us to feel one way or the other about ourselves.

A young child's self-concept, though, is determined mostly by the "messages" he receives from others, particularly his parents. These messages can be deliberate or unconscious, verbal or non-verbal.

Sometimes the message the child receives is not what parents really intend. For example, a parent may insist on doing everything for the child, even the most simple things that the child could do for himself.

The parent thinks he or she is sending the message: "I'm doing all these things for you because I love you." But the unconscious, non-verbal message the child may be getting is: "Always rely on parents to do everything for you because you're dumb and helpless."

Many of the suggestions made in *Growing Child* in previous months—playing, talking, games—have been aimed at developmental growth. But they also have been aimed at promoting positive self-concept, because self-concept is intertwined with achievement and competence.

To understand a child's self-concept, you have to try to see the world from his perspective.

A 13-month-old is occupied with developing competence—that is, learning to do things himself. It is this continued striving for competence that pushes him to try new challenges—such as learning to feed himself with a spoon. These challenges—and successes—lead him from one stage of development to the next.

The day your child grabs the spoon and tries to feed himself is a day to rejoice!

His best efforts to balance food on a spoon are certainly not the neatest or most efficient way to get the food to his mouth. But to the child, the feeling of accomplishment and self-worth are much more important than neatness and efficiency.

Whereas the parent might be upset by half-a-spoonful of pudding on the floor, the child will be proud that he managed to get the other half-spoonful into his mouth!

One of the most important factors in the development of self-concept is the parent's attitudes toward the child's successes and failures.

If the most important people in his life view him as "dumb" or "helpless," it will be almost impossible for him to develop positive feelings of self-worth.

Mockery and sarcasm are like the hot sun that causes a flower to wither. But praise is like the nurturing food that helps the self-concept develop and blossom.

So watch for the things a child can do for himself and encourage him to do them—even though he can't do them perfectly.

The more he learns to do for himself, the more positive his self-concept will be. ■

Baby's Feet

As you look at your child's feet you may wonder if she has flat feet because you cannot see a long arch.

When Baby begins to stand, her feet and ankles are barely ready for weight-bearing.

She looks quite flat-footed as she stands holding to the side rails of her crib or playpen, feet spread apart and often rolled inward at the ankles. But this flat-footed look is somewhat deceiving.

Baby's bones are still quite soft, and her foot and ankle muscles are not yet strong enough to support her arch as she stands.

However, she has some natural arch in the form of fat pads which support her arches when she stands. It is these fat pads which make her feet look as though they are flat.

As Baby walks more and more, the muscles which support her arch grow stronger.

Later she will learn to run and to jump, first flat-footed and then with the strong push-off and flexibility which only strong arches can provide.

In societies such as ours where shoes are worn, the fat pad under the arch gradually disappears when it is no longer needed, and the fully developed arch can be seen by about age five.

It is important to your child's motor development as well as to her future comfort that her feet have the best possible chance to grow straight, flexible and strong.

Keeping Baby's feet clean and dry also helps to prevent skin problems and infection.

Most babies start to walk at about 12 months of age. Those who start to walk a little earlier or a little later are still within normal limits.

At first, your child may appear to be knock-kneed or bowlegged as she takes her first steps. This is perfectly normal.

Her legs, which are in the process of developing and strengthening, may still be somewhat curved.

Besides, infants will walk with feet wide apart in order to improve their balance.

Once your child begins to walk, she will need her first pair of "real" shoes to protect her feet from injury.

Although many infants will appear to be flat-footed (due to undeveloped arches) or to have in-toeing ("pigeon toes") when they first start to walk, there is no need to purchase shoes with special arches, wedges, or reinforced heels, unless specifically recommended by the pediatrician.

For most children, the most important considerations when purchasing shoes are size and comfort.

Because children's feet change so rapidly, it is necessary to check the shoe size about once a month. As a rule of thumb, a new pair of shoes will be needed at least every two to three months.

It's better to purchase reasonably priced shoes, such as sneakers that can easily be replaced, than to buy more expensive shoes that become too tight.

Hand-me-down shoes from one child to another are not a good idea. Shoes that have previously been worn have conformed to the shape of that person's feet.

When selecting new shoes, make sure there is about half an inch to spare when you press down on the toe.

Less space than that will not allow room for growth, whereas more space would indicate that the shoe is too loose-fitting.

Children who are learning to walk need shoes that bend easily and have good traction. Avoid shoes that have rigid or slippery soles.

Baby's first walking shoes should have sturdy but flexible soles which are not slick on the bottom (so-called intermediate soles).

Uppers should be soft and preferably without a back seam. Moccasin-type toes without stiffening are best.

The shoes should be fitted so that they grip the heel firmly and there is plenty of room to wiggle the toes. Stores that specialize in children's shoes generally have staff who can provide expert advice and assistance.

At the end of the first day of wearing new shoes, it is wise to check your child's feet for any signs of soreness or irritation.

The fit of your child's socks is as important as the fit of her shoes. Properly fitted shoes are of no help if his socks are too short. Be careful with stretch socks. After you have pulled them over Baby's feet, pull them out at the toes to relieve any pressure.

Your baby should also have plenty of opportunity to walk about barefoot so that she experiences the feel of the floor against her feet and learns to grip it with her toes.

If floors are chilly, confine her barefoot experiences to her crib or playpen. In general, though, she will walk better at first in her shoes.

Later, sneakers may be substituted for bare feet during cold weather. These must be as carefully fitted as her other shoes. (Don't forget—if you wash sneakers, they tend to shrink.)

Once your child becomes used to her new shoes, she may try to move too fast. Don't be surprised if she falls when she tries to turn or stop.

It's important not to become unduly alarmed by these frequent falls. If parents are upset, then the child may become upset, which may inhibit her desire to walk.

If parents give the child a hug and reassurance in a matter-of-fact way, the child will learn how to deal with this aspect of growing up.

Before long she will master the skills needed to walk, trot, turn, stop, or squat to pick up something off the floor. An exciting new world of exploration is opening up for her. ∎

Problems for Little Minds

This month we're going to suggest some problem-solving activities that will stimulate Baby's thinking and reasoning processes in various ways.

Our problem-solving tasks have two aspects. First, there is something which Baby wants and will make an effort to reach.

Second, there is a barrier of some kind set up between Baby and his goal so that he cannot directly reach it. He must experiment by trial and error to find ways of removing or getting around the obstacle.

In doing so he discovers principles and ideas which expand his knowledge of how the world around him works.

The barrier can be anything that forces Baby to refine or use his ideas in a new way, or to put two separate ideas together.

A goal or reward motivates the greatest efforts and thus increases the number of experimental actions Baby tries. It also seems to make the lesson stick more vividly in his mind.

What kind of goal would be best? The answer is anything that keeps Baby's inter-

est long enough to let him try several ways of reaching it.

In the following activity it may be a favorite small toy or a tidbit of fruit or cheese.

In previous months we gave you two games that involved removing a cover to find an object and pulling on a string to bring an attached object within reach. Now we can combine the two tasks into a new problem.

Get a large square plastic container with a snap-on lid. (The lid must be loose-fitting enough for your child to pull it off.)

Punch a hole in the lid near one edge. Put a heavy string through this hole so that you can tie it around the rim of the lid.

If the string is too heavy to allow good closing, make two holes in the lid near the edge and tie a knot on the string which passes through both holes.

Place the container on its side with the open end facing Baby. Then, in Baby's full view, place his toy (reward) inside the container and snap on the cover.

There is now a barrier between Baby and his goal. But with his experience in using the string, he should hit upon the idea of pulling on the string to pop the lid. (Hold the container to prevent it from sliding off the tray or table.)

Eventually Baby will learn to hold the container with one hand while he pulls the lid off with the other.

The first time you might have to shake the string to bring it to his attention, or even show him how to use it to pull the lid off.

If he isn't interested in the container, put it away and try again on another day. ∎

Language Games

Here are a number of games that contribute to a child's growth of concepts which are vital to language acquisition.

1. Picture Books. Look at the book together while you name the objects in the pictures.

At this age Baby may not pay attention for more than two or three minutes, but it is still a useful game. Also, Baby will begin to turn pages herself.

2. Get the Clothespins. Drop a colored plastic clothespin into a wide-mouthed, shallow, clear plastic container. Tell Baby "Get the clothespin!" She may not solve

the problem on her own at this age, but she will imitate you.

If she doesn't respond to your instruction, show her what to do. Then get her to repeat what you did.

3. Where's the Block? Put a block beneath one of two different sized cans. Ask Baby to guess which can it is under by asking, "Where's the block?"

Change the position of the cans but always put the block under the same can.

Be sure to compliment her when she guesses the right can—she won't have many successes right away, but tell her

about her success: "The block is under the big can."

4. Rhythmic Action Games. With Baby either seated or standing on your lap take her hands in yours and, facing her, sing, "Row, Row, Row Your Boat."

Make your song vary in speed—slow, fast, faster, slower. At the same time move her arms in a back and forth rowing movement.

"Row, row, row your boat, (fast)
Gently down the stream. (slow
Merrily, merrily, merrily, merrily, (faster)
Life is but a dream." (slower) ∎

A Sense of Direction

After Baby is regularly pulling the string to open the lid, (see previous article) we can switch signals on him to create alternate conditions that stimulate learning.

Instead of having the lid face Baby, turn the container a quarter turn so that it faces to the side, the same side as the hand that Baby usually uses in pulling the string.

Now his old method won't work. If he pulls the string toward himself, the lid still stays firmly in place.

The solution to the problem is, of course, to pull the string to one side instead of toward himself. But the solution will not be obvious to Baby with his simple sense of direction.

One of two things is likely to happen: Baby may start by pulling in the usual direction, then begin making a random, left-to-right shaking motion of his fist when his first try is unsuccessful. The outward pulls may by chance open the lid.

In this case he will probably repeat this action on the next occasion, gradually learning that it is only one direction of pull that gets the lid off.

If Baby does not engage in this exploratory shaking or if it fails to pull off the lid, he may become frustrated.

The tipoff to Baby's frustration is crying or fussing combined with some movement that is repeated over and over again with no variation.

When this happens, no further learning can take place, and it is best to remove the frustrating container.

Depending on Baby's mood, you may want to wait a minute or two and then give him his toy without the container, or else simplify the task.

The best way to do this would be to turn the container at only a slight angle away from him so that smaller chance movements of his arm will cause the lid to come off. In later sessions you can gradually increase the angle as he learns to pull to one side.

After this new direction is learned, you can vary the task by turning the container upright so that Baby has to learn to pull in an upward direction.

Finally, you can turn the container toward the less-used side if he has a non-preferred arm.

Besides teaching Baby to move his arm in an unaccustomed direction, the solution to this problem has another important benefit. It matches the feeling of his arm as he pulls in an upward direction with the direction indicated by the lid.

Scientific evidence indicates that before directions in space can be understood in a useful way (such as moving the eyes from left to right in reading a line of print) there must be lots of actual experience in the basic directions of movements. The larger the body parts that are involved, the better.

If your child isn't interested in this problem, wait a week or two and try again.

All children develop at different rates and an activity that's exciting for one child right now may be totally boring for another.

Let your child be your guide. ∎

The Well-adjusted Child

At 13 months, Tim was nicely adjusted in life. He didn't mind the occasional hostility from his slightly older sister.

He responded nicely to suggestions from his mother and he was constantly curious about the world around him.

So how come he went haywire at the sight of two live kittens?

Of course, Tim didn't know much about right and wrong, good and bad, safe or dangerous.

So, as the occasion arose, over time, his mother made her point slowly and patiently and he usually went along.

But when two kittens were released into his play room, Tim got more excited than his mother had ever seen him.

He hopped up and down; he chased one kitten; he picked it by its head; he dropped it; he went after it again. All during this display, his mother tried to control him.

First she tried a positive response, suggesting, "We don't pick the kittens up, Tim. We just look at them."

When that didn't work, she responded in a negative manner. "Don't pick the kittens up, Tim, you'll hurt them. Don't touch, Tim, just look."

By actual count she tried 20 times to stop Tim from mauling the kittens. Finally, she had to pick him up while the kittens scooted for cover, and he hollered out in protest.

Now, would you say this was a time for discipline?

Tim's mother didn't punish, she tried distraction first (explaining how to handle the kittens) and when that didn't work, she removed him from the scene.

Thirteen months is really too young for punishment as such. In a month or so, Tim will begin to understand the meaning of right and wrong and probably will try it out both ways.

But at his present age, he simply got very excited and experienced what for him was a very exciting event.

Both kittens survived and at least the seed of an idea got planted in Tim's mind: Be gentle. ∎

Exercises in Learning

What kinds of things is Baby now doing on her own?

If you watch her carefully, you will notice she is likely to try to do something in a different manner the second, or at least the third time she tries to repeat an action.

For instance, when she discovers the fascination of dropping objects, she doesn't drop the same toy the same way each time. Instead she holds her arm in different positions. She also tries out all possible surfaces for dropping.

This is quite a change from her younger months when she used to do the same thing over and over, like banging an object or shaking her arms and legs to sway the bassinet.

What has happened is that she is no longer so fascinated with the effect she can produce when she simply makes the same thing happen over and over again.

Her interest has shifted to the world of causes and effects outside herself. She is willing and able to make variations in her actions to learn about the nature of the objects themselves.

Jean Piaget, the noted psychologist, divided a baby's learning experiences into two categories.

First, when she has learned a new idea through her experience, she tries it out with a number of variations.

She exercises the idea, so to speak. Baby's various ways of dropping an object is not just a one-time occurrence but a predictable happening.

Then, along comes a situation where an idea doesn't work. Let's say that Baby is exercising the idea that she can put objects into a box through a hole in the top.

All of a sudden an object refuses to go through the hole—push though she will.

Now comes a tiny crisis. Baby's idea, which had been so stable, suddenly be-

comes unsettled. She must either reconcile the idea with this new happening or give it up entirely.

Of course, Baby soon learns to modify her idea slightly: All objects will go through the hole except those that are "too big."

This process of adapting an idea to new circumstances is the second category of learning experiences and is really the more important of the two.

By this means, all of us have gained a more highly refined understanding of the world and its ways. ■

Growing Child

P. O. Box 2505 • W Lafayette, IN 47996
(800) 927-7289
©Growing Child, Inc.
www.GrowingChild.com

Contributing Authors

Phil Bach, O.D., Ph.D.
Miriam Bender, Ph.D.
Joseph Braga, Ed.D.
Laurie Braga, Ph.D.
George Early, Ph.D.
Carol R. Gestwicki, M.S.
Liam Grimley, Ph.D.
Robert Hannemann, M.D., F.A.A.P.
Sylvia Kottler, M.S.
Bill Peterson, Ph.D.

A Change in Sleep Pattern

Now that Baby is able to move around on her own, she is eager to explore. Everything new that she learns seems to motivate her to want to explore even more.

Not surprisingly, at about this age, some babies have difficulty going to sleep at night. They want to continue to explore rather than go to bed.

Even when they are comfortably lying in their crib, they may want to stay awake in order to replay some of the day's events in their minds.

If you look in on your baby after you have put her in her crib, you may sometimes find that she has pulled herself up to a standing position, while her eyes indicate she is already half asleep.

Even though your baby may not want to go to sleep, it's important that you stick with her regular bedtime routine (for example: getting undressed, bath, pajamas, story time, lights out).

If your baby continues to have problems going to sleep, there are some variations you can try without fundamentally changing her bedtime routine.

For example, before her bath, you might help her to relax by holding her in your lap while you read her a story.

Avoid anything that would cause her to become excited, such as game playing or loud laughter.

It's best to stay firm and not give in and let the baby stay up as this will create problems later.

After you have put your baby to bed, you may need to lengthen the story book time until she shows signs of nodding off. The extra time will be well worthwhile if it means that your baby goes to sleep sooner, in a more relaxed state, after a busy day. ■

Growing Child®

> There are only two lasting bequests we can give our children. One is roots, the other wings.
>
> Hodding Carter

Toddler Learns to Play

Friendliness, like courtesy, makes the give and take of life more enjoyable. And, like courtesy, friendliness is learned through experience as well as by example.

Now that your toddler is getting more steady on his feet, it is time to give him a good start in learning the art of being friendly.

At this age, Toddler is so busy exploring, so curious about people and things, that he has not yet become self-conscious about himself. This is the ideal time for him to encounter other children in a play situation.

Even though Toddler will not be ready to play with another child until he is about a year older, he is not too young to learn the fun of mutual exchange. His self-confidence will grow with each new acquaintance made.

Friendliness is basically a love of other people, an enjoyment of their company, and a spontaneous desire to please them. Your toddler has a head start toward friendliness, we are sure, because you have been delighted with him since he was born.

You have smiled at him, hugged him, talked to him. Now, between the ages of one and two, he will be ready to turn this warmth and love outward toward others.

Now is a good idea to take your toddler two or three times a week, if possible, to places where other children are present. Let him get acquainted with them in his own way and at his own rate. Don't push him, but quietly encourage him to respond to any overtures made by other children. Don't be over-protective either. Let Toddler learn some give and take: to hold onto a toy if another child snatches it. Let him find out that a little roughness and noise are not fatal. Often he doesn't mind so adults shouldn't insist on their ideas of fairness and justice.

This doesn't mean that you should let an older child bully your child. It does mean that Toddler should have the opportunity to learn to stand up for his rights.

These early play experiences will help your child learn how to play beside another child or in company with other children, to share and to exchange toys. You should not expect your child to share on his own at this age—he will need help. For the present, his communication with other children will be largely wordless. He will talk more to himself than to others.

This early play behavior is known as "parallel play" where two children will sit next to one another with each one engaging in his or her own activity.

Even though the children are not directly interacting with one another, you will notice that they are very much aware of one another's presence. For example, if one child moves to another part of the room, the second one will likely move to a place close by. Only after a long period of parallel play do young children begin to engage in cooperative play. This requires much more language facility than your toddler has now.

To provide him with the early play experience he needs, you may find it necessary to join or organize some type of cooperative play group with other parents of preschoolers. This may seem like quite a task—but this early experi-

At 14 Months Toddler Likes to:
- Eat finger foods.
- Participate in dressing and undressing.
- Hand objects to a parent.
- Stack blocks.

Give Toddler:
- A ball to roll back to you while she sits on the floor.
- Recordings of nursery rhymes and nonsense songs.
- Conversation about everyday things in her world.

ence with small groups of children is very important.

For those in childcare, the play experience is just as important. The presence of other children does not automatically ensure good play experiences. Parents can periodically monitor the kinds of interactions encouraged by their child's caregiver simply by observing the children at play.

The child whose first play experience with other children is delayed until he is three or four will most likely be frightened by the noise, movement and behavior of a group of children.

A child with very limited experience with other children near his own age will also likely have difficulty adjusting to kindergarten. Such children may be immature in their social responses. Some are over-stimulated by the large number of children. Others are so frightened that they withdraw into themselves.

If your child is to develop into a friendly, well-adjusted kindergartner, he needs early play experiences with other children. ∎

Programming for Independence

Toddler's beginning to walk was a milestone for all of you, in more ways than one.

Not only was it a triumphant motor achievement that allowed his hands to be free to manipulate and carry things, it was also a social achievement for him.

At last he could walk just like Mommy and Daddy, and he felt a little more a part of your big, important world.

It was also the beginning of a change in the way you look at him. To you, he became more like a real person, someone you could no longer think of as a "baby" in quite the same way.

He is not a helpless infant anymore. Almost without realizing it, your attitude has probably changed. His demands no longer get the quick, undivided attention you gave them before. You feel he must learn to respect the times you are busy and can't come to him immediately. This is as it should be, a tiny but important shift of responsibility onto his shoulders.

We want Toddler to mature with a sense of confidence and self-sufficiency. An important general principle to follow in helping him gain this confidence is to direct him toward independence.

Independence can be pursued by setting a reasonable goal and then using a series of steps to reach it. We will try to provide you with an accurate picture of what can be expected of Toddler, now and later.

The best approach to use in carrying out these various steps is an arrangement in which (1) Toddler does those steps already within his ability; then (2) you both cooperate in doing the steps within his ability that he needs to learn; followed by (3) your completion of the parts that are still too difficult.

This sequencing method has several advantages. First, by breaking the task down into steps, you come to appreciate that even a simple action is made up of a number of smaller motor movements, some of which are easy and some of which are hard.

By always doing what he can do, Toddler gets practice in the basic, previously-learned movements. This practice seems to be necessary before he can advance to more difficult movements.

Second, the cooperative or joint action approach gives a sense of importance to those skills that are a challenge to him at the moment. It puts you in the best position to judge when he is able to handle more of the task himself.

Third, as you interact with Toddler, you become more aware of the tasks which are too difficult for him because they are beyond his present level of development. These are the tasks which you can complete for him, talking with him as you perform each part of the action.

In developing independence and responsibility in a child, it is helpful to be aware of the two extremes to avoid: (1) being over-demanding and (2) being over-protective of your child.

Over-demanding parents are those who consistently have unrealistic expectations for their child. When parents are over-demanding a child is likely to become frustrated by repeated failure. This frustration may eventually cause the child to give up more easily. Over-demanding parents have a negative effect on self-concept. The child believes he has failed in his parents' eyes.

The child's apparent lack of effort may cause the parent to be more agitated. Which, in turn, may cause the child to be less motivated to attempt a new challenge.

On the other hand, parents who are over-protective tend to do things for Toddler which he is perfectly capable of doing for himself. In this way, the child is deprived of valuable learning experiences.

Over-protective parents generally find it difficult to "let go" of their "baby" as he strives to become more independent. They send the message to the child that he can't do it.

Parents are constantly challenged to reach a happy balance between the extremes of being over-demanding or over-protective.

What makes this challenge more difficult is that this balance must repeatedly change as Toddler develops new skills and abilities.

Here are some guidelines that will help to develop your child's independence and responsibility:

(1) If he can perform an action once or twice, he should be capable of doing it more often by himself.

(2) If there is something he can't do which you consider should be within his range of ability, try to simplify the task as much as possible so that he may experience success in doing even a part of it under your guidance.

(3) Watch for signs of frustration. He is not likely to learn anything positive when he is tired or when the task is clearly too difficult for him.

(4) Be attentive to what your child can and can't do, remembering that each child develops at his own unique rate.

Dressing and eating are "self-help" areas in which Toddler can progress through a number of steps toward greater independence. The next section, "Dressing As Partnership," provides an example of how to deal with that challenge in a practical manner. ■

Dressing As Partnership

Dressing and undressing are activities that involve a number of movement skills ranging from simply sticking an arm into a sleeve to the complicated acts of buttoning and shoelace tying.

Since the hardest parts are far beyond Toddler's present ability, some parents have a tendency to do the entire job themselves, even bending arms and legs into the desired position.

While this may be a quick and efficient way, it is apt to be less than pleasant for Toddler and does not let her take the first steps toward confidence and self-sufficiency.

The partnership method guides Toddler gently toward independence, while turning this activity into an exercise in communication and cooperation.

First, think of all the little things Toddler can do. In diapering you know that she usually holds still after you have positioned her on the diaper. This is at least a passive kind of cooperation, even though she is not yet ready to learn how to fasten a diaper.

What she can do is to raise and lower each foot alone while sitting and move her arms back and forth. She can also grasp pieces of clothing and then pull toward the upper half of her body.

So, she should be expected to put her own arm into the first sleeve of her shirt as you hold it open in front of the arm. As the shirt is brought around in back, the second sleeve comes into a more difficult position.

Here the cooperative approach comes in. Encourage her to pull her arm backward with gentle nudges and words like, "Reach back. Farther. That's good!"

When she has gotten her arm as far back as she can, put just enough pressure on her wrist to ease her hand the rest of the way into the opening.

As soon as her fist feels the opening she will thrust forward almost automatically,

and her arm will be through. Then you can take over the buttoning which is too difficult for her.

If the shirt is a pullover, have her put her hands into the armholes. Then you can fit the neck opening around her head. I

f the sleeves are long, hold each sleeve and have her "Push out!" until her hands are completely through.

At the times when she wears trousers, have her sit on a little chair (without your placing her, since she can do this by herself). Gather the trouser legs into "doughnuts" and lay them on the floor just ahead of her feet.

Her job is to "step into" the holes. When one foot is in, ease the "doughnut" around her toes and up around her ankle. Then she should put the other foot in.

Now find the tops of the trousers and have her take hold of one or both sides and "Pull up!" Her pull won't be very strong or effective. But your hands will be on either side of hers, providing most of the lift and guidance.

The important thing is that she is participating in the type and direction of movement that she will later have to do completely on her own.

A few months from now you can hold the gathered trouser legs slightly off the floor and have her point her toe and thrust her leg into them. All of these trouser movements will apply to underclothes, too.

Instead of putting her socks completely on for her, get them past her heel, then let her pull up the tops.

With shoes, after you have fitted in her toes, she should be able to push to get her heel in.

Many months from now you can teach her to hold the back of the shoe as she pushes so that the back part doesn't get rolled in.

In the process of undressing, several movements are reversed, like pulling down trousers and withdrawing arms.

Slide the sock most of the way off to leave a waving tassel. Toddler will love to pull on this and watch the sock suddenly pop off.

After Toddler learns this cooperative routine, the two of you will be able to do the job about as quickly and easily as you could by yourself.

When she has broad, flexible movement patterns, she is better able to go on to more complicated movements.

There will be times on Toddler's "down" days, that she is too fussy or fidgety to have much interest in cooperating. Then you can skip the cooperative items. But insist that she still do the things that she can do completely herself.

Undressing usually develops sooner and easier than dressing. If the parents take turns in dressing or undressing, it would be good for both of them to keep up with the developing stages so there won't be inconsistency.

It is an advantage for a child that both parents will do things slightly differently, (holding clothing at a little different angle and so forth), for Toddler will learn to be more flexible in how she performs the various movements. ∎

Tooth Saving

How excited you were when Baby cut her first tooth! By now she probably has most of her front teeth.

All parents hope their children will have strong straight teeth and an attractive smile. Unfortunately, hope is not enough.

If your child's permanent teeth are to have the best possible chance of being straight, her temporary or baby teeth must be preserved until her permanent teeth are ready to come in.

These first teeth help to shape the jaw and to preserve the size and shape of her mouth in preparation for the second or permanent teeth.

Decay can lead to pain, infection, early visits to the dentist for fillings, and even premature loss of these important space-saving first teeth.

If you have not already begun a regular program of careful dental care for your toddler, start now! At this age there are two important areas of care:

• **Your child's well-balanced diet helps build strong, healthy teeth.**

However, even good teeth can decay. Dentists agree that sweets are a major factor in tooth decay.

Tooth decay is the result of bacterial action in the mouth. This action uses sugar as the raw material to produce an acid which destroys tooth enamel.

In addition, a sticky, almost colorless film, called plaque, is constantly forming on teeth. Bacteria in this film cause not only tooth decay—but also gum disease.

Allowing your child frequent snacks during the day is a sure road to early tooth decay—unless you plan to brush her teeth after each snack! Begin now to limit your child's intake of sweets except at regular meal times.

• **Brush your child's teeth regularly.** If possible, brush immediately after each meal or snack to keep plaque to a minimum.

Bacterial action is strongest within the first 20 minutes after eating. Teeth should be brushed within this time to be most effective.

Your toddler is now at a very imitative age. Set a good example for her. Brush your teeth and hers regularly. Establish the habit of regular brushing.

By the time your child has all her teeth she will be old enough to brush them herself with only periodic supervision from you.

Choose a brush with a straight head, small enough to get at all teeth. Bristles should be soft and have rounded ends to prevent injury to soft tissue at the gum margin during brushing.

Keep the brush clean and in a place where it will dry quickly. Replace it as soon as it starts to show wear.

For the present, limiting sweet snacks and brushing regularly are enough. Plan to take her for her first visit to the dentist within six months after her first tooth appears, or no later than her first birthday.

At that time, ask your dentist about when flossing should begin. ■

Talking With Toddler

Child development does not proceed evenly and smoothly. Toddler has spurts and plateaus in her maturation.

When she is starting to walk, her energy is needed for movement. During this time speech may not increase in frequency or fluency. In fact, there may be less speech for a time.

Once walking is well underway, Toddler redirects her energies toward speech development. Meanwhile, she develops a gesture language to help convey her needs. She points, pulls you toward what she wants, screws up her face in different ways.

At fourteen months Toddler's sentences are single words. "Ball" is likely to mean "I want the ball," and "more" is used to indicate "I want more."

At this point a most valuable exchange between parent and child is what we call expansion. Toddler says, "car," meaning "I want to go in the car." The parent responds by repeating her word and developing Toddler's meaning into a full sentence. "Yes, we're going to ride in the car."

These suggestions for developing your child's language and speech may sound simple. But they are extremely impor-

tant. We urge you to do these activities regularly.

Expansions are made on the basis of various cues—what is going on in Toddler's life at that moment. You read the situation correctly, and as a result provide her with a proper sentence form for what she isn't yet able to express.

One study of grammatical development of children found that children of parents who more regularly engaged in this kind of expansion developed speech more rapidly and fully.

continued on next page

Toddler Games

We must not assume that just because Toddler only uses single words, her understanding is limited. Her comprehension exceeds her production of words. And this will generally be true for the rest of her life.

Does she understand all the words in a sentence? No. She depends upon a variety of cues.

If you say to her, "Would you like some juice?" she may go to the refrigerator where there's a container of juice. But she might have done the same thing if you had said "You don't like juice," or "Colorless red juice swings furiously."

"Juice" is the significant word. She knows "juice" and she associates it with the refrigerator. Each separate word is not attended to.

In fact, up to the age of ten a child rarely tries to understand each word—she simply incorporates what she hears into the general scheme of her perceptions at that time.

Other cues that Toddler uses for purposes of understanding are the rhythm and sound of your voice, your body posture, facial expression and hand gestures.

If we were in a foreign land, we would find ourselves relying upon these types of cues in order to understand what is said to us in an unfamiliar language.

In the same way, these cues help Toddler understand what we say. ∎

1. "How Will You Find It?"

Sit across the table from Toddler. Between the two of you place a sheet of clear acrylic plastic (it's softer and safer than plate glass) perpendicular to the table.

Behind the plastic place an attractive item such as a string of beads. Encourage him to find the object—"Come get the beads."

He will discover that he must reach around the plastic in order to succeed.

Be sure to hold the sheet securely because he may attempt to push it aside in his effort to retrieve the object.

Interpret his success to him by saying, "You found the beads. They were behind the plastic!"

As Toddler experiments with space and with objects in space, the experience is enhanced when he hears and learns the right words for each object.

2. "What's In the Sack?"

While Toddler is watching you, place an object such as a wooden block in a piece of tissue paper so that it resembles a loose, bag-like bundle.

Then tell Toddler to "get the block" (or whatever you selected). We want him to really seek out the object.

Let him know when he is successful by telling him "Johnny found the block!"

3. "Give and Take"

At last Toddler is ready for a pegboard toy. To make your own, start with a block of wood (or some similar material) into which you drill holes for four to six pegs, about two inches apart to allow room for Toddler's hands.

For safety, the pegs should be made from a dowel rod that is at least 1- 1/4" diameter.

We want Toddler to learn both to remove and replace the pegs. Since he's been about seven months old, he's been able to remove objects which protrude from containers. But now the challenge is purposeful.

Toddler won't learn the words for numbers and colors all at once, but every exposure to those words will add to his growing language ability.

Be patient if he can't replace all the pegs. Some children take two more months to learn the task.

Be sure to provide all the bonuses for learning the task by describing what he has accomplished: "You put the pegs in the holes," or "You took the pegs out of the holes."

4. "Can You Manage Another?"

One-inch wooden blocks, preferably colored ones, are the right size for Toddler's hands.

Offer him one block. As soon as he has taken it, offer him a second one. Present it in a way that will require him to reach and grasp it. If he takes the second cube, hold up a third one in front of him.

The natural tendency will be for him to put down one so he can grasp the new one. But the objective here is to get Toddler to work out a way to hold three cubes at one time.

He may hold a cube in each hand and hold the third against his body between the two closed fists. Or he may put one into his mouth.

Here is an excellent opportunity to start teaching number concepts and colors.

"Take one block."

"Here is a second block."

"Now you have three blocks."

Or you can label the blocks by color, "blue block, red block, yellow block."

Toddler may repeat the last word or two you say. He won't learn the words for numbers and colors all at once. But every exposure will add to Toddler's growing language ability. ∎

Something About "No, no!"

We have talked a lot in *Growing Child* about your child's need to explore his surroundings and to learn about objects in space through such exploration. We have also advised "child-proofing" large areas of your home so that he can explore safely.

By now you have learned from experience that, as he pulled to a stand beside furniture, his explorations expanded enormously.

To him a hanging table cloth looked just as solid as a table leg—and he pulled on it, sometimes with disastrous results.

Since he has been able to stand, your child's busy fingers reach much further than you expect. You have learned to remove fragile or dangerous objects from his reach.

However, "child-proofing" removes only obvious dangers. At best it can be only a temporary protective measure until your young explorer has developed enough language to understand your spoken warnings.

As Baby grows into Toddler, you will find it necessary to set certain limits on his explorations.

These limits are not meant to restrict his opportunities for learning but to teach him even more about his ever-enlarging world.

This larger world holds dangers from which you cannot protect him directly but which he must be taught to avoid.

It is also a world full of other people—his parents, other adults, other children—all of whom have rights as important as his own.

The first step toward teaching Toddler to control his own activities and to respect the rights and possessions of others is the use of a firm, but loving, "No, no!"

This phrase was usually an automatic response to the younger baby who grabbed at your glasses or wanted to poke a curious finger in your eye.

Now you can begin using "No, no!" as a teaching tool.

Toddler should be taught that "No, no!" means "Stop what you are doing—now!"

"No, no!" provides a way of controlling his activity when he is out of your immediate reach. His response will give you time to get to him when he is headed for trouble.

If "No, no!" is to be effective and useful, however, you must be selective in your use of it. Set reasonable limits to Toddler's activity. Restrict the use of "No, no!" Carry through to see that your child does indeed stop.

Growing Child®

P. O. Box 2505 • W Lafayette, IN 47996
(800) 927-7289
©Growing Child, Inc.
www.GrowingChild.com

Contributing Authors

Phil Bach, O.D., Ph.D.
Miriam Bender, Ph.D.
Joseph Braga, Ed.D.
Laurie Braga, Ph.D.
George Early, Ph.D.
Carol R. Gestwicki, M.S.
Liam Grimley, Ph.D.
Robert Hannemann, M.D., F.A.A.P.
Sylvia Kottler, M.S.
Bill Peterson, Ph.D.

The over-anxious parent who says "No, no!" to everything only confuses the child. You also need to restrict the number of adult "no, no's" so it doesn't become a meaningless game.

Don't expect miracles. It is not enough just to teach your toddler that "No, no!" means "Stop!" That is important for his safety and is necessary for that reason. But it is only a negative approach.

If you stop him from doing one thing, you should provide him with an acceptable substitute activity. After the "No, no!" let Toddler know what is acceptable.

Very young children have so very much to learn in such a short time. They must learn the names of objects, what they do, how they are used.

They must learn what objects may be touched safely and which ones can be handled, thrown, pulled, pushed, squeezed, sat on and jumped on.

As parents, you can help your child learn by naming objects, by using them properly and by talking about what you are doing.

But, if you want him to live happily and safely in his rapidly enlarging world of things and people, you must start now to help him learn to control his actions.

Begin by using "No, no!" wisely, firmly, and consistently. ∎

The most precious thing a parent can give
a child is a lifetime of happy memories.

Frank Tyger

The Mythical "Perfect" Parent

Have you ever felt that you were an "imperfect" parent—that your efforts to provide Toddler with good learning experiences were sometimes less than successful? And does this seem to happen most often on a day when you are in the mood to interact with Toddler—but Toddler somehow has other plans for herself that day?

On such a day, for example, you line up all those good educational materials. Toddler doesn't appear to pay any attention while you carefully demonstrate how to put one little block on top of another. You call Toddler and try in various other ways to get her attention. But to no avail.

You start to think of all the other things you could be doing very profitably with your time today. You finally have the last block in place on your tower.

Wham! With one sweep of her arm Toddler sends the blocks flying. You begin to feel you have failed in Lesson One.

Fortunately, you remember some "good psychology" about the importance of controlling your temper. So you calmly put away the blocks.

You try another "good learning experience"—like teaching Toddler the concept of "object-permanence." You carefully hide an object under a plastic cup—just like it says in "the book."

According to "the book," Toddler will lift up the cup and give a cry of joy upon discovering the object under the cup.

Instead, to your horror, Toddler picks up the cup and throws it straight at you. You abandon Lesson Two, feeling frustrated

and angry. But you wonder how a "perfect" parent would handle this situation. Your feelings of being an "imperfect" parent make you feel even more angry.

Just at that moment, Toddler grasps a corner of the tablecloth and starts to pull. As you see the plates moving, you forget all the good "parenting skills" you ever learned.

You scream: "Stop that!" To your amazement, Toddler stops! Lesson Three was a success. You think that somehow you must have done what a "perfect" parent would do!

Actually Lessons One and Two may not have been the failure you thought they were. Even though Toddler didn't learn what you intended to teach, she may have been learning something else. In Lesson One, you probably wanted to teach "fine motor skills." But Toddler's mind may have been more interested in the laws of gravity, or reinventing Newton's laws of motion!

In Lesson Two, Toddler may not have learned about "object-permanence," but she probably learned an important lesson from your patience and self-control.

In Lesson Three—unplanned—perhaps learning occurred for both Toddler and Parent. Toddler learned that there are limits to a parent's patience and to the amount of her own unsocial behavior that will be tolerated. Parent learned the need for quick parental judgment on occasion and the power of parental authority.

Parents should not be afraid to use their

At 15 Months Toddler Likes to:
- Walk alone.
- Fill and empty buckets, containers and cups.
- Imitate your actions.

Give Toddler:
- A small broom.
- Pots and pans.
- Play dishes, dolls, toy telephone.

Ask Your Doctor About:
- MMR vaccine (measles, mumps, rubella).
- H. Influenzae type b (Hib) vaccine.

own judgment when dealing with their child. While it is important for parents to acquire knowledge about child development, they should not be paralyzed into fear of asserting limits or taking appropriate action, lest they be violating some unknown psychological theory.

The message should be clear by now: There is no such thing as a "perfect" parent. Even psychiatrists and psychologists who work with children on a daily basis experience failures. When they find that one method fails, they try another one. Eventually, by using good judgment, they find one that works.

You too can rely on your own good judgment in deciding how to handle a difficult situation. In general, parents who use good judgment in other aspects of their lives can have confidence in that judgment when deciding what is best for their child.

When you experience some failures in your efforts to provide Toddler with good learning experiences, you can at least feel proud that you are a full-fledged member of the human race! ■

Experience and Meaning

For several months we were content to let Toddler explore the world on his own and this was as it should be. The ordinary home has plenty of shapes, sights and sounds to stimulate his curiosity.

So we have relied on Toddler's gift of curiosity to gain exposure to a variety of experiences with objects found in a home that he can see, hear, taste, smell or feel. Curiosity and varied experience work upon each other, each acting to increase the other.

Many studies performed on both animals and humans have shown that exposure in the early years to surroundings that are dull and monotonous can permanently reduce curiosity.

This results in a vicious circle of intellectual poverty where lowered curiosity resulting from inadequate stimulation leads to still less curiosity, and so on.

Toddler's lively explorations right now are a tribute to the fact that all along, this curiosity has had plenty of things on which to feed and develop.

Toddler's curiosity will continue to gobble up anything new. But you may ask, "Isn't it possible that too much variety will flood his brain with so much information that he can't make any sense out of it?"

That's not likely as long as he controls his own rate of movement and as long as parts of his world like his own home, room, and crib remain relatively unchanged.

With his physical and emotional home base steady and secure, he can sally forth confidently on ever wider trips, like walking with you in the neighborhood or riding in the car to new places.

While he may still be distrustful of strangers, you will notice that he observes them with long gazes as long as they keep their distance.

Every bit of newness has many tiny pieces of information, such as size, smell, and taste, so insignificant that we have forgotten they were there. But Toddler's brain has a remarkable ability to collect and store this information.

The many different experiences are not only retained but help stimulate further curiosity. Toddler's memory is like a sponge which soaks up things. He may not yet really understand what they are.

Only a small part of his experience has any meaning to him right now in the sense of knowing what something is for or why it differs from something else.

He has learned one kind of difference between objects through what is called "motor meaning." For example, the kind of physical action that Toddler can use on an object depends upon the nature of that object. Something that is small can be picked up, held or brushed aside. Most big things can't be picked up, and Toddler must walk or crawl around them instead of pushing them out of the way.

This motor intelligence lays the foundation for later concept formation. Toddlers' physical understanding of the properties of objects, gained through their ceaseless hands-on exploration, is assimilated into the brain as the best preparation for later learning and classification regarding shape, size, etc.

The dimension of "bigness" and "smallness" has very real, practical meaning for him—"motor meaning"—since it relates to his need to move easily and safely around in his world.

It is not surprising, then, that "big" and "little" will be two of the earliest descriptive words to appear in his vocabulary. Your role is to supply the language to describe the discoveries he is making in his physical explorations. ("Yes, that box is **big!**")

By contrast, while Toddler has experienced round and square objects, the distinction between them has little practical significance for him right now, except perhaps that square corners are sharp and hurt when he bumps into them while round ones do not.

A true appreciation for the difference must await some problem-solving task, like trying to fit a square peg into a round hole.

Color recognition is still further removed from the kinds of motor experiences that might give it meaning. While colors lend richness and variety to a child's surroundings, most early experiences are not color-coded. An object can usually come in any of several colors. So color is less significant right now.

While objects may vary in shape, color, size, and weight, only a few of these qualities have practical significance to the average toddler as he goes about his daily activities. There is likely to be a natural gap between a toddler's ability to perceive the difference between two things and later learning that that difference is important.

Research studies on preschoolers from poor homes have indicated that when these children were taught to experience, think about and identify differences between objects—such as color, size, and shape—they were more likely to do well in school at a later age. Their intelligence scores also improved.

It is likely that all children will benefit from learning about such differences in shape, length, weight and other similar concepts. This learning will take place more easily if the experiences are related to Toddler's own interests.

Keep the learning activities simple. And try to introduce only one new concept or dimension at a time.

Toddler will first experience the concept, by playing with his ball, for example. Then you will supply the language (A ball is "round.") Later he will understand the practical significance of this concept.

In future issues of *Growing Child,* we will continue to identify good learning experiences that help teach these concepts. This is the kind of problem-solving we discussed in Month 13 with the pull-string plastic container. ■

Individual Differences

As we've said before, not all children develop at at the same rate. Nor does any one child develop evenly in all areas. Any single child may vary a great deal at different periods in his rate of development.

For example, he may have gained control of his head at about average age, progressed rapidly to sitting balance, then spent a little longer-than-average time in progressing to creeping. Slight variations in the rate of development are perfectly normal.

However, during infancy and childhood, all children should go through the same stages of development and in the same order.

First, for example, the baby achieves head balance and control, then sitting balance, then creeping, standing balance, and finally walking.

You will remember from what we have told you previously that it is most unlikely that there will ever be a child who is truly "typical" in every aspect of development.

Usually a child may be somewhat ahead in some areas of development and somewhat behind in others. We use the word "typical" to describe the characteristics children normally exhibit at a particular stage of development.

The concept of the "typical" child is also a useful one in helping to identify the child who may be "slow."

Periodically we include in *Growing Child* age-appropriate checklists so that you can monitor your child's development.

When we speak of the "slow" child, we refer to those children whose slowness in relation to the average is very marked. An example may help to clarify what we mean and also illustrate the importance of knowing when a child is "slow."

If we consider, for example, a fifteen-month-old child who is unable to stand alone for 10 seconds or more, we would judge that child's development to be "slow."

We can say this because we know that, by eleven months of age, 50 percent of all children can do this. By thirteen months, about 75 percent, and, by fourteen months, about 90 percent of all children have attained this developmental milestone.

It is important to have this knowledge because once any developmental delay is recognized, something very often can be done about it.

In the example described above, the delay may simply be the result of consistently not providing opportunities for the child to practice standing alone.

In this instance, "treatment" might be simple: providing the child with appropriate developmental experiences such as the ones we have recommended in *Growing Child.*

However, there are many different reasons why a child may be delayed or slow in his development.

• The delay may be due to hereditary causes where the child has inherited some specific characteristics from the parents.

• A small percentage of children are seriously delayed in their motor development because of muscle or nervous system problems.

• Some children may be delayed in their development because of complications that may have arisen during the birth process.

For these types of problems, an examination by a neurologist may be needed in order to diagnose accurately the cause of the developmental delay.

But other children may be delayed simply because of a lack of opportunity if they grow up in a disadvantaged environment.

Whatever the reason for the delay, it is important to identify any such problem early, so that treatment may be initiated as soon as possible. Generally speaking, the earlier such problems are identified, the simpler and more effective the treatment will be.

That is why the concept of the "typical" baby is a useful one—it gives both professionals and parents a measure of whether the delay in the child's development is serious or not.

In this way, when parents suspect that a child's delay in development may be serious, they can consult a pediatrician or other appropriate professional and obtain whatever assistance may be needed. ∎

Listening To Differences

Listening curiosity is very strong now. Toddler is like a detective stopping to hear the pitter-patter sound of rain. He likes to distinguish peoples' voices from the background of radio, traffic or household noise.

In one research study it was found that toddlers at this age prefer and pay more attention to meaningful speech than to meaningless sounds.

Auditory discrimination is occurring also. For example, Toddler discovers how to distinguish the sound "b" from "p."

The sounds are made in exactly the same place, the lips meeting and then separating explosively. The only difference is that "p" is voiceless and "b" is voiced, a really subtle distinction.

Parents help support discrimination in sound with traditional nursery rhymes and rhythms, as well as repetitive books, like the Little Brown Bear series.

Toddler also discriminates between sounds which are made in the front of the mouth and sounds which are made in the back— "t" from "k"—and she differentiates lip sounds from tongue sounds—"b" from "d."

How does she make such marvelous discriminations? She links together the sensory information received from listening with her ears to the tactile information received from the feelings in her lips, tongue, mouth, and throat as they move to produce the sounds. Educators call this perceptual-motor learning. ■

Body Awareness

How do toddlers learn the names of their body parts? Parents name them—"eyes," "nose," "finger," "toes." They also learn body awareness when parents touch them while playing body games like "This little piggy went to market."

But when a toddler fingers his or her genitals, there's not much chance parents will joyfully explain, "There's your penis," or "That's your vulva." Nor do parents usually identify the genitals when they label the body parts. Very often they just say nothing.

If Toddler happens to touch the genital area, parents will probably remove the child's hand or distract the child with a toy.

Yet we know that infants are sensitive to sexual stimulation, indicating pleasure and relaxation when they are touched during diapering and bathing.

Even newborn boys have erections of the penis. Both boys and girls during infancy stimulate their genitals when they explore their bodies.

In the area of sexual awareness, it is the parents' responsibility to decide what behaviors are appropriate or inappropriate for their child. The parents' decision will be guided by their moral standards and upbringing, what is socially acceptable in their society, and their religious beliefs.

In deciding what to do about their child's behavior, parents should know that:

1. Interest in the genital area is a part of the child's natural curiosity and exploration of the world—including his or her own body.

2. Negative attention from parents ("Don't do that !") when Toddler touches genitals will only serve to stimulate Toddler's curiosity.

3. The most effective way to change Toddler's behavior is to acknowledge calmly what Toddler has discovered ("Yes, that's your penis") and then refocus attention on something else ("Look at this book I have over here") rather than correction.

Parent educators have long felt that it is wise to identify body parts and their functions and allow very young children to gain appropriate knowledge about their bodies.

Their attitude has been that it helps the child develop a clear body image and helps build a positive self-concept. ■

Don't Push Your Child

We'll say it again: Don't push your child. Even if she is ahead of schedule, be sure she has basic experiences which are typical for her age. Many children will be "ahead" in some areas of development, but "behind" in others. Sometimes a parent will push to advance the "ahead" areas, and neglect those that are "behind."

We are trying to identify the experiences a typical toddler is having which are getting her ready for learning in school. If she has the right experiences now, she will more likely do well in school later. In addition, she is preparing for success in overall development as a well-balanced child, a social being, with emotional control and a healthy self-concept.

We identify experiences in many different areas of development. To concentrate on only one, such as intellectual development, while neglecting others, such as social development, would not be helpful for your toddler's later overall adjustment to school life. Even at this early age she needs to do, see, hear and feel things. The more of these experiences she has now, the better prepared she will be for school — and life. ■

Special People — Like Grandparents, Relatives and Friends

Your growing child needs people. A large part of her development involves being part of a world full of people. She needs to see people, listen to people and feel people as a natural part of the world around her.

At this time, the most important people in her world are her parents.

Research studies have found that a very young child needs regular contact with her parents, and especially her mother. If a very young child is separated from her mother for several months, her development tends to suffer.

She does not explore her world as she should. She is not interested in finding objects behind barriers. She is not as curious as she needs to be for her best development.

One important result of such a lag in interest is that her ability to learn falls off. She does not develop some of the basic learning skills as well as other children who have ongoing contact with their mothers.

In addition to her parents, there are other special people who are very important: grandparents, relatives, neighbors, friends and caregivers.

Along with her parents, these special people provide one of the finest components of a young child's life. She learns from them that she belongs and that she matters.

The feeling that she is an important person, the feeling that someone cares about what happens to her—these are the feelings which give a child a strong self-image and a solid base for emotional development.

Parents and other special people provide an atmosphere in which the young child learns she is important. They notice the child, talk to her, laugh with her when she is happy and show their concern when she falls and hurts herself.

They say "hello" to her in a special way because she "belongs" to them and they "belong" to her.

In all these interactions they send a message to the child: "You are important. You matter. We care. You belong." Long before she can understand specific words, the child gets this message.

If these special people send out good messages to the child, then the child needs to be "in touch" with them. But it is a fact of modern life that grandparents, aunts and uncles seldom now live in the same community.

In today's world, families get separated. Most often children live in one community while many of their special people may be scattered from coast to coast. When this happens, the child doesn't get all the messages she needs because these special people simply are not part of her daily life.

Some years ago a psychiatrist studied two different towns in the same county in New Jersey. In one town, people usually were born in that town, grew up there and continued to live there as adults. In a town like this, a child's special people usually lived in the same place as the child.

The second town was quite different from the first. Practically no one there was

born or grew up in the town. There was a twenty percent turnover in population each year with new people moving in and other people moving out. Hardly any child had special people living there; they all lived somewhere else.

In general, according to the psychiatrist, people in the first town were much more relaxed than people in the second town.

His opinion was that children and young people in the first town had a solid feeling of belonging, and that this feeling made them better adjusted. He specifically pointed out the importance of being in contact with grandparents, aunts and uncles. He felt that contact with these special people gave children a solid sense of "I belong. I matter."

If you live in a town like the second one, you may well protest, "But what can I do? There are no special family people here."

One simple solution is to try for regular visits to your child's special people so that your child has a number of contacts with them. Such visits are extremely important and well worth the time and effort they require.

Telephone calls, notes and cards can help youngsters feel a connection to distant special people.

Another practical solution is to find substitute "special people" among your own circle of friends.

If you have several couples who are very special friends, you might ask some of them to play the role of aunts and uncles. Each time they are in your house, they would be especially aware of ways they could pay special attention to your child.

You might also have a relationship with one or two older couples who could serve as substitute grandparents—and you may be pleasantly surprised at how delighted such older people would be to play the role. ■

"Whazzat?"

The production of single words is increasing and Toddler uses them for commands, requests, names and actions.

One-word sentences will continue until about 18 months when Toddler will start to combine words.

Some early speakers may already be using word combinations such as "all-gone" or "whazzat?"

Toddler is feeling a great surge of satisfaction because of his word power. By saying "drink," he can get someone to produce water, or by saying "out" he can get the world transformed from indoors to outdoors.

While learning to talk is a natural developmental process, stimulation from one's environment is essential to this development. After all, children born in China learn to speak Chinese. In this country children learn American English.

Studies show that family experiences have an important influence on the process of learning to talk.

For example, in one study children between 10-30 months were read to by their parents.

At the end of the experimental period, these "stimulated" children were able to speak with greater fluency than those who did not have the same experiences.

Furthermore, the early stages of learning to talk are deeply emotional as well as intellectual.

One child development expert has stated that words may be produced earlier if they are first made to sound good in the "context of affectionate care and attention."

Many studies offer convincing evidence that the toddler's relationship with people has a definite effect on his own language behavior. ■

Behavior

Angry outbursts are frequent during the second year. This is because Toddler is eager to make choices and exercise her independence. But she has neither the experience nor the skills to control her behavior. So these outbursts result.

One of the best ways to help Toddler over this difficult period is to reduce tensions by meeting her needs while still maintaining reasonable but firm control.

Another factor that may trigger anger and frustration is the child's limited language to express wants and needs.

Expressions of fear may also appear during the second year. The kinds of fear are broad—fear of the dark, fear of new and different experiences, coping with a stranger without the presence of a familiar person.

Toddler may not be able to convey her fears verbally but adult reassurance, in terms of affection, will certainly pay off.

At the same time, parents should try not to be over-protective of their child since these fears are a normal part of growing up and Toddler must learn to cope with them. ■

Growing Child®

P. O. Box 2505 • W Lafayette, IN 47996
(800) 927-7289
©Growing Child, Inc.
www.GrowingChild.com

Contributing Authors

Phil Bach, O.D., Ph.D.
Miriam Bender, Ph.D.
Joseph Braga, Ed.D.
Laurie Braga, Ph.D.
George Early, Ph.D.
Carol R. Gestwicki, M.S.
Liam Grimley, Ph.D.
Robert Hannemann, M.D., F.A.A.P.
Sylvia Kottler, M.S.
Bill Peterson, Ph.D.

Michael and the Key

Do you know what can happen when you are 15 months old? What can happen is that you discover you are a person! A person who lives in your body, and then you can set out to fool around with that idea.

At 15 months, Michael certainly knew he was a person. He had learned how to bug Momma, if he wanted to, or how to make her smile and hug him. Despite his tender age, he knew he could be naughty or nice.

Michael was also extremely curious. He wanted to know how things worked. What might happen? Who might get mad?

So, when he and his mother were about to take off for the apartment house basement where she would do the wash, Michael was pleased when his mother let him hold the key to the apartment.

As they waited for the elevator to come down from above, Michael noticed something: there was a space between the hall floor and the elevator door, not a very big space, but wide enough that he could see it.

So he wondered, would a key fit through there. How long would it fall? Would he be able to hear it clink. How loud would Momma scream?

So, Michael did what he had to do. He dropped the key down the crack.

The experiment was a smashing success! Momma did scream! The superintendent had to be called! The elevator had to be shut off! There was a long search in the elevator bed, and Michael's name was mentioned many times. In loud voices, and soft ones.

Well, was Michael being a devil? Or was he simply responding to a powerful motive to his short life? Was it his curiosity to find out, to test?

Let's give him the benefit of the doubt. An active mind provides an opportunity for bold action. This is how children teach themselves. ■

A hundred years from now, it will not matter what my bank account was, what sort of house I lived in, or the kind of car I drove. But the world may be different because I was important in the life of a child.

Author Unknown

Learning New Words

The ability to understand what is heard (receptive language) is still growing faster than speech (expressive language). At 16 months, Toddler is using mostly single words, maybe as few as six to eight.

The bulk of these words are nouns, but she can use adjectives like "hot," verbs like "want" and "go" or even questions, such as "whadda?"

These words represent thoughts and serve as actual sentences. "Car" may mean, "We're going for a ride, and I can't wait to look out the window to see the world!"

The first two-word sentences are pieced together with the words said together but not really connected, as "Boy. Run."

You will observe that Toddler talks at least as much to herself as to other people. She may appear astonished when someone responds to this self-talk.

We have been saying for many months that receptive language is learned mainly in the home—in a context of feelings and actions which coincide with objects, people, and their gestures.

When Dad says "Come here," he holds out his arms to receive Toddler. When Mother says "Give it to me," she reaches out to accept the object.

When Mother holds the cup to Toddler's lips, she says, "Drink your milk."

In other words, Toddler's receptive language is the product of simple associations which have been going on since she was about six months old.

Imitation plays a big role in the life of the toddler. She uses it for learning new words. The parent says, "See the monkey," and Toddler echoes the word "monkey." Or Toddler points to an

At 16 Months Toddler Likes to:
- Play roughhouse.
- Carry things while walking.
- Imitate your actions and words.

Give Toddler:
- Stuffed animals, dolls, pots and pans.
- Small broom.
- Playdough.
- Toy telephone.

object and her parent supplies its name. There is a snowballing effect in learning language—the more a child is able to speak, the more she learns to speak.

Once Toddler discovers this power of speech, she has a new style of behaving and dealing with her world.

She demonstrates this mastery by manipulating the adults in her life. And they generally love it! ∎

Kitchen Play

Do you worry what Toddler is doing while you are busy in the kitchen?

Do you feel that you must keep him in a playpen to keep him out of trouble while you are putting away groceries or cleaning up the dishes?

How about arranging things for safe play in the kitchen instead?

By now you should have accomplished the child-proofing of your house. Be sure that all potentially harmful substances—cleaning compounds, detergents, metal and furniture polish, anything your child might swallow—are out of his reach. Knives and other sharp objects should

also be unreachable. Handles of pots on the stove should be turned in.

Now just look around your kitchen and you will find any number of safe things for play and learning. A cardboard carton turned on its side makes a house or a cave; on its bottom it can be a car or a boat or just a comfy place to crawl into and count one's treasures.

Pots, pans and spoons make wonderful "music." Give him shelf or cupboard space of his own. A collection of lightweight packages or cans will make Toddler's very own pantry shelf. A round cereal box or empty coffee can rolls

almost like a ball. Empty cans with tops and bottoms smoothly removed and paper towel or bathroom tissue rolls are fun to look through. Small ones fit into larger ones.

A salad basket or a small plastic pail will serve to carry objects from here to there. Measuring cups and spoons fit together and come apart endlessly and in many combinations. Small cardboard boxes make good hiding places for small toys and fit inside larger boxes.

And so it goes—all sorts of simple, everyday objects make for safe and exciting play in the kitchen while you work. ∎

Grown-up Gadgets

Grown-ups do all sorts of interesting things with the gadgets in the house such as doorbells, alarm clocks, light switches and water faucets.

Toddler doesn't know enough to use these household gadgets, so she just takes household happenings in stride.

But occasional experience with the everyday knobs and switches that make things happen can stimulate her curiosity and imagination.

Just be careful not to introduce her to any potentially dangerous experience—such as lighting a fire—because she may try to repeat that experience later on her own.

Here are some things that will interest Toddler as she rides on your shoulders or otherwise gains access to places beyond her usual reach.

Stand on the front porch with the door open. At your push of the button, the doorbell will make a very audible sound.

Show Toddler how you make the magical "visitors coming" sound. Then see if she can imitate you and press the button, too.

Her push is likely to be weak so you may have to encourage her to "push harder." Be aware that once she makes the sound, she probably won't want to stop.

The push of a button can also stop a sound, as you can demonstrate with an alarm clock. If she has trouble pushing with just her fingers, you can turn the clock so that she can push the button with the palm of her hand.

Toddler can also test the effect of turning the light switch both on and off. This effect is not only reversible but is quite dramatic to her.

When you take her to the bedroom you might sometimes lift her up to turn on the light for you, especially if she has been cooperative that day.

Tell her, "Lights on" or "Lights off" so that she can integrate the words and the physical action with her perception of what she's doing.

When a package arrives at your home, an intriguing change of appearance will result if Toddler pulls on the free end of a loosely tied bow. The same effect, though less dramatic, will result if she pulls out the bows of her own shoelaces.

The bathroom has a few mysteries, too. The toilet makes quite a "sound and fury" as it flushes.

Toddler may not have the strength to do the flushing by herself. But she can watch with fascination as she sees you flush the toilet.

She should be able to turn on the water faucets in the sink, if the handles can be pulled rather than twisted.

Caution: Check the temperature of your hot water—which should not be above 120 degrees—so that she won't be scalded if she turns on the water.

At tooth brushing time, she has seen you squeeze the toothpaste out of the tube. She should be strong enough now to

produce some toothpaste if you let her try squeezing. (She will use mainly the last three fingers against the heel of her hand). Just stay nearby to make sure she isn't strong enough to squeeze out too much of it!

Dispensing shaving cream from the aerosol can is a job best left to Daddy. The sight of all that white stuff coming out of such a little can should give her cause for pause.

Can she recognize Daddy with all the shaving cream on his face?

There are other possible grown-up activities to show Toddler. Remember, you can expect her in many cases to imitate you later on her own.

For example, the first time she sees you hammering a nail, she is likely to adopt a similar activity in her self-play, an action so much more purposeful than her banging action when she was six months old.

You can provide Toddler with one of these new adventures, such as participating in grown-up jobs, as a special reward for being cheerful and cooperative on a particular day.

You can also make your own simple gadget board with a thin piece of plywood and purchased or recycled gadgets from the hardware store. These are far more satisfying than traditional "busy box" toys as they are the real thing.

As always, consider the safety aspects of all items you add to the gadget board—can any of them be dangerous if misused? Usually the simpler the item, the safer it is.

One final thought. It is best to introduce these new experiences sparingly, perhaps only one a day. If you hold your bag of tricks in reserve, you will avoid crowding her with more than she can comfortably absorb.

Pop a single one on her when she is in a curious mood and is interested in things that you are doing. ■

Some More Sleight of Hand

Around nine or ten months, Baby began to look for objects that you placed under covers.

This was an important milestone in the development of her thinking because it showed that she was beginning to form pictures in her mind.

At first she pictured the hidden object only in connection with the cover under which it had disappeared. She did not usually look under a new cover, even when she saw the object transferred from the old cover to the new one.

So, her sense of "object permanence" was not very flexible. An object was not something that could exist just anywhere.

Instead it had to be identified with another object with which it had originally been seen. Seeing one object then called up the picture of the other.

But now your sleight of hand doesn't fool toddler, whether you hide the object under a single cover or under several covers in succession. She will search correctly in the last place where she saw it disappear.

There are still a few gaps, however, in how Toddler reasons about what makes things happen.

An important gap at this stage is the fact that she understands only what she sees. She cannot grasp an action, even the simplest, that happens out of her sight.

Try this as a sleight of hand trick: let Toddler see you place in your hand some small object of interest to her. Close your fingers around the object to cover it completely. Then bring your closed hand around behind your back.

While your hands are hidden behind your back, transfer the object from one hand to the other. Then close the fingers on your empty hand and bring it back into Toddler's view.

When you open your fingers to reveal an empty hand, Toddler may show some surprise or agitation, but she will not look behind you to find the object. If you close your fingers again, she will probably open them in search of the object.

After all, this was the last place she saw it before it disappeared.

What seems like a simple bit of reasoning—that you must have released the object at the place where your hand was hidden—is not possible for Toddler at this stage.

The thinking process is really more difficult than it looks. Toddler must not only be able to form mental pictures of unseen objects but she must also be able to picture unseen actions, and to picture an action in its proper place.

An adult example may help you appreciate this problem. From your school mathematics courses, you may remember times when the book said, "It is obvious that ... " in describing how one step led to another.

But unless you were gifted or experienced in mathematics, you may sometimes have had trouble telling how to get from one equation to the other.

It was not at all "obvious" how the change was made, if certain operations had been done without a full explanation being given. You needed each little step to be spelled out.

So it is with Toddler in this much simpler problem. She has to be able to picture, in proper order, each of the actions we mentioned above in describing the sleight of hand trick.

Of course, you can show her how you transferred the object from one hand to the other before making your hand reappear.

If you repeat the trick after your demonstration, she will probably look in the right place for the object.

But it isn't likely that this understanding will transfer to a new situation where you use different objects and covers. Two or three months of experience will be needed.

Before Toddler can truly reason the relationship between cause and effect, she must be able to reconstruct the chain of events.

Before she can do this, she has to have direct experience with all of the individual links in the chain, and how they fit together.

Thus the hiding of hands and the transfer of object are two links that must be fitted together. Transferring of object and closing of fingers is another necessary pairing, and so on.

Yet even this is not enough. To reason backwards, from effect to cause, requires something called reversibility.

Once Toddler learns the chain in a forward direction, she must be able to "read it" in a backward direction—run the movie in reverse, so to speak.

That way she can deduce what must have happened to cause the later effect.

Reversibility isn't an ability that a child either has or doesn't have. Her ability to reverse an idea depends upon how complicated the idea is.

Reversibility will continue to develop over the next few years. It must be practiced on every new experience so that it can keep pace with increasingly complex experiences.

Eventually a child reaches a point, well into her school years, where she can make fairly complicated reversals in her mind without performing them physically.

These reversal learnings explain the fascination of repeatedly filling and emptying containers, stacking and unstacking (or tearing down) blocks.

She is practicing simple one-step reversals in her growth toward higher thinking and reasoning. ∎

Introvert or Extrovert?

The study of temperamental differences in children has received much attention in recent years.

Temperament refers to personality characteristics by which different individuals relate differently to the world around them. It is generally assumed that these temperamental differences remain fairly stable over time.

Indeed, several research studies have indicated that infants who scored either high or low on measures of such characteristics as, for example, shyness, sociability, irritability, activity level, and attention span, responded in a similar manner during later childhood, and, occasionally, even into their adult years.

There is also increasing evidence that one's temperament is largely genetically determined.

Several studies of identical twins who were separated shortly after birth and were then raised in completely different environments showed such remarkable similarities that these similarities could only be accounted for by genetic factors.

This is not to say, however, that temperament is completely unchanged for life. On the contrary, several studies have indicated that many children undergo changes in temperament, with only those at the most extreme ends of temperamental characteristics being unlikely to experience much change.

Alexander Thomas and Stella Chess have conducted the most comprehensive study of temperament. They found that a majority of the individuals in their study could be placed in one of three categories:

(1) the easy child (40 percent of the sample) who, during infancy, quickly established a regular routine, was generally cheerful and adjusted easily to new experiences;

(2) the difficult child (10 percent of the sample) who didn't establish regular daily routines during infancy, generally displayed a negative attitude, and reacted intensively to any changes of environment; and: (3) the slow-to-warm-up child (15 percent of the sample) who generally had an uncooperative mood and reacted slowly and reluctantly to any new experiences.

It is interesting to note that 35 percent of the subjects did not fit any one of these three categories, which indicates how complex the study of temperamental differences in children can be.

One of the most important conclusions that emerged from the study is that parents cannot be blamed for a child's negative temperament. Nor, by the same token, can they take full credit for raising an easy child.

Another important outcome of this study was the development of the concept of "goodness-of-fit" between specific parenting practices and each child's individual temperamental characteristics.

In essence, this means that different children have different child-rearing needs related to their individual temperaments.

While recognizing and respecting each child's basic temperament, parents need, at the same time, to help their child develop appropriate strategies for dealing with any problems associated with his type of temperament.

We can illustrate this point by considering an aspect of children's temperamental characteristics which has received considerable attention in recent studies, namely differences between introverts and extroverts.

While most children will, at some time or another, exhibit both introverted and extroverted behavioral characteristics, they generally display a distinct leaning toward one style or the other.

Children who are introverted are reflective, shy and generally inhibited in social situations. They prefer to interact with just one or two close friends.

Surrounding them too quickly with lots of other children could be an overwhelming experience that may cause them to retreat even deeper into their shell of solitude.

Introverted children are generally protective of their possessions and are often reluctant to share. In group activities they prefer to look, listen and learn, rather than be active participants. Even when they know the correct answer to a question, they prefer to let someone else respond.

Extroverted children, on the other hand, are talkative, friendly and outgoing. When someone asks a question, they want to be the first to respond, even if their answer is incorrect.

They also like to keep talking even as they are working out a solution to a problem. They are generally at ease in a large group of children. They become restless when left alone and can be very demanding of a parent's time and attention.

In adjusting child-rearing practices which take into account each individual child's temperament, two considerations should be kept in mind:

(1) It is very important to recognize and respect the strengths of each child's temperament. This can be difficult for parents whose own temperamental characteristics differ from those of their child.

continued on next page

New Social Skills

Social competence involves the ability to interact with other people in an age-appropriate manner. In order to develop new social skills, it is important to provide your child with opportunities for peer interactions.

At this age, children are not yet capable of establishing friendships. But they will smile at a familiar friendly face and may sometimes even try to comfort a crying playmate.

When visiting someone else's home, it's important to allow infants time to adjust to a new setting. In a new environment, children this age usually feel most safe and secure when sitting in a parent's lap.

If there are two or more toddlers in the room at the same time, it's fascinating to observe how they will interact.

At first, they will generally ignore one another—until the more adventurous one decides to get down from the parent's lap in order to explore the room.

When toddlers begin to explore a new environment, they often like, at first, to hold on to some familiar adult for security.

This may take the form of grabbing the adult's clothing or scurrying across the room to be near another familiar adult. From that secure position they get a different perspective of the room.

Eventually when it appears to be safe, they will muster the courage to venture out on their own—especially if they see something in the distance that they would really like, such as a favorite toy.

While one child is busy exploring the room, another may prefer the comfort of her parent's lap. From this safe vantage point she can watch carefully what the other infant is doing.

Eventually she too may decide to venture out on her own if her curiosity or interest is aroused.

Once two or more toddlers become mobile, they may attempt to make some type of contact with one another. This may include making vocal sounds, gazing into each other's eyes, smiling or touching the other's mouth, nose or ears.

Most times these interactions do not anticipate any response from the other infant.

To foster successful social interactions between toddlers, careful planning by parents is essential. Most successful are cooperative play activities such as marching in step or beating drums to the sound of music.

While most children this age are capable of simple forms of taking turns in play situations, they are not yet ready for sharing of prized toys and possessions.

Therefore, when you invite other children to your home, it is wise to put away your own child's favorite toys. If possible, provide toys for which you have duplicates available. In this way you will help keep the peace and avoid jealousy between the children.

Don't stop arranging play dates, however, if you find that the children ignore one another or don't seem to get along too well. For some children it takes more time and repeated exposure to peers before they acquire appropriate social skills.

Sometimes a neutral site, such as the playground at a park will be an environment in which toddlers will get along better.

In their own home, some children become highly possessive of their own toys. In another child's home, they may cling to a parent because of being nervous in a strange environment.

While parents need to keep a watchful eye on children's play activities—to prevent accidents and avoid either of the children getting hurt—it is best not to involve yourselves too closely in these peer interactions.

Studies indicate that when adults and peers are both present in the same activity, the children will interact seven times more often with the adults than with peers.

Likewise parents don't need to become involved in minor squabbles between children, unless one child is likely to hurt the other. It is better for young children to develop the social skills needed to resolve minor problems than to be dependent on parents always coming to their rescue.

The basic interaction skills which children learn in early childhood become the foundation on which they will build later social development. ∎

continued from previous page

(2) It is also important to help each child to broaden his ways of dealing with and responding to his environment.

For example, in the case of the introverted child, while it's important to respect his desire to have time and space for personal reflection, it's also important to help him expand gradually his circle of friends, so that he will eventually feel more at ease in larger group settings.

In the case of an extroverted child, he needs patience and understanding whenever he blurts out an answer without thinking.

To him, interacting with you has a higher priority than giving you the correct answer. You can help him to learn gradually to wait his turn, listen carefully to what others have to say and, in general, become more reflective.

One of the secrets of good parenting is having the ability to recognize and respect the specific strengths of each child's temperament while, at the same time, helping him to broaden his ways of adjusting to and dealing with the realities of the world around him. ∎

A Problem-solving Toy

Here is an easy-to-make toy you can give to your child to see how he solves a problem.

Tie a heavy string around a large rectangular block. Pass the string through a hole cut in the middle of a foot-square piece of the stiffest cardboard you can find.

The hole should be square and just large enough to let the block pass through when it is turned the right way.

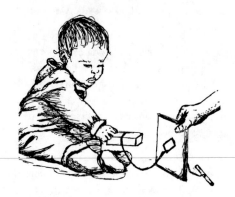

Tie the other end of the string around the middle of a Lincoln log or stick (be careful to avoid sharp points!) that is longer than the hole.

Make the string long enough so that when the block is against the cardboard, the stick can be turned perpendicular to the cardboard with an inch or so to spare.

This will allow the stick to be turned and brought through the hole.

Give this toy to Toddler and see what he does with it. After he gets used to the toy he will probably try to pull one or the other through the hole.

But neither object will go through just any old way. The block has to be turned to match the shape of the hole.

The stick must be turned perpendicular and then passed through the hole. Even though it may take a while, see if Toddler can solve the problem on his own.

If he doesn't seem to know what to do, you might suggest how to get the block through the hole.

When he accomplishes this, praise him and tell him what a good job he has done.

When he has learned to manipulate the block through the hole, wrap some more string around it to make it too big for the hole.

See if he can figure out the alternative solution to the problem, which is to turn the stick so it will go through.

If he initially turned the stick to go through the hole, make a knotted loop in the string to shorten it. This will prevent the stick from being turned perpendicular.

Now he will have to use the alternative solution of making the block go through the opening.

Note whether Toddler is flexible in trying new approaches or whether he doggedly clings to the method that was originally successful.

This will give you some insight into how he operates when solving a problem.

It should also suggest whether it will be necessary for you to help him look for alternative solutions to problems. ■

Growing Child®

P. O. Box 2505 • W Lafayette, IN 47996
(800) 927-7289
©Growing Child, Inc.
www.GrowingChild.com

Contributing Authors
Phil Bach, O.D., Ph.D.
Miriam Bender, Ph.D.
Joseph Braga, Ed.D.
Laurie Braga, Ph.D.
George Early, Ph.D.
Carol R. Gestwicki, M.S.
Liam Grimley, Ph.D.
Robert Hannemann, M.D., F.A.A.P.
Sylvia Kottler, M.S.
Bill Peterson, Ph.D.

Nancy Knows

Things are suddenly different in Nancy's house: Nancy knows who Nancy is. Nancy is almost 16 months old, and has she changed! You'd think she is the only one in the house. At least, she seems to think so.

Her five-year-old brother picked up her push toy for a little idle play while waiting for lunch and Nancy grabbed it back.

Her mother asked her to take her fingers out of the orange juice pitcher, and she stuck in her whole fist.

Her mother finished folding a whole basket of clothes. Nancy pulled out everything until she found a favorite blanket to drag around.

Ask Nancy to do something and she will most likely refuse even if it is fun to do. She might even say, no, two or three times. Or even, Nancy, no.

Her older brother and sister are baffled and sometimes hurt by Nancy's new attitude. But, her mother knows how to comfort them. She says, "That's just Nancy, Nancy. Forget it."

Nancy's mother remembers the same sort of period from her other two. She knows that Nancy, Nancy will come very close to being nasty, but that this, too will pass.

There is a rule that prevails, however, Nancy doesn't get away with it. When told to do, or not to do, she must or she must not. As painful and patience-straining as it sometimes is, Nancy's mother makes her stick to the rules—unless the matter is a trifle and she can afford to let Nancy win one now and then.

Nancy's mother has concluded that since each of her three children went negative in their second year, maybe most kids do. Well, she's right.

Many parents have found that just about all of their children go through just a stage. If dealt with sensibly, firmly, and consistently, most of them will come out of it as fairly nice people again.

Even Nancy, Nancy. ■

Play teaches children to master the world.

Jean Piaget

Moving Toward Independence

Toddler's feet are now taking him everywhere. No place into which he can squeeze his little self is safe from his busy explorations. Each day dawns on a world of exploration and he shows a growing desire for independence. So, take advantage of his interest in new activities to start him on the road to independence.

One of the ways Toddler learns independence is by imitating parents, brothers, sisters and others in his environment. He follows Mommy or Daddy around the house acting as a "helper."

Every parent who has tied a toddler's shoelaces in a double knot knows that even this is not really proof against the prying, pulling and poking fingers of a persistent child.

He also begins to explore his own clothes—pulling off as much as he can. He may even enjoy the freedom of running around without any clothes.

Don't let your child's apparent determination to set up his own nudist colony worry you. He is just as interested in exploring his clothes and himself as he is in exploring the rest of the world.

As you get Toddler ready for his bath, encourage him to help. Untie his shoelaces and loosen them as you say, "Now we'll take off Jimmie's shoes! We untie the knot. We pull the laces. And off comes the shoe!"

Let Toddler pull the laces out. Pulling these strings through the little holes is great fun—and good training in hand-eye coordination, too.

Soon he can unlace his shoes all by himself. What an accomplishment! But look

out, because as Toddler kicks his feet in excitement, that shoe might really fly!

Before that happens, show him how to pull it off gently. Then say, "Now give the shoe to me, please." Get a grip on it before he throws it to see if shoes will fly, or drops it on the floor to find out what kind of noise it will make.

And don't forget to say, "Thank you!" as he lets go of it. From your example, he will learn to say "Thank you," too.

Socks must also come off. Push the top down over Toddler's heel and pull the toe loose. Twitch it and pull it a little say-, ing "You pull it off!" When he pulls it off with a flourish, be ready with "Give the sock to me. Thank you!"

As you and Toddler go about getting the rest of his clothes off, follow the same procedure. Get the garment part way off and allow him to finish pulling it off. And talk about what you and he are doing together.

Does all this sound like just play and perhaps time-consuming for a busy parent? It is play and it is time-consuming, but Toddler is learning important lessons about his clothes and himself, about concepts of "on" and "off," about how to balance himself while he pulls off a shoe or sock.

He also learns about the characteristics and textures of shoes, shoelaces, socks and shirts. And how about the lesson on neatness ("Give the shoe to me") and the lesson on politeness ("Please," and "Thank you")?

During this period it is necessary to be a diplomat. If you intervene too soon

At 17 Months Toddler Likes to:
- Play with water.
- Wave bye-bye.
- Carry and move things.
- Be chased.

Give Toddler:
- Pull-toys.
- Small wagon.
- Small cars.
- Large blocks.
- Scarves, hats, purses, or wallets for simple imitative play.

or try too hard to help him undress, he may become angry. If he is deprived of the opportunity to undress because you are so helpful, he may not develop the motivation and desire to try for himself.

If, on the other hand, you never assist him at all, he won't succeed and will feel frustrated.

As in many other management techniques, there must be a middle ground—thus our suggestion to pull off his sock or shirt part way and allow him to complete the job successfully.

Lastly, a word to the wise: Eager little hands are hard on shoelace tips (if his shoes have shoelaces) and there is nothing more frustrating than trying to push a bushy-tailed shoelace through a small eyelet when the shoe is on a wiggling foot.

So when you buy Toddler a pair of shoes, always buy at least one extra pair of shoelaces. Keep a bottle of white glue handy for hardening the ends of a shoelace that is bushy-tailed. This will make it easier to thread the shoelace through the eyelet. ∎

Big People's Little Helper

There are times when Toddler wanders into the kitchen while you or your spouse are cooking dinner. She is apt to come in just to see what is going on. The sights, sounds, and smells are very attractive when she is hungry.

There are moments when you might wish she were in another room and not underfoot. But instead of saying, "Go away, I'm busy," take a moment to involve her, in a small way, in what you are doing.

As Toddler hangs around, take note of what you are doing. Is there any action or part of an action that she can do?

If you are opening a can, hoist her up and show her how the opener works.

Then put her down, finish opening the can and show her how the lid can be raised to reveal the contents.

You might point to the picture on the label, say "Peas," for example, then dip out a few peas with a spoon and hold them beside the picture. "See, here are the peas."

The significance of the picture as an indicator of the contents will be a new learning experience for her.

Now you can bring the pan down to her eye level and show her how the can's contents are poured into the heating pan.

Pouring is and will be a fascinating operation to her. She can be shown the pouring anytime she is around.

Her hand is too small to hold the can, even with your guidance. But you can give her the empty container, with the lid safely removed—provided it has no sharp edges—and direct her to properly dispose of it.

If Toddler should show up when you have something that needs to be stirred, show her how to do it. Then let her take a couple of turns at it with you holding the bowl with one hand and steadying the spoon with the other.

She will gain the feeling that she is helping and have the warm sense of acceptance and participation in a part of the adult world.

How many jobs should Toddler participate in at one session? She will provide you with the answer. She will stay with you for one or more activities, then seem to lose interest and wander off.

That's so she can digest in her mind what she has experienced. She has to ponder the idea that grown-ups pour, stir things, and push buttons. You may even see her pouring and stirring with new purposefulness in her self-play not long after she has helped you in the kitchen.

There will be times, of course, when you are too rushed to let her join in your activities. In these cases, she must accept the idea that you have nothing for her to do.

On more relaxed occasions the kitchen can serve as a center for new experiences, an interesting place where important things happen, and a laboratory where she has a chance to learn about the way "big people's jobs" are done. ∎

Beginning to Talk

What can we expect now of Toddler's speech production?

He will have a vocabulary of about ten words, such as cookie, drink, ball, bed, dog, milk, candy, daddy, baby, airplane, water, mama, doll, car.

As you see, these are words associated with his experiences—the objects and people important to him.

Sometimes first-time parents or those overly conscientious anticipate their child's needs and provide what he wants before he asks for it.

In such cases the words the child understands—his receptive vocabulary —may be equal to other children his age. However, since his needs are met so easily, he may have no motivation to talk or experience

any need for self-expression. Rather, he points, pulls or tugs to direct an adult toward what he wants.

To become a proficient talker in the coming months, Toddler must be encouraged to produce more sounds in addition to pointing in order to obtain toys, food, or treats.

His pronunciation is often not precise at this age. So, if we expect too much and make him repeat the words correctly, he may feel insecure and not speak as much or as often as he should.

Instead, allow him the luxury of being his age by not demanding too little or too much. Require him to attempt to tell you what he wants or needs, but accept less than perfect pronunciation.

After all, when his errors are fairly consistent, ("muk" is always "milk"), there really is no problem understanding him. You can, of course, repeat his request ("You want some milk?") so that he hears the correct sound long before he can reproduce it himself.

You can also expand his one-word utterances. "He says "Juice?" and you reply, "You want some more apple juice?"

Meanwhile, you can expect to hear jargon, in addition to meaningful speech, until about age two. It will have plenty of expression, similar to your own speech, but only occasionally do specific words stand out.

Don't be shy about entering into his jargon-talk. As he develops more words it will lose its attraction for him, gradually fading out toward the end of the second year. ∎

When Anger Emerges...

Anger is one emotion that may emerge about this time.

In a comprehensive study, "Anger in Young Children," psychologist Florence Goodenough analyzed the angry outbursts of a large population of children under eight years of age.

There was a marked peak in such outbursts during the second year, and then a rapid decline.

Sex differences were unimportant until the preschool years when boys demonstrated more outbursts than girls.

Toddler may learn to use anger for solving some of her problems, depending upon how successful the behavior is.

When she wants to "do her own thing," any adult interference may bring on expressions of anger such as crying, screaming, kicking, jumping up and down, throwing objects, even biting or hitting.

Of course, there is a variety of genuine reasons for children feeling upset: hunger which emerges just before mealtime; illness, even a slight cold; an "accident," if elimination control has been introduced; a shift in the daily routine which appears to suit a parent's rather than Toddler's needs.

If a parent makes it a habit to wait until Toddler's frustration erupts into anger, the child may learn to "use" this anger.

Simply put, a parent reinforces anger when he or she reacts to the child's anger with attention—which is satisfying to the child.

An association is formed between the angry behavior and the parent's attention.

Even if the attention happens to take the form of punishment, it may be rewarding. For a child, negative attention is often better than no attention at all.

Dr. Goodenough offers these conclusions: The control of Toddler's angry behavior is achieved if it is viewed with tolerance. When you adhere to your standards or expectations with consistency, the child learns through experience what is expected of her.

Self-control in parents is a pretty good guarantee of self-control in the child as she matures.

The following recommendations may help you to deal more effectively with negativism or ornery behavior at this age:

1. Be aware that this negative behavior is perfectly normal and healthy in a child during the second year.

2. Try to understand the reason for the negative behavior, namely, that your child is probably "testing the limits" in her probing search for her own individuality and independence. Frustration can play a role as well.

3. Be aware that if your only technique for dealing with negative behavior is "head-on" confrontation, you are unwittingly offering yourself to the child as a role model for more negative behavior.

4. Directing your child's attention to some positive activity will be more effective than scolding.

5. Realize the consequences of either extreme. Always giving in will create a spoiled child, while always putting Toddler down will result in a poor self-concept—and a crushed ego.

A balance is needed in order to transform a potentially unpleasant parent-child conflict into a positive learning experience from which Toddler can learn appropriate and desirable social skills.

6. Yielding occasionally to the child is not abdication of control by the parent (as some would think) but it is instead a selective, responsible choice in the interest of the child's self-concept and sense of individuality. Adults can decide on the battles that are important enough to pursue.

7. For the parent to remain calm but firm is not only best for the child but is in the best interest of the parent's own mental well-being. ■

Games Toddlers Love

Toddler will love to play these games that encourage movement and language skills.

1. Hide and Seek. This is an older child's game which you can modify for Toddler. In her presence you "hide" by pretending not to see her. Then you ask, "Where's Judy?" In response she may point, giggle, jump up and down, laugh, or say "me" or "here."

2. Copycat. Introduce animal sounds and their actions—walk on all fours and growl like a lion. Or, in a squatting position jump up and down like a bunny. Make the sounds and actions of objects such as an airplane, a car, a boat. This is a period of strong and natural imitation on Toddler's part.

3. Jack-Be-Nimble. Read or recite the rhyme: "Jack-be-nimble, Jack-be-quick, Jack-jump-over-the candlestick." Jump when the word "jump" is said. This will help associate the movement with the word. Next play it as a partnership with Toddler, getting her to make the jump.

4. Blowing. Show Toddler how to blow a cotton ball or ping pong ball across a table. Be sure to tell her the word "blow" at the same time.

All of these games are fun to play. More importantly they help Toddler put together the different pieces of her world—coordinating auditory, visual and motor development. ■

Learning To Eat Can Be Messy!

Toddlers who have been practicing with both finger feeding and holding a spoon, are probably becoming pretty good self-feeders by now.

On the other hand, if you have been feeding Toddler, now is the time to encourage her to take over and do it herself.

You can expect an occasional mess—being a neat eater takes lots of practice.

Some toddlers will feed themselves certain foods but want a parent to feed them others.

If this practice continues, it is possible that Toddler will build up faulty eating habits—she will discriminate between the foods she wants and the foods you want her to eat.

In this period of self-assertion such a practice can develop into a parent/toddler tug-of-war. In the future you may find that she may not have an appetite for your foods.

We urge you to allow Toddler to feed herself in spite of the mess she may make, but don't insist.

Between the first and second years many youngsters will give up certain foods, particularly some vegetables. Accept her preferences and return to the rejected foods in a few weeks.

By pushing a temporary dislike on her, you increase the probability that the particular food may become permanently distasteful to her.

Toddler's preferences may result in an occasional lopsided meal but from day to day or week to week her choices should even out to a well-balanced diet.

There is no doubt that the quality as well as the quantity of her appetite will change during this period. She may drink less milk, but a pint a day (in any form) is satisfactory to cover her needs if she's receiving a reasonable diet.

If she rejects milk, don't force it; just quietly take it away. Experienced parents

report that each time Toddler says "no," her determination becomes stronger.

Should it happen that she is without a daily pint of milk or other calcium-containing products (such as cheese or yogurt) for more than two weeks, it might be good to report this to your physician.

Toddler requires variety in her menu just as we do. Chewy foods, especially finger foods like shredded carrot strips, a chicken leg or a pork chop bone are excellent for her emerging teeth and for exercising the muscles of her mouth.

The identical muscles used in chewing are used in speaking. Regular vigorous chewing practice will make the movements of tongue, lips and jaws more proficient.

Caution: Finger foods should be introduced with care and in small amounts, such as shredded carrot, not sticks.

Meat bones should be checked carefully to make sure there are no small fragments that can come off and choke Toddler.

Likewise, don't give Toddler hard foods that have to be chewed completely before swallowed—Toddlers aren't always sophisticated in their eating and chewing—and even small pieces of food can cause choking. ■

Self-Awareness

At 17 months, most children can point to some of their body parts when you name them. They can identify hair, nose, mouth, eyes, ears, hands, feet, legs, fingers, toes.

All you have to do is ask, "Where is your nose?" and your toddler will show you. In addition, she often says the name immediately after you.

For example, if you say, "Touch your feet," she may say "feet" before touching them. And some advanced 17-month-olds will already have the vocabulary for head, eyes, feet, toes, nose, arms.

If you haven't as yet introduced body-image games, play them in the bathtub.

Give Toddler a sponge and tell her "wash your tummy" or "wash your legs."

If you have made it a habit to name her body parts for her as well as describing their actions to her—"arm up" when her arm is guided through a sleeve—she will join the bathtub game easily.

On the other hand, if naming and describing have not become a way of life, it is not too late to introduce both right now. And expand the "self" vocabulary: elbow, knee, vulva, belly, tongue. ■

Toilet Learning

We discussed toilet learning in a previous issue of *Growing Child.* We said that toilet learning was a learning process and that three basic skills are necessary for success:

1. Muscle control. A child must be able to control his sphincter muscles to hold and let go of bowel and bladder contents. This physical ability does not usually develop until the second year and is often not fully achieved until later.

The child must also be able to get himself to the toilet and have mastered the coordination necessary to manage his clothing.

2. Communication. A child must be mature enough to understand what it is you want him to do, and to communicate with you—by word or action—when he wants to use the toilet.

3. Desire. A child must want to be trained, whether the reason is a desire to be clean, to be like his friends, or to please you.

Bowel and bladder control are developmental behaviors. As with other milestones, there are wide variations in the age at which a toddler reaches a stage of development that will allow him to control his elimination.

In toilet learning, the concept of "readiness" is central. This is a process of the child slowly learning control, rather than the parent "training" the child.

If the parent begins the process too early, there can be frustration for the parent and unnecessary pressure and failure for the toddler.

The age of beginning lessons about elimination control—and the rate of progress in becoming trained—is no indication of the child's other developmental achievements.

Being early or late in bowel or bladder control will not predict being advanced or backward in school, nor the rate at which other developmental milestones will be reached.

Observation and experience suggest that certain parental attitudes and actions encourage the success of elimination control when the child shows by words or actions that he is ready. These are:

• Calmness and patience and a matter-of-fact attitude.

• Clarity in telling the child what is expected of him (i.e. to put his feces and urine in the toilet or potty chair).

• Acceptance of gradual, rather than instantaneous, success. Praise and encouragement for successes. Appreciation of this success must not be out of proportion to his other accomplishments because this could cause fear of failure.

• Understanding of failure. Casual responses to failures indicate that you have confidence in him to do better next time.

Readiness

When is the best time for toilet training? Here are words or actions that show the child is ready:

• Pausing and making sounds or grimaces while having a bowel movement; telling you when he has had or is having a movement.

• Being regular in bowel movements.

• Staying dry for an hour or two in the daytime; waking up dry from naps.

• Complaining when wet or soiled; generally liking to be clean and tidy.

• Being aware that urine and feces come from his body.

• Wanting to imitate adults or be grown up.

As a way of preparing for toilet training, you can begin to comment when you know your child is having a bowel movement or when he tells you so. This will help him begin to associate the physical feelings and the result. Tell him that when he has those feelings, he should tell you so you can help him get to the toilet. Then introduce him to the potty chair or booster seat.

At first your child may let you know he needs to go to the toilet after he has wet. This is not an act of defiance. It is a sign that he recognizes what is happening, a necessary step to being able to "go potty" by himself.

Wait until the child is ready and he will learn without battles. As one wise pediatrician said, "Don't worry about it. He won't want to go to kindergarten in diapers."

An investigation of what a group of American mothers said they did about toilet learning indicates that seven months was the average length of time it took to complete bowel training, but there was a range from a few weeks to 1-1/2 years.

What emerged was the fact that the later the training began, the less time it took.

As the toddler matures, he is better able to recognize the signals of elimination and "hold it" long enough to reach the toilet.

Another study involved the achievement of twins. One twin's introduction to elimination control began at seven months and was almost complete at two years when the

continued on next page

Learning by Exploring

continued from previous page

During the past seventeen months, Toddler has been learning about the world around him, mainly by looking, listening and exploring.

Psychologists call this the "sensorimotor" period of development.

For example, if you gave him a fleece or cloth ball, he may have watched as he rotated it around and around.

Then perhaps he rubbed it against his arms, legs, or cheek and even brushed it against his lips.

From all of this sensorimotor activity he learned about the shape, size, and feel of the ball.

He is now ready, however, for the beginnings of real thought, namely, forming mental images and symbols that represent objects or actions in his environment.

Over the next several months he will develop the ability to learn about a ball in a more intellectual way.

And he will need you to provide the labels for the ball's qualities—its color, roundness and softness, for example.

Casually interpreting the child's explorations to him is a very good teaching method that helps him to learn more efficiently.

For example, tell him: "Feel the ball, it's soft like your teddy bear. And it's round like this other ball. See how round it is when you turn it? Your ball is red, like this red block."

Use simple, brief descriptions because his comprehension is still very limited. You want him to be able to absorb all of the ball's qualities you describe.

Toddler should be ready at this age to move from purely sensorimotor learning (seeing, hearing, touching) to a higher form of learning involving symbols and images.

You can encourage this process by continuing to identify the objects in his environment and by naming their various qualities. ∎

Growing Child.

P. O. Box 2505 • W Lafayette, IN 47996
(800) 927-7289
©Growing Child, Inc.
www.GrowingChild.com

Contributing Authors
Phil Bach, O.D., Ph.D.
Miriam Bender, Ph.D.
Joseph Braga, Ed.D.
Laurie Braga, Ph.D.
George Early, Ph.D.
Carol R. Gestwicki, M.S.
Liam Grimley, Ph.D.
Robert Hannemann, M.D., F.A.A.P.
Sylvia Kottler, M.S.
Bill Peterson, Ph.D.

second twin was introduced to the process of control.

Within three months, their toilet learning achievement became equal. Apparently, the second half of the second year is the time for easiest toilet learning.

Another study showed that the average age for learning to use the toilet reliably for bowel and bladder is 28 months.

Many professionals and the majority of experienced parents currently advocate delaying efforts to start the toilet learning process child until just before or after the second birthday, when control is much more likely to proceed gradually and with less conflict.

Because of the larger bladder capacity of little girls, they are often more quickly able to achieve control than are boys.

Again, generally speaking, you can expect daytime control between the ages of two and three.

Nighttime control occurs at approximately the same time or may be slightly delayed.

It is very important that you be rational and realistic about the toilet learning process. A parent who has an intense desire for the child to achieve control and who uses severe measures to bring this about is asking for trouble. This is no time for competition with others or pressure on the child.

Indeed, the whole process could become a major confrontation between parent and child because the parent wants the child to do something which the child often cannot or will not do.

A battle in the area of toilet training is a losing battle. Two factors are in direct opposition here.

(1) The child is entering a developmental stage where he wants and needs to be independent.

(2) At the same time the parents insist that the child control the "when" and the "where" of bowel and bladder movement to their satisfaction. ∎

A child is a person who is going to carry on what you have started. He is going to sit where you are sitting and when you are gone, attend to those things which you think are important. The fate of humanity is in his hands.

Abraham Lincoln

Good Parenting Means Being a Relaxed Parent

At regular intervals in *Growing Child* we try to make you aware of the appropriate developmental milestones (see "Developmental Milestones—18 Months") that a "typical" child will have reached.

Each month we try to send you helpful suggestions for your child's growth and proper development.

Even allowing for the individual differences in children, it would appear from the letters that we receive from our readers that our suggestions are perceived as "on target" and come to parents at a time in their lives when such help and advice are much appreciated.

At the same time, we are concerned about how you use the newsletter.

First of all, we fear that *Growing Child* might make some of you unduly anxious about how your child is developing.

It is one thing to be aware of real lags in a child's development. It is quite another thing to get uptight about it.

When you get overconcerned about a real problem, your emotional energy gets drained away in worry. You find that you are not up to dealing with the problem in the best way you could. Worry is nonproductive and inefficient.

Being genuinely concerned is different from being worried. If you are genuinely concerned, you can see a problem for what it is.

Then you can focus your energy on finding the best solution to that problem.

We have another concern which is harder to describe. Perhaps an example may make it clear.

One of Norman Rockwell's illustrations shows a young mother with her child face down on her lap.

The child is positioned in such a way that the viewer expects he will be soundly spanked. In one hand the mother holds a hairbrush. In the other she holds an open book on the subject of proper child raising.

It is part of Norman Rockwell's art that the expression on the mother's face clearly conveys her frustration. Should she "whale the daylights" out of this kid or should she try to find out what the experts say she should do?

We certainly do not want our newsletter to be like the expert's book in Rockwell's painting. We don't want to frustrate you or inhibit you as you care for, enjoy and play with your child.

Your child will thrive best if you develop a relaxed atmosphere for him in which he can enjoy his parents and himself. And you will find parenting richer and more satisfying.

Whatever you may be doing with your child at the moment, it should be done naturally. But it won't be natural if you're always wondering, "Am I doing this right?" or "Should I be doing this at all?" or "Have I done all the things in *Growing Child?*"

This kind of nagging, fretful self-questioning takes away the naturalness and even the joy of being parents.

So, read *Growing Child* and get all the benefits you can from us. Try to get our information "wired in" with all the other information you've learned from your total experience with life.

Then when you are "doing your thing" with your child, your know-how can flow naturally and smoothly into the immediate situation as needed.

You do not have to spend every waking minute with your child, but when you are with him, you really should be with him. You are giving something of yourself to each moment you spend with him. ∎

At 18 Months Toddler Likes to:
- Communicate with hands.
- Climb on chair or sofa.
- Play in the bath.
- Use the word "No."
- Explore objects with hands.

Give Toddler:
- Names for the different parts of the body.
- A ball to roll and throw.
- Storybooks with pictures to "read" with you.
- Games that require activity, like running and chasing.

Ask Your Doctor About:
- DTaP vaccine (diphtheria, tetanus, acellular pertussis).
- IPV (inactivated polio vaccine)
- Influenza vaccine.

Developmental Milestones—18 Months

Motor (Gross)
- Pushes and pulls objects.
- Walks with feet slightly apart.
- Does two things (only) at once—for example, walks and carries an object.
- Climbs into a large chair, rotates body, and sits.
- Creeps backward when going down stairs.

Communication
- Speaks 6-20+ recognizable words.
- Likes listening to nursery rhymes and joins in.
- Echoes the last word spoken to him.
- "Talks" to self while playing.
- Enjoys looking at picture books.
- Points to 2-3 parts (eyes, nose, hair, shoes) on doll or self.

Vision
- Watches and retrieves a rolling ball as far away as 10 feet.
- Points to distant objects out of doors.

Social/Emotional
- Raises and holds cup with two hands.
- Drinks from a cup without spilling.
- Removes shoes, socks, cap.
- Imitates familiar actions such as sweeping floor, dusting, reading a book.
- Amuses self, but prefers to be near an adult.
- Alternates between independence and dependence on caregiver.

Motor (Fine)
- Scribbles with a crayon on paper.
- Builds a tower with three blocks after a demonstration.
- Picks up food and small objects.
- Explores objects more frequently with hands than mouth. ∎

These milestones are guidelines only. All babies do not develop at the same speed, nor do they spend the same amount of time at each stage of their development. Usually a baby is ahead in some areas, behind in others and "typical" in still other areas. The concept of the "typical" child describes the general characteristics of children at a given age.

A Potential Rival—The New Baby

A problem parents may face is how to help young children cope with the arrival of a new baby.

Unless Toddler is prepared for a new baby, she may perceive him as an intruder and may demonstrate her negative feelings actively.

The term "sibling rivalry" is used by psychologists and child specialists to describe the feelings that brothers and sisters may have toward one another. Jealousy is a normal and natural feeling for all of us.

While Mother is attending to the needs of the newborn, Toddler may feel abandoned, even if her dad, grandparents, or brother and sister pay more attention to her than to the baby.

It is customary for friends, relatives and neighbors to come and ogle Baby, sometimes bringing him presents and frequently expressing their pleasure with his cuteness, size and weight.

It should not be too surprising, then if Toddler may sometimes resent Baby.

It is possible to help reduce Toddler's negative feelings by preparing her for the newborn. Tell her about the forthcoming birth at least a month before delivery and start to practice a real-life situation. Introduce a rubber baby doll which you bathe, diaper and tend. Then allow Toddler her turn as caretaker.

When you prepare for the hospital, or if you will need to be away from home (to arrange for an adoption, for example), hide some special things for Toddler about the house.

Then, call her on the telephone and tell her about your surprises, using very simple language.

Finally, when you return with the new baby, make a special effort to indulge Toddler a bit.

Even with good planning, things might not be ideal. You may expect two possible kinds of behaviors:

(1) Regression—infantile behavior such as wanting a bottle, nursing at the breast or eating erratically.

(2) Anger or hostility toward the baby. We offer this advice: (A) Give Toddler her opportunity to regress a little if she wants to. The period will be brief—a few days or a week. (Older children will respond differently and may not satisfy their infantile needs as quickly or as easily.)

(B) At this time, ignore as much as possible any negative behavior. It is Toddler's way of expressing resentment toward the baby.

At the same time, watch carefully to make sure Toddler doesn't try to harm the newcomer. No matter how well-meaning, threatening behavior toward the baby should be promptly and effectively stopped. ∎

Sand and Water: Good Playthings

Children learn important concepts from unstructured play with natural materials, such as sand and water, which generally are easily accessible. Such materials are particularly valuable in play-learning because they have no form of their own but assume the form of the container which holds them.

Play with such materials is "unstructured" in the sense that there are no fixed ways for using them. It is precisely this aspect of flexibility that makes these materials so unique and useful for learning new concepts—concepts which might not be learned in any other way.

Consider the "tools" of the sandbox: little shovel and pail, old spoons, pans, sieve, plastic bowls or cups of assorted sizes.

As Toddler fills his pail with shovelful after shovelful of sand, he learns about adding small quantities to make a larger quantity.

He has no difficulty lifting a small shovelful of sand—but wait until he tries to lift the full pail! Weight begins to have more meaning for him. And when he upends the pail, the dry sand in the pail loses its pail-shape and returns at once to the general shapelessness of loose sand.

When sand is wet it feels, looks and acts in different ways than it did when it was dry. If he stirs a little sand in a lot of water, they will mix, but when he stops stirring, the sand will settle to the bottom.

Even though it will be a long time before Toddler understands why this happens, his experiences teach him that it does happen again and again. This new knowledge then becomes the foundation on which later learning—such as the nature of the laws of gravity—can be built.

Sand play is continually fascinating to a child. He picks up a handful, only to have it trickle through his fingers until only a small amount is sticking to his damp hand. He fills a small pan and pours it into a large pan—but when he fills his pail first and then tries to pour it into the pan, the pan overflows!

Pouring, patting, shoveling, carrying, transferring sand from one container to another—all of these are stimulating pastimes from which your child learns important concepts such as hard, soft, heavy, light, wet and dry.

We usually think of bath toys as floating toys—but consider what a child can learn from squeezing sponges and washcloths, dipping up water in a cup, filling a bowl.

He will find that a bowl may float when empty but it will sink if he fills it with water. Some things will float, some things will sink! His young mind is already taking mental note of these differences and the seeds of scientific curiosity are being sown.

During the summer a plastic wading pool will provide hours of outdoor pleasure as he pours water, fills containers, kicks, splashes or dips. (Even though these wading pools seem shallow, they can be dangerous; **DO NOT leave a child unattended in a wading pool.**)

A variety of containers in his pool will add to his experiences, so give him old aluminum or plastic bowls and tumblers of several sizes.

As Toddler fills, pours and refills he practices coordination of hand and eye. He is also learning about some of the properties of natural elements such as sand and water.

Truly, play is learning. As Toddler plays with sand or water, he builds a valuable background of experiences from which he will later develop important concepts about quantification. These concepts will be basic to his later success in arithmetic. ∎

Thumb Sucking

Are you concerned because Toddler has not given up thumb sucking? If you look closely, you will observe that most thumb sucking at this age occurs at times when Toddler feels fatigued, insecure or is just in a mood to relax.

Sometimes there is a thumb substitute, the "security blanket"—a rag doll, soiled teddy bear or an old piece of blanket or towel which she won't discard.

She may suck, lick, chew or just hold it near her nose to sniff. It has some special meaning for her; maybe it reassures her that while a parent isn't around, she still has something familiar close to her.

Some children prefer pacifiers, which are often easier to take away.

Not all children suck their thumbs or carry security blankets. That's why some parents are concerned. But we want to assure you that you are not alone. Parents have always reported the problem of thumb sucking to their physicians.

At this age, if you ignore the sucking and try not to let it bother you, Toddler will most likely give it up and substitute more acceptable behaviors.

Be tolerant and allow her these pleasures when she is 18 months old. At this age some children may need the security provided by a thumb or a blanket and this habit probably isn't going to harm her teeth ... yet. It is best to discourage thumb sucking by age three.

Parents may wish to discuss this habit with their dentist if they have questions, or wish to learn about positive effects of stopping it. ∎

Teach Toddler To Read?

Several years ago there was a big stir over whether parents should teach toddlers to read. Some people said that most three-year-olds could learn to read if parents would just teach them. It was even suggested that some children younger than three could get in on this bonanza.

Although some of the excitement seems to have died down, we still get questions about teaching toddlers to read.

We advise parents not to be concerned about reading at this early age. At the same time, we feel strongly that parents should help their toddlers get ready to read. In fact, what we are writing about in *Growing Child* is aimed at helping you prepare your toddler for school.

We want him to be ready for reading, arithmetic, and writing. In one sense, nearly all the things we suggest you do are things which will lay the foundation for later school success.

There is no beginning point at which children learn to read. Instead, children use language continually; they experience how print language functions and gradually move themselves into print media experiences. Continuity exists between all language experiences, from birth through the primary years, not a discontinuity of "now it's time to learn to read."

Experts in early literacy point out the need to offer children abundant experiences to help them develop the various components of literacy. Parents have a key role in encouraging spoken communication and in fostering pleasurable adult-child interaction.

It has long been recognized that children who come from homes in which communication and literacy are valued and demonstrated move more easily into school reading and writing.

There are seven components of literacy that parents can support:

1. Vocabulary and language. As children learn to read, they use their listening and speaking vocabularies to make sense of printed words. Most vocabulary is learned through everyday experiences and conversations. Researchers find that increasing children's oral language skills can prevent the majority of reading problems.

2. Phonological awareness. A continuum of skills in hearing and understanding the different patterns of spoken language is necessary for reading. Listening to sounds in the environment, developing the skills of rhyming and rhythms, and nonsense language games all promote this awareness.

3. Knowledge or print. Understanding the functions and forms of print comes when children are given materials for drawing and writing; help make cards for family members, and make shopping lists.

4. Knowledge of letters and words. Far more than learning to recite the ABCs or recognizing letters, this understanding allows children to match spoken to written words. Children develop this ability as they learn to recognize and then print their names, and look at alphabet books.

5. Comprehension of meaning. Children's background knowledge helps them to understand the meaning of language. The more firsthand experiences that children have, the more they increase their understanding of the world.

6. Awareness of books. As children have books in their environments and are read to aloud, they discover the many purposes of written language, as well as learn the mechanics of using books—holding them right side up and turning pages.

7. Seeing literacy as a source of pleasure. Children who have had abundant, pleasurable experiences with books are highly motivated to learn to read for themselves.

When activities involving books include fun, play, and positive relationships with parents and others, children develop positive attitudes toward reading and writing.

These seven components of early literacy are specifics that parents can provide in the toddler years, rather than explicit teaching to read. ■

Progress in Speech and Language

Toddler's understanding of what she hears and says has now developed to the point that she:

1. Understands simple requests.

2. Carries out two consecutive directions, such as, "Please get the broom," and "Bring it to me."

3. Associates new words with old ones and understands categories such as "food," "clothing," "animals."

4. Can choose correctly two objects named by you from a choice of four or more items.

5. Perceives time in a very simple way—she understands the word "now."

6. Likes listening to stories, rhymes, songs and jingles if they do not exceed two or three minutes.

Toddler's expressive abilities have also been developing. For example:

1. She uses "words" in preference to gestures in order to express wants and needs.

2. Her vocabulary is about 10 words.

3. Repetition of words she has heard is not uncommon.

4. She employs a few word combinations or two-word sentences—"all gone," "what's 'at?", "come here," "see that?" ■

Language and Learning

As we have repeatedly stressed in *Growing Child,* the quality of Toddler's expressive language and speech will depend upon how well you, the adults in his life, have enriched his receptive language—how much you have been talking to him and playing with him through the medium of language. No educational toy can teach language like a parent can.

We want to continue sharing with you the teaching techniques which researchers have found to be most effective.

"Amplification" is a technique by which you develop more fully a statement or command. For example, over the past several months you have been telling Toddler, "No, no," whenever there was need for some prohibition.

Now that Toddler is older it is better to amplify the use of "No, no" with some words of explanation: "No, no, the stove is hot", or "No, no, don't go into the street because you might get hurt."

There are several advantages to using amplification: (1) it enriches Toddler's speech and language; (2) it helps Toddler become aware that the "No, no" refers to a specific object or situation—a hot stove or dangerous street—rather than implying that everything in his environment is hazardous or off-limits; (3) it helps Toddler understand there is a good reason for the "No, no": the stove is hot or going into the street could result in injury.

"Echoing" is another technique for language and speech enrichment. It is used if you understand only a few words of Toddler's particular message.

Rather than irritate, frustrate or embarrass Toddler by asking him to repeat the message, you imitate ("echo") him insofar as you can and replace the unintelligible part with one of the "wh" words. For example:

Toddler: "Goin owa nah."

Parent: "You're going where?"

The parent is asking a question to which Toddler, we hope, will give a more articulate response.

Incidentally, at this age Toddler is frequently unable to respond accurately to direct questions, such as "Where are you going?" This type of response takes more time to learn. However, you will observe that when you modify your question so that it resembles an "echoing" question—"You're going where?"—Toddler can answer you more often.

"Expansion" is another important method for aiding Toddler's language acquisition. In "expansion," Toddler's speech is repeated, but not exactly. The adult adds something to the statement, thus providing a good model of English grammar. For example:

Toddler: "Daddy car."

Parent: "Daddy is in the car."

In a study conducted by linguist Roger Brown, he noted that "middle class" parents expand about 30 percent of children's utterances. On the other hand, he noticed that "working class" parents expand their children's language much less often.

Another researcher, Dan Slobin, observed that children whose language is expanded tend to imitate the adult model. As a consequence their imitations are more advanced than their own spontaneous speech.

"Elaboration" is still another device to promote language development. In the use of "elaboration" the adult produces well-formed sentences, but they are not just expansions of what the child says. Instead they are elaborations of the content, that is, additional information related to and relevant to what Toddler has said. For example:

Toddler: "Pick mitten."

Parent: "Pick up the mitten. It will get dirty on the ground."

Courtney Cazden, a developmental linguist, investigated the effects of "expansion" with one group and "elaboration" with another group of very young children.

There was also a third group—a control group of children—who received only a regular nursery program with no attention to language enrichment.

At the end of the experiment, a progress score was computed. The language production of the "expansion" group had advanced more than the control group.

However, the language of the "elaboration" group advanced even more. Keep in mind that "expansion" and "elaboration" are not mutually exclusive. Use them both generously!

Finally, let's not neglect the use of picture-story books as a means of stimulating language and speech.

What is best is a book with bright, simple, childlike objects arranged on a page in a realistic scene. This kind of presentation helps the child begin to understand that these are objects in his life, ones that he can see in his environment.

Favorite authors for this age include Sandra Boynton and Bill Martin whose books provide rhythm and repetition.

When you sit down with Toddler, begin by naming or identifying the picture. Say something descriptive or functional about the object—"Orange juice tastes good. We drink orange juice from a glass."

As Toddler gains experience with picture reading, ask him to "find the dog," "point to the police officer," "show me the kitty."

Next, after he is familiar with the pictures, point to one and ask, "What's that?"

You will note the three step sequence: (1) You introduce the pictures. (2) Toddler is asked to select the pictures, which you name. (3) He is asked to name the one to which you point.

These simple techniques have been found to greatly enhance a child's receptive and expressive language. They are also a wonderful way for parents to enjoy interacting with their child in a manner that is both playful and educational. ■

Early Brain Development

You've heard about early brain development. Now here are some facts, free of the "hype" that is often employed by entrepreneurs who want to offer you gimmicks to make your child the "smartest" one around.

There is a four-year period of "potential" growth, which is the most critical period of human development. This time is from conception until about the third birthday.

By the 17th week of pregnancy, the fetus already has one billion brain cells, more than the adult brain. There are millions of neurons (nerve cells) that are connected to each other by synapses. These synapses and the pathways they form make up the wiring of the brain.

The number and organization of these connections influence everything, from the ability to recognize letters to the maintenance of relationships.

Neurons develop rapidly before birth. The brain is the only organ in the body that is incomplete at birth.

Following birth, brain development consists of wiring and rewiring the connections (synapses) between neurons. New synapses are formed, while others are pruned away.

Between birth and eight months, the synapses form more quickly, with possibly 1,000 trillion synapses at eight months. After age one, pruning occurs more quickly. By 10 years of age, children have nearly 500 trillion synapses, about the same as an average adult.

Early experiences, both positive and negative, have enormous effects on this formation of synapses. You might say that the brain operates on a "use it or lose it" principle, with only those connections that are frequently used being retained.

Consider the process of language development as an example of this principle. At three months of age, the brain has the ability to distinguish several hundred spoken sounds—all those of all languages.

During the next few months, the brain organizes itself to recognize only the sounds it hears, by reinforcing those neural connections.

However, during early childhood, the brain retains its ability to discriminate sounds it has discarded, or not organized into neural pathways. Final "pruning" has not yet taken place.

This is why young children can easily learn foreign languages, accent-free. But after age ten, when the pruning takes place, more effort is required to learn foreign languages.

Thus from early infancy to early childhood, these vital brain connections are being strengthened and made permanent. At this time, the brain is most flexible and prepared to learn.

There are ten things that children need in the first three years need to help the brain grow. These are:

1. Interaction with people and objects.

2. Touch, that literally sends signals to the brain telling it to grow.

3. Stable relationships that prevent the stress hormone cortisol from affecting brain development adversely.

4. Safe, healthy environments, including protection from lead; a high fat diet that facilitates the absorption of fat (necessary for growing children), as well as necessary amounts of sleep.

5. Self esteem, mirrored from calm, nurturing, predictable caregivers.

6. Quality child care, since poor care does not provide the necessary elements for brain development.

7. Communication and conversation to learn the complex skills of language.

8. Play experiences, including sensory and motor exploration that aid brain growth.

9. Music, since it brings many learning elements together.

10. Reading, over and over again, making ever more connections in the brain.

Find more about early brain development at: www.zerotothree.org/brainwonders ∎

Growing Child.

P. O. Box 2505 • W Lafayette, IN 47996
(800) 927-7289
©Growing Child, Inc.
www.GrowingChild.com

Contributing Authors
Phil Bach, O.D., Ph.D.
Miriam Bender, Ph.D.
Joseph Braga, Ed.D.
Laurie Braga, Ph.D.
George Early, Ph.D.
Carol R. Gestwicki, M.S.
Liam Grimley, Ph.D.
Robert Hannemann, M.D., F.A.A.P.
Sylvia Kottler, M.S.
Bill Peterson, Ph.D.

I love these little people; and it is not a slight thing when they, who are so fresh from God, love us.

Charles Dickens

19 Months Old

At nineteen months Toddler is well into a transition period from babyhood to early childhood. He has made enormous gains in control over his body.

For several months he has been able to stand independently. He walks well with arms down or uses his arms to carry, pull or push something.

When he hurries he moves along with a stiff, rapid, uneven lurching gait which is not exactly running, but which is faster than walking.

Toddler can seat himself in a child's chair with fairly accurate aim and can climb into an adult's chair unassisted. He settles himself with an air of having completed an important task—much as if he were saying "There! That's done!"

Toddler is steady enough on his feet now to have begun to walk upstairs with help.

He needs no help to come down because he either bumps down one step at a time in a sitting position or backs down on his hands and knees or hands and feet.

He delights in pulling a wheeled toy around after him as he walks—particularly if it makes a noise as it moves along.

While Toddler's balance has been improving and his legs have been brought under better control, he has also been learning better hand-eye coordination.

He spontaneously stacks two, three, sometimes even four blocks in a tower. Although his ability to grasp is quite precise, he has not yet achieved the same precision when he puts objects down. He enjoys building the tower—but

enjoys knocking it down even more! He loves to gather many blocks or toys into a pile—and then spread them out again.

He is interested in "many" and "more." For example, he will store six or more blocks in his arms when they are handed to him one at a time. He may then open his arms and delightedly watch them scatter far and wide. And the more noise they make, the better!

During the period from 18 to 24 months, Toddler learns many relationships. He knows where things are. For example, he will go to the refrigerator for his drink or to the door to go out into the yard.

He remembers where things were—where he left his ball or toy. He knows where things, such as his jacket, belong and will go there to find them if asked to do so.

Pictures now have meaning for him and he excitedly finds and points to pictures of familiar objects such as a car, dog, or clock.

Toddler has begun to claim "mine" and to make a distinction between the concepts "you" and "me." He is developing a sense of personal identity and of personal possession.

His spontaneous play is almost completely self-absorbed. He does not yet play with another child, but rather beside or near him. However, he may cry if his companion leaves and may try to follow him.

Toddler has probably been imitating the actions of his parents for several months. His imitations are now less crude and he duplicates more completely what he sees. He may pretend to read the paper or struggle with a parent's briefcase.

At 19 Months Toddler Likes to:
- Climb, climb, climb.
- Dance to music.
- Identify body parts— Eyes, nose, mouth ...
- Play pretend games like driving the car, or ironing the clothes.
- Have stories read to him.
- Hear you count numbers.

Give Toddler:
- Different size boxes, blocks.
- A chance to feed himself finger foods.
- Milk cartons, spoons, clothespins, and other (safe) items to put in containers.
- A pegboard with pegs to fit in and take out.
- Simple 2-3 piece puzzles with knobs.

He loves to do little fetch-and-carry errands around the house. He wants to place things in the grocery cart, to unwrap packages, and peer into paper sacks. His satisfaction in these activities seems to come from doing things which appear to him to be important.

He is almost always busy at something. His "busyness" is learning about objects and their relationships, where things go, what you do with them.

As yet he has shown little interest in how things work. It is enough for him to learn what they are used for. He learns by impersonation—of Mom, Dad, or the family dog.

At nineteen months our Toddler's world is full of wonderful things to do and to try. No wonder he seems to be busy every waking hour! ■

'It's Time for Bed'

Sleep needs: Nineteen-month-olds require an average of about 12 hours of sleep at night. Most also generally need to take a nap in the afternoon.

It is important to be aware, however, that children, like adults, have individual sleep needs. What may be too little sleep for one child may be more than enough for another.

The best way to determine your child's sleep needs is to observe his behavior when it is time to get up in the morning. If he is wide awake and eager to get up, then he is probably getting enough sleep.

If, on the other hand, he is drowsy and reluctant to rise, it is likely that he needs more sleep—even if, at bedtime, he is reluctant to go to sleep.

Bedtime ritual: Most children, at one time or another, try to delay the time for going to bed. They will usually do this for one of two reasons: either they want to prolong their time for being with other people, or they fear the solitude of their bedroom.

The best way for parents to help their child make this transition is by establishing a consistent bedtime ritual.

When handled well, the bedtime ritual can become the most enjoyable part of the day—something to which both parent and child can look forward, a time when they can give undivided attention to one another in a warm and affectionate atmosphere.

The bedtime ritual should usually begin with a calm and quiet time when the child can gradually unwind and relax.

It's wise to give a child some indication that the day's activities are coming to an end, saying, for example, "It's almost bedtime. You can play quietly for a few more minutes. Then it will be time for your bath."

The bedtime ritual should proceed in the same manner every night: quiet play time, getting undressed, taking a bath, putting on pajamas, reading or telling a story, followed by a hug or goodnight kiss, then turning off the main light.

Children at this age will occasionally try to stretch the limits of this bedtime ritual. They may try to engage the parent in rough-house play or want to laugh and giggle uncontrollably while getting undressed. Or they may plead for "just one more story" in order to get the parent to stay longer in the bedroom.

The most effective way to deal with a child's efforts to disrupt the bedtime ritual is by calm and consistent firmness. Establishing a consistent bedtime routine early in a child's life helps establish good habits for years to come.

Bedtime stories: It's important to give some consideration to the choice of appropriate bedtime stories. Involve the child in selecting the book he would like you to read.

Don't be surprised if he selects the same book night after night. To an adult, it may seem boring to read the same story over and over again, but to a young child, it is comforting and reassuring to listen to the same favorite story time and time again.

Parents can help a child choose a book that will help him relax. Just don't let him pick ones which are scary or which over-excite his imagination.

Once the bedtime story has been read, and the light has been turned off, the child should not be allowed to get in the habit of making purely manipulative requests, such as wanting "another drink of water" every night or being escorted to the bathroom "just one more time."

Nighttime fears: Parents can generally distinguish between manipulative behavior and genuine nighttime fears. When a child awakens in terror because of a bad dream, parents should not ignore his fears. At nineteen months of age, children experience genuine nighttime fears.

There are number of things which parents can do to lessen the impact of nighttime fears.

First, it is wise to provide a night light so that the child's bedroom is never completely in darkness.

Second, parents can encourage their child to bring to bed a favorite blanket or stuffed animal which can provide comfort in time of stress.

Nighttime fears, however, are never completely preventable. The best way to help a child deal with them is through some form of physical contact such as a hug or a holding of hands while saying reassuring words in a calm, comforting voice. ("I know you got a bad fright. Everything is okay now. You're safe in my arms.")

Nightmares: Children's nightmares are more intense than fears. They are usually triggered during sleep either by a fear of "monsters" or by a scary daytime experience. Sometimes the child may cry without even awakening. In such cases, it is best to gently wake him up to end the frightening nightmare.

In dealing with nightmares, the most important thing is for the parent to remain calm while providing the child with the reassuring warmth of physical touch.

If your child has frequent nightmares, it is wise to explore if there is some experience in the child's life that is causing emotional discomfort or stress. Sometimes the cause may be obvious, such as inappropriate TV viewing. At other times, the help of a psychologist or physician may be needed to determine the cause.

Night terrors: There is another phenomenon, called "night terrors" which young children sometimes experience.

Typically, the child falls asleep and shortly thereafter experiences hallucinations. Although his eyes may be open, he is not yet awake.

He is so focused on what is terrifying him that he may cry, scream, wrestle and kick while his parents are trying to comfort him.

continued on next page

Progress in Speech

Toddler's repertoire of expressions is increasing steadily. The words which give the essential meaning are the ones used first. At this stage sentences consist of nouns and verbs.

Although the words are usually put together in the correct order, sentences are often incomplete and articles, pronouns and prepositions are usually omitted.

The ability to communicate verbally shapes the child's experiences more fully. As he becomes aware of the fact that everything and everyone has a name, he begins to understand how much he can do with words. His power to influence and control the world and the people in it, including himself, is growing.

He may sometimes resemble a parrot because he now imitates so much of what

continued from previous page

While this behavior may be very distressing to the parents, it is important to remain calm while holding the child and using comforting words.

Even though it may take as long as a half hour for the child to settle down, he will usually stop crying abruptly and go back to sleep. The next day he usually won't remember anything about his "night terror" experience.

Summary: Getting a 19-month-old child to bed can sometimes be a problem in the home. The best way to deal with bedtime problems is:

(a) Determine your child's individual sleep needs;
(b) Establish a consistent bedtime ritual;
(c) Give careful thought to the selection of appropriate bedtime stories;
(d) Give your child the support and comfort he needs whenever he experiences genuine nighttime fears, nightmares, or night terrors.

With proper handling, getting ready to go to sleep can become the most enjoyable part of the day. ■

you do and say. One mother tells a story about the day she despairingly cried, "Oh, Molly!" when her daughter threw down all of the canned goods in the kitchen cabinet.

Immediately after this happened, Molly was heard to mimic her mother's "Oh, Molly!" with identical intonation.

Following this episode, whenever Molly caused trouble, such as spilling milk or soiling her underpants, she would say, "Oh, Molly!" She knew she had done something wrong. Yet mother and daughter could share a laugh about it.

In addition to verbal imitations, you will see Toddler imitating your gestures like applying shaving lotion or spraying deodorant under his arms.

You are probably hearing more "no's" than you like. He understands and uses "no" vigorously. Even though he knows the word "yes," he tends to use "no" or a negative response.

The use of "no" is sometimes serious. But sometimes it means "yes."

Sometimes it is just a demonstration of his independence. For example, you may say, "Bill, will you please come here?" Instead of coming, he runs away, only to return a few minutes later.

This kind of behavior suggests that we not ask Toddler a question unless we are prepared to abide by his "no" response. Better to use the statement, "Bill, Mother wants you to come here," and thereby avoid a conflict.

While each day Toddler comprehends more complicated speech, it is easy to be misled and assume that he understands more than he really does. For example, he has a ready response—"good" or "fine"— to the question, "How are you?"

However, if you happen to ask other questions beginning with "how," you are likely also to get "good" or "fine" as an answer. Similarly, "where" questions may elicit identical answers. You will ask "Where's

Daddy?" and he may say "Downtown." Later, if you ask, "Where's Nicki?" (the dog), he may also answer, "Downtown."

Even his parents will not understand some of Toddler's speech. For example, he may reverse consonants so that the word "cup" is pronounced "puc," or "shoe" may come out as "oosh." Syllable reversals are frequent and sometimes funny; for instance, "hamburger" may become "hamgerburg."

Be prepared for speech sound substitutions (for example, "bite" for "write") and for omissions ("bock" for "block," "ky" for "sky"). And don't be alarmed if you hear sound or syllable repetitions such as "wa-wa-water" for "water."

Above all, don't expect perfect speech from a 19-month-old toddler. Sometimes parents may become unduly irritated by Toddler's imperfect pronunciation. When adults seek perfection in a young child's speech, (for example, demanding that he say "water" instead of "wa-wa"), Toddler is likely to become discouraged.

As a result he may give up trying to talk and revert back to physical gestures, such as pointing, in order to express his needs and wants.

So, if you find yourself being irritated or frustrated at times by Toddler's imperfect speech, be aware that you are not alone. Other parents frequently experience those same feelings. Just try not to let Toddler know that you are irritated or frustrated.

You can correctly repeat the word he has mispronounced, not as a correction but to let him hear the proper sounds. Also, Toddler needs all the praise he can get for making his best effort.

To understand what Toddler's world is like, imagine that you are living in a foreign country where you can't speak the language of the people. Just think how much you would appreciate a word of praise for your best attempt to make yourself understood in that language, even if your speech were likely to be mainly unintelligible to others. ■

More About Containers

In Month 11 of *Growing Child* we talked about Baby's fascination with containers. In the months since, Toddler has continued her interest in objects that hold other objects. But her use of containers has become more mature and advanced.

Earlier, Toddler was interested in the very idea of containment, and in the acts of putting in and dumping out. She would put just a few objects into a container before dumping them out again.

But now she will try to put in as many objects as possible, seeming to prefer a large number of small items rather than a small number of large items.

She will notice how they sound when they strike the empty container, how the sound changes when the container is partly full, how the items look when they are all crammed together.

She will take delight in completely filling the container if she can, especially if the job does not take too long. In fact, you can get a rough idea of her developing attention span by observing how long she will stay at the task of filling a container.

All of this is in line with Toddler's gradual shift of interest from the action she can perform with an object to the way objects relate to one another.

The clinking sounds, the appearance of partially filled and completely filled containers are lessons in relationships between objects. They are further adventures in time and space.

She seems to need innumerable repetitions and variations before her curiosity is satisfied. Each of these deceptively simple concepts of time and space involves an enormous adventure in discovering laws of nature in the world around her. These are lessons that Toddler takes very seriously.

Very soon now will come another dimension of Toddler's interest in containers:
the idea that the way in which objects are put into containers determines whether or not they can go in at all.

That is, if an object is anything but perfectly round, whether it will go through a small opening will depend not only on its size but on the way it is held, turned and fitted into the opening.

Our description of this idea, while it took several words, doesn't begin to describe the complexity of the learning task for Toddler as she encounters the task for the first time.

Consider the act of putting a rectangular block through the neck of a jar. It involves the perception of size and shape of both the object and the opening as well as the finer coordination of hand with eye.

These are the kinds of judgments and skills that we use constantly throughout life without realizing their complexity.

For Toddler, the experience is one of learning the relationship between cause and effect. This gives her a further understanding of how the world works and a greater sense of power.

This fascination with new discoveries, given proper materials with which to work, leads her to higher levels of knowledge and performance.

Let's consider again the jar problem a little more carefully. By now Toddler's sense of relative size is fairly well developed. She will not try to insert an object if it is definitely too large for the opening. This in itself involves a fairly complicated judgment.

For an object that is approximately the same size as the opening, Toddler will test the fit. If the block is nearly square, Toddler will use the "force" method: slamming the block against the opening.

If it is not turned the right way, it will not go in, and Toddler will probably give up the attempt if she is left to do the task by herself.

Suppose the block is longer, say twice as long as it is wide. Toddler will probably attempt to insert it, evidently sensing that it can go into the jar.

That is, there is an awareness of the similarity of the small end of the block to the jar opening.

Even so, she is likely to start out by forcing the block against the opening any old way. Then she may attempt to turn the block so as to match the small end to the opening.

When this idea does not work, she may try the more highly differentiated actions of which she is capable, such as holding the block in her fingers and bending her wrist, so as to position the block more exactly.

This two-stage order of actions will occur even though she may have used a more refined method on a previous container. The idea of first turning the block a certain way has not yet developed as a consistent idea.

Now think of an object that is very long in relation to its width, such as a clothespin. Its length determines the way it should be turned so as to go into the jar. Toddler will have no trouble turning it the proper way to begin with.

Yet even with this strong visual clue, Toddler's contact with the jar opening may be partly a matter of feel. The tip of the clothespin may fall across the opening, then be guided inside by feel.

At this stage, Toddler's visual system has not become dominant over her sense of touch. For new tasks, her hand and sense of feel lead her eye rather than the eye directing the hand.

If you watch Toddler closely while she fills containers with various kinds of objects, you will see the actions we have described.

continued on next page

You will notice that she shows more interest in smaller containers, especially those that have constricted openings.

This suggests the kind of toy containers that will hold her attention in the future. Right now a one quart plastic jar will give her an excellent chance to practice new ways of putting thing into containers.

An ordinary quart jar has a less constricted mouth but may be easier for her to start with if she has not filled small containers before. In-between in difficulty is a square quart jar

Toddler will learn more quickly how to turn the objects if you first give her long narrow items like clothespins or spoons. She should have enough to fill the jar completely if she wants. (Just remember not to get upset if Toddler just wants to play with the clothespins or spoons rather than put them in the container!)

The narrow neck poses another challenging problem when it comes to emptying the objects. Simply tipping the container or holding it upside down will not empty out all the items.

She must shake the jar, an activity she will do very happily and industriously. She will perhaps even insert her hand or finger to break up any logjams that form.

After she has found it easy to insert and retrieve these long narrow objects, you can give Toddler some shorter items like dominoes or rubber erasers. These require closer inspection to tell how they should be used.

Toddler will now be ready for a more difficult task: fitting a specific object into a hole that is just its own size and shape.

As a start, you might cut from the side of a small cardboard box a square hole the size of her blocks and a round hole big enough for a small ball. Or perhaps a slot just big enough to accept bottle caps or poker chips.

A three-sided cut on another side will make a handy retrieval flap for the blocks, ball or caps.

The slot is the easiest to fit. It requires only that she present the edge of the disc to the slot, holding it the way she normally holds such an object anyway.

The block is more difficult. To fit it to the square holes she must hold the block properly in three different planes by rotating her wrist in unaccustomed directions.

If you use balls and blocks you will notice that, while her hand-eye coordination is less than perfect, it doesn't take her long to learn which opening takes which object, even if the overall sizes are nearly the same.

Telling a circle from a square, or more exactly, telling a round figure from one that has corners, is a perceptual skill that develops very early.

In a few months Toddler will outgrow the cardboard box. We suggest you look for a commercial shape-sorting box that will serve her for a long time to come.

These toys are colorful, durable, and have fairly complex shapes that will test her growing discrimination and visual-motor skills. ∎

Care of Teeth

One of the best ways to protect your child's dental health is to be a good role model. Parents are their child's first teacher and regular care for your own teeth is a good place to start.

"Baby" teeth

An often-repeated remark is that cavities in baby teeth don't matter because they'll soon be replaced by permanent teeth. That isn't necessarily true. Your dentist is your best advisor —permanent teeth can be effected by cavities in a child's baby's teeth. That's why an early dental check is important.

Dental visits

• The first routine dental exam is usually scheduled sometime during the child's first year or within six months after the first tooth comes in.

Most often little treatment is required and the first visit helps the child become acquainted with the dentist and aware of the surroundings in the dental office. Parents can also use this time to ask questions about the care of the child's teeth and the dentist's recommentations.

Your child's physician may refer you to a dentist earlier if he or she notices any abnormality before that time. After that first visit, regular dental exams usually occur every 6-12 months.

Brushing

• The most important times to brush teeth are before bed and after meals.

• Young children's teeth should be brushed with a soft-bristled infant toothbrush.

• Parental supervision of a child's tooth-brushing is recommended until six-eight years of age.

• Children under four years of age need a different brushing technique than adults.

The "scrub" technique is recommended in which the surfaces of the teeth are cleansed by using a small circular scrubbing motion with the bristles of the toothbrush. The direction of the scrubbing doesn't

Children under four years of age need a different brushing technique than adults. The "scrub" technique is recommended in which the surfaces of the teeth are cleansed by using a small circular scrubbing motion with the bristles of the toothbrush.

Growing Child.

P. O. Box 2505 • W Lafayette, IN 47996
(800) 927-7289
©Growing Child, Inc.
www.GrowingChild.com

Contributing Authors

Phil Bach, O.D., Ph.D.
Miriam Bender, Ph.D.
Joseph Braga, Ed.D.
Laurie Braga, Ph.D.
George Early, Ph.D.
Carol R. Gestwicki, M.S.
Liam Grimley, Ph.D.
Robert Hannemann, M.D., F.A.A.P.
Sylvia Kottler, M.S.
Bill Peterson, Ph.D.

matter but each tooth should be cleaned thoroughly—top and bottom, inside and outside.

Young children, naturally, spend the most time on the front teeth, so a quick check after brushing and gentle suggestions help the process.

• For optimal brushing, the toothbrush should be changed every three-four months.

• If a child has had a cold or flu, the toothbrush should be changed to avoid the transmission of germs.

• No more than a pea-sized amount of fluoride toothpaste should be used. If a larger amount is used, it is more likely to be swallowed—which, for children under six years of age, may lead to white or brown spots on teeth.

Also, tell your child not to swallow the toothpaste even though it is difficult at this early age to teach a child to rinse and spit.

Flossing

• Flossing may be introduced when any baby teeth are touching each other.

Once the teeth start to fit closely, usually between the ages of two and six, parents should begin to teach their children to floss daily.

Don't worry if the child's gums bleed a little at first: this is quite common.It should stop after a few days but if not, consult your dentist.

It is important that flossing is carefully taught and supervised by parents until the child reaches 10 years of age.

A number of factors are necessary for good oral hygiene, starting at a very young age including proper nutrition, brushing and flossing, dental check-ups and fluoride needs.

Parents are in charge of the habits and attitudes which are essential to maintain a healthy dental care routine for life. Help make those smiles beautiful for life. ∎

Play is children's way of perceiving the world they have been called upon to change.

Maxim Gorki

Gaining New Heights

From now until Toddler reaches the ripe old age of two, you may wonder whether she could be part mountain goat!

In previous months she learned that her arms and legs could move her from one place to another horizontally. Now she begins to move with her body in a vertical position.

When Toddler explores her surroundings from an upright position, her world begins to look quite different. She can now see objects which remained hidden from her while she crawled on hands and knees.

Even if she could have seen them previously when she pulled to a standing position, she couldn't reach them, no matter how hard she stretched. Being able to reach these objects now stimulates her desire to explore.

Her feet are serving her pretty well. She walks easily, often carrying with her a favorite toy or some object of interest. She doesn't really run yet, but she hurries along when excited about something.

She has also already begun to creep up short flights of stairs. She may even walk up these short flights when her hand is held or when she is holding onto a convenient railing.

Of course, she brings one foot, then the other, to each step in turn in what we call "marking time." However, she cannot descend the stairs that way for some time. Instead she will creep down backwards, first one foot, then the other.

It will be several more months before Toddler develops the coordination necessary to achieve the left-right alternate foot movement that adults use when going downstairs. Even then, she may prefer to back down on her hands and knees.

Chances are Toddler won't stop with climbing stairs. She will climb onto chairs and from there to a table to reach what she wants.

Of course, some children are by nature more daring than others. They will climb anything climbable, moving from chair to bookcase or dresser or chest of drawers.

The adventurous spirit leads the child to reach upward and explore things above her. The ability to climb up comes soon after walking. Once she has climbed up, she may cry indignantly because she doesn't know how to get back down. The ability to climb down comes after learning to climb up.

How can you handle the panic that strikes when you find your child on a table or atop a chest of drawers?

You don't want her to fall and hurt herself. Neither do you want to dampen her enthusiasm for exploration. Certainly you don't want to make your child a "fraidy-cat," too timid to explore and try out new skills.

So, be calm. Don't communicate your fright to Toddler. Help her down, but don't snatch her up while comforting and scolding her simultaneously. When you help her down you are teaching her how to get down safely.

Communicate the fact that tables and chests are not safe for climbing. But reserve your instruction until after your child is safely on the ground and after you have had an opportunity to calm down. In that way, your words of instruction will more likely be helpful to your child.

Toddler's urge to climb is your cue to provide climbable objects other than furniture. Outdoor play equipment with a short ladder to climb or steps up to a slide would be good. Small slides are ideal because a child climbs up—but slides down.

Small plastic slides with three steps up to the top are available at toy or department stores. "Do-it-yourselfers" can find plans for other outdoor equipment in home improvement magazines.

Instead of discouraging climbing, provide Toddler with safe climbing experiences such piles of cushions or bolsters, and boxes to climb into and out of.

By climbing, Toddler is learning about height and depth, about how to work her arms and legs together, about balance and holding on, and about how things look from "up there."

We want her to learn all these things and to learn them safely. ■

At 20 Months Toddler Likes to:
• Dig and make a mess.
• Take things apart.
• Carry and help.

Give Toddler:
• A case to carry things in.
• Little chores to do.
• Things to take apart.
• Your patience.

Good Discipline

With an active almost-two-year-old in the house, now is an appropriate time to think about good discipline—what it is and what it is not.

Toddler is now at a stage when he needs good discipline to learn acceptable behavior. Good discipline should: (1) Provide structure; (2) Be positive; (3) Be specific; (4) Be consistent; and (5) Reward desirable behavior.

Providing your child with structure in his life is a key ingredient for the development of his self-concept. Structure implies order and the setting of boundaries.

At twenty months Toddler has difficulty finding order in his many new experiences. Parents can help if they break a task into small components. ("Pick up your teddy bear off the floor. Put it on the couch.")

A child who spends part of the day, for example, with one parent and part with another, weekends with grandparents and the rest of the time in still other settings, is living his life in several different worlds.

Just when he thinks he has mastered the rules of one environment, he discovers a contradictory set of rules in a different environment.

No wonder he becomes confused—and at times rebellious.

Even within the same home environment, keeping to a regular schedule for mealtime and bedtime will help Toddler more easily develop patterns of desirable behavior.

The second guideline is to be positive in your approach. Positive commands ("Walk to the table") are more effective than negative ones ("Don't run to the table!").

Being firm with your child does not mean that you have to shout or spank. For discipline to be effective it must be geared to your child's stage of development.

Knowing that it is perfectly normal for a 20-month-old to be very active—and that

activity is necessary for learning—should help you to avoid yelling at him for being so active. Your authority will be more effective when it is asserted quietly and with warmth.

Before you impose a new rule or issue a command, make sure you have temporarily removed all distractions so that you have your child's full attention.

If you allow him to continue playing with his truck or other toy while you are talking to him, you can be sure that you do not have his attention.

Once you have gained his attention, be as specific as possible about what you want him to do. "Watch what you're doing" is too vague a command for a twenty-month-old child to understand.

Instead, saying "I want you to keep your trucks on the floor—and not on the good dining room table" is more specific and easier for your child to understand and obey.

Above all, be consistent in your disciplinary practices. Both parents should strive for basic agreement about what is considered acceptable behavior.

Otherwise your child will become frustrated and even defiant as a result of the basic unfairness of inconsistent treatment.

Another source of inconsistency is idle threats ("That's the last time I'll take you to the store with me.") which a parent won't or can't carry out.

Eventually the child will learn to "tune out" what the parent says and a breakdown in discipline will occur.

The most difficult times for parents to be consistent with discipline is when they are tired or in a hurry. Parents who have been working all day are likely to come home tired.

In such cases their loss of patience with their 20-month-old's very active behavior may be more the result of their tiredness than of Toddler's specific behavior.

Parents of children of this age have often been heard to ask: "Why is it that it's always when I'm in a hurry that Toddler decides to act up?"

The reason is simple. At this age Toddler is not able to handle the pressure of being rushed. For example, before going to the store, it will be good to take the time to tell him in advance what you plan to do. That way his mind has time to absorb the change in his environment and adjust accordingly.

Lastly, good discipline implies rewarding good behavior, much more so than punishing undesirable behavior.

One of your child's most basic needs is the need for attention. Undesirable behavior may often be the child's way of seeking attention.

If the parent can ignore undesirable behavior and reward the opposite, desirable behavior, then the child not only gets the needed attention but he gets it in a way that teaches him desirable behavior.

What kinds of rewards should we give to Toddler? At this age tangible rewards are the more effective way to get good habits started. A tangible reward need not be a new toy—it may be a hug or a kiss.

Later, as good habits become established, praise and the child's own sense of self-satisfaction will gradually take the place of purely tangible rewards.

For rewards to be effective at this age, they should be immediate. Toddler doesn't yet have the same sense of time that adults have.

The sooner the reward is given after the desirable behavior, the easier it is for Toddler to form the link between the behavior and the reward.

Good discipline in the home not only makes life easier for the parents but it also provides the child with a more structured, more positive, more specific, and more consistent environment in which to grow and develop. ∎

Blocks Are The Perfect Playthings

Of all the toys that have been invented, perhaps the most versatile and widely used by preschoolers is a set of blocks. Their appeal is universal, and Toddler will play happily with them for hours.

In understanding the fascination that blocks can hold at this age, it is helpful to look at a perceptual principle that affects Toddler's behavior, now and later. The principle is called "emergent form." An example will help clarify what we mean.

Suppose we have a stick of a certain roundness, length, texture and so forth. We can learn about the stick's appearance and become quite familiar with it.

If we take another identical stick, and cross it with the first, we form a cross, or X shape.

A new unit has been created, one that has its own individuality and uniqueness. The appearance of this new unit is quite different from what we would imagine by simply considering the two sticks alone. It is more than the simple sum of the parts of which it is made.

A more striking example is the square. It is composed of four simple straight lines, all alike. But when these single lines are placed at right angles to each other, a new impression emerges, that of squareness.

This form has a distinctive quality all its own. Again, it is more than the sum of the parts. It has its own perceptual existence.

In each case the new form has "emerged" almost magically from simpler parts. Thus it is called an "emergent form."

Emergent forms do not have to arise from items that are connected to each other.

The following picture might be thought of as six lines, but we usually see them as three pairs of lines.

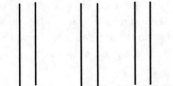

Our perception organizes the lines automatically into pairs because of the difference in spacing between the lines.

This is called the "principle of proximity". It is another kind of emergent form.

Or consider the following picture:

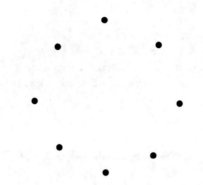

Here we see a circle rather than eight dots. The dots make a bare outline of a circle. Perceptually we close it in to recognize its circleness.

The principle here is called "closure," and it is still another kind of emergent form.

Gestalt psychologists believe we are born with the perceptual ability to organize some basic elements into emergent forms. But other kinds of emergent forms may arise or take on special importance through learning.

It is likely that Baby's reaction to the face described in Month 5 is a result of his learning about the form of a "face" through experience with many examples of people's faces.

A brick house is rarely seen as a collection of bricks, since its function is well known. But we might be very conscious of the bricks and their arrangement in a different structure such as a brick cistern if we were not familiar with such a structure.

A printed word is an emergent form composed of letters. If we know the word, we see it as a single unit. As we read it, we may not even be aware of the individual letters.

If we look at Toddler's blocks in this way, we see that they can be put together to create emergent forms which, to Toddler at least, are completely new experiences in vision.

Blocks are wonderfully easy to manipulate. Toddler will group and regroup them to form as many combinations as he can.

When the blocks are piled together, they look different than when they are apart. Two small groups look different than one big group. If two or more blocks touch each other, they form a distinctive pattern.

When he stacks the blocks, two, three or as high as he can, the tower formed is a far cry from individual blocks scattered on the floor. Patterns can be undone and the tower allowed to fall.

Toddler takes as much pleasure in the undoing as in the doing. This is not only because a falling tower creates an interesting effect in itself, but because it demonstrates to him that the original effect is reversible.

When he can reverse an effect at will, the principle behind it becomes more understandable, permanent and meaningful to him.

Gradually Toddler will see the resemblance between his block creations and objects in his world. He will begin to give some of these structures names, like "house," "chair" and "chimney."

As these structures take on new meaning, he will concentrate his attention on them, striving for greater accuracy in modeling the structures after real objects or embellishing or varying them according to his imagination.

A basic set of wooden unit blocks is a good investment to be used for many years. ■

Fun With Blocks

There are many things that can be done with blocks. In your play with Toddler, you can introduce him to new possibilities. You can help with some fascinating activities that he cannot do by himself.

This kind of guided adult participation helps lead a child to learn new abilities that are not yet at the child's developmental level of independent play and problem solving.

Here are just a few ideas to get you started.

• Hold a block in a big spoon without dropping it. Can Toddler imitate what you just did?

• If blocks are placed exactly together, they make their own floor that a little man could walk on. Space the blocks like stepping stones and let your two fingers "walk" the blocks.

Does Toddler imitate you? Can a little doll hop or step along the blocks without falling off?

• Stacking blocks is an activity of recurring interest to him. It challenges his developing hand-eye coordination as he creates new and interesting forms.

When Toddler reaches his limit as to the number of blocks he can successfully stack, you can place the blocks against the side of a cardboard box. See if he catches on to this method as a way to build a taller tower.

Many months from now he will get the idea of starting with many blocks as a base and gradually tapering the size of the tower as he builds it up.

• Place the blocks at intervals around the outside of a round canister, then remove the canister. Trace their circular pattern with your finger and say, "See how the blocks make a circle."

Similarly you could create a square. Here the blocks can be unconnected, and the shape can be identified as a square by the principle of closure. Toddler should be able to describe such forms as soon as he knows the names for shapes like circle and square.

• Lay a flat piece of wood across the top of a can, and place a block at each end so they are in balance. Have him pick up one block and notice his surprise as the other block and the piece of wood tumble to the floor.

• Arrange four blocks so that their sides enclose a square. Then cover the opening with a fifth block. You have a container, a secret compartment that can hide a small object.

Blocks are nearly limitless in their possibilities for learning. Playing with your toddler in order to add activities and ideas for using blocks is a good idea. He also will need lots of time to explore and manipulate them on his own.

Let Toddler drop something small into the hole. You can then cover the hole with the fifth block. Does Toddler quickly remove the top block to rediscover the object?

• Fasten a paper napkin across the opening of a coffee can with a rubber band. How many blocks can be stacked on the napkin before it breaks and they fall into the can with a clatter?

This is apt to be a startling effect for Toddler. After watching you make such an interesting thing happen, he will probably be eager to try it himself.

• How high does one end of a book have to be tilted before a block sitting on the end will slide?

• A fascinating effect is to let a block slide down an inclined surface and drop into an open can.

Toddler will be eager to try sending the object down the ramp. He will gladly accept your help, for he cannot hold the runway and the object at the same time.

If, after a few hits in the can, you tilt the ramp slightly to the side, the object will no longer find its way into the can.

This is a fine mystery to him, for the cause of the error is not at all evident. But it should keep him coming back.

Before long you can show Toddler how to use the blocks to support an inclined surface for use when he is on his own.

• A "snake" can be made by tying several blocks a few inches apart on a string. Toddler will be interested as you slowly lift one end of the string to make the snake rise from the floor into the air.

Let it collapse in segments as you lower it again.

When he takes the string he will probably make broad sweeping movements of his arm, causing the string of blocks to weave back and forth on the floor.

• Can Toddler hold the string of blocks at one end and lower it into an upright shoebox with its end cut out?

• While the blocks are on the string, weight the unheld end of the string. Over a sink lower the blocks into a coffee can nearly full of water. Soon the water will overflow.

Toddler will not begin to understand the principle that the volume of the blocks displaces an equal volume of water. But he will experience the effect. That is really the important thing at this stage.

You could ask him, "What made the water go out? Did the blocks push the water out?"

Next, pull the string of blocks out. The water level in the can will fall. Ease them back in and the level will rise again. This is a readily reversible effect.

continued on next page

Learning Games

In order to help Toddler develop better language and perceptual-motor skills, here are some good games you can play using simple materials that are probably available in your home.

1. Materials: Toddler's favorite doll or stuffed animal.

Playacting can help Toddler increase his vocabulary of action words (verbs) and directional words (prepositions).

Have Toddler act out commands using his animal or doll: "Shake his head," "wave his arm," "sit him down," "stand him up."

2. Materials: Doll, doll furniture, cup, spoon.

Here is a second playacting game to increase his vocabulary of objects (nouns).

Place the doll near a suitable doll chair and put a cup on the doll table.

Tell Toddler, "Dolly wants to sit down in the chair." If the doll and chair are very small, he'll need some help.

Next tell him, "Dolly wants a drink. Give Dolly a drink." Don't expect precision. He may offer the cup to an area between the forehead and navel.

Should he inform you that Dolly has nothing to drink, you can increase the drama by putting a few tiny pieces of paper in the cup. Finally offer him a facial tissue and tell him, "Wipe Dolly's nose."

3. Materials: Blocks.

Toddler will learn about direction and sequence through many activities using a variety of materials.

You start a tower by handing Toddler blocks, one at a time. Use gestures and tell him, "Put it up here." Pointing to another block, invite him to continue: "Take the block, put it up here!"

You may find him becoming absorbed in knocking down the tower. But don't be disappointed. Use the experience to teach the directional word "down"—"The blocks have fallen down!"

4. Materials: Three small boxes and a toy dog small enough to be easily covered by the boxes.

Place the boxes in a row about three inches apart. Tell Toddler, "Look, I'm going to hide the doggie." Be certain he is watching as you hide the animal, first, under the middle box.

Hold his hands briefly in order to delay his response. Then say "Find the doggie."

Next hide the animal under the box on the left and repeat the instruction: "Find the doggie." Finally, hide it under the box on the right, repeating the same instruction.

In playing these learning games, it is best not to spend too much time on any one activity as a child of this age becomes tired easily. It is better to return to the games for several short periods throughout the day than to have one long session.

Better learning will occur if these activities are planned as fun games for both Toddler and parents. ■

continued from previous page

Toddler should have enough muscle control by now that he can raise and lower the string in imitation of what you did.

A single block will float on the surface of the water. "The block is light. It floats."

Drop a penny in. "A penny is heavy. It sinks." No matter that the penny is lighter and smaller than the block. Toddler will see each in relation to the water.

Be sure that you leave Toddler lots of time and supervised freedom to explore the blocks and water independently.

All of this illustrates that blocks are nearly limitless in their possibilities for learning. Occasionally playing with your toddler in order to add activities and ideas for using them is a good idea, but he needs lots of time to explore and manipulate them on his own.

Watch him and you will be amazed at the ideas he comes up with independently. You may now have some idea why blocks have been favorites of preschoolers for quite a long time.

Not only does Toddler have lots of fun with blocks, but through using them, he is gradually discovering basic scientific concepts of shape, space, balance, weight and number—all of which are important in establishing a foundation for later learning.

■

Bruce: A True Story

Bruce was in the fourth grade and he was having some problems. He was intelligent, but he couldn't do his schoolwork. When he took standardized achievement tests, he always scored near the bottom.

He also had a real knack for getting into trouble. He wouldn't stay in his seat, he teased other students, and he talked out of turn.

When the teacher gave him an assignment, he would begin to work right away, but he seldom finished. He was constantly disrupting the class, and his teacher was "climbing the walls" over his behavior.

When things got completely out of hand, she would send him to the principal.

One day while Bruce was cooling his heels in the principal's office, back in his classroom the teacher was giving out the test booklets for a standardized achievement test, the sort of test where Bruce always wound up on the bottom.

About ten minutes before the allotted test time expired, in walked Bruce, newly returned from his encounter with the principal.

"Oh, no," thought the teacher. "I really wanted every child to take this test and here comes Bruce at the very end of it."

She solved the problem in a very straightforward way. "Bruce," she said, "let's you and I go over to this quiet corner. I'll read the questions on this test to you. You tell me the answers and I'll write them down in the test booklet." And this is just what they did.

When the teacher scored Bruce's test results, she was astounded to discover that Bruce was at the very top of the scale instead of at the bottom where he usually stood.

Why did Bruce do so well on a test where the teacher read the questions to him and then marked down his answers on the score sheet?

Why did he do so poorly when he was left on his own to deal with the printed instructions?

The thing that comes to mind first is that Bruce understood quite clearly what he heard, but he had problems in getting information visually from the printed page.

It seems that he learned well with his ears but learned poorly with his eyes.

Growing Child

P. O. Box 2505 • W Lafayette, IN 47996
(800) 927-7289
©Growing Child, Inc.
www.GrowingChild.com

Contributing Authors

Phil Bach, O.D., Ph.D.
Miriam Bender, Ph.D.
Joseph Braga, Ed.D.
Laurie Braga, Ph.D.
George Early, Ph.D.
Carol R. Gestwicki, M.S.
Liam Grimley, Ph.D.
Robert Hannemann, M.D., F.A.A.P.
Sylvia Kottler, M.S.
Bill Peterson, Ph.D.

When he had to read the questions in the test booklet and then write down his answers or make marks in the proper places, he was in trouble.

So we need to find out if Bruce has an eye problem that results in a reading disability, or has a problem in writing down his answers due to poor eye-hand coordination.

Bruce is not all that unusual. We who write for *Growing Child* have worked with several thousand children who were very much like Bruce.

There are several million children like him in schools today. Our experience suggests strongly that the typical classroom has several Bruces in it.

Each of these children, like Bruce, is very special and each has his own particular cluster of problems. But we are convinced that each child like Bruce has one thing in common: What he sees, hears and feels somehow doesn't "match up."

In Bruce's case, what his eyes saw did not match what his ears heard or what his hand was doing.

Whenever we really dig beneath the surface with a child like Bruce, we often find that he may not have had enough of these early developmental experiences which we tell you about each month in *Growing Child*.

For example, if you look back at "More About Containers" in Month 19, you'll notice that a major emphasis is upon Toddler's using his eyes and hands together.

It is in such early explorations that a child learns how to "put it all together." We think it is extremely important that toddlers have such early experiences.

This is really one function of *Growing Child*—to tell parents about the importance of early childhood experiences.

We want to cut down, if possible, the number of children who later might experience learning problems in school. ∎

Children are small people who are not permitted to act as their parents did at that age.

Josephus Henry

Helping Toddler Express Feelings

As Toddler continues his path toward self-identity, he will be expressing his feelings more and more often.

Sometimes he will use words. At other times he will act out by using negative behavior.

Believe it or not, it is healthy for Toddler to express negative feelings to get them out of his system. In this way he can eventually learn how to express those feelings in an appropriate manner. He will also learn how to control the actions that may accompany his feelings.

When adults with psychological problems go to a therapist, they usually must learn how to express their feelings appropriately.

Children, on the other hand, have a natural tendency to express their feelings openly as long as their parents don't try to repress them.

How often have you witnessed two little children fighting fiercely in the morning and becoming intimate "buddies" in the afternoon? And how often do their parents take a long time to overcome the grudge aroused by a disagreement?

Little children should be permitted to express themselves. They also should be helped to understand that their parents appreciate how they feel. How can parents do this?

Psychologists Carl Rogers and Haim Ginott have recommended that parents should "reflect feelings"—demonstrate that you genuinely understand how the

child feels by putting his feelings into words and reflecting them back to him, like a mirror.

With a toddler this is sometimes easier whenever you can borrow his very own words. Let's take an example: Toddler comes to you crying because older brother Billy hit him. Our usual response may have been to call a conference and conduct an interrogation: "Now, tell me, who started it?"

However, the approach of reflecting feelings removes you from the role of police officer and referee.

Instead, when you receive a complaint like, "Billy hit me," you can answer with more understanding: "You're crying and you're angry because Billy hit you."

What you have done is put his feelings into words and these feelings are reflected back to him.

At 21 Months Toddler Likes to:
• Point to things in books.
• Turn pages.
• Put things together.
• Make marks on paper.

Give Toddler:
• Books with pictures.
• Toys to build with.
• Crayons and paper.
• Small vehicles, animals and figures for beginning pretend play.

When you do this, he knows that you not only know what happened, but you also understand how he feels. This also shows acceptance and respect for his feelings, a basis for healthy emotional development.

This is particularly important for the child whose vocabulary is not yet adequate to convey his feelings. He is reassured that you understand him and his feelings when you say the words for him.

Finally, when you reflect feelings, you help a child to make a perceptual-motor match: He matches the words to an action and to the feelings that accompany the action. ■

Children have a natural tendency to express their feelings openly as long as their parents don't try to repress them.

Toddler's First "See-Feel-Talk" Notebook

A "See-Feel-Talk" notebook will arouse Toddler's interest. Its purpose is to stimulate his perceptual-motor development.

It will also stimulate his speech and language comprehension.

You can make this book by getting a simple organizer notebook with pockets on each page. Into each pocket put one of the items listed in the table. (See box).

This notebook will be tailor-made for Toddler since it is multisensory. It offers plenty of opportunities to see and feel things that you can talk about and ask questions about.

Before each playtime you can think of some different items to put in the pockets.

For example, if you want to teach Toddler about nature, you could put a leaf in one pocket, a flower in another, a twig in a third, pictures of each of the four seasons in another, and so on.

Because of the variety, Toddler will look forward to seeing what is in his notebook each playtime.

Just remember to repeat some of the items used earlier.

After a while, you will discover which items are Toddler's favorites.

Next time you use the notebook, these will be good items to begin with. They will immediately arouse Toddler's interest in what you are doing. You can then introduce new items to increase his learning.

Toddler will have fun identifying the objects with which he is already familiar. This helps to reinforce the vocabulary and perceptual-motor learning that has previously taken place.

It also becomes the solid foundation on which new learning can be built. If Toddler appears to lose interest in what you are doing, it is best to put the notebook aside for another time.

Then begin again with the items he appears to enjoy the most. ∎

Some Items for the "See-Feel-Talk" Notebook

MATERIALS	HOW WILL THEY STIMULATE PERCEPTUAL-MOTOR DEVELOPMENT
Heavy duty zipper	Hand-eye exploration and manipulation.
Unbreakable mirror	Self-awareness; identification of the parts of the head by pointing to each one (eyes, ears, nose).
Bright, colorful pictures of familiar objects	The pictures should be two-dimensional likenesses of some three-dimensional objects he has experienced.
Scrap materials (terry cloth, vinyl, sandpaper, velvet, corduroy, satin, fake fur)	Visual-tactual discriminations of different textures which he can first see without touching, then touch with his eyes covered and finally experience by both sight and touch.

MATERIALS	HOW WILL THEY STIMULATE SPEECH AND LANGUAGE COMPREHENSION
Heavy duty zipper	Learning words to accompany the action. For example, "open," "close," "zip," "un-zip," "up," "down."
Unbreakable mirror	Examining and naming different body parts. For example, "hair," "eyes," "teeth," "mouth," "chin," "tongue."
Bright, colorful pictures of familiar objects	Naming the people and objects in each picture; discussing their size, shape, color, sex, dress, or actions.
Scrap materials (terry cloth, vinyl, sandpaper, velvet, corduroy, satin, fake fur)	Identifying the individual sensations: "rough," "smooth," "soft," "hard," "fuzzy," "bumpy."

Talking: Getting It Together

Nearly all children at age 21 months are making spontaneous word combinations such as "eat cookie." Jargon is dropping out in favor of speech with gestures accompanying it.

Examples of his speech indicate how egocentric and self-centered Toddler is—everything he says involves himself, his actions, needs, desires, and possessions.

What kinds of combinations are most frequently heard? "Give me a cracker," "Do it," "Come here," "Drink water."

You will observe that Toddler's two-word combinations generally omit the unimportant words, those which don't convey meaning. He will say, "Sit lap," "Build blocks," "Come me." In each of these it is the pronouns and prepositions which are ignored.

This is called "telegraphic speech" which uses only important words. The child may refer to himself by name, in the third person.

At 21 months Toddler hasn't straightened out the use of pronouns. When he refers to himself he doesn't use the word "myself." Instead he may substitute "me" by saying, "Hurt me self." On the other hand, when asked "Where's Billy?", he answers, "Here he is!" rather than "Here I am!"

If he wets his training pants and wants to be changed, he may say "Change his diaper" not "my diaper." As a matter of fact, whenever possible he uses his own name, "Billy do it" instead of "I'll do it." Should you ask who something is for, Toddler may reply "Billy for" rather than "for Billy."

Before now, one of Toddler's most frequently used words was "no." Now he can use the word "yes" appropriately.

Toddler's speech is increasing at such a pace that it is sometimes difficult to understand many of his new words. He may, for example, say "gog" for "dog," "dood" for "good," "sish" for "fish," "talebec" for "table."

We have said in earlier issues of **Growing Child** that distinct speech cannot be expected for at least another year. Insisting that Toddler repeat a word correctly is rarely useful. If he could say it right, he'd do it without your reminder.

Baby talk is only of concern when a youngster is no longer a toddler. Preschoolers can be corrected in their speech in later years when they should have the skills to do something about it.

Research studies indicate that:

(1) Parents who talk frequently to their yound child, and (2) who listen uncritically at this age to Toddler's word combinations, play an important part in their child's language development.

There also appears to be general agreement that (3) for the first two or three years, girls are generally more advanced than boys in language development, and (4) the period between 21-24 months is one of rapid language and speech acquisition for both boys and girls.

Knowing then how important the next three months will be, the accompanying article includes some new activities to enhance Toddler's comprehension and production of language. ∎

Finger Play Games

At 21 months, Toddler loves to watch you play finger games which help to stretch her imagination. We suggest you try these:

"Here's a ball for Baby," (Make a ball by cupping both hands together.)
"Big and soft and round."
"Here is Baby's hammer," (Use right fist to pound on the left hand.)
"See how she can pound."
"Here are Baby's soldiers," (Hold up fingers of both hands.)
"Standing in a row."
"Here's the Baby's trumpet," (Form trumpet by putting right and left fists in front of mouth.)
"Toot, toot, toot, toot."
"Here's the way the Baby,"
"Plays at peek-a-boo."
(Cover eyes with both hands and peek through fingers or side of hand.)
"And here's the Baby's cradle
To rock the baby bye." (Interlace fingers of both hands with fingers down. Shape cradle by pointing index fingers and little fingers).

Here's another one:

"The teensie weensie spider went up the water spout." (Put together thumb of one hand and second finger of the other hand to "walk" upwards.)
"Down came the rain and washed the spider out." (Spread fingers out wide and make downward trickling motion.)
"Out came the sun and dried up all the rain." (Make circle with fingers and hold up high.)

"Then the teensie weensie spider went up the spout again!" (Repeat first gesture.)
Visit your local library and look for additional finger play games. ∎

Deductive Thinking

Every few months we look at significant milestones in the development of Toddler's thinking and intellectual ability.

We've talked before about Toddler's tendency to try doing the same thing in different ways, such as dropping things, to see what happens to them under different conditions.

This shows she can get the idea that these objects and actions are apart from her body. Some things go their own way without her. Other things need to be examined to be better understood.

Toddler is developing a new ability, one that will help her use her imagination and solve problems faster than before. It is the ability to combine two or more ideas in her head. She can then understand what the outcome will be, to "put two and two together," so to speak.

Such reasoning is more complicated than trying variations of ideas which involve learning by trial and error.

While experimentation by trial and error is a simple process which develops earlier, however, it is never completely replaced. It will continue to be useful, especially in new situations.

For Toddler, learning is still much more trial and error than cognitive. She is really not looking ahead and knowing what the consequences are. She is more like a pure researcher: What will happen if I do this?

Let's look at some examples that will compare trial and error experimentation with Toddler's new thinking ability.

Toddler has had lots of experience with dropping things. She knows that heavy objects fall harder. They also make a louder sound than lighter ones.

She knows that if she lifts objects higher before letting them go, they will land with more force.

When things have chanced to fall on her foot, she has found that it has hurt.

Through experience she may have already learned that if she drops something heavy, she risks having a painful consequence if it lands on her foot. So, when she learned the principle through experience, it was an inductive form of reasoning.

Suppose she comes upon a new object that she has never handled. She knows that she is now strong enough to lift it. She also knows it might fall if she lifts it.

It is unlikely that she will let the new object drop, as an experiment. By the process called generalizing, she knows that heavy things may break or hurt her if she lets them fall.

In a simple way, her ability to generalize has taken away the need to discover a consequence only by performing an experiment.

Her mind is doing this kind of reasoning: (1) Here is a heavy object. (2) Heavy objects may hurt when they fall. (3) Therefore, this object may hurt if it falls.

The ability to apply a principle she has learned to a new situation is a simple form of the thinking process called deductive reasoning.

The important thing to realize is that Toddler can take two pieces of information and come to a conclusion without actually having to try things out by experiment.

In this case, she has combined the information that this object is heavy with the knowledge that it might hurt her if it falls. Another example will illustrate this idea in a different way.

How does a toddler of 12 to 14 months learn to use a stick to rake in an object that is out of arm's reach?

She must first discover what the stick can do to the object. Thus she will start by poking the object with the stick, tipping it over, and pushing it away or to the side.

Then, she will discover that she can place the stick beyond the object to sweep it

toward her in order to retrieve the wanted item.

This is trial and error learning. With repeated practice, she will have learned the general principle that a stick can be used to retrieve an object beyond her reach.

Now, at the age of 21 months, she is given a stick and a toy just out of reach. After trying unsuccessfully to reach the toy with her hand, she will quickly pick up the stick and use it to fetch the toy.

This is thinking by deduction, a brilliant deduction from her point of view. What she is doing is mentally applying her earlier knowledge of how a stick can be handled to the needs of a specific situation where a stick has never been used before.

She seizes upon the solution immediately, without going through the trial and error process that a younger child would have to do.

If Toddler were to pull a chair over to the counter for climbing up to reach a high

continued on next page

continued from previous page

cabinet, she would be demonstrating this more advanced kind of reasoning, namely, deductive reasoning.

It is more advanced than simply trying available footholds because the chair, being in a separate location, is a separate idea.

This is an idea about climbing that must be mentally transferred to the new problem to provide a solution.

An important point must be made, however. In order to put two ideas together or to transfer an idea to a new situation, the ideas involved must be very familiar to Toddler.

For example, she must have enough experience in playing with sticks or chairs to know that they can help her to reach objects that are otherwise beyond her grasp.

Dropping of various things must be tried before the effect of dropping heavy weights can be predicted.

Experiments with both young children and chimpanzees have shown that the idea of using a stick to reach a distance object is not arrived at unless they have had earlier experiences in using the stick by itself.

Toddler's sense of cause and effect is now more highly developed, too. She can link a cause to an effect that occurs sometime afterward. Or she can look at an effect and figure out what the probable cause was.

For example, she can now begin to understand why you put wood on a fire. When you ask her what the wood makes the fire do, she may tell you that the wood makes the fire get hot. (You can also use this opportunity to explain to Toddler why fires are a "no-no" when adults are not with her.)

If the fire is low, she will realize the cause as being the need for more wood.

You can show Toddler her empty plate and ask her, "Where did the food go?" She should be able to say something to the effect that she ate it. ■

Activities for an Expanding Mind

Here are some activities that will help Toddler to develop her intellectual abilities.

Note that not all children of this age will be interested in playing these games, so some adaptations may be needed.

As you read these tasks you may think of similar ones that will challenge your own child's ability to perceive relationships between separate ideas.

• When you get her clothes together in the morning, omit one piece of clothing (one sock, for example) and see if she can figure out which item is missing.

If this is too hard, lay out the pieces on the bed just as they would be worn and see if she can name the article that is now more obviously missing.

• Tie a ribbon around the bottom of the leg of her pants before she puts them on.

Does Toddler realize ahead of time that she will not be able to put her leg through?

If so, she is relating two ideas together (If the leg of the pants is tied, I won't be able to put them on) rather than operating on a strictly trial and error basis.

• When you are out of soap in the bathroom or need a towel or toilet paper, ask Toddler if she knows where to find some more.

If she doesn't know, let her see you stock the linen cabinet with such items. But don't take things from there to the bathroom while she is around to see.

Eventually she should make the connection between what is in the linen closet and what is needed in the bathroom, even though she has not seen you make a direct transfer from one place to the other.

In addition to playing games with adults, toddlers' minds grow with independent exploration. They have a nearly insatiable curiosity, and use all of their manipulative abilities to explore objects in their envi-

ronment, always looking to create a new effect, rather than merely repeat the same old results.

This is one reason why balls are such an attractive plaything for this age as the results of playing with a ball are not always predictable.

Supply a variety of balls of different materials and sizes, with others objects children can use in their exploration: a pan of water for creating a splash effect; boxes in which to drop the balls, including some that have various sizes of holes cut in their tops; and containers for carrying the balls.

Objects with moving parts provide endless fascination such as hinged boxes, casters and springs, hinges and slide mechanisms. Check out your workshop for safe hardware that can be explored.

continued on next page

The Pre-Tricycle Period

continued from previous page

Toddler will not be ready to ride a tricycle for almost a year. But she is ready at 21 months to learn about wheels and how to make them go.

She will delight in a wagon to pull. She will busy herself loading, unloading and transporting toys, blocks, and assorted objects.

Of course, Toddler will love having Dad or Mom give her a ride in the wagon!

Many children will be ready to tackle riding a kiddie-car by this age. Kiddie-cars are the little three-wheeled "trikes" without pedals.

The child sits on the seat and moves herself along by "walking" her feet and steering with the handlebars.

Be sure to get a sturdy kiddie-car because it will take a lot of punishment in the next six to 12 months!

Don't be alarmed if your Toddler pushes herself backwards at first.

It is much easier to push with the thigh muscles that straighten the knees than it is to pull yourself along by muscles that bend the knee.

Toddler may also push or pull herself along using both feet together.

Using the legs alternately will come as Toddler tries to imitate tricycle or bicycle riders in the neighborhood.

Some children may push the car around for several months before even being willing to sit on the seat.

Other toys ridden by children this age are wooden engines, trucks, and horses, These are not guided by handlebars.

Toddler can push or pull herself around on them using her legs and feet.

They are good toys because your child will enjoy them in many different ways for several months to come. ■

Growing Child®

P. O. Box 2505 • W Lafayette, IN 47996
(800) 927-7289
©Growing Child, Inc.
www.GrowingChild.com

Contributing Authors

Phil Bach, O.D., Ph.D.
Miriam Bender, Ph.D.
Joseph Braga, Ed.D.
Laurie Braga, Ph.D.
George Early, Ph.D.
Carol R. Gestwicki, M.S.
Liam Grimley, Ph.D.
Robert Hannemann, M.D., F.A.A.P.
Sylvia Kottler, M.S.
Bill Peterson, Ph.D.

In addition to exploring, older toddlers are beginning to represent their understanding of the world through simple pretend play.

To support this play, at first they need simple objects that look like realistic replicas of items that are familiar from their surroundings: toy dishes, brooms, telephone, babies, blankets, and beds.

Then they can imitate the activities they have seen at home, such as cooking dinner and cleaning house, putting the baby to bed, and talking on the telephone.

They also need small replicas of real objects that they can use, such as cars, trucks, and animals.

You will notice them making the sounds for these items as they manipulate them. This kind of imitative play is the precursor for the rich pretending that will be coming.

Pretend play is the height of indicating intellectual development. As toddlers begin to pretend just before their second birthday, they are actually using symbolic reasoning, indicating they understand the concept they are substituting.

For example, a toddler who holds a block to her ear is representing the idea of a telephone without actually needing the realistic object.

This mental substitution indicates that Toddler has used her growing intellect to "put two and two together."

That is to say that she has developed the ability to relate one idea with another idea in her mind.

The thinking process of symbolic representation shows us that she has gone beyond her earlier thinking that relied largely on trial and error experimentation.

Symbolic representation has great importance for success in later learning.

Researchers tell us that there is a strong correlation between child-initiated pretend play and school success. ■

If I could say just one thing to parents, it would be simply that a child needs someone who believes in him, no matter what he does.

Alice V. Keliher

Avoiding Bedtime Uproar

Around the age of two years, many children suddenly object to going to bed. Until now going to bed was accepted willingly, or at least without much objection.

Now, suddenly, Toddler begins to resist. He hangs back. He clings. He wants this or that. He cries. He may even have a temper tantrum.

Why this sudden reluctance to go to bed? After all, Toddler is probably tired. He is almost certainly sleepy. Why then is he fighting about going to bed?

To try to answer this question, we need to consider how Toddler's thinking has been developing in relation to the world around him.

Toddler has learned that objects and people do not just vanish when they are out of sight. If he goes into another room leaving his favorite toy behind, he knows that it will be where he left it when he comes back. The permanence in his world gives him feelings of possessiveness. It also gives him a sense of security.

But with sleep it is different. Toddler becomes aware that sleep is different from waking.

He is afraid of what might happen to his familiar world while he sleeps. So he clings to the security of the known, the security of whom and what he can see and touch.

At this stage of development, a bedtime routine will help both Toddler's behavior and general peace in your home.

Perhaps you have already established a bedtime routine. Just what this includes will depend, of course, on the lifestyle

of your particular family. The routine should be structured so as to provide a nightly ritual which prepares Toddler for sleep.

You may say that you are just not a person who follows a daily routine. You don't like to do the same things in the same way every day. You say you need the freedom of flexibility. Perhaps as an adult you find your security in this very freedom.

A two-year-old, however, is not ready for that kind of freedom. He must feel that his world, as he knows it, is stable. It will be the same tomorrow as it has been today. He must feel secure if he is to explore his world further. Every explorer needs a base camp from which to move out into the unknown.

Toddler needs reassurance that his world will be there when he awakens in the morning. A bedtime ritual serves to provide this reassurance because it moves him along familiar paths toward sleep.

As part of this nightly ritual, a realistic bedtime hour—flexible within reason—should be established.

Often this can be cued to an after supper playtime or after a special cuddle with a picture book story. This leads naturally into the ritual of getting ready for bed and for sleep, which reduces bedtime uproar to a minimum.

For one child the nightly ritual may include saying "good night" to favorite toys. Or it may involve giving a good night kiss to every member of the family.

Another child may want to take a favorite toy to bed with him. Or he may insist

At 22 Months Toddler Likes to:
- Imitate what adults do.
- Put lids on containers and take them off.
- Match familiar shapes.
- Take favorite playthings to bed.

Give Toddler:
- Some time alone for self-communication.
- Encouragement for new verbal skills.
- Simple picture puzzles.
- Plastic jars with screw caps.

that his new shoes be placed where he can see and touch them. This can happen if he has developed a strong sense of possession. He wants "his" things around him.

For yet another child, sleep may come only with the corner of a favorite wooly blanket clutched in his fist.

The bedtime routine that is appropriate for your child should be adhered to night after night. Following a familiar ritual reassures him about the stability of his world.

This helps him to organize and understand this world. It also gives him a feeling of security. It prepares him for the separation from his daytime world that sleep will bring.

If your child appears fearful about darkness, you may find that a small glowing night light provides the reassurance needed. It is also a sensible safety measure for a child who may have to use the bathroom in the middle of the night. ∎

Learning at Work and Play

Toddler's accomplishments are substantial by now: He is able to drink through a straw, eat with a spoon, and blow his nose with a tissue.

He is moving from babyhood toward childhood in several ways. He wants to do things for himself.

He demonstrates his independence in the mastery of his own body (walking, climbing up, climbing down, running, jumping). He prefers now to push his stroller rather than ride in it. He wants to transport objects from one place to another and back again.

He knows where things are kept. But he may not yet appreciate the fact that one object cannot be in two places at the same time.

For example, during a ride with a toddler in the family car, a father once joked, as they passed a car identical to theirs, "Say, somebody must have stolen our car!" The toddler immediately began to cry because he was unmindful of the fact that they still had their own car.

In addition to the mastery of the larger space in which he now moves, he is learning space relationships between objects. He takes apart things like pressure cookers and percolators and may even put them back together.

He stacks wooden or plastic donuts on a peg. Most likely he cannot arrange them in the correct order if they are of different sizes.

He can understand gross differences in size. But he cannot consistently differentiate small differences as can be observed when he tries to put larger objects inside slightly smaller ones.

Language is now very much a part of the child's daily activity. It is not an isolated skill such as riding a bicycle or dressing oneself.

Language deals with moving, perceiving, feeling, thinking, and expressing oneself. At 22 months, Toddler is word-hungry. He goes around cataloging his environment by naming objects, actions, situations. Or he comes to you and asks, "What's that?"

From now on, Toddler is likely to be highly verbal. Speech is self-rewarding and self-motivating.

More verbs are coming into his vocabulary. He matches words to his actions: "climb up," "climb down," "run," "eat," "fall," "cry."

However, he may frequently misuse the vocabulary of space—prepositions such as "up," "down," "over," "under," "in," "out."

He can generally count to "two." To him "two" stands for any quantity greater than one! He may even be able to count higher than two. But it is a rote recital of a learned sequence.

For example, if there are objects on the table, he may count to five. At the same time he's likely to skip an object or touch the same object twice. There is not yet a one-to-one correspondence between numbers and objects.

In addition, counting and summing are unrelated to him. If he counts five cookies—1, 2, 3, 4, 5,—and you then ask, "how many are there?" he may reply, "two," or repeat "1, 2, 3, 4, 5."

He doesn't realize that the last number is the sum. This kind of awareness will come much later.

He is also beginning to understand and use time-related words, such as "day," "night," "now," "first." He demonstrates that he has a memory for past events and can anticipate future events.

If he is told before napping that he will visit his grandmother when he awakens, he will likely awaken from his nap with a loud reminder—"Go nana" or "Now go nana!"

Self-communication is Toddler's way of enhancing his language and speech development. Talking to oneself at this age takes four forms:

(1) **Self-direction.** Toddler dictates to himself step-by-step how to do something as he goes about doing it. You can observe this, for example, in his sand play as he pours, mixes, stirs, and bakes.

(2) **Self-control.** He admonishes himself with words like "no-no" or "don't touch" as he approaches the candy dish.

(3) **Daydreaming.** As he stares into space, you may hear Toddler repeating certain phrases to himself. Or he may just chat to himself in a world of his own.

You may find him sitting quietly and even sucking his thumb or holding his security blanket when only a second before he was active.

If you are sitting or working nearby, he will appear to be totally oblivious of your presence.

It's best not to interrupt this daydreaming chatter. Toddler needs this time to communicate out loud with himself in order to organize and integrate his own experiences.

(4) **Dramatic play.** Toddler tries out the roles of the models to which he has been exposed. He acts out the events of daily life which he has observed.

The types of actions are simple ones that he has seen frequently in his own life such as when he imitates driving the car or using the telephone.

Both boys and girls pantomime shaving. They also play with dolls—feeding them, pushing them around in strollers, bathing them, putting them to sleep.

Doll play is important for both sexes. There is no loss of masculinity when boys engage in doll play. Rather it helps them to develop feelings of tenderness, care, and affection.

Dramatic play helps Toddler learn about himself. It is an essential ingredient in the process of identification, of learning to become a member of his family and his community. ∎

Learning by Imitation

Imitation combines both play and learning for Toddler. She imitates you on her own for fun. She is learning new action patterns at the same time.

When you want to teach Toddler something new, you can simply tell her what things should be done.

A more efficient method, however, is to have her watch while you demonstrate how to do the activity. You can then have her imitate what you just did.

You may notice that Toddler's imitations have become increasingly more complicated. She may imitate not only people but animals and machines, a sign that many things are now represented in her mind.

These imitations are quite realistic. They are accurate enough that you can easily recognize what she is pretending to do, such as imitating your food preparation actions in the kitchen.

When you attend to Toddler's imitations, you realize that they can be rather remarkable feats for someone so young.

In imitating someone, she must be able to observe accurately what the person does. Then she must call upon her body to perform movements that are similar to what she saw.

To do all this, she needs to develop a wide variety of individual motions.

In the last few months she has built up a fund of movements such as pulling, sliding, turning, stacking, and rolling things.

A really interesting aspect of her present imitative ability is that she can put together for the first time two or more simple motions to reproduce an action which she has seen only once.

She does this even though she may never have combined the movements in such a way before.

Let's take an example. You have probably played the game where you touched some part of your body and tried to see if Toddler could touch the same part of herself.

By now she is probably pretty good at touching her nose, eyes, ears, mouth and other major parts in imitation of your movements. You could also have her do this by naming the various parts of the body.

Now suppose that in a play session, you grasp your nose between your thumb and the knuckle of your forefinger. At the same time grasp your ear the same way with your other hand.

The chances are that Toddler can imitate your actions fairly closely, including the particular kind of grasp.

She will do this even though she may never before have combined grasping her nose and ear at the same time.

Even if she fails at first, she usually can get it after being shown the difference between what she did and what should be done. She can do the right combination without having to do several trial and error attempts.

This was not true earlier when she learned the simpler movements, like grasping or touching a part of her body.

Those movements had to be repeated again and again, at first exactly the same way, then later with little variations.

Eventually her muscles were able to do the movements dependably, at her will. But now two or three simple movements can be combined immediately. ∎

Self-Identity

At 22 months most children are still the center of their own universe. And we have been helping Toddler to develop a sense of self when we teach the names for body parts.

It is important that we do not omit words like "penis," "urethra," "vagina" and "rectum." If we're casual in our naming, Toddler will have a relaxed and positive acceptance for the organs of elimination and sex.

Here's a body image game that may be recited or chanted:

"Eyes to see with" (point to eyes);
"Ears to hear with" (point to ears);
"Nose to smell with" (point to nose);
"Teeth to chew with" (point to teeth);
"Hands to work with" (point to hands);
"Feet to walk with" (point to feet);
"My behind to sit on or to go potty" (point to your behind). ∎

Burns: Prevention and Treatment

It is estimated that over 2 million Americans suffer severe burns each year and that over 8,000 die from these injuries. Thousands are disfigured for life.

Saddest of all, the vast majority are young children who are involved in accidents, which are often preventable, in their own homes.

We sincerely hope that none of our extended family of *Growing Child* children will ever be counted among those statistics. For that reason we believe that all parents and other child caregivers should have some basic information about the prevention and treatment of burns.

Scalds: Scalds are burns that are produced by any hot liquid or steam. Scalding ranks as the most frequent cause of burns, with children under five years of age being most at risk.

It's important to remember that water can still scald even 30 minutes after boiling.

To avoid scalding, the thermostat setting on a water heater should never exceed 120 degrees F. Even at that temperature, third-degree burns can occur after 30 seconds—while at 140 degrees F, they will occur after only 5 seconds.

A water heater temperature setting of 120 degrees F should be adequate for most household uses.

The temperature of the water in a child's bath should be about 100 degrees F but should never exceed 104 degrees F.

When filling the tub, it's a good idea to run the cold water first, then warm it with hot water, as a safe way to prevent accidental scalding.

Always check the temperature of the bathwater with your hand or elbow before letting a child get into the tub.

Matches and lighters: To a young child who is unaware of their danger, matches and lighters look like very attractive toys. They are small enough to be held in one's hand, are relatively easy to use, and

produce a most fascinating, colorful flame. Because they are so attractive to a young child, they are all the more hazardous.

The U.S. Consumer Product Safety Commission reports that approximately 9,000 individuals receive hospital emergency treatment each year for injuries—mostly burns—related to the use of matches.

Hospital personnel who deal with these injuries recommend that children under five years of age should never be allowed to use matches, even under adult supervision.

After five years of age a child can be instructed in the safe use of matches to light a fire or a candle, provided they do so always under adult supervision. Matches should always be kept out of reach of young children.

A field study conducted by the U.S. Consumer Product Safety Commission has found that about 200 deaths each year are the result of fires started with cigarette lighters. An estimated 140 of these deaths are caused by children playing with lighters, with over 75 percent of the victims being under five.

It has been found that young children—because they don't understand the consequences of their actions—are more likely to hide in a closet or under a bed rather than inform their parents that they have started a fire.

Emergency treatment: Very often emergency treatment is needed immediately—even before getting medical help:

• Make sure all family members know what to do if clothing catches on fire—STOP-DROP-ROLL—to extinguish the flame.

• Before swelling occurs, remove shoes, tight clothing, belts, jewelry, etc.

• Don't try to remove clothing that adheres to a burn. Simply cut around the fabric that is stuck to the skin.

• In the case of thermal burns which are caused by a flame, hot liquid or other

source of intense heat, cool the burn with cold water as quickly as possible.

• In the case of chemical burns, it's important to be familiar with the emergency treatment information provided on the package or container involved.

• Any injury to the eyes usually requires continuous flushing with water until medical help is available.

• Burns on any part of the face, hands or feet should always receive prompt medical attention.

Some household precautions to prevent a fire:

• In the living areas of your home, don't leave electrical cords dangling to tempt busy little fingers.

• Keep covers on all electrical outlets not in use.

• Keep all chemical, flammable or combustible materials in a cool, well-ventilated place which is out of reach for children.

• Make sure that all fireplaces or wood-burning stoves have a protective screen around them.

• In the kitchen, make sure that the handles of all hot pots and pans are turned inward.

• Don't allow young children near you when you are carrying hot liquids or removing a hot dish from the oven.

If necessary, establish a "No Trespass" zone, marked off with Scotch™ tape, in front of the oven, until your child is old enough to recognize the danger area.

• At table, use tablemats rather than a tablecloth. Young children will sometimes grab the corner of a tablecloth—with disastrous results—when trying to pull themselves up from the floor.

• Keep all hot dishes close to the center of the table, away from the edges where they could easily be knocked over.

continued on next page

continued from previous page

• Around your home, it's wise to install smoke detectors and carbon monoxide detectors on each level and in each bedroom.

It has been found that fires in homes are most likely to occur between midnight and 6 a.m. when family members are likely to be sound asleep in their bedrooms.

It's important, therefore, to check the batteries periodically in all smoke and carbon monoxide detectors.

• Fire extinguishers are an extra precaution. Keeping some water in plastic bottles in all bedroom closets will enable you, in the event of fire, to moisten a cloth that will help block smoke from your mouth and nose as you make your escape.

How to survive a fire: Knowing what to do before a fire occurs can be the difference between life and death for you and your family.

• It's wise to develop an escape plan for the entire family, with at least two possible exits—windows and door—from each room.

• Be sure to identify a meeting place for all occupants of the house at a safe distance from the home.

• If you are in your bedroom with the door closed when you first discover there is a fire, first feel the door and door handle with your hand. If they are not hot, open the door slowly.

If, however, you notice smoke or hot gases are entering the room, close the door immediately and seek your escape through a window, if possible.

• If you find it's safe to exit through the door, cover your mouth and nose with a dampened cloth, if available, in order to prevent smoke inhalation.

• As you make your escape, crawl, if necessary, rather than walk, in order to keep below the level of the smoke.

• Once outside, never try to go back inside. Only trained firefighters should enter a burning building.

Everyone who has ever experienced a fire in their home undoubtedly once thought that those things only happened to other people—but never to them!

Those who take the precaution of knowing what they should do in the event of a fire most likely will improve their chances of survival. ■

A Positive Attitude

A positive attitude can lead to better parenting. In life, two people can look at the same glass: while one sees it as "half full," the other sees it as "half empty." It's just a matter of positive versus negative attitude.

An attitude is something we can work on changing. If I perceive that my attitudes on life are more negative than positive, I can deliberately make a greater effort to focus on the positive (versus negative) aspects of each situation.

Here are three good reasons for seeking to develop and maintain a more positive attitude as a parent:

1. My attitude helps to determine how I perceive my child's behavior. For example, if my almost-two-year-old has recently developed the habit of saying "No!"

I can perceive that as either (a) "My child is developing a healthy sense of autonomy and independence" (a positive attitude) or (b) "My kid is becoming a little monster" (a negative attitude).

2. My attitude helps to determine how I will react. If I perceive my child's behavior in a positive manner ("He's learning to develop a sense of autonomy and independence"), I'm more likely to react to his behavior in a positive way.

For example, by showing him more love and affection to reassure him that it's natural and okay for him to want to demonstrate greater independence as he gets older.

On the other hand, if I perceive the same behavior in a negative manner, I'm more likely to respond in a negative way ("You'll lose your TV time if you keep doing that!")

3. My attitude will affect how my child will respond. When a parent can exhibit a positive attitude toward a child's behavior, the child will more likely develop a positive attitude toward life.

Giving him the reassurance that he is loved unconditionally will help him to be more in tune with his world and, therefore, behave more positively.

On the contrary, when a child feels threatened and unloved because of a parent's negative attitude, he is more likely to develop negative feelings toward himself, which ultimately will lead to worse misbehavior.

It's important to note, however, that having a positive attitude toward a child's behavior ("I think my child is terrific") is not the same as spoiling a child ("My child can do no wrong").

Whereas a spoiled child will eventually exhibit misbehavior increasingly more demanding of parents, the child who is treated by parents with a positive—yet realistic—attitude will more likely develop a similar, more positive outlook on life. ■

Movement Combinations

Suppose that Toddler is learning to unscrew the lid of a jar. She must combine a finger grasp with a turn of her wrist.

She is probably capable of performing each of these separate movements. But the unscrewing action requires a conscious combination of two separate movements. This is a process that takes some time to master.

You may notice a delay between the closing of Toddler's grasp and the beginning of her wrist motion. She is thinking about the order of motions to be performed.

If you try to talk to her while she is at the task, she will be frustrated. She does not have enough attention to spare for both the conversation and the task.

For you, unscrewing the lid of a jar is a simple movement. You can unscrew the lid while you are talking to someone else.

The movement is simple for you because it is automatic. For Toddler the movement is a movement combination.

Here we need to make a distinction between simple movements and movement combinations. Each of these changes in complexity as a child grows older.

A simple movement is one that can be done automatically, without conscious thought other than to give oneself the command to begin the motion.

Once the order is given to start the movement, the muscles do the entire job themselves without having to be consciously guided.

A movement combination is the conscious and deliberate joining of two or more simple movements, either at the same time or closely following one another.

A human being is marvelously flexible. She can create just about any combination of simpler movements that she needs in order to get a particular job done.

The next time you are learning a new skill such as learning how to play a musical instrument, you will find that three or four movements are the most you can put together at one time.

y

Growing Child®

w

P. O. Box 2505 • W Lafayette, IN 47996
(800) 927-7289
©Growing Child, Inc.
www.GrowingChild.com

Contributing Authors

Phil Bach, O.D., Ph.D.
Miriam Bender, Ph.D.
Joseph Braga, Ed.D.
Laurie Braga, Ph.D.
George Early, Ph.D.
Carol R. Gestwicki, M.S.
Liam Grimley, Ph.D.
Robert Hannemann, M.D., F.A.A.P.
Sylvia Kottler, M.S.
Bill Peterson, Ph.D.

Notice how you operate the next time you are learning a new skill (for example, if you want to learn how to play a musical instrument).

You will find that three or four movements are the most you can put together at one time as you learn.

Usually you will do only two things at once. The proverbial "one-track mind" is a limitation we all share.

So when we look at things this way, we see that Toddler is able to combine separate learnings at about the same rate that we do.

The marvel does not end here. For if the same job occurs repeatedly, the movement combination needed will become, through repetition, a simple movement.

The action will be performed automatically, as a single unit. Its control is actually shifted to a lower center of the brain, allowing conscious thought to be redirected to something else.

A movement combination can then become a simple movement. Most simple movements, including many that Toddler does at this stage, can be broken down into still simpler movements.

All of our motor skills are built from simpler movement patterns. This is how a concert pianist, for example, learns to play so many notes so quickly.

It is how a pilot is trained to fly the plane and operate the radio at the same time. It is the way a person is able to drive a car.

Right now Toddler is learning to combine simple movements into movement combinations.

When movement combinations become automatic, she joins them into more complicated combinations.

When Toddler can perform two or more simple movements in combination, she is performing almost as well as an adult. ∎

138

Growing Child

Seek the wisdom of the ages, but look at the world through the eyes of a child.
Ron Wild

23 MONTHS

The Great Explorer Becomes the Great Imitator

If there are three words which describe Toddler as he moves from babyhood into early childhood, those words might well be: "The Great Imitator."

True, Toddler continues to learn by doing—by touching, poking, handling, patting, pulling, and pushing. But now he begins to search for meaning in the activities of those around him by imitating them.

At first his imitations are simply a repetition of whatever you do without any real understanding of the purpose of those actions.

He is simply trying to become a more active participant in the world around him. By imitating what you do he will eventually understand why you do it.

His early attempts at imitation range from the endearing to the exasperating. He climbs into an easy chair and "reads the newspaper." He carries Daddy's gym bag or Mommy's briefcase because he has to "go to work."

As yet he does not "role play." That is, he is not pretending to be you or Grandpa.

He just goes through the motions as he sees them, using any grossly similar objects which he finds available.

Lipstick goes on Mommy's mouth, for example. So the Great Imitator puts it on his mouth—and his face—and on the wall if you are not watching as he shifts gears to imitate your writing behavior.

Imitator watches Daddy do some painting—and he tries to imitate by painting the wall with water as high as he can reach, using a bath sponge or washcloth as a brush.

He seems to be completely unaware of the sometimes disastrous results of his imitations.

Cause and effect are still not well understood. But he paints with total absorption, dipping his "brush" in the "paint" and rhythmically sweeping it back and forth over the wall.

Sometimes Toddler's imitations may take strange forms. For example, you may find him stomping around the bathtub in rubber boots because earlier in the day, he observed Daddy, in his rubber boots, stomping around in street puddles after an unusually heavy rainstorm.

He associates the boots with water. Water in the bathtub is a familiar part of Toddler's life. So, he progresses from boots to water to tub.

His inability to turn on the water and fill the tub doesn't really interfere with his chain of association. As he "walks" the boots back and forth in the tub he sees himself doing what Daddy does!

Perhaps this imitation may take a different direction if Toddler also finds water—in a puddle, a tub, even a birdbath. Now he tries to walk the boots through the water with his hands but the boots are heavy and awkward.

One falls over and water runs inside. Flash! A new idea! Water on the inside of boots?

At 23 Months Toddler Likes to:
• Run.
• Put pegs into holes.
• Stack blocks.
• Turn switches on and off.

Give Toddler:
• A puzzle to assemble.
• A toy to ride.

The Great Imitator happily explores the characteristics of this new container.

Often Imitator finds lots of scope for imitation in the kitchen. You may have just assembled all the ingredients for a cake when the telephone rings.

Imitator has been watching you. What could be more natural than for Imitator to carry on and imitate his version of your cake mixing.

So the eggs miss the bowl and drip onto the floor? And the flour gets pretty well scattered between bowl, counter, floor, and Imitator's clothes?

To the Great Imitator, all is well. Your exasperation surprises him. After all, he was imitating you!

As he grows past his second year, Toddler will amuse you, surprise you, puzzle you, exasperate you, and sometimes really frighten you as he produces his versions of what you do.

He is moving from exploring objects to exploring people through imitating what he sees them do. ■

Expect Some Changes

Before he turns two, Toddler may show some real behavioral changes.

First, his taste in food may change. The customary bland diet may no longer have the same appeal.

Is a bland diet necessary? No. If onions, garlic, or spicy sauces (in moderation, of course) make food more attractive, why not use them?

Many Toddlers exhibit gourmet palates. They eat with relish such things as strong cheeses, olives, salami, avocado, and seafood.

Before the age of three, cooked vegetables—except for sweeter ones like carrots—generally are not too popular. However, your child may eat raw vegetables. A raw vegetable is as nutritious and digestible as a cooked one.

Dentists report another bonus: The exercise which results from chewing these foods cleanses the mouth and retards tooth decay.

A word of caution: To avoid the possibility of choking, the vegetable pieces should be small enough to make them easy to chew and swallow.

Next, there will be changes in elimination control, where incidentally, there are more individual differences among children than in any other area of development.

At 23 months, Toddler may be inconsistent when it comes to urination. Sometimes he will report before, other times after, an accident. Often the report takes the form of pointing to the puddle.

Because of the increased amount and frequency of urination, lapses seem to multiply. Parents understandably may be impatient—changing diapers and wiping up puddles is extra work.

However, keep in mind that children don't develop their abilities evenly nor at the same rate as their siblings.

If you compare Toddler with another his age you will find that the early walkers are

The occurrences of "stripping" and going about in the nude are declining. Toddler is definitely interested in purposeful dressing and undressing now.

often the late talkers; those who learned elimination control early were likely slow in social behavior; or some children appear advanced in everything but toilet learning.

In regard to bowel control, if you delay this task until Toddler is ready, accidents will be fewer. Besides, you will avoid a "Battle of the Bowels."

Generally, Toddler's daily movement(s) occur(s) after meals or following the afternoon nap. He will usually give you some warning such as straining or grunting or having a "strange" look on his face.

This is the time to put him on the potty chair. Reward and praise him when he has a bowel movement in it.

If toilet learning is not emotionally charged, it can also be used for purposes of language lessons.

For example, when Toddler awakens in a wet bed or he alerts you to the presence of a bowel movement on the sheet, give him the words for the experience.

As you change him, say "Johnny is wet, see?" or "Johnny had a bowel movement, see?"

If he has an older brother, allow Toddler to observe him urinate and say, "Billy is wetting now, see?"

This is a good time to select the words you plan to use for elimination. Repeat them matter of factly whenever the occasion arises.

The occurrences of "stripping" and going about in the nude are declining. Toddler is definitely interested in purposeful dressing and undressing now. He can remove his shoes, socks and pants.

With dressing he is less agile—he may put two feet into one pant leg or put his hat on backwards.

In the bathtub he may still like to play. But now he seriously tries to wash himself with a sponge or washcloth.

His understanding of property rights is minimal. He has begun the first stage in a series of steps which are necessary for an appreciation of "mine," "yours," "ours." Right now he's at the "mine" stage.

At home he wants as much as he can get for himself. The word "mine" may precede every relationship.

However, away from family or home, he most likely won't insist upon his rights and will generally be more compliant.

Under supervision Toddler can be a parent's darling helper because he enjoys fetching and delivering objects and passing snacks around to people.

But left unsupervised, he may wreck any room in a flash, pulling out and emptying drawers, spilling and spreading cosmetics or toiletries.

He is beginning to be independent, to acquire a sense of who he is and what he can do. ■

Developing Independence

From time to time we have said how important it is for Toddler to feel that he belongs, that he really matters. Such a feeling makes for solid self-confidence. This is something that doesn't just happen—it is learned.

This month we want to suggest some practical things to do to build Toddler's awareness that he is important.

First of all, you should be aware that Toddler is growing up in a brand new world. There never has been a world just like the one we live in now.

The way the world is, and the way things happen have a powerful influence upon how Toddler sees and feels about himself.

One important fact about growing up in today's world is that children are nearly always on the receiving end.

Our world is full of many gadgets and labor-saving devices that do things for us that we formerly did for ourselves. There are machines to wash our dishes, take us from one place to another, sweep our floors, and so on.

In yesterday's world there were not nearly so many machines. Young children and teenagers did many of the tasks which machines do so smoothly now.

In yesterday's world children washed the dishes, took out the garbage, carried wood or coal to heat the house, walked to school or to a friend's house to play, swept floors with brooms, and dusted furniture with cloths.

We are not suggesting that Toddler do all these things now. But this does illustrate that children can no longer learn to participate in those activities which often gave them feelings of accomplishment and personal self-worth.

Toddler learns to be independent and self-sufficient in a very simple way: He learns by doing things for himself.

This does not happen all at once. He learns it gradually, but he needs your help in learning.

As time goes on, Toddler should do more and more things for himself. And you should do less and less for him.

This is the way development should occur. You must be alert to opportunities to help this process along.

Take dressing, for example. At this age, getting Toddler dressed is mostly your job. But he can do some of the simpler dressing tasks by himself.

He can learn to put on his hat, socks, and mittens with just a little help from you. Whatever he can do in dressing himself, let him do it. It will certainly take more time for him to do it by himself. But it will be time well spent.

The way you help him is also very important. There is a systematic way of giving your help which lets him learn to take over in easy stages.

To illustrate this point, suppose you want to teach him how to put on his socks. This involves: (1) starting the sock over the toes, (2) pulling the sock down to the heel, (3) pulling the sock over the heel, and finally (4) pulling the sock up.

Toddler should learn to do the simplest part of the task first. You first teach him to pull the socks up (which is the last step in putting on socks). In other words, you do all of the first three steps. Then he does the last step.

When he has mastered this, you begin working on the next-to-last step. This means that you put the sock over the toes and bring it to the heel.

Now Toddler must do the last two steps. He must bring the sock over the heel and then he must pull the sock up (steps 3 and 4).

You proceed in this way until finally he is able to do the whole task from stage one through stage four.

In addition to doing for himself, it is also very important that Toddler learn that he can help you. Start with very simple things.

For example, when you and Toddler are shopping at the supermarket, you say, "Johnny, where is the bread?"

If he can find where the bread is, he has learned some very basic facts about space. There is a special place where the bread is kept.

continued on page 144

141

Thinking, Planning, Doing

Last month we talked about motor imitation and the kind of learning that goes along with it.

We noted that a simple movement is one that Toddler can imitate automatically without the need for practice.

On the other hand, the imitation involved in movement combinations is more complex. Initially it requires the conscious coordination of several simple movements.

Practice can transform a movement combination into a simple movement. This takes place when Toddler can perform the action in an automatic manner without having to think about the different components of what she is doing.

So, what began as a conscious coordination of several simple movements has now become automatic.

We tend to think of coordination as being mainly physical. But as we have indicated, when the job is new, the skills involved are mostly mental.

One must consciously think about what parts of the body are to move, where they should go, and at what time and order.

Now consider an everyday situation requiring more complicated coordination than a simple imitation.

You have driven home with the groceries. Being lazy, you would like to carry two bags in the door instead of one.

To make everything come out right, you must be sure that the house key is in your hand before you pick up the second bag.

Then a knee must be brought into play to support the second bag as you unlock the door.

The skills involved are not only physical but mental as well. You find yourself thinking ahead, planning what the next move will be.

Or, if you have ever had to rearrange boxes or furniture in a tight space, you know what careful planning it takes to do the job efficiently.

The next time you literally have your hands full with some kind of job, notice how you must plan the little, individual motions so that each will be done at the proper time and place.

Toddler must do the same kind of planning with the simpler coordinations her life requires. Just avoiding furniture and objects on the floor as she walks takes con-

siderable motor planning on her part.

Now her explorations are leading her to climb over and crawl under many different kinds of objects.

She pulls wheeled toys around corners. She carries bulky objects through narrow doors. She can open doors without bumping her head or stubbing her toes.

Since no two situations are exactly alike, she must, for now, approach them individually, being conscious of what her various body parts are doing.

If she is successful in her endeavors, we say that she is adequately coordinated.

Toddler has to think just as hard about each new thing she does as we do when faced with any new, complicated task.

This has important implications for the development of her thinking and problem-solving abilities.

Activities which require Toddler to plan how to coordinate her body parts are useful to her intellectual as well as her physical development.

However, this does not mean that you should discourage all unplanned, rough-and-tumble play and concentrate instead on "pickup sticks." Toddler needs vigorous activity to exercise her growing muscles and absorb the energy of her metabolism.

It does mean that you should encourage her to try some activities where she must think and plan ahead, coordinating the parts of her body in new ways.

For example, you may remember that we suggested some months ago that you give Toddler several small blocks, one at a time, to see if she can devise ways of holding several objects at once. This is an exercise in planning and coordination.

Now you can play a reverse of that game. Place three objects, like a small ball, a block, and a shoe, into Toddler's cradled arms.

Then name one object and ask her to give it to you without dropping the other two.

Feet can be coordinated, too. Make several tracings of your shoes on paper. Cut them out and place these "footprints" on the floor.

If you walk on the footprints, being careful to place your foot exactly on each step, Toddler will want to follow your example and do the same thing herself.

Then you can play a game by inviting Toddler to arrange these footprints on the floor for you to follow.

But beware: Toddler will sometimes give you impossible patterns to follow. She doesn't understand your limitations and may assume you have two left feet!

continued on page 144

The Practice of Words

Until recently Toddler has spent much of her energy in practicing motor skills—creeping, climbing, walking. But now she is broadening her skills and redirecting her energies to the practice of words.

If you listen to her pre-sleep talk when she is in her crib, you may hear fascinating monologues which contain such features as rhythmic patterning, rhyme, and melodic sequences.

A distinguished linguist, Roman Jakobson, says the child's first speech resembles exercise drills which appear in textbooks for self-teaching of a foreign language!

Let's look at some examples: "Like a piggy had a pink one, pish, pish, piggy." Here the child is playing with the "pi" sound.

Next, she may play with word substitution: "What eat? Eat soup? Eat cookie? Eat Mommy?"

And then, without any motive except her own pleasure, she may play with nonsense phrases. Some people might label it alliteration or even poetry: "Lump go Teddy, not ring, ring, knock, knock, knock, lake, cake, cans clap, clap, clap, dan, dan, dan."

You may also observe what appears to be confused labeling by Toddler. For example, she may at one time have a variety of objects around her and name them, "comb," "hat," "car."

Then at another time when the same objects are in view, she doesn't call them "comb," "hat," or "car," but instead she says, "Daddy."

In fact, each of the objects belongs to Daddy. What is happening may be confusing to you but not to Toddler. Sometimes she chooses to label by class name. But often she labels by the owner's name.

This change-in-naming practice is evidence of Toddler's developing awareness of the concept of ownership.

It is this very ability which gives her a feeling of power. She can now manipulate in her mind the words and the objects they stand for.

Toddler's vocabulary is about to take a big spurt, if it hasn't already done so. Some children develop clear speech from the beginning. Others may be hard to understand and require an interpreter.

Common types of articulation errors are "tove" for "stove," "banket" for "blanket," "fank you" for "thank you," "Wodjer" for "Roger," "bedi" for "very" and "wif" for "with."

We hope no readers of **Growing Child** will be over-concerned with articulation errors. At this age they are to be expected. If you try to help Toddler correct her mistakes, it won't help if she isn't ready.

You may tell her to say "stove" but she will continue to say "tove." It isn't that she fails to hear you say the "s" sound in "stove." She knows it's there. She cannot yet blend it with the "t."

When you correct errors directly, you make the new talker very conscious of her speech. You imply that it is not satisfying you, or that she's not very adequate because she requires so much coaching.

A better way to bring Toddler's attention to particular words is through play. You play with the sounds and words by repeating them in songs or stories.

For example, if Toddler says "tove" as she reaches to turn the knob, tell her, "The stove is hot. Don't touch the stove because it is hot!"

You can be creative and make up the words to familiar tunes. To the tune of "Three Blind Mice," for example, you might sing: "The stove is hot, the stove is hot, we don't touch, we don't touch, the stove is hot, the stove is hot, yes it is, yes it is, the stove is hot."

Toddler is word-hungry. She wants to know the names of everything in sight. She asks in two ways: The first is by saying, "What's dat?"

Or she names the object, raising her voice as in "Cookie?"—which is her way of asking you to verify the accuracy of her naming.

Actually she wants to know more than just the object's name, but only a bit more.

In an investigation to discover the cause of delayed speech in normal, middle-class three-year-olds, it was found that insufficient conversation between parents and child has profound effects.

Even when television was played in the home, it did not serve as a stimulant for speech. It was only a stimulant to the understanding of words. The crucial missing element was verbal exchange.

Moreover, the investigators determined that there was a critical level for the amount of conversation that must be present in order for speech to be acquired.

So we encourage you to set some time aside for those all-important parent-child conversations.

We hope that Toddler's torrent of questions will not overwhelm you. Try to look at it this way: You are her educator. Every time you respond, she becomes brighter and more intelligent.

Ideally it would be nice to answer all her questions, but this is impossible. Do the best you can.

Then be honest with Toddler. When you run out of stamina or patience, tell her, "Mother (or Father) is tired now. No more questions until later." ∎

continued from page 141

When you get to where the bread is, you can enlarge upon his basic learning: "Now, what kind of bread do we buy here?"

From previous trips to the supermarket, Toddler may select the correct loaf and put it into the shopping cart.

There are other ways he can "help." He can carry small parcels for you. He can hold the door open when your arms are full of bundles.

He can put clothes and other things in their appropriate drawers or cabinets (at first with careful help from you).

He can hand you things you need when you are washing dishes or clothes, or when you are cleaning, vacuuming, or dusting. The list could go on and on.

These opportunities for Toddler to learn to do things for himself are very important. It would be a mistake to deprive Toddler of these chances to learn just because he won't do the job as perfectly or as quickly as you would have done it yourself.

Leave yourself enough time for whatever job needs to be done so that you can afford to relax and enjoy Toddler's first stumbling efforts to be your "big helper."

Whether you are working for independence or to help Toddler feel he is a helper, there are some general principles which apply throughout the whole process.

First of all, the whole atmosphere should be one of enjoyment and fun. If it does not come off naturally, try again later.

Next, Toddler should receive genuine and consistent rewards whenever he displays either independent or helping behaviors.

Perhaps the best reward is judicious praise: "Hey, Johnny, you're growing up! You can almost get the sock on by yourself." Or, "Thank you, Susan, for holding the door for me."

These are only a few of the ways Toddler learns independence. He is also learning the gentle art of helping.

Right now he can learn in only a limited way about these most important aspects of living in a fascinating world. But we think it is important that you begin now.

He needs to learn, slowly but surely, that he can be self-sufficient and that he is needed.

In today's world you can help him learn these very profound lessons by providing him with the kind of good learning opportunities we have just described. ■

Growing Child

P. O. Box 2505 • W Lafayette, IN 47996
(800) 927-7289
©Growing Child, Inc.
www.GrowingChild.com

Contributing Authors

Phil Bach, O.D., Ph.D.
Miriam Bender, Ph.D.
Joseph Braga, Ed.D.
Laurie Braga, Ph.D.
George Early, Ph.D.
Carol R. Gestwicki, M.S.
Liam Grimley, Ph.D.
Robert Hannemann, M.D., F.A.A.P.
Sylvia Kottler, M.S.
Bill Peterson, Ph.D.

continued from page 142

Eyes with hands is an important kind of coordination. With Toddler watching, have another adult roll a ball across the floor toward you while you hold a cardboard box on its side a foot or so above the floor.

As the ball approaches, drop the box so as to trap the ball inside.

Then let Toddler try it, but roll the ball as slowly as possible and don't be surprised if she tends to wait too long.

Releasing the box in anticipation of where the ball will be when the box reaches the floor requires a high level of advance planning. She will find this a fascinating test of her skill.

Can Toddler take two medium-sized balls (about the size of a small basketball) and roll them toward each other so they collide? The difficulty of this game can be controlled by the size of the balls.

A simpler level at which to start is rolling two balls around and round, one under each palm at the same time.

Another game which teaches eye-hand coordination is to fill two cardboard boxes as quickly as possible with an assortment of small objects.

Two objects must be picked up with each hand at the same time, and then the two dropped simultaneously into the two boxes.

Variations of grasp also require new coordination skills. See if Toddler can pick up an object between her two flat palms, without closing her fingers around it.

Can she use one hand and one foot together to lift an object off the ground?

Eventually she can try to pick up objects by using only the backs of her hands.

These are some simple and not-so-simple coordination tasks that should be new to Toddler. They should be of appropriate difficulty for now and for the near future.

We will have more to say about coordination as time goes on, and we will continue to provide more ideas to stimulate development of these important skills. ■

Growing Child®

In the final analysis, it is not what you do for your children but what you have taught them to do for themselves that will make them successful human beings.

Ann Landers

Now That We Are Two—

Your two-year-old child has really come a long way in 24 months.

He has moved from helpless infancy to the edge of early childhood.

TWO is busy all the time. He has learned to run, although his running is still somewhat stiff and flat-footed.

Once he starts to run, he sometimes has trouble slowing down. He usually stops himself by colliding with someone or something.

Stairs are no longer a barrier. He can walk independently both up and down short flights of stairs. Of course, he must still bring both feet to each step in turn.

Although he usually holds the stair rail for support, sometimes he can climb a few steps without any support.

TWO also likes to jump off the last step of stairs or off the curbing as he walks down the street. When he jumps, he leads with one foot but lands on both feet, usually in a deep squat or sometimes on all fours.

He also can jump forward and loves to show how far he can jump. In general, he now loves rough and tumble play.

TWO can now hold a cup or small glass in one hand, lifting, drinking, and replacing it without spilling.

He can feed himself pretty well with a spoon—although he still spills a moderate amount. So eating can sometimes be pretty messy. Just try to ignore this as he continues to gain experience.

Dressing and undressing are gradually being mastered. He can take off his shoes if they are untied. He can put them on

again—not always on the proper foot. He can also put his socks on although heels sometimes cause trouble by ending up over the instep instead of the heel.

He also helps pull up or take down his pants. When he tries to pull them on by himself, he continues to get both legs in one side—sometimes even from the wrong end. He hasn't yet mastered the top and bottom or the front and back of pants and pullovers.

When playing he squats down to pick up objects from the floor. He also squats to get a closer look at interesting things such as a tiny ant, a fuzzy caterpillar, or a shiny pebble.

Paper and crayons are beginning to be of interest to him. He likes to scribble holding a pencil or crayon in his fist. If you make some vertical or horizontal strokes on paper, he will try to imitate them.

In general, TWO is getting more skillful with his hands. He can turn the pages

At 24 Months Youngster Likes to:
• Play "hide and seek."
• Use three-word sentences.
• String beads.
• Point to pictures in a book.
• Jump down a step.

Give Youngster:
• Different things to smell.
• Paper and crayons.
• Blocks for building.
• A ball to throw.
• Giant pegs and pegboards; beads to string.

of a book or magazine one at a time. He can turn a doorknob and unscrew a jar lid. He can even snip with blunt-ended scissors.

His grasp and release are now quite precise. He can build a "tower" with about six, 1-inch blocks or make a "train" by laying the blocks end-to-end on a table. He can push snap-it beads together and string large wooden beads on a shoelace.

Most children have developed handedness by this time so parents can be aware of the child's hand preferences.

TWO wants to wash and dry his hands by himself but cannot do either very well. It will be some time yet before he learns not to wipe dirty fingers on a clean towel.

Balls are often favorite playthings to be shared with an adult. He can throw overhand but still does it very poorly. He can walk up to a large ball on the ground and kick it.

continued on next page

Developmental Milestones—24 Months

Social/Emotional

- Uses a spoon to feed self.
- Chews food well.
- Raises and drinks from cup, then replaces it on table.
- Plays beside but not with other children.
- Is very possessive about toys—no sharing.
- Clings to caregiver when tired or afraid.
- Goes into tantrums when frustrated but can be distracted readily.
- Demands a lot of caregiver's attention.

Motor (Fine)

- Removes a wrapper from a cupcake.
- Builds a tower of six blocks.
- Imitates a vertical line with a crayon on paper.
- Turns pages in a book one at a time.
- Picks up tiny objects as small as a crumb.
- Names familiar miniature toys at a distance of 10 feet away.
- Enjoys picture books, pointing to details on command.

Motor (Gross)

- Runs on whole foot, but stops by falling down or by colliding with something or someone.
- Climbs stairs holding onto the railing (two feet to each step).
- Pulls wheeled toy by string, forward and backward.
- Throws a small ball.
- Walks into a large ball when intending to kick it.

Communication

- Engages in simple pretend play.
- Uses 50-200 or more recognizable words but may understand as many as 300 words.
- Puts together two or more words to formulate a sentence.
- Asks: "What's that?"
- Joins in nursery rhymes and songs.
- Refers to self by name.
- Points to and repeats the names of body parts such as eyes, nose, hair, feet, mouth.
- Understands simple commands and conversation. ∎

These milestones are guidelines only. All children do not develop at the same speed, nor do they spend the same amount of time at each stage of their development. Usually a child is ahead in some areas, behind in others and "typical" in still other areas. The concept of the "typical" child describes the general characteristics of children at a given age.

continued from front page

By now TWO has probably had considerable experience with a slide and is no longer satisfied just to slide down on his "seat."

He has begun to explore new and different ways of sliding—such as a "belly buster" on his stomach and sliding down backwards. (Your watchful eye will be needed as he attempts new experiments.)

TWO still prefers to play by himself. Although he enjoys being with other children, he plays beside them rather than with them. This has sometimes been aptly described as "parallel" play.

He can ride a kiddie-car and enjoys steering around obstacles.

TWO can now understand about 300 words. He likes to listen to stories you tell him.

He especially enjoys stories about himself and about his belongings.

TWO also likes for you to read him a story. As you read, he will want you to point to the pictures in the book. Sometimes he will want to do the pointing. Eventually he will spontaneously name a familiar person, animal, or object.

TWO is also eager to talk about his own experiences. He can now use about 50 recognizable words and can combine them into two-word sentences, such as "Dada go."

He likes to emphasize his newly experienced feelings of possession by labeling objects as "my ball", "my chair", "my house." In other words, "me", "my", and "mine" now become an important part of his vocabulary. But in a sentence he may use his first name ("Bobby do") instead of "I" or "me."

Simple questions are also getting more numerous. "What dat?" and "Why dat?" will become very familiar sounds around the house during the coming months.

Yes, indeed, your two-year-old child has really come a long way in 24 months—with even more exciting developmental changes to come in the months and years ahead. ∎

Homemade Toys

At two years of age, Youngster has much to learn from interacting with good educational toys. Here are some simple suggestions for toys you can make at home:

Xylophone. The basic principle of this sound-producing instrument is that of different tones produced by striking different lengths and thicknesses of metal or wood.

To make your own xylophone, use pieces of discarded copper tubing, steel pipe, or wood of different lengths and thicknesses.

Lay the wood or metal pieces next to one another on top of a piece of foam rubber. Now they're ready to play! Give Youngster a cooking spoon to tap out her music.

If you prefer a hanging instrument, hang up each piece of wood or metal using strong fishline.

Rubber Stamps. Any piece of rubber such as an old inner tube may be used.

First, trace a design such as a square on the rubber. Then cut it out with a sharp knife or razor blade.

Next glue the piece of rubber onto a block of wood—one that fits comfortably in the child's palm.

For variety you can substitute flat rubber erasers with the designs cut into them.

Now she can stamp the design on paper if she has a stamp pad. To make a simple stamp pad, soak a piece of foam rubber-sponge with tempera paint.

Youngster will have a lot of fun with these homemade toys. More importantly, these simple toys are providing her with opportunities to explore new dimensions of experience.

Table House. Every two-year-old would like to have her own house. Make her a house by throwing a blanket over a small table (a card table is excellent).

The opening in the blanket can serve as "front door."

Youngster will have a lot of fun with these homemade toys. But, more importantly, these simple toys are providing her with opportunities to explore new dimensions of experience.

From these explorations she can gain a better understanding of the world around her.

Safety note: The fishline, knife, and razor blade suggested in preparing these activities are not appropriate tools or playthings for youngsters this age without adult supervision.

They should be handled carefully and put away in a secure locaation after use. ■

Toilet Learning Reminder

In months 12 and 17 of *Growing Child,* we identified three basic prerequisites for successful toilet learning: adequate muscle control, development of communication skills, and a desire or willingness on the part of the child to participate in learning.

We mention the topic again in this issue simply because it appears to become a concern for parents of children around this age.

If your toddler is showing signs of readiness, it would be a good idea for you to refer to the longer articles in the previous two issues of *Growing Child.*

But if you find that your toddler is not showing any signs of readiness for toilet learning, our advice has consis-

tently been that you not try to rush the process. True, the lack of toilet learning can be hard on some parents' levels of tolerance and patience.

But a tolerant and patient attitude can be helpful both to the parent and the child.

Studies have even shown that the later the toilet learning starts, the less time it will take.

If you are tempted to rush the process, consider what the cost may be in terms of your child's loss of self-esteem.

Also consider the impaired parent-child relationship that your haste may induce.

Remember that every child is different.

Therefore the appropriate time for your child's toilet learning to begin is when—and only when—your child is ready. ■

Growing Pains

We have suggested that you can expect a growing negativism in Youngster's behavior during the next few months.

It may come as no surprise that Youngster now uses the word "no" often and forcefully. Sometimes it seems as if "no" is her favorite word. This behavior may cause you to reflect on your own use of the word "no."

Actually, we think the word "stop" is generally better for parents to use than "no." "Stop" is a little more specific than "no." "Stop" conveys rather explicitly that whatever she is doing is supposed to cease. "No" is more vague. We think you will find many occasions where "stop" will be more explicit.

How can one explain Youngster's growing resistance and stubbornness? Is it a reaction to having lost her former position at the center of the universe?

As an infant she was the kingpin about whom all adults revolved. They heeded her beck and call. Her every need was satisfied with little or no delay.

But now she is expected to control her bowels, wait for meals that are served only three times a day, and entertain herself for long periods at a time.

Has the loss of her former status created tensions and frustrations? Her desires must be delayed for a longer time before being fulfilled. She reacts with general stubbornness and unwillingness to cooperate with adults.

While this explanation has some obvious merit, it is probably not the most basic reason for Youngster's present behavior.

For one thing, Youngster's "fall from grace" has not been all that sudden. It has been happening gradually for quite some time.

We noted in an earlier issue how her learning to walk caused adults in her world to see her differently and treat her in a different way than when she was a sitting and crawling infant.

For another thing, Youngster's increasing maturity, both physical and social, permits her to handle more stress and responsibility than before. As long as your demands match up with her abilities, she should be able to handle the situation.

What then is likely to be the reason for her more negative and stubborn behavior? We think it is not the loss of power but rather the discovery of new power that leads to her negativism.

Youngster has discovered that "no" is a powerful word. It is an expression of her increased ability to assert herself. It brings people up short, draws attention and elicits lots of words from them.

"No" is a term of control over a situation whereas "yes" is merely going along with the situation.

The world of smoothly flowing events stops suddenly when she says "no." New happenings begin to revolve around her in an attempt to get her to say "yes."

This new attention and her control of events lead her to experiment with being resistive in a variety of situations.

There are several ways to handle Youngster's negativism. The first step is to recognize that this type of behavior is normal at this age. This will help you be less disturbed when she is contrary.

Second, it is often useful to tell Youngster what to do rather than asking a question with a possible "yes" or "no" answer.

You could say, "Here are some nice carrots," instead of asking, "Would you like some carrots?" Obviously if you give Youngster the option of saying "no" and she then says "no," you are in a bit of a bind.

If you expect resistance, such as at bedtime, start her down the road you want her to go, then insert some pleasant experience into her activity.

Thus, you could say, "Let's get your pajamas on and then Daddy will give you a ride." Or maybe a bedtime story is the inducement that will set the wheels in motion.

What you are doing is rewarding (that is, reinforcing) the first step in the right direction. After that, Youngster's own momentum can more easily carry her through the task to be accomplished.

Finally, it may sometimes be necessary to ignore resistance and proceed gently but firmly along the course you have chosen.

If Youngster refuses to leave the house for the planned visit to Aunt Sharon's, you may have to lead her firmly by the hand or even carry her to the car.

It is important not to be impressed by the fuss that she raises when you do this. In other words, try not to show you are angry. Pay as little attention to the fuss as possible and avoid looking at her.

Don't try to reason with her or "sweet-talk" her while she is actively resisting. Such extra attention merely reinforces the resisting behavior since she learns quickly that resisting brings her more attention.

Note that negative attention, such as scolding, actually reinforces (or strengthens) the resisting behavior you would like her to change. The reason is that children crave attention, even negative attention.

continued on next page

Learning New Words

Now that Youngster is becoming more verbal and less physical in her communication, it is possible to observe more easily her language development.

She is beginning to arrange words so that they make sense. Although she doesn't know all of the rules of grammar, she will be more inclined to say "Daddy eat pie" than "pie eat Daddy."

By listening to you, she learns the correct arrangement. This doesn't mean that she is simply repeating your speech. Children are known to utter sentences they've never heard.

What the child has acquired is the underlying subject-verb-object pattern—"Daddy eats pie" and many other sentences like it. In other words, she has abstracted the pattern and can order other words in a similar manner.

Even when Youngster uses longer sentences, she is more selective about her choice of words, preferring the content words—

nouns, verbs, adjectives—because they carry the information. She omits articles, prepositions, and conjunctions because they lack content.

In addition, the content words receive most of the attention or stress in our own speech. When she hears "Daddy is eating the pie," the most vivid words are the content words, "Daddy," "eating," and "pie."

In Youngster's spontaneous speech, the pronouns "this" and "that" are used abundantly. However, she must either look at, point to, or pick up the object when she uses these words. In most situations "this" or "that" are spoken in response to your "what" questions.

Her understanding and use of new words is increasing so rapidly it is hard to keep account of them.

When she talks to herself—especially when she is alone, such as in bed—she repeats and repeats new words and usually puts them into a meaningful context.

She can be heard repeating familiar words, too. Only now she generalizes them into new situations. Swiss psychologist and natural scientist Jean Piaget calls this kind of behavior "practice play."

How is she absorbing so much so fast? She wisely observes the speaker's use of body language—facial expressions, hand gestures, body movement—in order to help her understanding of words.

If you have watched people speaking a foreign language, you know that it is sometimes possible to interpret what is being said by following the speaker's use of body language.

When communicating with Youngster, we recommend that you continue to use gestures and body language to accompany your words.

Another way Youngster learns new words is through your interpretation of what is happening.

Haim Ginott, author of "Between Parent & Child", used this approach as a means of managing behavior to establish good family relationships.

For example, when Youngster falls and is crying, if you tell her, "You're crying because you fell and hurt yourself. It hurts when you fall so hard," she will likely simmer down.

You will have matched words to her feelings and conveyed to her your understanding of her feelings. This technique borders on magic if employed consistently and immediately.

Another effective vocabulary-builder is the habitual use of choices. For example, you ask "Shall we put on the jacket or vest?" "Would you like an apple or an orange?" Or, "Do you want to read this red book or that blue book?"

Youngster has to compare and contrast two different concepts by considering some of their similarities and differences. Her learning of both concepts is thereby strengthened. ■

continued from previous page

That is why it is important to pay little or no attention to her undesirable, resisting behavior.

After she has quieted down and has begun to cooperate, it is wise to reward her by giving your attention to something she enjoys doing, such as playing with her favorite toy.

We talked earlier about temper tantrums. If Youngster is still throwing tantrums with regularity, it is time to sit down and think about how you are reacting to them.

Giving in or fussing will perpetuate this behavior that you would rather see your child change or eliminate.

It is important to establish a routine in Youngster's life—so that she knows what to expect next. Routine and ritual—knowing what will come next—helps to prevent

resistance. There may be other stormy outbursts, short of a tantrum, however, and these also deserve a word of comment.

A child this age characteristically shows no gradation of emotion. That means her response is all-or-nothing with little or no moderation in her reactions.

She has not yet learned to express mild irritation when such behavior would be more appropriate to the particular situation that is bothering her.

Instead, the irritating situation will provoke an outburst that is sudden and violent. But it is over just as quickly as it started, like a summer rainstorm.

This is something to be lived with for awhile. Both her behavior and your nerves will be better off if you avoid overreacting to these emotional storms. ■

Activities for All Senses

Youngster is well along in naming objects and stringing two or three words together into sentences. He is starting to describe in simple ways the interesting things that happen to him.

Since he communicates with the world around him through all five senses, every avenue of sensing is his learning laboratory. His words reflect not only what he sees, hears, and feels but also the tastes and smells of things he comes in contact with.

Here are some activities that will appeal to Youngster's growing awareness of the world around him.

Show Youngster how to rub his hand lightly over a piece of sandpaper. Describe its feel. "The sandpaper is rough. It feels scratchy." But the wooden floor has a different feel. "The wood is smooth."

Similarly you can have him compare the feel of a bedsheet with a nailbrush. "The sheet is smooth but the nailbrush feels rough."

You might want to test his understanding afterwards by bringing him a rough and a smooth object. Tell him to feel them both.

Then ask him to give you the one that is smooth (or rough). A piece of bark, for example, will be rough compared with one of his smooth blocks.

Don't worry if at first he doesn't get it right. He may need many more examples to understand these concepts.

The important thing right now is that he experiences the differences and learns there is a name for each. This method of using two contrasting things to teach a principle is one we will continue to use.

Youngster also can learn to make a loud clap or a soft clap by changing the force with which he strikes his hands together.

As soon as he can follow your instructions to clap either loudly or softly, you might see if his understanding will transfer to another situation, like hitting a cardboard box or jar lid with a wooden spoon.

You can explain "sticky" by sticking a piece of cellophane tape to Youngster's finger.

While he is trying to get it off, you can explain that it is sticky so it sticks to his finger. Or let him have some fun by walking on Contac paper that is upside down.

Tearing paper with two hands is an interesting sensory experience that Youngster may not have encountered yet. In the past he may have ripped a page out of a magazine by pulling on it with one hand, but that is not the same thing.

Show him how you can tear a piece of paper in two by drawing one hand toward you and one away from you. When he tries it, he will pull both hands away from his centerline. But he may still get two

Growing Child®

P. O. Box 2505 • W Lafayette, IN 47996
(800) 927-7289
©Growing Child, Inc.
www.GrowingChild.com

Contributing Authors

Phil Bach, O.D., Ph.D.
Miriam Bender, Ph.D.
Joseph Braga, Ed.D.
Laurie Braga, Ph.D.
George Early, Ph.D.
Carol R. Gestwicki, M.S.
Liam Grimley, Ph.D.
Robert Hannemann, M.D., F.A.A.P.
Sylvia Kottler, M.S.
Bill Peterson, Ph.D.

pieces, even if they are of widely different sizes.

Blowing is an activity at which Youngster is gaining increasing skill. He can now blow out a candle. You might set a tall piece of glass between him and the candle before he tries to blow it out.

Does he know enough to move the glass out of the way?

You could ask him, "What made the candle go out?" He will say, "I did." Then you ask, "But, why can't you make it go out when there is a piece of glass in front of the candle?"

A New Year's Eve blow toy will be fascinating to him now, as he learns to direct his blowing more carefully.

If you make a musical sound by blowing across the top of a pop bottle, Youngster will try in vain to imitate you. He also cannot blow up a balloon. But you can use a balloon to demonstrate what air is and how it can fill things.

Then, if he has any doubt as to what made the balloon get bigger, you can let him feel the rush of air and hear the squeak as you slowly let the air out through the neck.

Smell and taste should also have his attention. Have Youngster close his eyes while you let him smell some aromatic food with which he is familiar. Then, with his eyes open, see if he can choose that food from among two or three choices in front of him.

The same thing can apply to taste. You might use the old saying, "Open your mouth and close your eyes and I'll give you something to make you wise."

You can accompany his tasting with descriptive words like, "This tastes sour (sweet or salty)." See if he can tell you what he tasted or point to it when he opens his eyes.

Experiences like these will keep Youngster attuned to all five senses. All of them are important in learning about the world. ■

Growing Child®

> . . . a child should not be denied a balloon because an adult knows that sooner or later it will burst.
>
> Marcelene Cox

The Challenges of a Two-Year-Old

You may have heard some people refer to this period in a child's life as the "terrible twos." Actually, with a little understanding of the important development taking place, you may come to view the "terrible twos" as the "terrific twos!"

Right now, Toddler is striving for a sense of autonomy, a feeling of being his own person. He is fascinated with expressions of his own will (for example, his frequent use of the word "No!").

He is also striving to be less dependent on his caregivers. Here are some ways to encourage independence and at the same time avoid negative parent-child interactions:

(1) The two-year-old constantly wants to help you, a sure signal of extra mess and more clean-up. We urge you to accept his offer and exploit it. Assign him simple tasks that he can do with you. If he wants to dust, for example, give him his own dusting mitt.

This practice is training for the future when he will enjoy bigger responsibilities such as setting the table and putting objects away.

Many parents of older children wonder why their children don't pick up after themselves. The lack of early experience in helping around the home is probably part of the answer.

Special Note: *Now that your child is two years old, the sections titled "Youngster Likes To" and "Give Your Youngster" are being omitted. At this age the comments in the body of each monthly issue more appropriately describe your child's development.* ■

As you and your child work together, talk about what you are doing. Even in an ordinary household situation you can casually teach valuable concepts, new vocabulary and good grammar.

Consider the task of "picking up and putting away." Don't wait until late afternoon or evening when Youngster is tired and fretful. You'll both enjoy more success if you shelve toys immediately after he's through playing with them.

At this age he needs specific instructions rather than general statements. He most likely will be unable to respond to the broad command "put all your toys away." But he will happily participate in a playful duet: "First we'll pick up the big cars. Let's put them down here. Now we'll find the little cars. We'll reach up high to put them on this shelf."

As you complete these simple tasks together, a lot of learning is taking place about the concept of space: spatial organization, position of himself and objects in space, and their relationship to each other.

• He is stretching both his mind and his body. He must squat and stretch in order to pick up and deposit the cars. Meanwhile you are interpreting his movements to him and he is matching words to actions: for example, "up" and "down"— very important direction words.

• He is developing his understanding of relative size, "big" and "little," for example.

• He is listening to your use of language from which he will increase his word supply and later construct his own sentences.

(2) Two-year-old dawdles, and when you press him to hurry, he resists more. How can such situations be handled? There are several approaches you can try:

(a) Make it a habit to talk about the next thing that will happen: "Pretty soon we'll be going to Granny's. We'll leave in five minutes."

(b) Allow him some time to say goodbye to whomever is present or to whatever he is doing.

(c) Offer him a choice. "Do you want to walk or do you want me to carry you?" Abide by his decision once you have offered him a choice you can live with.

(d) If all else fails, entice him away. "I'm going to show you some magic when we get to the kitchen." Then reward him with the demonstration of something simple.

In addition to avoiding a confrontation, some important learning is taking place. Each time you alert Youngster to anticipate an event, his ability to understand and organize the concept of time will increase.

And the vocabulary associated with time ("pretty soon," "five minutes") will become understandable. Also, he will appreciate the fact that you respect him and honor his choice.

Finally, Youngster will get practice in making an important language transformation when he indicates his choice.

He will transform the information you pose in a question, "Do you want to walk or be carried?" to the answer he gives, "me walk." ■

Young Stutterers

Stuttering—an involuntary repeating or prolonging of sounds, syllables, words, or phrases—is often first noticed when a child is between two and five years of age. The child at this age is developing many complex motor and linguistic skills at a rapid rate.

He is learning, for example, to handle longer sequences of speech, muscle movements, developing a larger vocabulary, and trying to put words together in longer sentences. So, it is not surprising that many children go through a "stuttering" stage.

For many years speech-language pathologists thought that stuttering was caused by paying too much attention to the child's speech and was made worse by attempts to correct it.

Some speech-language pathologists still believe this to be the case. They recommend ignoring the stuttering and letting it run its course.

We now know, however, that there are a variety of causes for stuttering. Many contemporary experts have demonstrated excellent results through early intervention and treatment approaches that provide direct feedback to the child to encourage easy speech.

Some stuttering may be caused by faulty breath control, causing children to break their sounds and breathe mid-word. This situation can be helped by practicing rhymes and singing, so children absorb the concept of when to breathe.

Parents are often alarmed by their child's stuttering. The best way to reduce concerns about stuttering is to learn more about it and to know what things will help the child.

Here are some indicators suggesting a further consultation would be appropriate:

1. There is a history of stuttering in the family.

2. The child repeats or prolongs some sounds at the beginning or middle of words.

3. The child typically repeats the same sound three or more times.

4. The child prolongs a sound for more than two seconds.

5. The child makes faces or uses exaggerated movements of his head, arm, or body whenever repeating or holding speech sounds.

6. There is too much vocal or throat tension each time the child repeats or holds onto a sound.

7. The child demonstrates frustration in trying to communicate.

If some of these characteristics are present, it is a good idea to consult with your child's physician. After examining your child, he or she may decide to refer you to a speech-language specialist.

This individual can provide additional information and, if needed, develop a program for prevention or treatment of stuttering.

Some things a parent can do to help a child develop more natural speech are listed below. Remember, it is always easier and wiser to do something ahead of time than try to stop something later. These recommendations will reduce the possibility that stuttering will occur.

1. Make family life less hectic by scheduling events carefully and allowing more time to prepare for them. (All children tend to repeat words more frequently when they are excited or hurried.)

2. Plan more communication time that includes individual, undivided attention

continued on next page

Hearing Impairment

The child who is hearing-impaired has trouble understanding the meaning of the sounds she does hear, no matter how alert or intelligent she may be. She also has trouble learning to talk.

In order to detect hearing loss early, three-fourths of the States require hearing tests on all infants born in hospitals. These tests are helpful but are not a substitute for regular hearing evaluations done by a physician.

The prevalence of defective hearing in school age children is estimated to be five percent. But this figure usually represents only those children who are placed in programs for the hard of hearing. It does not represent children with mild hearing loss which frequently goes undetected.

Absence of speech, delayed speech development, and speech that is impossible to understand are all symptoms of a possible hearing impairment. Mild hearing loss may be the result of repeated ear infections.

Parents are a most important source of information in helping a physician or other professional detect any hearing problem. The physician will observe Youngster in order to answer questions such as: "How well and what does she learn?" "What sounds are absent from her speech?" "How many words or phrases does she have?"

Your physician will want to check Youngster for possible infection which may contribute to the problem. He may also suggest that you see another professional, an audiologist.

Early detection and remedial treatment are very important. ∎

152

A Reasoning Game

We have at times in the past suggested activities that we called sleight of hand or magic. The unseen hand does something to an object while Youngster is asked to figure out what happened.

Such games show us the level of her reasoning ability. She must be able to reason, for example, about cause and effect in order to explain a particular result that she observes.

There are many activities that a parent and child can do together that will help to prepare her for later problem-solving. A child of this age will generally be too young to solve these problems by herself. But she will enjoy the parent-child interaction in working together on these projects that will stretch Youngster's thinking about the world around her.

Here is a trick that will challenge her present reasoning ability. Show Youngster a penny and a small ball of play dough. Then place both objects in a paper sack. While they are hidden, press the penny inside the ball.

continued from previous page

with the child. Help the child feel good about sharing ideas with others. Talking and listening should be fun.

3. Model good speech by using slower, smoother speech with the child and encourage such use by the child. Talk in terms of "easy" speech.

Parents should convey an attitude of patient attention so children don't feel they have to rush while they have their attention.

4. Encourage members of the family to allow time for the child to talk and to complete all sentences without interruption.

5. Help the child with vocabulary and use of language, and provide opportunities to reinforce success.

6. Consult the child's physician if there are any questions about the child's speech. ■

After smoothing over all signs of the penny's entrance, uncover the ball. See if Youngster can figure out what happened to the penny. Will she first look for it in the paper sack?

It is not likely that Youngster will solve the mystery without help. Her sense of how the clay can be molded to engulf another object is hazy, even if she has had some experience in squeezing and reforming play dough.

In providing her with hints, there are a number of ways to proceed. One way is to repeat the problem using a container for the penny, such as a small box. Show Youngster how the box can be opened to reveal something inside.

Once the idea of containment is planted in her mind, Youngster has a better chance of solving the clay problem, if it is repeated soon thereafter.

Another possibility is to manipulate the clay in ways that may provide hints. Twisting the ball apart into two halves may show her that something might have been hidden inside.

Another approach is to select some other small object. Let her see you press it into the ball of play dough. After such a demonstration she will readily dig into the ball for the second object.

With this concept of the ball containing something, she should then go looking for the penny as well.

Now test her understanding further. Do the trick with a playing card that is slipped inside the cover of a book. As Youngster's understanding of the principle deepens with additional examples, she will be able to apply the solution to new situations that are different from the original one.

She may even be able to see through a deliberate distortion of reality, as with a false-bottomed container. You can create such a container by taping a false paper bottom about two-thirds of the way down inside a paper cup. Leave enough untaped area that you can slip a small object, like a short

Whether Youngster correctly "solves" these problems is relatively unimportant at this age. What is important is that she is being introduced to new concepts and new problem-solving techniques that challenge her thinking skills.

length of yarn, under the false bottom.

At first glance, of course, the cup will appear empty to Youngster. But by now her well-established idea of containment should cause her to look more closely at the cup.

If the false bottom is sufficiently high, she may realize that the inside depth of the cup is less than the outside height, and poke the bottom with her finger to discover the secret.

However she discovers the yarn, she won't feel unfairly tricked by the false bottom. She will just accept it as something to be remembered in a world that is always producing something new and unexpected.

Another activity is to give Youngster lots of containers to fit together. Some do fit together and some don't. She can create her own problems to solve.

Whether Youngster correctly "solves" all these problems is relatively unimportant at this age. What is important is that she is being introduced to new concepts and new problem-solving techniques that challenge her thinking skills.

Besides, Youngster will enjoy the special attention involved in helping Mom or Dad to "solve" a particular problem, even though her role at this age may be primarily one of observational learner. ■

'She Bit Me First!'

As a parent, it may be embarrassing to be told that your child is guilty of biting another child. A parent's first reaction is sometimes disbelief: "No, my sweet child wouldn't do such a thing!"

This can be followed by shock and horror, "What kind of savage has my child become, biting another human being?"

The reaction of the parent whose child has been bitten is usually no less dramatic, "I can still see the marks of that monster's teeth."

If you question your own child about the matter, you may be told, "She bit me first."

It's generally not helpful to take sides or try to determine who really "started it" or who first said what to whom. It's better to make it perfectly clear—in a no-nonsense tone of voice—that biting another person is **never** acceptable under any circumstances.

Contrary to what some people may think, occasional biting by a two-year-old child who is angry or frustrated, is not a sign of deep emotional disturbance.

It is behavior, however, that must be changed. Every child who bites another must learn that the biting has got to stop.

Biting behavior usually peaks between two and three years of age and then starts to decline as verbal abilities improve.

In their efforts to stop this behavior, some parents have tried washing out their child's mouth with soap and water.

Others have tried biting the child back "to let her know what it feels like."

We definitely do not recommend such drastic and undesirable measures. Besides, they have been found to be ineffective ways of dealing with the problem.

To stop biting behavior, it's not enough to treat the symptoms without dealing with the underlying causes. At two years of age, a child does not yet know how to control her feelings when she gets over-excited, angry, or frustrated. So, she may hit, kick, or bite the child who upsets her.

In reality, biting is usually no more aggressive or harmful than hitting or kicking. But biting is often perceived as much more malicious.

It usually evokes a greater howl from the victim—and from the victim's parent. That's because (a) biting appears so animalistic and uncivilized, and (b) the bite not only hurts but usually leaves a visible mark.

All normal children experience feelings of anger, frustration, and aggression at some time. They must learn to control these impulses in order to avoid aggressive behavior.

Although boys are generally more aggressive than girls, girls are just as likely to bite as boys.

How then do you stop your child from biting? Here are some recommendations:

1. **Provide closer supervision.** The child who bites other children needs more structure and supervision.

The person who supervises (usually the parent or teacher) must watch for signs of anger, frustration, or tiredness which often precede biting behavior.

2. **Intervene early.** Many children's problems can be better controlled or prevented by early intervention. For example, if you see the child who bites being teased or provoked, don't wait for trouble to occur. Separate the children from one another as soon as possible.

3. **Reprimand calmly but firmly.** Whenever one child bites another, it is important to reprimand as calmly and firmly as possible: "You must never bite another child. That **hurts** her."

Then quietly take the child to a room by herself. Give her time alone to settle down and get herself under control.

If she continues to yell or scream, it is best to ignore these behaviors as much as possible, unless, of course, you think she will do some damage.

Left alone in a room, a two-year-old will usually calm down in about ten to fifteen minutes.

4. **Teach her alternative behaviors.** In dealing with her feelings of anger or frustration, she must ultimately learn to express her feelings verbally rather than physically.

That is a skill that will need much practice. It is also one which will usually improve as children get older and can better express themselves verbally.

In general, thoughtful management of the problem, rather than severe punishment, will improve the likelihood of changing the child's biting behavior.

In summary, among normal two-year-olds, most cases of biting are due to the child's lack of self-control. The child who bites can usually be helped by closer supervision, early intervention, calm but firm reprimands, and by learning alternative ways to deal with feelings of anger and frustration.

What should a parent do if these techniques don't work and the biting becomes more frequent?

This may indicate the child has a more severe problem. If the biting behaviors continue for more than a few weeks, it would be wise to consult a pediatrician or child psychologist. ∎

Poisoning Prevention

Sad to relate, most poisonings in young children are caused by substances commonly found in the home, such as medicines and household products.

Accidents in the home are most likely to occur when a parent is preoccupied in some activity, such as preparing dinner or talking on the telephone.

Young children are, by nature, curious about the world around them. They are fascinated by little bottles with colored pills and by containers and sprays of all kinds.

They also like to imitate whatever they have seen an adult do. Parents of a young child, therefore, need to be aware of the possible dangers of poisoning in the home and how they can prevent such accidents from happening.

Here are some recommendations to prevent possible poisonings:

1. Keep all medicines and household products in a cabinet that is locked or out of reach of children.

Don't underestimate a young child's curiosity and ingenuity in reaching a desired object.

2. Don't leave a young child alone for a moment—even to answer the telephone—if there is any poisonous substance within reach.

Young children can act fast, and most poisons, unfortunately, also act equally fast.

3. Avoid taking medicine while a young child is watching. Children are great imitators but are usually unaware of possible dangers of poisoning.

4. Buy medications and other potential poisons in containers which have child-proof caps.

The U.S. Consumer Product Safety Commission estimates that hundreds of children's lives have been saved by the use of child-proof caps.

5. Keep all products in their original containers with their original labels. Accidental poisonings have occurred when someone was not aware what product was in a container.

6. Check the label every time that medication is taken to be sure you are using the correct medicine and the correct dosage. A mistake can easily be made because medicine containers often look alike.

7. Medication should never be taken in the dark. Always be sure to turn on a light when giving or taking medicine.

8. Read the label on all household products to become aware of any potential dangers. Be aware also of what steps need to be taken if a particular harmful substance is swallowed or inhaled.

9. Prescription medication should be taken only by the person for whom it was prescribed. The doctor knows an individual patient's medical history and uses this information in writing a prescription.

It is highly dangerous for parents to give a child—even in a small dosage—medication that was originally prescribed for someone else.

10. Periodically clean out the cabinets of all old medications and old household products no longer in use.

After the products have been disposed of, the containers should be cleaned out and then discarded or recycled in a safe manner.

11. Be truthful with a child when talking about medication. Tell the child the name of the medicine being used and for what purpose it is being taken.

Don't ever refer to medicine as "candy." This would give the child the wrong impression that medicine, like candy, is safe for children to eat at any time.

12. Talk to your child, in a calm manner, about the danger of poisoning.

Include possible harmful effects of improper use of medication or household products. They should eat and drink only those substances they are absolutely certain are safe. When in doubt, they should always check with an adult.

What to do if your child takes poison:

If your child swallows or inhales a substance which you believe is poisonous, **call your local Poison Control Center immediately.** There are more than 100 such centers nationwide.

It is wise to keep the number of your local Poison Control Center near every telephone in your home.

In case you cannot find the number of your local poison center, contact your doctor or the nearest hospital or call your local emergency number (usually 911).

Prompt action is important. Most children who receive immediate treatment are not permanently harmed.

Parent awareness of the dangers of poisoning is the most effective way to prevent such accidents from happening. ∎

What Will the Water Do?

Unstructured materials like sand and water are useful in building up Youngster's experience with shapeless quantities, the kinds he must later learn to judge, measure, and understand.

If Youngster has had several months of playing and experimenting freely with sand and water, he is now ready for you to test his understanding in a few simple ways.

The following activities will require him to use his experience to predict effects. They should also give him a chance to see some new relationships.

Select three drinking glasses that have approximately the same diameter but different heights so that they hold different quantities of water.

Line them up before Youngster. Fill the middle size glass with water. Then, pointing to the larger empty glass, ask him, "Will this glass hold all the water that is in this full one?"

Whether he says "yes" or "no,' say, "Let's find out," then pour the water into the larger glass. "Yes, the big glass held all the water."

Pour the water back into the middle glass. Repeat the question, this time with the small empty glass. Then make the test.

"No, the little one couldn't hold all the water; some of it spilled out." Needless to say this would best be done with a catch basin underneath.

This comparison of heights is fairly simple, and Youngster will quickly learn to make the correct judgment.

Next you can repeat the problem with containers that are the same height but of different widths. A good trio would be a 4-inch-high pan, a two-cup glass measuring container, and a small soup can.

Again, Youngster will quickly be able to judge the containers by their widths and make the right decisions after a few tries.

Now combine the two sets of containers and add others to provide a variety of capacities. Fill one container and point to another, asking him whether it will hold the water of the first.

Here the problem becomes much more difficult, for Youngster must take into account the height and width of a container at the same time.

In fact, for all but the most obvious differences in capacity, Youngster will make

Note: For safety reasons, never leave a child (or children) alone in the bathtub or another area where a quantity of water is available.

Growing Child®

P. O. Box 2505 • W Lafayette, IN 47996
(800) 927-7289
©Growing Child, Inc.
www.GrowingChild.com

Contributing Authors

Phil Bach, O.D., Ph.D.
Miriam Bender, Ph.D.
Joseph Braga, Ed.D.
Laurie Braga, Ph.D.
George Early, Ph.D.
Carol R. Gestwicki, M.S.
Liam Grimley, Ph.D.
Robert Hannemann, M.D., F.A.A.P.
Sylvia Kottler, M.S.
Bill Peterson, Ph.D.

the correct judgment only about half the time, which is the same likelihood as getting it correct purely by chance.

But the game will give him practice in judging the capacity of one container in comparison with another.

The knowledge, built up in free play, that water can be held in a container and poured will now allow him to use water in comparing the sizes of different containers.

The water is a way of measuring. It matters not to him that the yardstick may seem to change its size.

In this, as with other activities, the motivating gamelike quality will be enhanced if you take turns. If he answers a question right, he gets to pick a container to fill and then choose another for you to judge, and vice versa.

This game can also be played between two children under your supervision.

A few more interesting questions can be posed for Youngster. Ask him whether the tea strainer or flour sifter in your hand will hold some water.

Fill an empty milk carton with water. If you punch a hole in the middle of it, will all the water run out? What if the hole is punched near the bottom?

Half fill a dish with sand and pour in a little water. "Where did the water go? Is it hiding in the sand? Let's tip the dish and see if the water comes out."

With a plastic glass full of water and a rock in your hand, ask, "What will happen to the water in this full glass if I drop in the rock?"

Youngster can't express or understand the principles involved in these effects, but experiencing them is what counts.

Parents don't need to teach all of these concepts directly; provide lots of time for children to make discoveries on their own through exploratory play. ∎

Open the door to a lifetime of learning
with the right books for your child.
Author Unknown

Learning to Wait

The ability to delay satisfying a need, and the ability to be good-humored about the delay, are most attractive and endearing traits in a child or in an adult.

The person who doesn't get upset or angry when she can't have what she wants just when she wants it, is a pleasure to have around. Usually she is a happy person.

Further, she is probably an effective and productive person. The ability to tolerate reasonable delay is essential to being able to stick to a task, solve a problem, or complete an assignment.

This quality of personality doesn't just suddenly happen when a person reaches adulthood. It develops slowly from early infancy.

Strange as it may seem, it appears to develop better in young children whose needs are adequately satisfied. That is, the baby who is *not* frustrated appears to be better able to tolerate and deal with frustration.

A study sponsored by the National Institutes of Mental Health indicates that there is a close relationship between the degree of pleasure a baby experiences during her feedings and the gradual development of her ability to delay having her needs met.

The study found that, as a baby learns to look forward to pleasurable relief from the tension caused by hunger, she gradually begins to tolerate necessary periods of waiting—provided, of course, that in the beginning the delay is brief and bearable.

At the end of their first year, children who had their physical and emotional needs adequately met showed increased ability to pay attention to tasks and to handle testing situations well.

Introduced to activities such as fitting pegs in holes or dropping blocks into a container, these children showed interest in the tasks and pleasure when they succeeded. Further, they were not usually frustrated by failure.

In contrast, children whose feeding experiences had been less pleasurable showed less interest, less patience, and less concentration. Many showed signs of anxiety about what was expected of them.

The study was careful to point out that it is the *repeated* good or unhappy experiences that matter—not the occasional interference such as normal illness, teething, fatigue, or family stress.

As a child moves from infancy into early childhood, her ability to tolerate frustrations will continue to develop as her changing needs continue to be met.

Wise parents learn to recognize early signs of frustration in their child. Thus they are able to relieve the child's tension before there is loss of control, disorganized behavior, or temper tantrums.

This avoidance of frustration does not imply over-permissiveness. Rather it results from setting and maintaining realistic limits on behavior. A child feels secure when she knows what her parents expect of her and what she can expect from them.

Further, recognizing the early signs of frustration includes being aware of the effects of over-fatigue or over-stimulation and protecting the child from these stresses when possible.

It includes providing a pleasurable distraction at such times, such as reading a favorite story. It also includes allowing the child freedom to make mistakes as she grows into independence.

The emotional security provided by consistent meeting of her physical and emotional needs frees the child from the anxiety of uncertainty. Thus freed, she can concentrate better on a task, wait her turn, and accept the inevitable disappointments of life with reasonably good humor.

Later in her life, the social, behavioral, and learning demands of school will include the ability to wait to have a need or wish satisfied.

The gradual maturation of the child's ability to wait is therefore an important preparation for later life. ■

A More Independent Youngster

Around a child's second birthday one can observe a shift from dependent Toddler to more independent preschool Youngster.

Since this phase will continue over the next several months and years, it is worth discussing in more detail.

Parents who have an understanding of the changes that are occurring in their child will be better prepared to handle the behavior that accompanies this developmental process.

It appears that a number of factors converge to produce this shift from passive dependence to active independence. Among the most important are: (1) increased movement skills, (2) improved language ability, and (3) newly emerging social skills.

Youngster's newly acquired movement skills enable her to explore new territories. Just being able to run more easily or to climb stairs one at a time allows her to experience the exhilaration of independent discovery.

At the same time her improved language ability provides her with new opportunities to express her own independent thoughts and engage in more social interaction.

As Youngster begins to play with her peers—at first alongside them in "parallel" play and later in face-to-face play—her newly emerging social skills also help her to make the transition from dependence to independence.

Often this striving for independence on Youngster's part can be very trying for parents.

She may insist, for example, on doing things for herself—like dressing—even though Mom or Dad are quite sure they can do the same things for her more efficiently and more neatly.

It is also trying on parents when Youngster constantly seems to want to "test the limits." It is often at this stage that she may suddenly decide to give up her afternoon nap—just when parents most need a midday break!

It is obvious that some adjustments in family living need to be made to take into consideration these developmental changes in behavior.

Parents also have to be willing to let their child stop being a baby for independence to really thrive.

These adjustments are initially often difficult for parents to make. But Youngster's newly acquired skills and, above all, her increased independence will eventually contribute to having a happier child in the home.

Ultimately her new behaviors will become a source of pride and joy for the parent who has learned to observe and handle this exciting developmental change. ∎

Toy Safety

A two-year-old is an imitator and an experimenter. Not only does she imitate, she is continually experimenting with her toys—poking, pulling, prying, pinching. There appears to be no end to her curiosity.

This is a time for you to be particularly aware that some toys can be dangerous for your child.

Some stuffed animals, for example, have cute button eyes that pull off easily, exposing the sharp points which fasten them on. These points sometimes do not lock like staples but are just pushed in like a double- or triple- pointed thumbtack. Such toys should be inspected carefully to avoid those that are dangerous.

This type of stuffed animal is apt to be found in souvenir shops or carnivals. They are often attractive to children and may be bought casually or given as a spur-of-the-moment gift.

Your two-year-old can be rough on toys. She experiments by dragging them, banging them, and even sitting on them. Avoid letting her play with anything that has sharp or rough edges which will cut or scratch.

Be sure to read age-related information on toy packages. Those with small parts should be labeled "Not Recommended For Children Under 3 Years."

Avoid toys or objects with small removable parts that can be swallowed or—perish the thought—pushed into an ear or even up a nose. No one knows why a child will push a small object up her nose—but we know that children do such things and the consequences may be serious. Other points to check for toy safety:

• If a toy is painted or has painted decorations, be sure that the paint is non-toxic. Imported toys may contain lead-based paint which can cause lead poisoning.

• Some plastic toys may be flammable if exposed to heat.

• Decorative beads, beans, or seeds may also be poisonous.

Although there are laws and regulations to protect young children from toys that may be dangerous, accidents that were avoidable are reported every year.

It is therefore wise for you to assume direct responsibility for checking the safety of any toy or other object with which your child may play. ∎

Let's Read a Story

Numerous research studies have indicated that children whose parents regularly read to them during the early childhood and school years will generally do better in school.

That is why we continue to encourage parents to read aloud to their children. A child's parents are generally his first educators and his most important resource for developing a love of reading.

Let's consider some of the things your child can learn while you read a story aloud:

Vocabulary. As you read, your child is acquiring new words. Let him see the pictures in the book. Point to an object as you read its name. See if he can point to some objects which you name.

Information. Your child is also acquiring new knowledge and expanding the horizons of his mind. Reading helps to open a whole new world for him.

Comprehension. From books a child acquires new understanding of his world. He perceives new relationships between words and can relate new knowledge to what he already knows.

Listening and attention skills. Reading helps to sharpen your child's listening skills and improve his attention span.

Mental awareness. As a result of your reading to him, he will also likely become more aware of and take greater interest in his everyday surroundings.

Sequencing. From your reading he can learn about sequencing in time ("Once upon a time ... ") and in space ("In the first place sat ... ") which are important skills for school learning.

Emotions. Use expression and drama in your reading to bring the story to life. As he identifies with the characters in the story, he can sometimes gain a better understanding of his own emotions.

Love of books. As you read to your child, you are imparting an important value in your life, namely, your own love of books.

Be willing to repeat favorites again and again. This is how children really learn the flow of language and pre-reading skills.

Also, read to your child daily. This isn't always easy to do, but the habit, once instilled, helps create lifetime readers and learners.

Personal love. Above all, by setting aside uninterrupted quiet time for reading, you are letting your child know how important he is to you.

You are thereby conveying your own personal love for him. ■

Reading Together

Here are some suggestions that will help you and your child get the most enjoyment out of reading together:

1. Try to make reading time a fun experience, both for you and for your child. So choose a time for reading that is good for you and for your child. Don't try to "impose" reading time—as though it were a daily duty—if you and/or your child are feeling tired.

2. Give Youngster your undivided attention while reading to him. If you have an answering machine for your telephone, use it. Also, turn off the radio, television and other media devices.

3. Become aware of the kinds of books your child enjoys the most. A trip to the public library will enable him to know more about the different kinds of books available.

4. Encourage your child to make his own choice of books. Ask him what he likes about the books he chooses.

5. Involve your child as much as possible in what you are reading.

Here are some suggestions:

• Point to pictures in the book as you say a word or ask your child to point to objects he recognizes.

• Get him to join you, if possible, in reading recurring sentences.

("Run, run, as fast as you can. You can't catch me, I'm the gingerbread man.")

• Ask him open-ended questions about the story. ("What do you think will happen next?")

• Help him to relate the story to his own experiences. ("Has that ever happened to you?" "What would you have done?")

6. Help your child develop a sense of sequencing in space and time. ("What happened first, second, next ... ?")

7. Relate the pace of your reading to your child's interest in particular aspects of the story.

Children often like to create their own "side-road" stories, becoming more fascinated with what happens along the way than with the story's ending.

Parents, on the other hand, are often the ones who are most eager to reach the story's ending.

8. Let your child cuddle up beside you or sit in your lap while you read with your arm around his shoulder.

The warm, loving feelings you convey are as important to your child—and often even more important—than the content of the story you are reading. ■

Expressions in Play

What an active period! Youngster touches, explores, and investigates everything everywhere. Her inquisitive nature and growing interests are limitless. Every obstacle, crumb, crack, or crevice is her immediate business.

In order to satisfy this enormous curiosity, she needs games, toys, and other objects.

However, don't give her too many toys, nor too expensive ones. Excessive generosity doesn't help her learn respect for her possessions. She may only learn that she can have more toys or better ones if she breaks them or becomes bored with them.

Too few toys, on the other hand, will not provide the mental nourishment she needs.

Games or toys made at home are an excellent learning resource. We encourage you to develop your own ideas related to your child's interests and abilities. Here are some examples:

(1) An old handbag for make-believe. Fill it with old keys on a key chain, a pocket flashlight (the kind which is sealed against removal of the battery or lamp), a hairbrush, and a comb.

(2) A cardboard box to help develop form perception. From the lid cut out various simple shapes (square, circle, diamond) through which she can deposit a matching object.

This box is more than a formboard. When she drops the object, she can watch it disappear, hear it land in the bottom of the box. Then she can remove the lid and observe where it went.

Further, after several trials, she will discover that the ball will go into the round hole while the cube will not.

(3) Tin cans for nesting or stacking. Remove the lids from fruit, vegetable, or juice cans. For safety, check the cans for sharp edges.

Having collected a variety of sizes, cover the exteriors of the cans with colorful adhesive paper.

Now Youngster can build towers to demolish. She can hide small cans inside large ones and discover some of the mysteries of space relations ("near" and "far," "up" and "down"). She can also learn about gravity, such as what happens when objects fall or drop off tables.

(4) A sandbox and basin of water for discovery. Give your child some different-sized containers from which to "pour" either sand or water. Dry beans and rice also can be used for emptying and filling practice.

By transferring sand or water from one location to another Youngster learns the various properties of these substances. (The water that was spilled on the ground just disappeared!)

(5) Plastic containers and lids for the development of size discrimination. Use an assortment of different-sized containers and lids, preferably ones made of non-breakable plastic. Screw one container securely to a board. Then let the child attempt to place the appropriate lid on the container.

For variety and complication, change the container on the board or change the location of the board.

In each of these activities your child enjoys a new learning experience. From new experiences emerge new ideas, new concepts, new understanding of the world around us.

In this way her enormous curiosity is being put to good use. Best of all, these new learning experiences are really fun. ∎

The Injuries of Childhood

Injuries, like illness, are a part of growing up. Knowing how to prevent and treat them is part of being a well-prepared parent.

Bumps and bruises happen to every active child every day, beginning with his first roll as an infant and continuing with the tosses and tumbles of later years.

Bumps and bruises happen when the child trips, falls, or collides with something as he walks or runs about. Occasionally injuries can happen in a tussle with a playmate.

Regardless of the cause of a bruise, the result is the same—a painful swelling that at first is red, then becomes blue, and after several days turns yellow or green.

Naturally parents try to prevent injury by developing good safety habits. But when injuries occur and a bruise develops, several first aid measures can be employed.

First, cool compresses or an icepack can be applied to the hurt area. This will decrease the pain and stop the bleeding that is occurring beneath the skin.

Wrapping a piece of ice in a cloth or paper towel may help relieve the discomfort. Getting Youngster to hold the ice in place is often more successful than having a parent try to do it. Parents can be prepared with ice by freezing water in Ziploc™ bags or small paper cups.

The pain of a bruise usually lasts only a short time (20-30 minutes) and then, although it may appear serious, seldom interferes with play.

If the bump continues to enlarge or becomes increasingly painful, it may mean there is continued bleeding. In such cases the cool compresses or icepack should be reapplied and your physician notified.

continued on next page

Numbers and Sizes

Over the last few months Youngster has probably had lots of experience with filling and emptying containers.

Our suggestions for learning activities have included using containers of different shapes and sizes with a variety of objects to fill them.

Now we can use Youngster's knowledge of container-object relationships and his growing understanding of "more" to take another step toward awareness of numbers.

First, though, Youngster needs to know what it means for a container to be full. For our purposes, "full" means that a container holds as many objects as possible while still permitting the cover to be put on without forcing. With this understanding established, a game can be played involving sizes and numbers.

Find two shoe boxes, coffee cans or other containers that have large openings and thus are easy to fill and empty.

You and Youngster each take one container. Then gather up a number of toys and durable household objects and place them in a pile between you and Youngster.

The objects should cover a wide range of sizes. The largest ones should be big

continued from previous page

Most bruises are gone within seven to 10 days although a little blue, yellow, or brown color may remain for two to three weeks.

There may also be a "knot" under the skin. This should get smaller and smaller as the weeks go by. If it does not, or if it becomes tender or inflamed, your doctor should be consulted.

Additional care and observation is necessary for head injuries. In the case of an injury around the eye, an icepack may be applied , but *never* directly on the eye. If the eye itself is injured, consult your child's physician immediately. ■

enough that three or four of them will completely fill a container. The smallest could be as small as a clothes pin. Try to have a few objects for each of several different sizes.

Take turns selecting an object, with each one putting the object selected into your own container. The goal is to fill one's container with as many things as possible. When each of you has filled your container as described, compare the number of objects in each one.

How can this be done since Youngster can't count? Pour out the contents of each container and arrange the objects from one of the containers in a straight line. Then form the other container's objects in a parallel straight line so that each of your objects lines up with each of Youngster's. This is called one-to-one correspondence.

If you have more objects, as will probably be the case, your line will be longer and it will be easy for Youngster to see that you have more objects.

If there are 10 or fewer objects in your line it would be good to count each one out loud as you point to it. Then do the same with Youngster's line. This will give him experience in hearing someone count. (Soon he will be able to do it, too,

although such behavior right now would probably be a result of rote learning rather than a true understanding of the counting process.)

The main purpose of this game is to show Youngster that there is a relationship between the size of the objects and the number that can be placed in the container.

In technical terms the number of objects that will fill a space is inversely proportional to their size. In more down-to-earth language, the smaller the objects, the more can be put in the container.

While Youngster can't express the idea even that simply, he should grasp it intuitively after playing this game a few times. Don't give away the winning method by selecting only the very smallest objects. Try to be just slightly better than he is and see if he finds his way to the correct method as he gains more experience.

As Youngster begins to grasp the principle, you can anchor his understanding by using new containers and new objects. His judgment of size will improve if you reduce the difference between the sizes of the objects to make them more alike.

This little game is a small but fun step on the long road to learning about numbers and sizes and their practical application. ■

Show Respect for Feelings

Both research studies and experience with child rearing reveal what marvelous imitators children are—"child see, child do."

It is therefore essential to start right now to model the positive traits you want your child to possess. For example, if you demonstrate respect for her feelings, she will grow up to exhibit this same quality.

At this age Youngster is likely to experience feelings of inadequacy with regard to her speech.

The late Dr. Haim Ginott championed an approach, a feedback technique, which not only helps the child overcome this sense of inadequacy but also helps to build a strong self-identity.

Let's consider an example. You're having morning coffee with a neighbor when Youngster rushes in to tell you something that is important to her.

Since she's not yet a fluent speaker and she's speaking in a hurry, you don't know what she's trying to tell you.

First, let's talk about what to do:

(1) Echo what she has said as best you can and replace the part you can't understand with one of the "wh" words. For example:

Youngster: "Sam broke too me ever."

Parent: "Sam broke what?"

(2) Assure her that you truly understand her feelings (even if you do not understand her speech). Reflecting her feelings back to her is very reassuring to a child and helps her develop self-confidence.

None of us ever outgrow the basic need for emotional support. For a child, this can be expressed by a hug or a squeeze accompanied by some simple feedback: "I know you are upset right now. I understand how you feel. Let's sit down and talk about it."

Treating Youngster as an individual with her own personal dignity will enable her to overcome her feelings of helplessness or inadequacy. It is also the best way to help her gain self-confidence and thereby build a positive self-concept.

Now, let's talk about what not to do.

(1) Don't belittle the child with criticism, that is, by asking, "Who can understand you when you talk like that?"

(2) Don't threaten her, "If you don't talk better, I'll have to send you to your room."

(3) Don't bribe her, "If you say it nicely, you can have a cookie."

(4) Don't command her, "Say it properly so we know what you mean."

(5) Don't overprotect her, "You poor girl—you haven't yet learned to talk."

In summary, by knowing how to deal appropriately with your child and by knowing what not to do, you can help to build your child's self-esteem and develop greater self-confidence. ∎

Growing Child®

P. O. Box 2505 • W Lafayette, IN 47996
(800) 927-7289
©Growing Child, Inc.
www.GrowingChild.com

Contributing Authors

Phil Bach, O.D., Ph.D.
Miriam Bender, Ph.D.
Joseph Braga, Ed.D.
Laurie Braga, Ph.D.
George Early, Ph.D.
Carol R. Gestwicki, M.S.
Liam Grimley, Ph.D.
Robert Hannemann, M.D., F.A.A.P.
Sylvia Kottler, M.S.
Bill Peterson, Ph.D.

View—or not

The plethora of "educational" videos and programs, including cable channels designed just for babies, may suggest to parents that they should be sitting their little ones in front of the TV. Other videos are often marketed with the slant that parents are denying their youngster an educational advantage if they do not provide regular viewing sessions at home.

In fact, the American Academy of Pediatrics (AAP) states exactly the opposite. AAP has a position statement titled: "Children, Adolescents, and Television" (Committee of Public Education, 2001).

This statement says that pediatricians should discourage any television (or video) viewing for children younger than two, and should encourage more interactional activities to promote proper brain development.

Education with babies and toddlers is more about interaction than pure information. Research on early brain development shows that babies and toddlers have an actual need for direct interaction with parents and other caregivers for healthy brain growth and the development of appropriate social, emotional, and cognitive skills.

The position statement goes on to say that the effects of television on brain wiring and eye development in children under age two are not yet known and are a matter of some concern.

Other statements from AAP regarding television find a link between childhood obesity, lack of exercise, and behavior, sleep, and attention problems in children who are exposed to television early in their lives, who view more than two hours a day, and who have a television in their bedrooms. (A Kaiser survey indicates that one child in five under the age of two has a television set in his/her bedroom.)

Certainly television is a part of our lives, but parents would do well to monitor and control its use in their children over age two and to avoid altogether television and videos for babies and toddlers. ∎

> Don't gossip about the children of others
> while yours are still growing up.
>
> Jewish Proverb

'The Operator'

Our young "almost-two-and-a-half-year-old" is rapidly extending her range of operations. And, she is an "operator."

By now she walks with a smooth heel-toe gait. Sometimes she combines walking with pushing, pulling, carrying or dragging almost anything movable. When not engaged in this sort of "work," she hurries from place to place as if afraid she might miss something.

Her running is still somewhat stiff and awkward. Although she is fairly sure-footed, she still has trouble turning sharp corners or coming to a quick stop. This means that she frequently trips, runs into things, or knocks them over.

She is curious about everything—so she continually must try things out for herself. She may stand on tiptoe to see something or to pull it down to her

level. She will also try to climb anything climbable.

Earlier she climbed just for the sake of climbing. She was interested in exploring all the space around her—vertical as well as horizontal. Now she climbs with a definite purpose—to see better or to reach something otherwise unreachable.

Her determination can be surprising. She will pull, push, and tug anything on which she can climb, such as a chair, to the right place for its effective use. A drawer in a chest of drawers can be pulled out to make a convenient step.

Once she has reached the object of her momentary heart's desire, guess what? She probably can't climb down again! You may find her in strange places—in a dry bathtub, on top of a chest of drawers,—or sitting in a chair "reading" a

newspaper!

Youngster has also learned to jump up, getting both feet off the floor. She bends her knees, then bends some more and swings her arms most energetically. With great effort, she clears the floor by an inch! Of course, our high jumper expects applause for such an enormous effort.

Youngster is busy learning many things and beginning to show more independence every day. If you haven't yet heard "Me do it!" you'll be hearing it soon—and often.

Be patient. This is a child's "Declaration of Independence"—a sign that Youngster is beginning to see herself as "Me," an individual, someone who can learn to cope effectively with this big, wide, wonderful world.■

Funny Sounds

Youngster's expressions are becoming increasingly funny. He reverses sounds in words so that biscuit sounds like "bik-sit," elephant is "efilant," bunny rabbit is "runny babbit."

If he doesn't know the precise words to express an idea, he creates his own. (By now you probably know that "pema bunny" is peanut butter.

From now until he is about three years old, Youngster will acquire approximately 50 new words a month.

In some cases you may not recognize them as bona fide words — "mardapane" for marmalade, for example —until you

hear him use them repeatedly in similar situations.

Youngster is also hard at work using many different parts of speech. While his first words were interjections ("hi," "bye," "ouch"), nouns are presently the words he uses the most, followed by action verbs ("go," "carry," "eat"), and prepositions ("up," "out," "in," "again").

His chatter is constant. It is as if his use of new words helps him to think aloud. Words help direct his perceptions and his motor activity.

In addition, words help him to associate

past experience to what he is presently doing. Thus words help build up a time world in which he can develop time concepts and the specific vocabulary to represent them.

It is often tempting for a parent to intervene by trying to redirect the child's chatter. However, parents can learn to understand their child better by listening as he talks to himself.

It may sound something like this if he is playing with a ball: "Ever you be, ball?" Or, looking through a picture book, he finds a picture of a dog. Then he closes the book and asks, "Ever can Lassie be?"■

Learning to Make Decisions

One of the most important skills a person can develop is the ability to make intelligent decisions. Throughout our lives our decisions will range from big ones like the choice of a mate or a career to small ones like deciding whether to buy something now or wait until it might be on sale.

Sometimes one decision is important because as a direct consequence it leads to a particular set of choices later. Some decisions cannot be reversed.

Thus, when one buys a new car, the decision cannot be undone for it can only be sold as a used car with a corresponding drop in value.

The question then becomes how long to keep the car, weighing reduced depreciation over the years against increasing maintenance costs. In this case there is generally no right or wrong decision, just a matter of personal preference.

Other decisions require careful reasoning and good judgment. These qualities are not universal. We all have known people who seemed to be lacking in good judgment or even "common sense."

Decision-making ability has its roots in early childhood. Like personality, it is usually well-formed by the time a child enters school.

By elementary school age, the quality of a child's decisions as well as the style of his decision-making—reflective or impulsive—are fairly predictive of the way he will make his choices as an adult.

His decisions, like those of an adult, are based on how he views the chances of being successful and the consequences of success or failure.

But since his judgments of the chances and the consequences are likely to be inaccurate, his decisions are often the wrong ones.

He might toddle into a closed door in the dark because he is used to its being open. He needs to learn about the injury he could suffer by bumping into something.

Similarly, a young child might dart into the street without looking because he is unaware of the possibility of a car coming. The likelihood and the consequences of being hit are too abstract for him to fully grasp.

So we see that a child must be able to take into account both the probabilities and the consequences of an event in order for him to make wise decisions.

You can stimulate Youngster's decision-making powers with a little game. Here's how it works: Cut a hole in the top of a cardboard box, a hole that is large enough for toys of a certain size to be dropped through.

Then gather up several toys, some that are smaller than the hole, some the same size, and some that are too large to go through the hole.

Point to each toy in random order and ask Youngster if he thinks it will go into the box. After he has answered, let him try the toy in the hole to see if it will go through without forcing.

If he correctly judges that the toy will or will not go through, you can give him a little reward such as a piece of cheese or fruit and a verbal reward, "good choice" or "good decision."

As the game progresses, Youngster will tend to say yes to any toy that appears to have any chance of going through the hole.

The next time you play the game, change the rules slightly. Tell him that for every judgment he makes correctly he will receive a reward.

But if he makes an error by saying, for example, that it will go through the hole and it doesn't, he will lose one of the rewards he previously earned.

As soon as he understands the scoring system, you will notice he makes his judgments with greater care, for now the consequences of a wrong decision are greater.

In judging the size by eyeball comparison, he is learning to make size discriminations as well as learning to judge the probability of success in each case.

You will need to change the toys or the hole size often so he doesn't merely memorize which toys fit. The shape of the hole can also be changed: round, square, rectangular, slit-like.

Other activities can be used, provided Youngster is capable of making the appropriate decisions and understanding the consequences of each decision.

With any of these games, Youngster is likely to be reckless and inaccurate at first. But after he gains some experience, you can almost hear the wheels turning in his head as he weighs the elements that go into making a decision.

At this age tangible rewards will provide your child with the motivation needed to stay with a task. Tangible rewards should be combined with positive approval — smiles, touch and attention, for example.

Some thought should be given to weaning off tangible rewards to just praise and positive feedback before a child gets "hooked" on needing them.

Later in life, after he has learned to experience success, success will provide its own reward.

In choosing rewards for your child, it will be helpful to keep the following in mind:

1) What is rewarding to one child (for example, a 15-minute visit to a playground) may not be considered rewarding by another. So, try to be sensitive to your child's likes and dislikes.

2) Rewards that are immediate ("Right now you will receive ... ") are more effective at this age than rewards that are long-term or delayed ("Sometime next month you will get ... ").

3) Rewards should be tangible and concrete (for example, a favorite treat).

4) Rewards can be strengthened by praise ("You did a good job!"). ∎

New Play Materials

Finger painting. This is a favorite of most two-year-olds. Here is a recipe for homemade finger paint.

• Thoroughly dissolve one tablespoon of cornstarch in 1/2 cup cold water.

Stir constantly while cooking over medium heat until mixture comes to a boil, loses whiteness and starts to thicken.

Lower heat, and continue stirring for about two minutes until mixture is very thick and smooth.

Let it cool slightly.

Color by stirring in powdered or liquid tempera, or food coloring. One color at a time is enough for a beginner. Leftovers can be stored in a covered jar in the refrigerator.

The cornstarch mixture may be divided into separate jars, and a different color mixed into each one if you wish.

The surfaces for finger painting are numerous—plastic, aluminum or steel trays, oilcloth over floor or tabletop.

If a permanent record is desired, shiny shelving paper or finger paint paper may be used.

To begin, moisten the surface—tray, oilcloth or paper—with a sponge because the surface must be damp.

Deposit a tablespoon of paint and encourage your Youngster to cover the area with the palm of her hand.

Continue to provide spoonfuls, one by one, until the entire surface is coated.

Now she can do her own thing—painting with knuckles, fingertips, front or back of hands, and wrists.

When finished, she can assist with the cleanup which requires only a wet sponge and some paper towels.

Use finger painting as another language experience for Youngster, describing to her what is occurring: "How red the

paint is!" "Your hands go round and round." "The line is long—it goes all across the tray."

Finger painting can be varied by using yogurt or pudding for a different sensory experience.

Clay. Working with clay resembles finger painting because it allows direct contact with the material and permits a child to make a mess in a constructive pursuit.

If a child needs a release from too much excitement or stress, clay play is a good way to "blow off steam."

She can pound, hit, squeeze and punch without fear of destroying something and without fear of punishment.

A water-based clay sold as moist clay is preferable to more colorful modelling clay.

Modelling clay is frequently too hard for Youngster's hands to mold. She must therefore depend upon an adult to soften it for her.

Water-based clay may be stored in a

plastic bag to prevent it from hardening. A wet cloth placed on top of the clay will keep it in good condition.

Play dough is a good substitute for clay. Here is an easy and inexpensive recipe:

• Mix together in a large bowl 2 cups flour and 1/2 cup salt.

Keep stirring while gradually adding 1 teaspoon salad oil and approximately 3/4 cup water.

Add the water very slowly at the end so the mixture doesn't get too wet. Knead together until a consistency similar to bread dough is obtained.

When you first introduce the clay, work a piece of it yourself, without making anything specific.

Now, here's another opportunity for language learning because adjectives appear so automatically.

For example, you might talk as you play together: "My, that's round!" "Look how long the clay can be pulled."

Or, "Feel how smooth it is."

As you work with your clay, talk about what you're doing. "Let's see: What can I do with this clay?" "What will happen when I push my finger into it?" "

"Can I divide into two pieces and then put it back together again?" "What can you do with your clay?"

Your child also learns by watching and listening.

Cleaning up should include Youngster. She can roll up the clay into a ball and place it in a container.

Then she can use a wet sponge to wipe off the tabletop.

Play dough may be stored in a tightly closed plastic bag in the refrigerator.

If it is too sticky the next time it is to be used, roll it in flour and re-knead to the original consistency.■

The Ebb and Flow of Time

Time is something Youngster is learning about. We don't mean he is learning how to "tell time" or even "what time it is." But he is learning that time is always flowing, that there are rhythms and patterns in time and that there is a "before," a "now," and an "after."

When Youngster notices that "getting-up time" is different from "going-to-bed time" he is experiencing events as they unfold over time.

Time is also a part of activities that involve rhythm. Rhythm is actually a pattern of things which happen in time.

If a youngster lives in a confused time world where things do not happen with dependable frequency, he may become confused about time itself.

For instance, when you clap your hands in rhythm, you are actually organizing movements in time.

Rhythm also is involved when a child learns to creep on all fours. This activity demands that the infant make organized movements.

The right hand goes forward and then the left knee. Next in time the left hand goes forward and then the right knee.

If the infant learns to creep well, he has also learned to organize his movements over time.

In teaching him about the regularity of events in his daily life, you are helping him structure his own personal time world.

If a youngster lives in a confused time world where things do not happen with dependable frequency, he may become confused about time itself.

What can you do to assure that your youngster develops good organization of his time world? The following practices will be helpful.

Getting Acquainted With How Time Works

1. Give Youngster a consistent schedule with a predictable sequence of events. There should be some dependable landmarks in every youngster's typical day—certain things should happen in a certain time order so he can learn about time itself.

2. Going to bed and getting up should happen on schedule. That is, there is a time to go to bed and a time to get up.

3. Another important part of his schedule is the time for eating. Meals—breakfast, lunch and dinner—should occur at dependable times each day. As he learns about eating, he also learns about time.

4. There should be a time for getting undressed, having a bath, and going to bed. These important events should happen with dependable regularity.

5. You can add much to his time learning by talking to him about time throughout the day. A child doesn't need consistent time on the clock; order and sequence is what counts.

"Hey, John, you just got up. This is your first meal today. After breakfast you'll play until lunch. After lunch, you'll have a nap.

"Then we'll play some more and after a while we'll have dinner.

"After dinner you can play with Mom and Dad.

"After that you can go to bed and sleep until morning.

"Then we'll have another nice breakfast."

Note that the words emphasized are all time words. You may want to use different ones. Just be sure to use words which help him learn about time.

6. Be careful to monitor his experiences with time. For example, many television programs create an artificial time frame.

In some, the action unfolds over a number of years while the actual time space is just 30 minutes. Such experiences are likely to be confusing to Youngster.

As a general rule, we think Youngster should have limited exposure to television except for educational programs designed specifically for preschool children.

7. Help Youngster understand that the same time span (such as 15 minutes) may appear short or long, depending on the circumstances.

If Youngster really enjoys what he is doing, he may lose all sense of time passing.

On the other hand, if he has to wait for something he wants immediately, then a few moments may seem like an eternity.

Use these opportunities to talk with your child about his time world so that he will be able to deal effectively with the ebb and flow of time which confronts every human being. ∎

Problem Behaviors

No one will deny that a two-year-old can exhibit a very strong will, such as refusing to eat or to go to bed.

But parents ought to recognize that problem behaviors are not always Youngster's fault. They may occasionally be precipitated by a parent's lack of understanding of the child's behavior or by ineffective discipline techniques.

A good starting point for establishing good discipline is to set reasonable limits for Youngster's behavior. These limits must be specifically defined and clearly explained to the child.

It should be noted that, for successful discipline, the limits must be reasonable. In other words, there won't be an unreasonable number of "no-nos," "stop that," or "don't touch this."

Parents who use physical punishment may accomplish short-term compliance with their wishes. But in the long-term they may be creating new problems for themselves since children have been found to learn aggressive behaviors from parents who are aggressive.

Thus parent and child may be feeding the flames of each other's passions by temper tantrums, followed by physical punishment, leading to more temper tantrums, and so on.

Other parents may try using psychological or emotional punishment—"I don't love you anymore" or "You make me sick" or "Why can't you be more like your brother?"

In these cases, the scars left by the parent's rejection may produce more serious consequences than the child's initial acts of misbehavior.

But there are effective ways to handle problem situations. Parents who respect their child's feelings and take into account her individual temperament can develop great skill in deflecting anger.

They can become experts in defusing potentially explosive situations. Or they may

provide their child with emotional release by reflecting her feelings back to her: "I know you feel angry because your brother just broke your favorite toy."

Even though no discipline technique can ever restore the broken toy, the caring/understanding approach can help a child gain the self-control needed to deal with a difficult situation.

A common problem situation faced by parents and child is the hassle over going to bed. Here parents have an opportunity to apply the principle of "reasonable limits."

Once these limits have been specifically defined, they should be clearly explained to the child—along with the consequences for any misbehavior. Then the parent must adhere consistently to those limits and consequences.

A child will occasionally "test the limits" to find out what are the real consequences for misbehavior—as distinct from a parent's threatened consequences. Here is where parents need to be thoroughly consistent.

A child will inevitably become angry and confused if parents apply one rule at one time and another at a different time.

If temporary changes need to be made in the rules or in the consequences—because

of special circumstances—the child should be alerted in advance about these changes.

Anticipation on the part of the parents is a most effective way to prevent problem behaviors in the child.

For example, before bedtime a parent might announce: "You have just five more minutes to play before it's time for bed." In this way the announcement about bedtime doesn't come as a sudden shock.

Similarly, a parent might say: "I will play one game with you before bedtime," or "I have time to read you one story before you go to sleep."

The same technique can be used before it is time to leave the playground, the park, or end some favorite activity.

If a parent anticipates that Youngster may not go to sleep immediately or may awaken early in the morning, it is wise to provide her with some soft toys she can hold before she falls asleep. The same soft toys will also be at hand for her amusement in the early morning.

Anticipation demonstrates respect for a child's needs, and can also prevent many other problem behaviors.

If the last trip to the supermarket was disastrous in terms of Youngster's misbehaviors, it is time to think through those problems and rehearse that situation.

Before leaving for the supermarket, sit down with Youngster to explain acceptable and unacceptable behaviors in the store. You might even promise a specific reward for good behaviors at the end of your trip to the supermarket.

And if Youngster behaved well on this trip to the store, be sure to tell her in very specific terms what it was she did that particularly pleased you.

By focusing attention on positive behaviors—rather than their opposite negative behaviors—you are taking a most important step toward avoidance of future problem behaviors.■

Travel Tips

After making several long distance journeys by car with their young children, parents usually begin to think about how to make traveling more enjoyable.

Here are some travel tips that may help:

Plan ahead of time. Trips that are well planned are usually more enjoyable for young children.

So take the time to plan the details of your travel: how far you will travel each day, where you will stop for lunch, and so on. Having made your plans, you can then be flexible if any changes should be necessary along the way.

Try to involve your children as much as possible in making these plans.

Even though a young child is not capable of reading a map, she will enjoy being shown the line on the map that indicates where you will be going.

She will also enjoy seeing and hearing about local sites as you travel and hearing the sounds of the places through which you will be passing.

Her imagination will help her to conjure up fairyland visions of where these travels will take her, especially if you have travel brochures with pictures, which are usually available from a tourist office or convention bureau.

What to bring? Once you have completed your initial plans for the trip, it is now time to consider what to bring with you in the car to make the journey more enjoyable.

A first consideration would be a basic first aid kit—adhesive bandages, thermometer, medicines, etc. that you regularly need at home.

Have your child pack a bag of some toys to bring. Monitor the selections, pointing out to her why one toy would be more appropriate for the car than another. Just make sure that she is involved in the final selection.

It is also wise to bring a pillow as well as a child's favorite stuffed animal. That way, even though she will be sleeping in a strange room, she will have the comfort of a familiar friend.

Be sure to bring some snacks which might include fruit or fresh vegetables as well as something to drink. In the summertime especially, young children can become dehydrated inside.

It is also wise to pack a picnic lunch so that you can stop and eat and relax a bit. Children will have more freedom to stand, stretch and exercise than would be possible inside a restaurant.

On the road. Now that all the preparations have been made, you are ready to take to the road.

The first step is to make sure that everybody is wearing a seat belt or is in a safety car seat. Statistics on safety have documented the wisdom of wearing seat belts—so that it is now the law in all

states.

It will be most beneficial for young children if adults perceive the journey by car as a part of, not a prelude to, the whole vacation.

Parents will learn that traveling long distances without a stop may result in "making good time" but it will also result in having a carload of very unhappy and unpleasant children.

Rest stops should therefore be planned at regular intervals along the way, preferably at locations where children can run and play.

The closer parents can adhere to a child's normal schedule for eating and sleeping, the less aggravated the child will become while away from home.

Even though a child may not be able to eat or sleep well because of excitement, it is best to try to restore and maintain the child's normal schedule.

A good way to pass the time on the journey is to play some simple games together, such as counting trucks or identifying colors.

As the child grows older these games can become increasingly more sophisticated—even to the point where the child performs better than the parents!

Some parents like to bring along a DVD player with recorded cartoons or storybooks, some sing-along tapes or a songbook whenever they travel.

Whatever you do, try to make this time on the journey quality time together as a family.

The more enjoyable you make the journey, the happier your children will be. And, vice versa, the happier your children are, the more likely you too will enjoy the journey.■

Growing Child

P. O. Box 2505 • W Lafayette, IN 47996
(800) 927-7289
www.GrowingChild.com

Contributing Authors
Phil Bach, O.D., Ph.D.
Miriam Bender, Ph.D.
Joseph Braga, Ed.D.
Laurie Braga, Ph.D.
George Early, Ph.D.
Carol R. Gestwicki, M.S.
Liam Grimley, Ph.D.
Robert Hannemann, M.D., F.A.A.P.
Sylvia Kottler, M.S.
Bill Peterson, Ph.D.

Growing Child ®

The supreme happiness in life is the
conviction that we are loved.
Victor Hugo

28 MONTHS

Childhood Fears

One of the problems of dealing with a youngster's fears is recognizing when he is scared. When he cries, clings, hides, resists—or is generally "being impossible", it may be that he is frightened. Why?

He may often be unable to express his feelings clearly because of his limited vocabulary.

Then, too, he may not yet recognize or identify his own feelings as "fear." He just knows that something is wrong. He feels upset inside.

Two-year-olds can also experience a kind of magical thinking that results in limitations of logic or reasoning along with an enormous desire to protect themselves (now newly important).

Objects such as bathtub drains, flushing toilets, and vacuum cleaners all seem to present a threat for things that disappear suddenly, even though a toddler is far too large to be affected.

Dealing with these behaviors can be very frustrating for parents. It is easy to think a child is just being stubborn or having a tantrum.

Even if a parent does recognize that the reason for such behavior is fear, it is often difficult to decide just how to cope with this fear. A good first step is to try to gain a better understanding of this emotional response.

Fear is a normal human emotion—a natural means of self-protection. Certain fears appear to be inborn, such as a newborn's response to loud and sudden noises. Such responses are usually reflex reactions.

Some fears we consciously teach a child because he needs to be wary of persons, objects, or situations which are potentially harmful to him—such as strangers, fire, or a busy street.

Some fears a child learns on his own. For instance, if he sees another child fall from a swing, he realizes that he too might fall. The next time he rides on a swing he will likely hold on tightly!

Fears such as these are healthy because they tend to protect the child from real dangers.

Parents need to avoid two extreme reactions when dealing with a child's fears. One extreme is to express alarm at every sign of childhood fear. The other is to ignore completely all manifestations of fear by the child.

In between these two extremes lies a happy medium that involves giving thoughtful consideration to a young child's fears because they may indeed be a parent's first indication that all isn't well with the child.

Parents will want to help their youngster overcome unrealistic fears, both for his benefit and their peace of mind.

Recognition of a fear and reassurance to the child are important parts of dealing with a child's fear. Without this reassurance, a child may become more confused and even more fearful.

When coping with Youngster's fears it is important to remember that no matter how unreasonable, even ridiculous, his fear may seem to you, it is very real to him.

It is important, therefore, to respect his feelings as real and valid. Parents can reassure him that he need not be afraid, that you will keep him safe until he feels he can handle whatever is frightening him.

Some of the more common fears include fear of certain animals, loud visitors in the home, the dark, going to bed, going to sleep, and separation from parents.

Fear of animals may have its beginnings in an alarming experience with a neighbor's pet or a fright while visiting a zoo. This initial experience may lead to avoidance of even stuffed animals or those pictured in a book.

If he shows an abnormal fear of animals, introduce him gradually to their presence.

When you're driving, point out dogs and other animals you see. When possible, stop and let him watch from the safety of the car.

Several visits to a children's "petting zoo" also may be helpful. Don't force your child to go near the animals.

On the first visit just walk casually around the zoo and let him look. If he shows anxiety, quietly and gently pick him up and hold him. Somehow it is harder to be

continued on page 174

Sibling Rivalry

In previous issues of **Growing Child** we have talked about the idea that during these formative years, young children gradually develop a sense of who they are and what they can become.

In this process it is not uncommon for them to experience feelings of jealousy toward another child.

Parents frequently are upset by a particular form of jealousy known as **sibling rivalry.** This rivalry involves expressions of hostility between children of the same family who look at themselves as rivals competing for the love and affection of their parents.

Sibling rivalry most commonly occurs with the arrival of a newborn baby. It is important for parents to recognize that—even though the older child's behavior may be considered obnoxious by them—it is a common and normal reaction on the part of the child.

The older child is expressing distress and anger at being knocked off the pedestal on which he had previously stood.

The author Judy Blume humorously reflected these feelings of distress and anger when she described Fudge, in the book **Superfudge.** Fudge tries to "sell" his new baby sister, Tootsie, whenever there is company in their home. "You like the baby?" he asks. "You can have her for a quarter."

When that doesn't work, he even tries to pay people to take her away: "I'll give you a quarter," he says to strangers on the street, "if you take her to your house and never bring her back."

Sibling rivalry is most likely to occur if parents show favoritism toward the new arrival and don't give adequate attention and affection to the older child.

It also will develop if a parent is over-indulgent toward one child while being overstrict with another. A young child also may feel slighted if parents are heard to compare one child with another.

A child's feelings of jealousy may be expressed either by aggressive or regressive behaviors. The child's aggression may be expressed either directly toward the parents or toward the "intruder" in the family.

Parents should assume that some of these feelings are present and that they occur naturally. When these feelings are openly expressed, it comes as a great relief to children who are worried that their parents won't love them as much.

Regressive behaviors, on the other hand, involve a return to babyhood activities, such as thumb-sucking, bedwetting, or soiled pants.

There are many things that parents can do that will lessen or prevent sibling rivalry.

The first step is to prepare the child for the new baby's arrival before the event occurs. It is most helpful to communicate this information in a way that is personally meaningful to the child, for example, "**You** will soon have a baby brother or sister."

Even though a young child may not understand all that a parent tells him, it is most important to take the time to talk about any changes that may occur in his life and to talk openly about the feelings that may accompany those changes.

The second step is to involve the older child as much as possible in the preparations for the new baby. This might include preparing the baby's crib or getting the diapers ready.

Even though a two-year-old is very limited in terms of what he can do to help, it is important that his contributions be perceived as an integral part of the family's preparations for the new baby.

The third step is for the parents to set aside some time exclusively with the older child after the new baby arrives. This can often be arranged while the baby is taking a nap.

Such interaction time provides reassurance to the child that he is still loved as much as ever by his parents, even though they now have to devote much time to caring for the baby.

It is important to realize that feelings of jealousy toward a newly arrived baby are a

normal reaction on the part of an older child.

Even if parents are unable to totally **prevent** sibling rivalry, the same procedures—talking with the older child, involving him in activities to care for the baby, and providing him with exclusive time for love and attention—also are the most effective ways to help him **adjust** to this new family situation and thus keep sibling rivalry at a minimum.

Even apart from the birth of a new baby, children in the same family will most likely continue to experience some sibling rivalry during the preschool years.

It is as though they think of parental love as being limited in quantity: if you show love for my brother or sister, you will have less love left for me!

It is important for parents to be aware that because children's personality characteristics differ, parents may express their love differently for each of their children. For example, one child may like hugs whereas another may enjoy praise but dislike being hugged.

It is a good idea to explain these differences to children. This will help them to avoid feelings of jealousy and will ultimately help prevent sibling rivalry. ■

Motor Skill Development

When parents see the title "Motor Skill Development," they might ask: "Haven't we already dealt with that topic in previous issues of *Growing Child?*" Of course, the reason the topic keeps recurring is because motor skills are developed at different stages of growth.

In this issue we will discuss the specific gross motor skills and fine motor skills which children normally develop between two and three years of age.

Parent Involvement

Can parents stimulate their child's development of motor skills? Before answering that question we need to clarify two issues related to the purpose of stimulating a child's development.

It seems that there will always be some parents who want to know if "being ahead" in some area of development means their child will be a whiz in school or will some day become a professional athlete.

To those parents there is a straightforward answer: It is not possible to predict later success based on performance at this early age. The earlier the prediction is made, the more likely it will be wrong.

The purpose of stimulating a child's development is not aimed at "getting ahead" of one's peers but rather to ensure that normal growth and development will take place.

Being aware of what constitutes normal development also enables parents to keep an eye out for possible coordination problems which they could discuss with their pediatrician.

A second question related to stimulating development is: "Am I challenging my child enough or too much?" In responding to that question, two considerations must be kept in mind:

(1) Young children like to be challenged and will get bored if they are "stuck in a rut";

(2) When faced with new challenges, young children need to experience some degree of success in order to be motivated to do their best.

If the challenge is too difficult, or if parents push too hard, children are likely to become discouraged and their development may even be impeded. The secret is finding a happy balance.

Having addressed both of these issues, we can now answer the question about parent involvement by saying that parents have a most important role in a child's development of better motor skills.

The first secret is to focus on the here-and-now without being preoccupied with predicting the child's future.

The second secret is for parents to strive for a happy balance between providing appropriate challenges while ensuring some degree of success for the child.

Keep in mind that what children need are exciting challenges, opportunities to succeed, encouragement in defeat, and some involvement in selecting the activities which they will perform.

It's usually a good idea for parents to perform the same activities as the child. Parent participation in movement activities has several advantages:

1) It lets the child know that motor activities are important;

(2) The parent can serve as a role model for new physical challenges;

(3) It provides good exercise for the parent as well as the child;

(4) It adds to the fun for both.

As parents participate in motor activities with their child, they will also become aware of adaptations that may be needed for a child to succeed.

Adaptations might include simplifying a task by breaking it into simpler components, slowing the pace of the movements such as the tempo of a musical activity, and using materials or equipment which are more appropriate for the child to work with.

The key is to initiate an activity at a level which enables the child to participate safely and successfully. Once a child becomes competent and comfortable at that level, it's time to move on to new challenges which not only increase the skill difficulty but should also add to the child's enjoyment of the activities.

Benefits of Movement Activities

Movement activities help two-year-olds to develop not only motorically, but also cognitively, emotionally, and socially as well. Playing interactive games, for example, can involve such cognitive skills as counting, sequencing, vocabulary development, and color identification.

In motor development play activities, children also experience and learn to deal with emotions such as happiness and sadness.

Participation with peers inevitably involves social interaction and social communication.

When a number of children are involved, the emphasis should be on cooperation rather than competition. So, even when the focus is on the development of motor skills, these movement activities foster cognitive, emotional, and social development. In other words, the whole child—not just arms and legs—will benefit.

Expensive equipment and materials are not necessary for a child to participate in motor skill development activities. Gross motor activities can include simple stretching, bending, and lifting, as well as walking, running and jumping. Fine motor activities include drawing, scribbling, stringing beads, or using play dough, for example.

An obstacle course can be constructed very simply with rope, an old tire, and a cardboard box. Children can practice jumping over a rope or crawling under

continued on page 172

continued from page 171

it. They can climb through an old tire or into a cardboard box. The items in the obstacle course can be selected to match the child's interests and level of accomplishment.

Gross Motor Skills

Here are some activities which are appropriate for children between two and three years of age to develop gross motor skills:

Walking: In walking, what was once a stiff, jerky gait is now becoming a smoother stride. Steps become more regular and feet are not planted far apart as they used to be.

But children this age prefer short, quick little steps rather than a longer stride, which means they grow tired more quickly.

Running: As walking becomes smoother, running begins to appear. It starts out more like fast walking until it eventually becomes true running.

Galloping: Many two-year-olds prefer to gallop than to run. The uneven clip-clop rhythm of galloping seems more attractive and playful than straightforward running.

When children are particularly happy, they like to gallop up and down with joy, without really going anywhere.

Stopping: Once a child gets going, whether running or galloping, the next problem is learning how to stop. In the meantime, until they master the skill of being able to stop, children usually become adept at finding a soft landing spot.

Jumping: Two-year-olds generally like to try out their jumping abilities. As we watch an Olympic gymnast perform a perfectly graceful dismount, it's important to realize that those wonderful skills began by jumping as a two-year-old from one step to the ground.

Jumping down a step is easier than jumping upward or across a flat surface. By about three years of age, children learn to use their arms to propel themselves forward, but a broad jump of a few feet will not be accomplished until about five years of age.

Throwing: At first children throw all balls in the same way—generally with a two-handed forward lurch—irrespective of the size of the ball.

As their skill develops with practice, they will begin to throw a small ball with one hand and with more wrist action.

With a bigger ball, they will bring it over their head in order to get a longer arm movement. But control of the throw will only come with practice.

Catching: Catching usually begins by having someone drop a ball into the child's outstretched arms. As the person throwing the ball moves a little farther away for the throw, many young children close their eyes as soon as they see the ball coming toward them.

Once they have overcome this reaction, they eventually learn to close their hands and fingers around the ball to prevent it from popping out of their outstretched arms. It's another motor skill that will improve with practice.

Fine Motor Skills

Between two and three years of age, children show progress in fine motor coordination. This depends not only on the development of new physical skills but also on the way a child's brain develops.

For example, prior to 24 months, when faced with the task of placing a wooden square block in a square hole of the same size, a child will likely use a trial-and-error approach, pounding on the block if it doesn't fit right away—as though sheer physical force and will power will make it go in the hole.

Sometime before three years of age, most children gain a cognitive insight that the side of the block must be aligned with the side of the hole in order for the block to fit in the hole. And they now have the fine motor skills to act on this new cognitive insight. Each new discovery like this brings a new sense of excitement and interest to the child's explorations.

Most public libraries have simple puzzles appropriate for children of this age. Children seem to love the challenge of a puzzle they haven't seen before. But once they have mastered how to do it, they are ready to move on to a new and more challenging task.

One of the fine motor activities which all children appear to enjoy is drawing—which, at this age, might more accurately be described as scribbling. They enjoy experimenting with crayons, pencils, paintbrushes or markers.

Although the drawings may appear to an adult to be meaningless scribbles, to the child they may represent a particular person ("That's my mommy.") or object ("That's my house.) or feelings ("Joey is sad.").

Young children show great pride when their artwork is displayed in some prominent place in the home such as on the refrigerator door.

Fine motor skills are also involved in many routine activities throughout the day, such as getting dressed, washing hands, brushing one's teeth, eating with a spoon, or turning a doorknob.

With some tasks a child may need some help just to get started. For example, when zipping or unzipping clothing, a parent may have to take the initial step, then let the child take over the task.

The more practice children have with these activities, the sooner they will develop the skills.

In summary, motor skill development isn't something that happens all at once. It takes place over a long period of time.

As new skills are developed, new challenges can be faced, leading to new learning opportunities. From these motor activities the whole child benefits. ∎

Vision Problems

During the early childhood years good vision develops as a result of normal and proper use of the eyes.

For example, while a young child plays with blocks or uses finger paints, many important visual skills are being developed.

When vision problems occur, treatment is more likely to be successful the earlier the problem is detected.

Parents who are well informed about some of the most common eye problems of young children will better know when to seek appropriate professional help.

An eye examination is generally part of a physician's routine physical examination of a child. It is recommended that all children have a thorough eye examination at least once before their fourth birthday by a physician or by an eye specialist.

By that age, a child's vision can usually be measured fairly accurately.

Because vision is so important, parents should know something about how it is measured. Normal vision is labeled as "20/20."

The first number indicates the distance in feet from the eye chart to the eye being tested. The second number refers to the distance at which a normal eye can clearly identify a certain sized letter or picture on the chart.

"Twenty/twenty" vision, then, means that the eye being tested sees at 20 feet what a normal eye should see at that distance.

"Twenty/forty" vision, on the other hand, means what a normal eye is able to see at 40 feet can only be seen at 20 feet by this eye.

One common finding in vision screenings in preschool children is hyperopia, or farsightedness. Here, the eye must exert increased focusing to keep things clear.

While farsightedness may cause problems for an adult, particularly while reading, it rarely produces any symptoms in preschoolers.

If a child has to come closer than 10 feet to recognize what a normal eye sees at 20 feet, a check for myopia, or nearsightedness, by an eye specialist is in order. A nearsighted child will sometimes squeeze his eyelids together to produce a slit or pinhole effect (like a camera) in order to get a sharper focus.

Another vision problem to watch for in a young child is strabismus, a disorder which involves the inability to direct both eyes simultaneously to the same object.

When the eyes seem to be looking at the nose, the condition is called "cross-eye;" when they both appear to be looking to the opposite sides, it is known as "wall-eye."

The eyes may be crossed or divergent from birth, even though this may not be obvious until later. But strabismus can occur at any age.

In infancy a pediatrician watches for this condition. But as visits to the doctor become less frequent, it is possible for the problem to occur unnoticed.

You can check for this problem by watching Youngster's eyes while she is playing. It is especially important to do this when she is tired, for that is when crossing or divergence will most likely occur.

An eye that turns in or out during the early childhood years may sometimes lose its vision unless treated.

Therefore, if you suspect that your child's eyes may be crossed or divergent, you should consult an eye specialist.

A problem occurs when one eye noticeably deviates outward or inward and then stops working to avoid causing double vision. This is what is known as amblyopia or "lazy eye." The eye really does not stop working. The brain simply ceases to receive the image from the deviating eye.

This is similar to the ability of some people who can look through a microscope or telescope with one eye while keeping the other eye open. The vision in the unused eye is "suppressed" by the brain.

If the use of one eye is suppressed for a period of months or years, its ability to see sharply will decrease. It can only be restored by treatment such as putting a patch over the good eye for several weeks or months to force the defective one to resume its function.

The earlier this is done, the more likely the "lazy" eye will develop normal vision. That is why it is important to identify eye deviations and amblyopia as early as possible.

Parents need to be aware that a child will generally not "outgrow" vision problems. These problems require professional treatment, such as eye muscle exercises, covering the good eye, wearing glasses, or other measures.

A little watchfulness by parents will go a long way toward early detection of vision problems.

This watchfulness is especially important if there is a history of vision problems (for example, crossed eyes) in either of the parents' families.

If vision problems are discovered early, a lot can be done by a skilled eye specialist. That is why early examination and diagnosis are so important. ■

continued from page 169

afraid of something that you can look down upon.

Let him watch other children play with and pet the young animals. Talk with him about baby animals and their mothers.

An over-enthusiastic relative or friend who greets a child with loud laughter and smothering hugs also may arouse considerable anxiety and fear in a toddler. In fact, he may not only hide from that person but show increasing fear of everyone outside the immediate family circle.

It is pretty hard to tone down loud and over-demonstrative relatives but sometimes visitors can be told in advance that your youngster is just learning to adjust to persons outside the family. They also can be asked to wait until your child approaches them on his own.

Another method is to pick up Youngster and hold him as you greet your visitors. This includes him in the eye-level greeting and gives him the additional security of your arms. If he struggles or cries, comfort him. Then try to interest him in something else.

A young child is naturally curious and will usually overcome his fear if visitors keep their greetings low-key and if he is allowed to exercise his own initiative in approaching them.

Fear of the dark, fear of going to bed, and fear of going to sleep usually are interrelated. They also usually involve fear of separation from parents. Here are some actions you can take that will help calm these fears.

Begin by letting your child help you choose an attractive child's nightlight—a clown, star, or happy face. Let him handle and examine the light so that he will be familiar with it.

Children's nightlights should be fully enclosed in plastic for safety. They should also be dimmer than the ordinary nightlight, if possible.

A half hour of quiet play and a warm bath are recommended to relax a child before bedtime. This routine will be a source of security to an anxious child.

Youngster must learn trust. When you put him to bed, reassure him, if necessary, that you are near and that you will be there in the morning when he awakens. He needs to know that his parents will be there when he really needs them.

Once he has been reassured, you must then be firm with bedtime rules. Firmness in carrying out reasonable bedtime rules will

Growing Child®

P. O. Box 2505 • W Lafayette, IN 47996
(800) 927-7289
©Growing Child, Inc.
www.GrowingChild.com

Contributing Authors

Phil Bach, O.D., Ph.D.
Miriam Bender, Ph.D.
Joseph Braga, Ed.D.
Laurie Braga, Ph.D.
George Early, Ph.D.
Carol R. Gestwicki, M.S.
Liam Grimley, Ph.D.
Robert Hannemann, M.D., F.A.A.P.
Sylvia Kottler, M.S.
Bill Peterson, Ph.D.

eventually help a child to overcome fear of the dark or fear of going to bed.

When you leave him in someone else's care, be sure that it is someone he knows and trusts. Explain the nightly routine carefully to that person so that your child will feel more secure as the same routine is followed, even if you aren't there.

Don't forget that in dealing with childhood fears, an "ounce of prevention" goes a long way.

If your child must undergo a potentially frightening experience, such as a visit to the dentist or doctor, prepare him for it carefully by talking about it calmly and reassuringly. Control your own fears.

Above all don't punish your child in fearful ways, such as locking him in a darkened room, or threatening to have the doctor give him a "shot."

When in doubt about how to handle your child's fears, discuss the problem with your pediatrician, physician, or mental health professional. He or she is interested in your child's emotional health as well as his physical well-being.

A physician, for example, will know if it is appropriate or necessary to refer your child to another professional with specific expertise in dealing with childhood fears. ■

"What do you mean, 'Don't touch?'
Touching is the way I learn."
Unknown

29 MONTHS

Courage–Now and Later

As a parent, you know some of the problems and heartaches life can bring. In a quiet moment you may have wondered what the future holds for your child.

Will your child meet whatever life brings with courage, sensitivity, and tenderness?

How can you help your 29-month-old develop the inner toughness—and tenderness—she will need?

You have already made a good start in this direction. When you recognized your Youngster's drive to learn about her world and made it possible for her to explore it safely, you were helping her to develop self-confidence and courage.

Your quiet observation of your exploring child has provided her with protection while allowing her to develop independence and the ability to meet and conquer new challenges.

As your child successfully overcomes small problems, she develops the confidence to tackle and solve larger ones.

Even children who demonstrate self-confidence and courage, however, may suddenly display unexplainable fears. A parent's first reaction is usually in the form of reassurance.

But a child generally will not overcome her fears just because we tell her there is nothing to be afraid of.

Fear of water is a case in point. Every child is familiar with water—but usually with the limited amounts found in bathtubs or puddles.

The new, large, and to her, seemingly endless amount of water in a swimming pool, lake, or river is different.

She wants to approach it gradually, to explore it on her own terms and in her own good time. Fear of water is not a shameful emotion in a young child. It is a natural feeling that needs to be understood and respected by parents.

Nothing is more certain to produce lasting fear of water than a parent's determination that *his* child—or *her* child—will overcome that fear immediately.

No matter how confident an explorer your child has become, she may be hesitant and wary when she finds herself in a new and strange situation.

An unknown relative who snatches her up for an energetic hug may reduce your child to tears. A large, friendly-but-noisy dog may instill panic in a child whose previous experience has included only a small, quiet dog.

Such fears, though they may seem trivial to an adult, are entirely sensible from the child's point of view.

If we are to help a child be brave, we must begin by respecting her worries and fears. Accept them for what they are—questions about her own safety and security.

"What is this? Will this hurt? What should I do?"

Talk to your child calmly. Don't pressure her to hug Aunt Mary or pet the nice, big doggie.

Give her a chance to recover her balance. Then over a period of time, give her frequent opportunities to learn more about the feared object or situation.

Work gently but persistently to help her conquer any fear which may hobble her independence. ■

Good Manners: Are They Important?

Good manners are not necessarily "formal manners" or even "company manners."

It is true that good manners, in part, consist of the simple courtesies—saying "please," "thank you," "excuse me."

These pleasant words help to make an increasingly impersonal world a little more personal, a little more gentle.

However, the key to good manners is not rigid obedience to social rules. It is our attitude toward others. It involves a respect for the rights, ideas, and feelings of others, even of those with whom we disagree.

When we look at good manners from this point of view, the importance of certain social conventions becomes a little clearer.

A few are essential. Others are trivial. Most lie somewhere in between, depending on circumstances and your own family customs. But whatever courtesies you decide are important, it is the qualities of caring and consideration expressed through the courtesies which are important for children to learn.

A child learns politeness from an example, so "caring" politeness is a better example than to display rudeness by <u>demanding</u> a child's politeness.

"Thank you" can express gratitude and appreciation. It also can be said in such a way as to offend or even hurt. What matters more than the words expressed is the attitude toward others which underlies those words.

A child's manners not only reflect his feelings toward others, but also help him develop new, desirable attitudes.

The young child who is trained to parrot "please" and "thank you" may not, at age two or three, be any more considerate than a child who has not been taught these courtesies.

But as his good manners bring him praise and smiles, he becomes pleased with himself. This in turn makes him feel more friendly toward others.

Through the practice of good manners, he begins to develop the new attitudes which courtesy should reflect.

These attitudes and the learned courtesies are further reinforced as the child sees them practiced by his parents.

He accepts his parents' valuation of others as being individuals worthy of care and consideration and he adopts the outward forms which are the reflection of this attitude.

Thus the child learns to make his desires known in ways which are considerate of others and to express his appreciation in an appropriate manner.

He learns good manners in much the same way that he learns to take turns or share with others, all of which become ways of expressing positive attitudes toward others. ∎

Tips for Effective Parenting

The following suggestions are from "The Hidden Hinge," by Rosa Covington Packard, published by Ballantine Books. We think they're excellent.

1. Be objective, not personal in your instructions. "Books go in this bookcase," rather than "I want you to be sure to keep your books in the bookcase."

2. Be positive, not negative. "Use the tricycle, it is your size," rather than "You are too little to ride the bicycle."

3. Give the social reason for rules rather than flat authority. "Hang the coat up before the baby steps on it and wrinkles it," rather than "Hang it up."

4. Give a solution to a problem rather than mere prohibitions. "Please move to this side of the table, John, so that Mary will be able to see," rather than "Don't stand in Mary's way, John."

5. Be specific. Give concrete information using concrete names and commands: "If you hold the card by its edge, it will stay clean," rather than "Don't mess up the cards."

6. Match objects and actions to your words. "Trays (pause and show) are held in the middle (pause and show)," rather than "Do it this way."

7. Give awareness of consequences. "Hitting hurts Peter," rather than "Don't hit Peter."

8. Act as an individual to defend the common law in specific instances. "I will not let you hurt John with the stick," rather than "We don't hurt people."

9. Recognize the validity of emotions when you limit destructive actions. Some examples:

(a) "I know you are angry but you may not hurt Mary," rather than "Why did you hit Mary? She is your friend."

(b) "I know that you are afraid but you must have the scratch cleaned," rather than "You are a big girl and that little scratch doesn't hurt."

(c) "I know you don't want to wear shoes but you must protect your feet when you walk on city sidewalks," rather than "You don't want your feet to get all dirty and hurt, do you?"

10. Use simple and scrupulously courteous manners to children and other adults.

(a) "Good morning, John, I am glad to see you (hand offered and withdrawn if not taken)," rather than "Can you say 'good morning' to me, and shake my hand, John?"

(b) "Thank you, Aunt Jane, for remembering Susan's birthday," rather than "What do you say to Aunt Jane, Susan?" ∎

Parenting Styles

Make-believe

In the previous article, "Tips for Effective Parenting," we offered you some suggestions for becoming a more effective parent.

Now we need to look at some behaviors that parents need to avoid.

We hope that so far you have been able to wisely avoid these inappropriate parental behaviors which unfortunately are all too common in our society.

The first of these is the half-hearted, monotonously repeated warning issued by the parent whose attention is elsewhere. Such warnings are usually non-specific: "Karen, don't do that."

These vague warnings are meaningless to the busy child. Don't do what? Since Karen isn't certain what she shouldn't be doing, she continues to pursue her interest of the moment.

Next comes a parent's shriek: "Karen, I said stop that!" But stop what? By this time perhaps, Karen, chair and all have toppled with a crash and a wail.

Then follows parental anxiety. Maybe even anger expressed by loud voices. Karen is left resentful and confused. There is little consistency or security in her world. She is sadder, but no wiser.

There are other parents who over-dramatize, over-protect, over-explain. Every possible hazard is described in gory detail, every act cautioned against.

Grass should never be walked on because it may be full of rusty nails lying in wait for bare feet. Dogs are always noisy, rough, dirty, and apt to bite.

Doors and drawers are just traps for fingers. Rain means there will be thunder and lightning—or the rainstorm might even turn into a tornado.

Johnny is cautioned, "Don't climb that. You'll fall." "Let me carry the glass. You'll break it and cut yourself!" "Don't"—"Be careful"—"Watch out."

Johnny is soon so full of horror stories, so overloaded with words, so smothered by protection that he becomes a passive onlooker at life, afraid to commit himself to any new experience.

We mention these parental behaviors because they are observed so frequently in our society. For that reason it is probably good to repeat some of the most basic principles of effective parenting:

1. Be prepared.

Try to anticipate problems if possible. Many unpleasant situations could be avoided if appropriate preventive measures had been taken.

For example, if you anticipate bad behavior from Youngster while shopping in the grocery store, be sure to talk with her about what is acceptable behavior *before* you leave for the store.

2. Be specific.

Even though a parent knows what bad behavior is, a child may not. Therefore, be as specific as possible in describing these actions.

3. Be fair.

As far as possible, make known to the child in advance what specific reward will be given for good behavior and what specific punishment will follow bad behavior.

4. Be consistent.

Although a parent may be in a good mood one day and in a bad mood the next, children are not able to "read" these feelings.

So it is important for parents to maintain consistent behavior from one day to the next and from one situation to another.

Developing effective parenting skills is not easy. It is an endeavor that demands constant effort.

But the effort is worthwhile because it will help a child become socially well-adjusted. It will also increase the joy of parenting. ■

Make-believe play is one of the best ways for a child to practice language skills.

Pretending also helps him understand events by re-creating them and then talking about them.

He can alter a stressful memory by imagining a pleasant one. He can play out the roles of different family members.

This kind of activity is vital in establishing his own identity and learning to be a member of his family and society.

While he pretends he also discovers how to manage some of his hostile feelings, particularly those which do not receive parental approval.

He may even be heard "reprimanding" a stuffed animal for misbehavior in a tone of voice that sounds remarkably like Mom or Dad!

What props are useful for make-believe? Clothes (hats, scarves, gloves), a toy telephone, heavy cardboard boxes (they can become shelves, counters, cars),

continued on page 180

Selecting Good Toys

What are desirable toys for the 2 1/2-year-old?

A sandbox with bucket, shovel, and spoon plus other containers of assorted sizes will provide hours of fun and lots of learning experiences.

Large peg boards also provide good learning experiences. Jumbo pegs are easy for small hands to grasp and push into the holes and they are too big to be swallowed.

The "peg board" is usually a 1/2- to 3/4-inch thick piece of crepe foam rubber which is easy to handle and soft enough that its edges won't nick the furniture.

Big, sturdy cars and trucks—not the small plastic type that are easily breakable—will be much used by two-year-olds as they travel many miles over the floors in your home.

A good sturdy wagon will last through several years of loading, hauling, and unloading.

At age three many children can ride a tricycle, but steering and pedalling are a little too much for one who is "just past two."

Tip-proof kiddie cars without pedals—little riding toys which the child moves by using feet and legs—come in a variety of forms. Just be sure the wheels are far enough apart for good stability.

The kiddie car gives practice in steering and in going both backward and forward but doesn't require the coordination needed for pedalling.

A low rocking horse is a toy that provides exercise and excitement for a budding buckaroo. For safety's sake be sure the toy is stable with a low center of gravity and that your child can mount and dismount unaided.

A small table and chairs will afford hours of entertainment as children imitate the family meals. It is nice to have child-size chairs and a table that fit them since everything else seems to be made for adults.

Children also enjoy using a small table and chairs for other activities—arts and crafts, and pretend play.

The use of large crayons will stimulate an interest in colors. You can help your child differentiate between colors by naming the ones he chooses.

Scribbling with crayons also helps a two-year-old improve eye-hand coordination. At this age a blank sheet of paper is better than a page from a coloring book.

Just be sure to let your child make free and easy gestures—even if the final product may appear to you to be "messy."

Simple, well-made musical instruments—drum, toy horn, toy autoharp, xylophone or piano—will be enjoyed by Youngster while he experiments with different sounds.

Generally speaking, toys with which your child can actively interact (such as the ones we have just described) will provide more fun and more educational benefit than mechanical toys (such as an electric train) that require your two-year-old to be merely a passive spectator.

Through his play with toys he discovers more about the physical world. He perceives similarities and differences between things in terms of color, weight, size, shape, odor, and taste.

Yes, taste! Tasting or mouthing is still an avenue for exploring the unfamiliar, although he uses this method much less frequently than last year.

He also uses sorting to help him classify things into a system—size, number, color.

Just watch what happens as he builds with blocks, Legos™, kitchen equipment, or construction materials. He orders and controls them.

A child needs creative freedom to reconstruct his world as he perceives it, rather than always trying to imitate your "real" world.

What emerges is what he has constructed; from his own head he has built what he thinks things should be like.

Be sure to leave him his creative freedom to reconstruct his world as he perceives it, rather than require him always to imitate your "real" world.

Since toys not only provide fun but also stimulate development, be sure to choose them carefully and wisely.

In choosing a new toy for your child, keep these questions in mind:

1. Is this toy safe for a child under three years old?

2. Is this toy appropriate for my child's age?

3. Does this toy require my child's active involvement?

4. What will my child learn from it?

5. Is the toy attractive? Will it attract my child's attention?"

6. Is the toy versatile and sturdy: Will it last, with different kinds of play possible at later ages?

7. Will my child have fun with it? ■

Content and Process

Everything Youngster learns (and everything we learn, also) can be considered to be either content or process.

Content. Children learn specific facts or skills. For example, they learn the specific *fact* that it gets dark after the sun goes down, and they learn the specific *fact* that a ball bounces when you drop it.

They learn the specific *skill* of stacking one block on top of another, and they learn the specific *skill* of making marks on surfaces like walls (which sometimes makes you wish they wouldn't learn certain things!).

All this learning of facts and skills is called *content* because it is seen as an assortment of facts and skills which makes up the content of the child's "learning bag."

Process. Youngster learns more than specific facts and skills, however. She also learns process.

This kind of learning is much more advanced. We urge you to help your Youngster develop her "process learning."

What is "process learning?" Stated simply, this involves learning to apply general principles to solve practical problems.

Before we suggest specific ways of developing this extremely important ability, we will consider a concrete example of "process learning."

Let's say that Youngster has learned the specific skill of stacking large blocks on top of each other.

One day she notices that you have put the cookie jar in a kitchen cabinet which is higher than she can reach. She wants a cookie, but the cookies are up high and she cannot reach them.

She moves a chair next to the kitchen counter, climbs onto the chair, then onto the counter, opens the cabinet door, reaches into the cookie jar, and takes out a cookie.

It is precisely at this point that your Youngster has demonstrated that she is learning about *process*.

She first learned the specific skill of stacking blocks. Then she applied the same *general principle* so that she could reach the cookies by climbing from the chair to the counter to the cabinet.

It is this kind of learning which we want to help Youngster expand.

How do you expand process learning? Here are some ways of going about it.

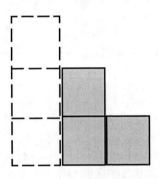

Build an incomplete stairway with blocks. The first step has one block, the second has two blocks.

Give Youngster about four or five blocks and tell her to build the next (third) step in the stairs.

To do this she must be aware that her (third) step must be higher than the second step.

At first she may fail to make her step high enough. Or, more likely, she will want to use all of her blocks and will therefore make the step too high.

You can explain to her that if one of her dolls wants to walk up the stairs, the steps must have an ordered (1, 2, 3) number of blocks.

It may take many sessions over several days before she can build the stairway accurately.

The next time she climbs the stairs in your home or in some other building she may note something that she had never noted before: The steps are each the same distance apart.

If you find that you have to demonstrate the solution to Youngster, first make sure that she can imitate what you have demonstrated.

Next, you can extend the problem by building the first three steps.

Give her five or six blocks and tell her now to build the next (fourth) step.

If you observe her making mistakes, don't rush in too quickly to solve the problem.

A child can sometimes learn more by trial-and-error than if a parent has provided the immediate solution.

After this task is mastered, it will be time to move on to another interesting activity.

Get three similar size glasses and fill them with varying amounts of water.

Then have Youngster point to the glass with the least amount of water, then the next least until finally she points out the one with the most amount of water.

After she has mastered the task of identifying the three glasses in order, you can extend the problem with a fourth glass which has even more water it in.

In each of these "process learning" tasks Youngster has had to identify some general principle which she could apply to solve a specific problem.

There is no need to be unduly concerned, however, if your child doesn't appear to immediately learn all about content and process.

Every child needs a great deal of experience and practice for learning to occur.

Sometimes her learning will take place when she is practicing alone after you have interacted with her. ∎

A Sense of Order

an old sheet, blanket or bedspread for draping over a card table, kitchen equipment (wooden spoons, bowls, pots and pans, empty plastic bottles or containers), eyeglass frames (without glass), tool chest, lunch box.

This is just a suggested starter list of ideas. It is not meant for just one day but for many make-believe performances. As parents watch their child engaged in make-believe play, they can become very creative in providing new props to stimulate these activities.

Later on Youngster may want a child-sized ironing board and iron, broom, vacuum, and play foods. Household furnishings scaled down to size are basics. Meanwhile, offer empty cans (after checking the edges for safety), boxes, containers, paper sacks.

Also real foods like carrots, apples, potatoes, and onions can be "purchased" in the child's "store," cooked in the child's "oven," and then served at mealtime.

Youngster will be very "busy" in these activities. He also will be very serious about this "work" he is doing.

It is important for parents to let him enter fully into his activity without making fun of him.

If you doubt the value of make-believe, just watch the serious expression on a two-year-old's face as he helps "wash" the family car.

It is by participating in this world of make-believe that Youngster learns to participate later in the world around him. ■

Youngster has been busy for the past few months acquiring new information, developing new skills, and processing new knowledge. In a very real sense she is putting things in order in her mind.

As she attempts to order her mental understanding of the world around her, it will help her greatly if she can readily find order in her immediate physical environment.

A sense of order will also help to make Youngster's learning environment more predictable—which, in turn, will help her develop a greater sense of security and of trust.

We know that many families cannot arrange their affairs in such a way that every object is always in its proper place or that every event always happens on schedule. What we are describing is an ideal—something to work toward.

By trying to get things in their proper place, and by trying to work out a schedule where events in your family's day occur with dependable regularity, you will be providing the stability and security that will enhance your child's intellectual and emotional growth.

There are a number of ways in which parents can create an orderly environment in the home: (1) **Provide some order for**

Growing Child®

P. O. Box 2505 • W Lafayette, IN 47996
(800) 927-7289
©Growing Child, Inc.
www.GrowingChild.com

Contributing Authors

Phil Bach, O.D., Ph.D.
Miriam Bender, Ph.D.
Joseph Braga, Ed.D.
Laurie Braga, Ph.D.
George Early, Ph.D.
Carol R. Gestwicki, M.S.
Liam Grimley, Ph.D.
Robert Hannemann, M.D., F.A.A.P.
Sylvia Kottler, M.S.
Bill Peterson, Ph.D.

your child's clothes. Have a special place for Youngster's clothes. Start with a drawer for pajamas and underwear. Label the drawer by sticking on pictures from ads so she knows what goes in this drawer.

Even though she won't immediately imitate the good habits you are teaching, you are using this opportunity to help her learn—little by little—about order.

(2) **Provide some order for toys**. Make shelves and clear, plastic containers available for playthings to be sorted and separated. Tape a picture from a toy package on the container it belongs in. Just as you organize your own cupboards and closets, so Youngster's "tools" should be organized and not junked together randomly.

(3) **Toys that are not currently in use should be stored out of sight in a box.** A child gets bored easily if she sees the same toys every day. But she will be thrilled when you bring back an "old friend" that has been hidden in the storage box.

(4) **Provide for the order of space, particularly if you have more than one child and limited area.** Decide what goes where—doll corner here, painting there, blocks and construction play right here.

You will find fewer conflicts when the territory is divided in advance. After all, in your own world you have a place for cooking and another for watching television.

(5) **Provide for the order of time.** You teach your child the order of time by providing some regularity to her daily life. Plan your meals at the same time each day so that the family eats together and meals are pleasurable.

This will help Youngster become sensitive to time order so that she can learn to anticipate events, to plan ahead, or learn to postpone until later what she is currently involved in.

Bedtime is consistently the same as is the sequence leading up to it—the bedtime story helps her to anticipate a happy experience. Such well-established habits will make Youngster's days more predictable and secure. ■

Growing Child®

The widest excursions of the mind are
made by short flights frequently repeated.

Johnson

Unpredictable Is the Word
for Two-and-a-half

Many people who study and work with young children agree that the period around two-and-a-half years old can be very exasperating.

You are no doubt finding it also to be one of the funniest.

Just keep your sense of humor well shined-up, draw on your hidden reserves of patience and objectivity, and both you and your child will weather this stormy period successfully.

Two-and-a-half has a well-earned reputation for going to extremes—sometimes shifting without warning.

Contradictory as this may seem, Two-and-a-half has her own reasons for being so changeable.

This is a transitional age. Youngster is just discovering opposites and alternate choices of action.

Her understanding of commands such as come and go, run and stop, give and take, grasp and release, push and pull, attack and retreat is still so evenly balanced that she is as yet unable to decide which way to go.

Her capacity for voluntary choice is weak. She is too inexperienced to make a reasonable choice and stick to it. She learns by doing—so she may sometimes try to go both ways at the same time.

This is not stubbornness. She just cannot yet weigh the relative advantage of one choice to the exclusion of the other.

This same quality characterizes her physical activities. Two-and-a-half doesn't yet have good control of opposing groups of muscles. She tends to squeeze too tightly, and let go too suddenly.

When being very cautious, as in building a tower of blocks, she may place one block carefully, then release it suddenly by spreading her fingers very wide.

She enjoys building and knocking down!

Two-and-a-half has not learned to unwind or relax easily before going to sleep.

She may demand a long and complicated bedtime ritual in order to prepare for sleep. Once in bed she may talk to herself for some time before falling asleep.

This same difficulty is exhibited in toileting. At two-and-a-half, a child may not easily relax her bladder sphincter voluntarily—and then may withhold too long.

A child who has generally been "dry" during the day since age two may begin to have "accidents." She may play so intently that she ignores the mounting bladder pressure until it is too late.

Characteristically, Two-and-a-half cannot modulate her social behavior. She is going through the growing pains of learning about opposites, and the developmental method of learning is to try both.

She is a sort of preschool edition of a confused adolescent. Yet by this very process, Two-and-a-half is finding her way.

Our lives are a series of choices—some simple, some complex.

For example, Mommy may try on a number of dresses before choosing the one that feels right.

Youngster is taking her first tentative steps toward meeting life's challenges. She does this by learning to choose

continued from page 186

"I Had It First"

Now that your child can talk, she will sometimes use language in order to get her own way.

When parents hear one child say to another, "I had it first," they know the statement is an open declaration of war.

Not surprisingly, parents are sometimes confused about what to do when their child quarrels with another child.

If they seek advice from other parents, they probably will hear conflicting solutions that range from unbridled permissiveness to strict authoritarianism.

And if they read what parenting "experts" have written about how to handle children's quarrels, they will find an equally bewildering array of opinions.

How then can you decide as a parent what you are going to do?

(1) One of the main reasons for **Growing Child** is to provide parents with the knowledge they need about typical child development. So, our readers should be very much aware that conflicts and quarrels are a normal part of growing up.

Getting along with others and sharing one's possessions are skills that a two-and-a-half-year-old child is just beginning to learn.

Sometimes these skills can be learned by the child herself through everyday interaction with other children.

At other times, a parent's direct intervention is needed. Physical fighting and scratching or biting, for example, require immediate parental direction.

(2) When the time comes for direct intervention, it is helpful for the parent to have knowledge about a variety of different strategies for dealing with behavioral problems.

Otherwise there will be an inclination to use the same strategy for every situation.

Unfortunately, a plan that works well in one circumstance may be too strong in a different situation or too weak to be effective in a third.

The books for parents listed on page 183 present different strategies for dealing with children's problems.

Even though you may disagree with the opinions expressed in one or more of these books, we recommend that you at least become aware of alternatives that other parents have found helpful.

(3) A parent needs to consider how and when to apply the parenting knowledge acquired.

Should the parent immediately intervene as the all-knowing, all-powerful authority figure? Or should the parent get the child to assume responsibility for solving her own conflict problems.

Deciding which strategy to use will involve consideration of your own needs, those of your child, and the specific characteristics of each particular situation.

Too often parents don't realize that they have their own inner feelings and needs when trying to settle children's quarrels.

Frequently these quarrels bother the parents more than they bother the children involved.

Becoming aware of our own inner needs as parents is a first prerequisite to effective intervention in children's conflicts.

We must also be aware of the individual characteristics of each child involved.

Conflicts in which one child is always the aggressor and the other child is always the victim will require more long-term interventions by the parent than a child's spur-of-the-moment outburst which is sometimes quickly resolved without any parental involvement.

Knowing the unique characteristics of the children involved is therefore a prerequisite in dealing with their conflicts.

It is also important to consider any special characteristics of the situation. For example, some conflicts are more likely to arise before bedtime when children are tired.

Being aware of the specific circumstances under which a conflict arises can be helpful not only in resolving it but also in preventing a similar recurrence in the future.

In short, there is no one solution that will resolve all children's conflicts in all circumstances.

But parents who have some basic knowledge of child development and of different intervention strategies and who are aware of the factors involved in applying that knowledge are the ones best equipped to make their decision about what they will do when they hear their child scream, "I had it first!" ■

The Feeling Game

Place three differently shaped toys under a blanket. They might be a small ball, a block, and a doll. Then find a fourth toy that is just like one of the hidden toys. Show Youngster this toy and say, "There is a toy just like this under the blanket. Reach under the blanket and try to find it. But don't look, just feel."

While you hold the blanket so that Youngster's hands stay covered, encourage her to feel each toy in turn to decide which is the right one. Then she should pull out the chosen toy and see if it matches the one on top.

If she chooses correctly, you can tell her how successful she is at matching. Or give her a little reward if you are used to doing so. However, just making the match may be reward enough.

If she doesn't get the right toy, show her all three of the covered toys so she can see what a true match looks like. Then cover all three up again, mix them around and let her try again.

The Feeling Game has some advantages over matching by looking. The main advantage right now is that it slows Youngster and makes her concentrate. This is because it takes longer for hands to feel a shape than for the eyes to see it.

Since the eyes can see a shape quickly, it is all too easy to take a quick look at something and then decide, even though that quick look could be wrong.

But when Youngster runs her fingers over the toys, she must build up a picture of them in her mind over a period of time. She must concentrate a little longer than she would by just looking.

For another thing, the game is new and different. You can keep it fun by playing it only once or twice at a session or by changing the objects. It is best to stop with Youngster wanting more. That way she will ask you to play the game rather than vice versa.

Finally, the game encourages her to make a match between one of her senses (touch) and another (vision). This is the passing of information from one sense to another. It is a skill that helps to make human beings unique, and will be very important later in school learning.

Start with easy items so Youngster can be successful the very first time. Begin with toys that are familiar and that she can tell apart by feel. Then you can use your own judgment in varying the hidden toys in order to challenge her.

There are other variations of the game that will work as well. One is to use a single object whose name she doesn't know, but with two or three visible choices above the blanket. After feeling the covered object, she should point to the object on top that is just like the one she felt.

You can also make her own feeling box using a shoe box with a hole large enough for her hand in the end. ■

Reading List

Growing Child seeks to provide helpful information for parents in a unique manner by following a child's development month by month. Parents sometimes ask advice about other reading materials that might also be helpful. This is a list of some good books about child rearing which should be available at a local bookstore or your public library.

Brazelton, T. Berry (1984), To Listen to a Child. Addison-Wesley.

Berends, Polly Berrien (1987), Whole Child/Whole Parent. Harper & Row.

Bush, Richard (1980), A Parent's Guide to Child Therapy. Delacorte Press.

Calladine, Carole and Andrew (1979), Raising Brothers and Sisters Without Raising the Roof. Winston Press.

Cristakis, Erika (2016) The Importance of Being Little: What Preschoolers Really Need from Grownups.

Crary, Elizabeth (1979), Without Spanking or Spoiling. Parenting Press.

Elkind, David (1981), The Hurried Child: Growing Up Too Fast Too Soon. Addison-Wesley.

Ferber, Richard (1985), Solve Your Child's Sleep Problems. Simon & Schuster.

Gopnik, Alison (2016), The Gardener and the Carpenter.

Kaban, Barb (1979), Choosing Toys for Children from Birth to Age Five. Shocken Books.

Lansky, Vicki (1980), Best Practical Parenting Tips. Meadowbrook Press.

Leach, Penelope (1985), Your Baby and Child From Birth to Age Five. Knopf.

LeShan, Eda (1985), When Your Child Drives You Crazy. St. Martin's Press.

Faber, Joanna and King, Julie (2017) How to Talk so Little Kids Will Listen: A Survival Guide to Life with Children Ages 2-7. Scribner

Lickona, Thomas (1983), Raising Good Children. Bantam Books.

Miller, Karen (1984), Things To Do With Toddlers and Twos. Telshare.

Newman, Catherine (2016) Catastrophic Happiness: Finding Joy in Chilhood's Messy Years. Little, Brown

Shelov, Stephen P., Editor (1991), Caring For Your Baby and Young Child: Birth To Age 5. Bantam Books.

Shiff, Eileen, Editor (1987), Experts Advise Parents: A Guide To Raising Loving, Responsible Children. Delacorte Press.

Siegel, Daniel (2012) The Whole Brain Child: 12 Revolutionary Straegies to Nurture Your Child's Developing Whole Mind. Bantam

Smith, Helen Wheeler (1982), A Survival Handbook for Preschool Mothers. Cambridge.

Tough, Paul (2012) How Children Succeed: Grit, Curiosity, and the Hidden Power of Character. Houghton Mifflin Harcourt.

White, Burton L. (1988), Educating the Infant and Toddler. Lexington Books. ■

Hang On—But Don't Get Hung Up!

Most of us at *Growing Child* are parents, too. We know what it is to worry about how well our children are doing. We also know how good it is to enjoy and savor our children's growing experiences.

In every child's growing up there are ups and downs. One day you think he'll surely be President. The next day you think you'll be lucky if he manages to stay out of jail. These wild swings between good and bad feelings about your child are all part of the business of being a parent.

Being a parent is a truly great experience, but at times, it can cause you exasperation! May we assure you such wild swings in your feelings are perfectly normal. We know that you sometimes wonder if you're doing the right thing because we have wondered the same thing about ourselves.

What we're really trying to say is that we do not write for *Growing Child* in a vacuum. We are with you in your suffering and your delight because we have been where you are now.

We know the joys of seeing our children and grandchildren grow and learn.

We also know the agony of how many mistakes we have made as parents. These feelings, some good and some painful, are all part of being parents. It "goes with the territory."

Our practical advice to you is simply this: "Hang on, but don't get hung up." Hang on because: (1) You know that almost every parent has felt what you are feeling now; (2) There are so many good things about your child's growing and development which can give you pleasure; (3) One or two problems now are not going to affect your child forever.

Hang on by: (1) Living with your child's developmental problems from day to day; (2) Enjoying him, laughing with him, holding him close when the dark moments close in upon both of you; (3) Simply getting through the ordinary routines of each day.

If you ever feel it's getting too difficult for you, talk to a close friend or other parents who can share their own experiences.

But, whatever you do, please do not get "hung up." Do not mentally bite your

fingernails or waste your emotional energy in wondering if you are a "perfect parent," whatever that may mean.

Do not hover over your child. Do not constantly ask yourself, "Is he doing all right?"

Above all, do not pressure your child into performing at ever-higher levels. Do not make him feel that you love him only if he performs well. He should know that you love him because he is your child.

He belongs to you. He is important to you. The knowledge that he matters, that he is loved for himself alone, is the greatest gift you can give your child. But you cannot give your child this gift if you are hung up over how well he is doing.

Above all, let Youngster know in a hundred different ways that you love him. Show him that he matters and that he belongs. Show him that he is a vital part of your world.

If you do this we think you will greatly improve his chances for success in school and also in the world beyond school. ∎

Is Dressing Your Child Getting To Be a Real Hassle?

Dressing a Two-and-a-half-year-old child can be enough to try the patience of Job! His demands for independence alternate unpredictably with times of complete dependence when he goes limp like he's a doll and refuses to help.

Temper tantrums are common during dressing. A parent pushes against time and Youngster balks or dawdles.

Running away as soon as a parent starts dressing him is a favorite game of children of this age. Two-and-a-half loves to be chased—and as soon as he is caught and brought back, he runs away again.

If caught, picked up and forcibly returned to the dressing spot, he may throw a temper tantrum. Or he may pull, tug, squirm, and wiggle until his parent is totally exasperated.

Be smart and change his game by having him follow you. For example, as you move toward the bathroom, you might say: "Come to the bathroom when you are ready to get dressed." Then go to the bathroom.

This usually brings Two-and-a-half running almost immediately, crying "I'm ready! I'm ready!"

When he finds you in the bathroom, quietly and calmly close the door—even lock it if Two-and-a-half is really fast-moving.

Dressing may also be easier if he is placed on the lid of the toilet seat or on a clothes hamper.

However, be prepared to return him to the floor if his activity makes it likely that he will fall.

As soon as he finds you are going to be firm with him, he is likely to be more cooperative so that he can go back to play as soon as dressing is over. ∎

Language and Music

It shouldn't be necessary to structure every moment of Youngster's play.

However, in bad weather, cold climates or periods of illness, when children are indoors a lot, they sometimes need ideas for constructive play.

The two- to three-year-old loves to listen to music. His preference will likely be for music with a strong, definite beat to which he may respond with total body movement.

It will not be unusual for him to want to hear the same music or stories-to-music over and over again.

If you happen to play the piano, guitar, or autoharp, you will become his favorite entertainer. Here are some ideas you can use for creating different songs:

I. Improvised songs

These are songs you "make up" to fit a situation or a need. The words are made to fit tunes borrowed from other songs.

(1) Washing Tune: **Mulberry Bush**

This is how we wash our face, wash our
    face, wash our face;
This is how we wash our face,
    Before we eat our dinner.

(2) Bedtime Tune: **Hey, Betty Martin**

Hey, little sleepy, sleepy, sleepy;
Hey, little sleepy, it's bedtime now.

II. Counting Songs

Tune: **This Old Man**

This old man, he played one,
He played knick-knack on his thumb,
Knick-knack paddy whack, give your
    dog a bone,
This old man came rolling home.

This old man, he played two,
He played knick-knack on his shoe, etc.

This old man, he played three,
He played knick-knack on his knee, etc.

This old man, he played four,
He played knick-knack on the floor, etc.

This old man, he played five,
He played knick-knack on his hive, etc.

III. Chants (to be clapped, beat out, or played with homemade instrument).

Teddy Bear—originally a rope-jumping
    chant.
Teddy bear, teddy bear, turn around,
Teddy bear, teddy bear, touch the ground.
Teddy bear, teddy bear, show your shoe,
Teddy bear, teddy bear, better skiddoo!

IV. Producing rhythm

Youngster also likes to make music, particularly with homemade musical instruments. Some examples:

(1) **Cymbals**—use two flat pot lids.

(2) **Razzle dazzle**—use dried peas or macaroni placed in a flour shaker.

(3) **Timpani**—use wooden spoons for striking metal pie tins and containers from canned goods.

(4) **Fife**—use a paper towel cylinder into which you have punched five small holes in a row down the top of the cylinder.

Next cover one end with wax paper which has been securely taped with cellophane.

Now when Youngster vocalizes into the tube, the sound will be amplified.

Should he cover some of the holes on the cylinder with his fingers, he will discover that he can produce different tones.

(5) **Maracas**—Use an empty salt box into which you place small stones and tape it closed. The maracas can be thumped or shaken.

(6) **Drums**—Use an empty 46 oz. round juice can or gallon paint can. Remove both ends.

From a sheet of flexible plastic material such as vinyl, cut out two identical large circles, large enough to cover the ends of the can.

Next, punch holes around the edges of the circles. Cover the ends of the can with the circles and lace them tightly to each other with a leather shoelace, lacing through the holes back and forth along the side of the container.

Large size pans also work well when turned upside down and tapped with hands and fingers.

(7) **Harmonica**—Use a large, clean comb covered with tissue paper which when blown with the mouth slightly open makes a real brassy sound.

(8) **Guitar**—Use the bottom of a shoe box with eight to 10 colored rubber bands of varying sizes stretched across it. It can be plucked with finger or teaspoon.

(9) **Sticks**—the simplest instrument to play is two sticks—perhaps two wooden spoons—that are tapped together to match the rhythm. ∎

Music as Education

continued from page 181

Music is more than just fun; it is education. As he sings along, dances, or "plays" an instrument, here are the sorts of things Youngster learns:

1. New vocabulary. Many songs, particularly folk songs and nursery tunes, repeat words or refrains over and over again.

For example, "We swing our arms so gayly, gayly; We swing our arms so gayly, all on a Saturday night." This type of repetition strengthens associations between newly acquired words and their meaning.

2. Time sense. When swinging the arms, moving the body, or tapping an "instrument" to music, the child is exposed to time relations between musical notes.

He becomes aware of order—this comes first, this comes next and this comes last. This kind of order is important in both understanding and using speech. It is also extremely important later in learning to read.

This is demonstrated by what happens to a sentence when just one word is put into a different order—"Now, I want to go"/"I want to go, now."

In addition, changes in the length of utterances, such as pauses within them, produce different patterns and thus different meanings.

For example, remember a song of the '40s, "Maresy Dotes and Dozey Dotes" ("Mares Eat Oats and Does Eat Oats"), or the prayer, "The Cross-eyed Bear" ("The Cross I'd Bear")?

Finally, take the sentences, "Let's eat Mother"/"Let's eat, Mother." The presence of word order is apparent in Youngster's own verbalization: "Here ball," "here daddy," "baby here," "dog here," or "more milk," "more up."

3. Counting. While at this age learning will be mainly by rote memory, he will learn to count from such rhymes as "One Little, Two Little, Three Little Pumpkins."

4. Self-control. It is necessary to really listen and attend to what the song says in order to carry out the actions.

When it says "clap," "jump," or "stop," he must translate what he has heard into a physical movement and clap, jump, or stop.

We urge you to make music a family affair. Before the days of television, families created their own entertainment, and singing together was very popular.

Develop your own song book from current rhythms, folk-rock, and old timers. ■

Growing Child®

P. O. Box 2505 • W Lafayette, IN 47996
(800) 927-7289
©Growing Child, Inc.
www.GrowingChild.com

Contributing Authors

Phil Bach, O.D., Ph.D.
Miriam Bender, Ph.D.
Joseph Braga, Ed.D.
Laurie Braga, Ph.D.
George Early, Ph.D.
Carol R. Gestwicki, M.S.
Liam Grimley, Ph.D.
Robert Hannemann, M.D., F.A.A.P.
Sylvia Kottler, M.S.
Bill Peterson, Ph.D.

between opposites, and to choose she must sometimes try both.

These characteristic behaviors are not equally marked in all children. They are particularly pronounced in very active children, but less conspicuous among more placid children.

It is relatively normal for a child of this age to show swings between the following extremes:

• From intense activity to quiet passivity, sometimes accompanied by thumb sucking.

• From boisterousness to shyness.

• From a keen desire to possess an object to sudden indifference once she has obtained it.

• From loud demands for food to rejection of it when offered.

• From loud laughter, shrieks and screams to whispering or talking in a low monotone.

• From loud demands of "me do it!" to dawdling.

These extremes of behavior are not necessarily mood swings. They are fluctuations due to Youngster's narrow base of experience.

She must try both extremes to find out which one works best for her at any given moment. Only by trying out the extremes will she eventually find a "middle way."

Parental "management" of problems, rather than overly strict discipline techniques, will lead to better parent-child relationships during this period. Forcing her into a given course of behavior is apt to bring on a temper tantrum.

With a better understanding of her present confusions and some wise anticipation of problems, she can be led to want to do what you desire.

So, love her, enjoy her unpredictability, and help her learn from experience during this complex developmental period. ■

Growing Child ®

The most favorable time for a child to learn is when she wants to do it herself.

Unknown

A Special Time

Youngster's major incentive for language development right now is her need to communicate something to somebody.

Parents should be a real audience, without pretending, even if the child produces only a few short sentences at a time. It is from these informal utterances that more formal language will eventually emerge.

Many parents think that because they are with the child most of the time, they, in fact, provide her an audience.

However, if one examines the routine of a typical home, Mom and Dad are involved with answering the door or telephone, washing clothes and dishes, making beds, or preparing dinner.

What is really needed is a "Special Time," however brief. This special time differs from the rest of the day because it belongs to Youngster exclusively. She isn't interrupting your work just to get attention.

Special Time differs from the rest of the day because it belongs to Youngster exclusively. It is entirely devoted to listening and attending to her.

Special Time is "special" because it is entirely devoted to listening and attending to the child. Of course, this means privacy—no answering phones or checking on food in the oven.

How much time is required? Only about fifteen minutes. That's about the maximum that parent and child can hold each other's attention at this age.

It is a good idea to plan for Special Time: (1) Explain simply what it is— you both will be together and she can tell you or show you what she wants to do. It is very important that you do not direct the program. Otherwise you will defeat the objective.

When she must tell you what she wants to do, her mind is more active, formulating and expressing her ideas and wishes.

(2) Help her to better understand the concept of "time."

If you have an alarm clock, set it to go off when the time limit is reached. Or show her the face of the clock and point to where Special Time begins and ends.

If during the day it appears that the child wants your attention and you

are too busy, remind her about the approaching Special Time. If it is a regular habit, she will learn to wait.

Because all good things end too soon, prepare her for the end of Special Time.

Even if she has no awareness of "five more minutes," continued daily use of such a warning will alert her to the fact that it is almost over.

Thus, in planning Special Time, you are educating Youngster to a temporal (time) order: the anticipation of Special Time each day, the length of time she will have your undivided attention, and the reminder about when it will be over.

(3) It may be necessary to set limits on what can or cannot be done during Special Time, especially if the child is inclined to want to do the same thing, such as hearing the same story every day for two weeks.

You may still allow her to choose and still set limits if you tell her honestly, "I'm tired of that book. Let's do something different in Special Time."

(4) As Youngster grows older, she will want to talk more—to express her feelings and to know that you are truly listening. Prepare yourself to be a good audience; this means active listening.

(5) Above all, make Special Time a good learning experience for your child by making it a fun time to be together. In that way, she will look forward to this Special Time.

Children learn more easily and quickly when the learning experience is an enjoyable one. ■

Playing with Toy Guns

"Should I allow my child to play with toy guns?" This is a question parents of young children frequently ask.

In the family where such forms of play are not tolerated, the troubling question still arises whenever the child visits a friend whose family has purchased toy rifles, revolvers, or laser guns.

In deciding what to do in such circumstances, parents need to consider three factors: The function of play in their child's development, the socially accepted aspects of aggressive play, and the "forbidden fruit" phenomenon.

Although many parents may think of their child's play as a time for "goofing off" rather than for learning, it is during play activities that some very important learning takes place.

Parents will have noted, for example, that during infancy it was mainly through enjoyable play activities that their infant learned to explore and eventually manipulate the objects in his environment.

Similarly, in the preschool years, eye-hand coordination and socialization skills are learned and developed during play activities.

In purchasing a toy, a most important question for parents to consider is what their child will learn from this new object.

For example, with skill-building toys, the child will acquire and develop new skills or improve those already learned.

It should be obvious that with aggressive-type toys, the child will learn aggressive-type behaviors.

Even though parents may teach their child to be peace-loving and respectful of other children, they are nevertheless faced with the reality that the environment in which their child is living is not always one of peace and harmony. That's why the socially accepted aspects of aggressive play need to be considered.

In our society, some forms of aggressive behavior—such as assertiveness, competitiveness, and physical contact sports—are not only socially acceptable but are even encouraged and rewarded.

In teaching a child not to be unduly aggressive, parents should also consider teaching him necessary skills, including self-defense, for survival in the real world.

A word of caution to parents who may try to forbid their child from ever playing with an aggressive-type play object, such as a toy gun:

Over-zealous efforts may backfire. By dealing too harshly with the problem, a child may become unduly attracted to the "forbidden fruit" which the parents have condemned.

Many parents have found that children can be endlessly inventive in devising ways to construct their own "guns" using a variety of materials and methods that vary from a simple stick to more complicated versions.

The most effective way for parents to deal with the problem is to approach it in a calm and reasonable manner.

They must first decide what are the most important values they wish to transmit

Many parents have found that children can be endlessly inventive in devising ways to construct their own "guns" using a variety of materials and methods that vary from a simple stick to more complicated versions.

to their child. They must then explain these values in a manner that will be meaningful to him.

For example, many young children find it difficult to share their possessions with others.

Parents can teach a child the value of sharing by pointing out the many ways in which he was made happy because others were willing to share with him.

After all, children first learn about sharing by receiving rather than by giving.

Later, when children learn to treat others as they would want to be treated, they begin to express the value of sharing in their lives.

If parents find that their child has violated the values taught, they should wait, if possible, to discuss the matter in private rather than try to deal with it in public which would only humiliate the child.

Children are more likely to learn from what a parent does than from what a parent says.

Parents who exhibit aggressive behavior in the home are likely to have an aggressive child.

And parents who exhibit loving, caring, and peaceful behavior are likely to have a child who ultimately will exhibit those same behaviors. ■

A good book on this topic: *The War Play Dilemma: What Every Parent and Teacher Needs to Know:* D. Levin and N. Carlsson-Paige (2005).

Development of Sex-Role Concepts

Am I a boy or am I a girl?
Will I always be the same?
Why do boys and girls
play differently?
What are some other differences
between boys and girls?

These and other questions about children's development of gender and sex-role concepts have been studied extensively by researchers in recent years.

In order to understand the research findings, the reader will need to be familiar with some definitions that are commonly used. (See "Definitions" in box.)

Research studies have revealed that:

• Most children between one-and-a-half and two years of age are aware of their own "gender identity" as either a "boy" or "girl."

• Children between two-and-a-half and three years of age are also generally able to correctly label the gender of adults and other children.

This ability to accurately label "male" or "female" is of course only a first step in the child's development of gender concept.

The child's response is frequently based on the type of toy another child is playing with, the type of clothing worn (pants or dress), or the length and style of the other person's hair.

As society changes, with some fathers having long hair, and with some mothers having short hair and wearing a shirt, tie, and pin-stripe suit, these cues to gender identity are becoming less clear for the young child.

Parents can easily test their child's ability to distinguish between the genders by pointing to pictures in a magazine and asking, "Which one is a woman/girl?" or "Which one is a man/boy?"

Once children have some initial grasp of gender identity, they begin to differentiate between the attitudes and behaviors associated with each gender, namely, the socially appropriate "sex-role stereotypes."

In each family, parents ultimately determine the values, attitudes, and behaviors they consider appropriate for their son or daughter. Being aware of important research findings will generally help parents provide well-informed guidance to their child.

Recent studies have found that:

• Between two and three years of age, both boys and girls consider that girls like to cook, clean house, and play with dolls, whereas boys play with cars and trucks, use tools, and build things.

Some sex-role differences between boys and girls are, of course, biologically predetermined.

Other differences are the result of cultural influences in the child's environment. Family, peers, and the media are three important influences which need to be considered.

(1) Recent research studies on the family have indicated that:

• During the preschool years parents generally provide both boys and girls with similar amounts of warmth and affection.

• Mothers did not appear to be concerned if their son or daughter played with a "masculine" or "feminine" toy, but fathers were found to disapprove strongly only when their sons played with girls' toys, even in homes where the parents expressed belief in gender equality.

• Among mothers, differences have been found between children of mothers who were homemakers and of those who worked outside the home.

Both boys and girls of mothers who worked outside the home were found to have less rigidly stereotyped views of male and female roles.

For example, these children considered it appropriate for women to be lawyers or doctors and for men to cook or clean house.

(2) Besides the family, the peer group hasan important influence on the child's

continued on page 192

Definitions

These are definitions for some of the terms most used in research studies dealing with sexual development:

Gender concept: The child's overall understanding of what it means to be either male or female—an understanding which progressively develops over many years.

Gender identity: The first step in the development of the gender concept by which the child can correctly label people, including him- or herself, as either male or female.

Gender constancy: Recognition that a person's gender will remain the same even if other aspects of the person may change (such as a man wearing a woman's wig and dress).

Sex-role concept: The child's overall understanding of differences in appropriate attitudes and behavior of a male or female in society.

Sex-role stereotypes: The attitudes and behaviors widely considered in society as appropriate or inappropriate for each gender. ■

Father Involvement

So much attention is naturally focused on the mother's role in child rearing that fathers may sometimes feel uncomfortable or out of place in this process.

The role of a mother is obviously very special during pregnancy, giving birth, nursing the baby, and generally taking care of a young child's needs.

Nowadays, however, fathers are more actively involved, not only in supporting the mother, but also in providing direct child care.

At the same time, psychologists are discovering that fathers have a unique and very important role—different from that of the mother—in a child's development, especially during the toddler years.

A study of history can help to understand some changes in society that have had an impact on the role of fathers.

Prior to the industrial revolution, many fathers were able to remain in close daily contact with their families as they worked on the land or had a home-based trade such as blacksmith, cobbler, or carpenter.

In this way they were able to take an active part in day-to-day family affairs.

At the same time, children had more immediate access to their fathers during the day, sometimes working alongside Dad either in the fields or at his trade.

With the coming of the industrial revolution, however, fathers (and sometimes mothers) were required more and more to work away from home. From early morning until late in the evening, they were separated from daily family life.

Mothers, who more frequently remained at home, became their children's primary caregivers. This eventually resulted in what sociologists have described as the "feminization" of the parent's role.

Two recent changes in our society have had a significant impact on family life, namely, the women's movement and the age of computer technology.

With more mothers working outside the home, it is not surprising that many fathers are now taking a more active part in raising their children.

Examples of more active father involvement in family affairs can be found even before a baby is born. More and more fathers are now attending pre-birth classes with the mother.

Also, the presence of fathers in the delivery room, either as coach or as supportive observer—a practice that was forbidden in most hospitals before the 1970s—is now more commonplace.

Studies have found that when a father is present during labor and delivery, the mother is likely to report lower levels of pain, receive less medication and is less likely to experience complications.

The coming of the computer age has also had an important impact on family life. Many parents—both fathers and mothers—can now perform at least part of their work at home where they can be in closer contact with their children.

Thus the potential for fathers to become more actively involved in childrearing is greater today than it was just a generation ago.

Studies also indicate that when both fathers and mothers are together involved in childrearing, they both more often express positive feelings toward their children. Ultimately, children are the ones who benefit the most from these positive relationships.

Psychologists have also been interested in determining if there are differences in children's attachment to fathers and mothers.

It has been found that from the age of eight months—when strong attachments are first observed in children—they show greater attachment to both their fathers and mothers than to strangers.

Between eight and 24 months an interesting difference emerges. In times of fear or stress, a child will more likely turn to the mother for comfort than to the father. In general, mothers are relied on in matters involving trust, sensitivity, and intimacy.

When both fathers and mothers are together involved in childrearing, they both more often express positive feelings toward their children. Ultimately, children are the ones who benefit the most from these positive relationships.

During the toddler years, however, a father's unique role becomes particularly important.

At this age, as children strive for more autonomous behavior, they seek and receive more support from the father in striving for independence. They still rely on their mother when they are in need of comforting and nurturance.

Both of these types of experiences—the striving for independence and the continued need for nurturance—are important aspects of every child's development.

The different roles of the father and mother thus complement one another in this developmental process.

Since it has been found that a child reacts differently to the father and mother, are

continued on page 191

continued on page 190

there then differences in parenting styles between fathers and mothers?

It has been found that the differences are indeed sometimes quite substantial. Whereas mothers are more likely to engage in quiet, peaceful, interactions such as smiling, talking or soothing, fathers are more likely to engage in more physical roughhousing with the child.

While the father is often perceived as the ultimate authority figure in the family, ("Wait until your father hears about this!") his interactions with the child are generally more playful.

And two-year-olds actively seek these playful interactions with the father. They particularly enjoy playing simple games such as hide-and-seek.

Through these playful activities, children will generally experience a broad range of emotions that they must learn to handle, laughing hysterically at one moment and being on the verge of tears at another.

During these playful experiences children not only learn better control of their emotions, but they also develop an important ability to "read" the non-verbal messages of others, as conveyed, for example, by Dad's facial expression or tone of voice.

These lessons that are learned from interacting with Dad will prove most useful later when interacting with other adults or with peers.

There are, of course, variations in father-child relationships. It has been found, for example, that fathers with low self-esteem have a more negative impact on their children than mothers with low self-esteem.

A father's work environment can also influence father-child interactions. A father whose job provides a great deal of autonomy is more likely to encourage independent behavior in his children.

In the contrary, a father whose job is highly supervised with little or no autonomy will expect a high level of conformity in his children.

Sometimes fathers experience difficulty in interacting with their children at the end of the day's work.

While Dad is ready and eager to read the child a story or play a game, he may find that Toddler is neither ready nor willing to engage in such interaction.

It may take the child some time to adjust from being with Mom or another caregiver throughout the day.

It's wisest for Dad to let the child set the pace for their interaction, allowing it to unfold naturally rather than trying to create "organized joy." Under these circumstances, children will usually give some indication when they are ready and eager for interaction with Dad.

If Mom has been with the child throughout the day, it may help the father-child interaction if she can find someplace else to go. This can be her time to enjoy a break while father and child spend some quality time together, giving one another their undivided loving attention.

In summary, although the industrial revolution caused many fathers to be removed from the daily lives of their families, recent changes in our society have resulted in more active father involvement in the home.

Father involvement in child-rearing not only enriches a young child's life, it also enhances the lives of all members of a family. ■

Single Parents

A note of clarification may be in order for single parents. While this article deals with father involvement in a child's development, it is recognized that, in today's world, there are many single parents engaged in childrearing without the support of a spouse.

Since it is not the purpose of this article to make single mothers feel guilty because of the absence of the child's father, the following points should be made clear:

1. A loving single-parent home is a preferable environment for a young child than one in which abusive relationships exist;

2. Single parents who raise a child alone under such circumstances deserve special recognition and encouragement;

3. It is often possible for a loving surrogate "father-figure" to fulfill a father's role in a child's life;

4. Children who grow up in a loving home environment can be extremely resilient in adapting to the conditions under which they live their lives. In their case, love seems to conquer all. ■

"Mommy!"

development of gender concept. It has been found that:

• Children as young as two-and-a-half years of age show a preference for same-sex playmates.

• They will also spend more time watching same-sex peers than opposite-sex peers.

• There are marked differences between boys and girls in their play activities even before three years of age.

When boys play with other boys they generally engage in loud and vigorous physical games, whereas when girls play together they usually prefer quieter, more artistic activities.

(3) Television and children's books also influence a child's thinking about male and female roles. The U. S. Commission on Civil Rights has found that:

• Role models presented on television are strongly sex-typed. Men and boys are more often shown as strong, capable problem-solvers.

Women and girls, on the other hand, are portrayed frequently as weak, dependent and conforming persons.

• Even cartoons convey a strong message to the child about sex-role stereotypes.

(4) Studies have also been done of cross-sex preference—boys who say they would rather be girls or girls who say they would rather be boys—a phenomenon that some-times causes great concern to parents.

These studies have found that:

• A child generally does not develop the concept of "gender constancy" until five years of age or older.

Prior to that stage, children do not have a clear notion that they will remain the same sex throughout life.

Nor do they understand, for example, that wearing a dress does not necessarily make a person a woman.

• In our society there are more girls than boys who exhibit cross-sex preference.

This finding may not be too surprising in an age when women are seeking greater equality with men.

Parents have also generally been more tolerant of "tomboy" behavior in girls than of "effeminate" qualities in boys.

Parents are often particularly upset if their preschool son expresses a desire to be a girl. Yet at this age this may simply be a child's way of expressing a desire for more emotional warmth and affection.

As indicated earlier, parents ultimately determine the values, attitudes, and behaviors they consider appropriate for their son or daughter.

In making that determination they need to take into account the child's own progressive development of gender and sex-role concepts.

They also need to be aware of important environmental influences such as family, peers, and the media.

Helping a child to develop appropriate gender and sex-role concepts is a most important element in the overall development of your child's positive self-concept. ■

P. O. Box 2505 • W Lafayette, IN 47996
(800) 927-7289
©Growing Child, Inc.
www.GrowingChild.com

Contributing Authors

Phil Bach, O.D., Ph.D.
Miriam Bender, Ph.D.
Joseph Braga, Ed.D.
Laurie Braga, Ph.D.
George Early, Ph.D.
Carol R. Gestwicki, M.S.
Liam Grimley, Ph.D.
Robert Hannemann, M.D., F.A.A.P.
Sylvia Kottler, M.S.
Bill Peterson, Ph.D.

Mildred is making cookies in the kitchen, and here is Ned, her 2.5 year old son, yacking away four miles a minute.

Maybe Mildred is a slightly uptight mother. She may be a little worried about whether or not she would do well by her kids. And then again, maybe Ned has learned to manipulate her.

He is kneeling on a chair at the kitchen table, playing with a set of toy automobiles.

And all the time, Ned is talking a polka-dot blue streak. "Mommy, do you think I should fix the motor on the blue car? Mommy, my yellow car only goes backwards. Do you think it can beat my blue car going backwards? Look, Mommy, I can get three cars in my garage if I put one of them on top of the others. Is it alright to put a car on top of some other cars?"

And, suddenly Mildred the Mom became another person: part wicked witch of the West, part bad queen from Snow White.

Without even knowing why. she suddenly, said, "Ned, you're driving me crazy! You are talking me right out of my mind!"

Ned became silent. His lip quivered. And Mildred felt worthy of falling through a hole in the kitchen floor.

Now, why had she blown up at her child? Had he really annoyed her? Was she an unfit mother?

Well, one of the things that every child must learn is how to gain and hold the attention of an adult, particularly his mother, in socially acceptable ways. Ned wanted to do that. And, eventually it got to be a strain. So, Mildred blew up. He got her attention, but his way was not socially acceptable.

Mildred need not feel guilty because Ned's silence might only mean that he is trying to find a more worthy means of getting her attention back again.

Ned is learning something, a little painfully, maybe...but still a lesson. He's learning something about not being a bore. ■

> We find a delight in the beauty and happiness of children that makes the heart too big for the body.
>
> Ralph Waldo Emerson

Dealing with Misbehavior

More than a few parents have expressed their feelings about their child by saying, "I wish I knew what to do about my child's behavior."

It would be nice to have a simple solution—like a magic wand—for parents to use when they feel frustrated by their child's misbehavior.

Unfortunately, the reasons why children misbehave are too complicated for a simple solution. We become aware of this complexity when we try to change the way a parent and child interact.

For example, most of us can appreciate how hard it is sometimes for a parent to control his or her temper after a child has misbehaved.

Even a simple analysis of such a negative interaction between parent and child would have to consider the characteristics of the parent, the child, and the specific situation in which the interaction occurred.

To make matters more complicated, each of these characteristics undergoes change from year to year, from week to week, and even from one time of day to another. It is also important to bear in mind that:

1) What works for one parent in disciplining a child may not work for another parent with the same child.

2) What proves to be an effective discipline strategy with one child may be ineffective or inappropriate for another child in the same family.

3) An approach that has worked well in one situation may not bring about the same desired result with the same child in a different situation.

How can *Growing Child* help you deal with misbehavior?

First, by reminding you that it is normal for young children to misbehave occasionally. It also is normal for parents to make mistakes and to lose their temper from time to time.

If you are thinking that you must be the only parent who can't handle misbehavior, then it is time to relax and realize you are not alone.

Don't be too hard on yourself—try to take a good look at the situation. Parents who can laugh at themselves are more likely to have a child who is happy and well-adjusted.

If you feel an extreme sense of "aloneness" in dealing with your child's misbehavior problems, you might consider joining a parent support group or parent education class in your area. Sharing concerns with a good friend or listening to the problems other parents are having can help remove that sense of aloneness.

Second, we want to help by making you familiar with a number of different approaches for dealing with discipline problems. For example, in "Why Children Misbehave" on page 194, we present an approach developed by Rudolf Dreikurs which many parents have found helpful.

Some misbehavior, in fact, may be mistaken behavior where a child just wants to learn and develop new, more appropriate ideas and behaviors.

Future issues of *Growing Child* will include other approaches that have been widely acclaimed. By becoming familiar with a variety of strategies for dealing with misbehavior, parents will be able to choose the approach best suited to the child, the parent, and the specific situation in which the misbehavior occurred. ∎

Needs and Wants

Now that Youngster is capable of expressing his requests verbally, it is important for parents to be able to differentiate their child's needs from his wants.

His *needs* are the things he must have for good physical or mental health.

His *wants* refer to the things he would like to have but may not need.

Needs must be responded to in the interest of Youngster's development. *Wants* may be considered but they may also be rejected in the interest of health, safety, or family priorities.

Parents who feel obliged to satisfy all their child's *wants* may discover that they are harboring a little tyrant. Some parents are afraid of losing their child's love if they deny him all he wants—especially if their child becomes easily frustrated and angry when thwarted. But parents who feel secure in their love for their child will place appropriate limits on his wants as an expression of their love and concern for his well-being. ∎

Why Children Misbehave

"Why does my child misbehave?"

"What is she trying to accomplish by her misbehavior?"

"And why does she continue to misbehave even after I have told her that what she is doing is unacceptable?"

Some years ago, Rudolf Dreikurs, a noted child psychotherapist, identified four basic goals of children's misbehavior: (1) attention-getting, (2) power, (3) revenge, and (4) inadequacy or helplessness.

These goals range from least serious psychological problems (attention-seeking behaviors) to most serious (feelings of inadequacy leading to discouragement).

It is not always easy to accurately identify these goals. One technique—which we discuss later in more detail—is for parents to identify their own feeling in response to the child's misbehavior. "How did I feel, how did I react when my child misbehaved?"

When parents have gained some insight and understanding of their child's goals, they are able to deal more effectively with the misbehavior.

On the other hand, when parents don't understand the purpose behind the misbehavior, they may respond in an ineffective manner (for example, "I don't know what to do with you.").

Sometimes the parent's response may lead to an increase in the child's misbehavior (for example, when the parent responds with negative attention to the child's attention-seeking goal).

The first goal of misbehavior identified by Dreikurs is **attention-getting.** The child who acts in this way thinks that to be important as a person, she must constantly receive recognition from others.

Of course, we all love recognition at one time or another. Positive attention has many desirable aspects, such as enhancement of our own self-concept.

Adults may seek attention by the clothes they wear or by the type of car they drive. Young children are less subtle. They shout, "Watch me, Mom! Watch me, Dad!"

Some children receive attention by their good behavior. Other children misbehave as their only way to get attention.

It is important to note that these children who misbehave to get attention would rather be corrected or even spanked than be ignored.

Consider the case of two-year-old Monica who is playing quietly with her toys while Dad reads the newspaper.

Suddenly there is a crash as Monica drops one of her toys which breaks on the floor. Dad jumps up and screams at Monica and she responds by running out of the room in tears.

The crisis in this home might have been avoided if Dad had paid more attention to Monica while she was playing so nicely. ("It looks like you are having fun with your dolls," or "You're doing a nice job building with those blocks.")

Secondly, Dad would be a more effective parent if he reacted with greater self-control. Parents are role models, and children are apt to act the way they see their parents act.

Since Dad jumped up and screamed, Monica is more likely to jump up and scream the next time she is upset.

What can you do if you find you are trapped into a negative response (for example, yelling, "Stop that. You're driving me crazy") whenever your child misbehaves (for example, by banging repeatedly on a drum with a big spoon)?

Here are some of the most effective ways for dealing with inappropriate attention-seeking:

(1) First, as far as possible, try to ignore minor attention-seeking misbehaviors. This isn't always easy. It requires a lot of patience and self-control on the part of the parent.

(2) Exercise self-control. The parent is the person who decides when to give attention rather than being manipulated by the child.

(3) Focus attention on the child's good behaviors rather than giving attention only to negative misbehaviors.

The second goal of misbehavior is **power.** This is exhibited by the child who wants to be the boss. She will not do what you want her to do.

A parent's reaction may be anger ("I'll show you who is boss") or helplessness ("I don't know what to do with you"). Unfortunately, both of these reactions only strengthen the child's desire for power.

In the first case, by engaging in a power struggle with a parent, the child becomes more aware of the power she wields. Even if she loses an occasional battle she will still strive to win the war!

In the second case, when the parent feels helpless the child assumes the role of boss, sometimes by crying loudly, screaming, or throwing a temper tantrum.

Consider the case of Joey, a two-year-old who recently has been very uncooperative with his parents.

When Mom tells Joey that it's time to go to bed, he responds that he is not going because he wants to play with his toys.

Mom feels very upset because she considers her authority as a parent has not only been challenged but has been taken from her.

When the child's goal is power, it is best for the parent not to get embroiled in a power struggle. The issue of power can be removed altogether by changing the topic, ("Let me see if you washed behind your ears") or just by smiling, which can quickly disarm the child.

Once the issue of power is removed, the parent can calmly tell the child what she

continued on page 195

continued from page 194

is to do without the child feeling humiliated by defeat.

It is also a good idea for parents to give a power-seeking child opportunities to experience power in a way that is socially acceptable.

This could be done, for example, by letting the child make some decisions about what clothes she might wear or what to serve for dinner.

In the case of the child whose goal is **revenge,** the parent is dealing with a more difficult problem. Such a child is aware of misbehaviors that are particularly irritating to parents.

Let us consider the case of Nancy, a two-year-old who is angry because she has been told to stay in her room while her mother entertains some friends for morning coffee.

Just before the guests arrive, Nancy sneaks into the dining room, grabs a corner of the tablecloth and pulls all the dishes and place settings on to the floor.

Because the revengeful child acts in a vicious and sometimes brutal manner, it is likely that she is frequently punished and feels unloved by others. But it is the unloved child who needs love the most.

The first and often the most difficult step in dealing with a revengeful child is to avoid getting pulled into a revengeful relationship. Taking revenge on a child—

for example, by hitting—only perpetuates the cycle of hatred, fear and revenge.

What a revengeful child needs most is positive unconditional love. This approach can be very difficult for parents whose feelings of anger are not under control.

Parents need to be firm yet caring when dealing with such a child. ("I love you and I care about you. And because I love you, I can't let you hurt either yourself or someone else.")

This caring approach—rather than an angry confrontational one—is ultimately the most effective way to deal with the revengeful child

If the child's goal is to demonstrate **helplessness or inadequacy,** it is because she is so discouraged that she won't even attempt a task at which she might experience failure. Such a child is frequently described as "unmotivated."

Consider the case of Jimmy, a three-year-old whose language development is delayed. When Jimmy was two, he was very vocal. But like many two-year-olds, he mispronounced many words — saying "college" instead of "cottage."

Jimmy's father decided he would insist on Jimmy pronouncing every word perfectly. After a few months Jimmy's parents noticed that he was no longer a vocal child.

Now when Jimmy is asked to pronounce a new word, he usually won't even try. Instead, his face tightens and his eyes convey a helpless look. He uses helplessness as his way to avoid the risk of failure.

In working with the helpless child, choose experiences in which the child is capable of enjoying some success.

If necessary modify the activity, such as a game, so that the child can participate successfully. Encourage positive efforts, no matter how imperfect they initially may be.

Above all, a parent must try to avoid despair (that is, giving up on the child) which would only discourage the child even more.

In order to decide which approach will work best with your child it is important to understand the specific goal of your child's misbehavior. How can a parent identify these different goals?

The first step is to try to observe your child's behavior as though you were an objective third party. ("She just insulted her mother," rather than "She just insulted ME!")

The second step is to determine the emotional and behavioral reaction you had because of your child's misbehavior. This will provide a most important clue in determining which of the four goals is involved:

(1) Do I feel my child is trying to occupy too much of my time and is getting a lot of negative attention from me? (Attention-getting.)

(2) Do I feel that my authority is being challenged or threatened? (Power.)

(3) Do I feel hurt, angry, outraged, or revengeful toward my child? (Revenge.)

(4) Do I feel helpless—just not knowing what to do—about an apparently hopeless situation? (Inadequacy.)

Your own reactions as a parent are one of the best indicators of your child's goals of misbehavior. Awareness of your own feelings helps you to decide the most effective strategy for dealing with such misbehavior.

This awareness also helps you to keep your own feelings under control so that you can guide your child more effectively toward socially appropriate, positive behaviors.

Parents who wish to read more about this approach for handling misbehavior should consult the following books:

Dinkmeyer, D. & McKay, G. (1973). Raising A Responsible Child. New York: Simon & Schuster.

Dreikurs, R. & Soltz, V. (1974). Children: The Challenge. New York: Hawthorn. ∎

On Novelty

Young children respond to new events in their lives in ways that can't always be predicted.

One city child may eagerly explore everything in sight on his visit to a farm.

Another may find the animals strange and frightening, the sounds and smells unpleasant. Or the same child may dislike the visit to one stranger's house but enjoy a visit to another's.

Much of this has to do with the feeling of security the child has in a particular situation. This in turn depends a great deal on how the new situation differs from what he knows and is used to.

If we could always see the world the way Youngster does, it would be much easier to explain his behavior. An understanding of how most children behave at a given age will generally help provide clues to your child's feelings, perceptions, and needs.

Youngster seems to do best with a combination of sameness and variety.

First of all, there are some activities where he demands a highly structured routine. He wants to do things the same way each time and he gets upset if the routine is changed even a little bit. This is most evident in the bedtime ritual.

He also shows a desire for routine at meals and in his style of using the potty. These activities are the ones that satisfy his most basic physical needs.

Adults have long since taken these foundations for granted, but not so with Youngster. He feels very keenly that they have to do with his well being and his dependent-on-others existence. As a result, they arouse strong emotional feelings for him.

When eating, sleeping, and eliminating he is sensitive to his parents' love and concern. Predictability means security to him. If his basic needs are consistently met in the same way, he is able to face the rest of the world with much more confidence.

In the world of ideas, a little more variety is

preferred by Youngster. But even so he starts out with the security of some fixed ideas.

After discovering that a toy car has wheels and can roll, he spends some time strengthening this idea by rolling it back and forth under his hand or giving it short pushes.

Only later does he begin the inevitable variations, like rolling it on all kinds of new surfaces or letting it coast down an incline.

Once the basic idea is down pat, variations are interesting and a challenge for him. But just so much change and not too much.

In Month Five, we noted that Baby is most interested in new faces that are slightly different from those he is used to. If he is shown a face or a picture that is too much different, he loses interest.

The same principle applies for Youngster and even for adults. We all like new ideas which relate to what we already know.

If something is too unfamiliar, we can't handle it. For instance, we rarely find it pleasant to read an article about a subject with which we are completely unfamiliar.

For Youngster, a completely new toy may not be appreciated during the period he is still trying out the possibilities of an old one.

It is best to give new toys to him one at a time, at least a day or two apart, even though you may have bought him two or more toys on the same shopping trip.

Sometimes Youngster may not be ready for the advanced ideas a new toy entails. If so, he will use it in a manner that is consistent with his present level of development.

A father who bought his not-yet-three-year-old a fancy battery-powered electric car was dismayed to see his son continue to push the car around by hand.

The child was operating at an earlier level and was not ready for the novelty of such a completely new idea.

There are few times when novelty is so great as when you take Youngster on a trip away from home. The only familiar things may be his parents and the car. Even these seem different as new scenery rushes by and the conversation focuses on unfamiliar trip-related topics.

It will help to take along a few of his favorite toys and picture books to keep him entertained while riding in the car.

A most difficult situation for many Youngsters is sleeping in a strange place, whether in a motel or at someone's house.

At such a time, his feeling of security will be greatly increased if you surround him with some things brought from home, especially from his own bedroom.

The strangeness of a new bed can be lessened by substituting his own pillow and giving him whatever he normally takes to bed with him, such as a teddy bear. Throughout the trip, the softness of a familiar fabric like a small blanket or an afghan can be enormously comforting.

Of course, the most comforting thing of all in a strange place is your own presence. Stay within range of his voice whenever possible. Then he can be assured that no matter what else changes, one thing stays the same: His parent is near when needed.

Thinking of Teeth

If your child hasn't already visited the dentist, we suggest you do so without delay.

About 50 percent of the population seeks dental care only in emergency situations. Yet the major causes for dental disease begin in early childhood, even before the arrival of the second teeth.

Promoting care of teeth is in the interest of good health, articulate speech, and attractive appearance.

Even though you can't see them, there are various bacteria that are present in the mouth.

Some of them actually help digestion and protect our teeth and gums. Unfortunately, there's another kind that feed on sugar and starches in the food and beverages we consume. These bad guys can cause tooth decay and gum disease.

That's why parents are urged to avoid the intake of sugary and starchy foods and beverages their children consume.

Good oral care also means brushing after meals to control and remove harmful bacteria. But young children often are not able to brush their teeth properly.

It may be necessary for a parent to accomplish the daily toothbrushing, permitting the child to participate in whatever way he can, until the skill is learned.

We might add that since tooth-brushing is a motor skill, once learned, it is not forgotten. But it must be learned correctly.

Obviously parents can't always say "no" to sweets. Such a blanket rule usually makes children more desirous of what is forbidden.

Rather, parents should encourage good eating habits by making available the kinds of snacks which are both nutritious and less likely to cause tooth decay.

There are also some foods that are known to promote healthy bacteria and promote a healthy mouth and teeth.

So, what's the prescription for healthy teeth and gums?

1. Avoid sweet, starchy food and drinks.
2. Brush after every meal.
3. Make regular visits to the dentist. ∎

Looking, Listening, Learning

One of the main ideas behind *Growing Child* is to tell you about effective child development practices so you can help your child to grow and learn. In that way you are also helping your child get ready for school.

During the preschool years, your child is building the foundations for later school learning.

Many research studies indicate that children who develop more slowly than normal frequently have trouble later in learning to read, write, spell, and "do" math.

So, proper development now is most important for your child. If she develops well now, she should learn well later.

We are trying to inform you about child development and, at the same time, present ideas to stimulate good development in your child.

Here are some everyday things you can do to encourage normal development:

1. **At the supermarket:** Let Youngster participate in your shopping. Let her share in getting some items and in making some simple decisions.

Talk to her about what you and she are doing there. For example, you may be getting things which are needed for breakfast, lunch, and dinner.

She can get some items from the shelf and put them into the cart, with your help, of course, when needed.

She can learn to identify certain items, such as her favorite cereal, and learn where they are located in the supermarket.

Ask her to help you find where other items are located. Then let her go to their places, find the items, and place them in the cart.

All this is far superior to being wheeled passively through the supermarket where she only looks but does not do anything. When she only looks, she is like a sponge that soaks up sights, sounds, and smells. This is one form of learning.

But when she also does specific things like helping you look for a particular item, she is developing and learning—and this is the name of the game. She develops best when she is actively involved in doing.

2. **In the car:** You can even use a trip in your car to promote normal development.

As you drive through your neighborhood, talk to her about the major landmarks which she can see.

"Billy lives here and Susie lives there." Try to determine if she really has the idea about where Billy and Susie live.

There are other landmarks which should be important to her: the toy store, the bank, the service station, the post office, the supermarket, the library.

continued on page 198

continued from page 197

Later let her tell you how to get to all those places from your house, including where her friends' houses are located.

The main idea is that you talk to her at times such as these so that she gets the basic connection between language—what she hears and says—and the places she sees as you drive.

3. At home: In any home there are many happenings which can be turned into good learning experiences. For instance, the laundry.

Laundry activities can provide great learning experiences. As you put clothes in the washer, let her help you.

As you pour detergent into a measuring cup, let her learn to do this.

As you take the clothes out of the washer, let her open the dryer door, help you to put the clothes in, and then close the door.

In helping you to do the laundry, she develops a sense of order. Her thinking is stimulated as she does her part. She begins to understand how all these activities take place in sequence.

The best part of laundry learning comes after the dryer has stopped. Then the clothes must be removed, folded, sorted, and finally put away.

At this point much good learning can take place once you know the secret for making it happen.

The biggest secret is to let her do as many of the activities as she can.

Let her take the clothes from the dryer. Help her sort them into appropriate piles because sorting is an extremely important ability. When she learns to sort, she is actually learning about categories.

When she learns about categories, she is beginning to develop her first tentative abilities to do abstract thinking.

Here are the sheets, here are the towels, here are Dad's socks, here are Sister's socks.

If you help her learn to sort the clothes in the laundry, you also are helping her begin to learn to do the abstract thinking she'll need later in school.

There are even more good learning experiences from the home laundry. After the clothes are sorted, she can help to fold them and put them away.

Help her learn where things go. Teach her to place the various objects in the correct places.

Dad's socks go in this drawer. The towels go here in the linen closet. The sheets go over there. Her undershirts go in this drawer.

As she learns that the different items of laundry go in particular places, she is really learning about the location of objects in space.

4. In the outdoors: There are probably many activities in your backyard in which she can participate. For example, if the flowers or the grass need to be watered, she can probably help with this activity.

If you take her to your local park, there are many things she will experience—the different trees, the flowers, the birds—all of which can become sources of new learning. ■

Growing Child®

P. O. Box 2505 • W Lafayette, IN 47996
(800) 927-7289
©Growing Child, Inc.
www.GrowingChild.com

Contributing Authors

Phil Bach, O.D., Ph.D.
Miriam Bender, Ph.D.
Joseph Braga, Ed.D.
Laurie Braga, Ph.D.
George Early, Ph.D.
Carol R. Gestwicki, M.S.
Liam Grimley, Ph.D.
Robert Hannemann, M.D., F.A.A.P.
Sylvia Kottler, M.S.
Bill Peterson, Ph.D.

'My New Play House'

The Gillmores got a new refrigerator and Patty Gillmore got the carton it came in.

The men who delivered the new refrigerator offered to take the new carton away, but Evelyn Gillmore told them to leave it.

Then she opened the flaps on the bottom, flattened out the big carton and stashed it out on the crawl space in the back of the house.

Then she waited for a rain storm or boredom, whichever came first.

Boredom won about three days later.

Her daughter, Patty, nearly three years old, was having one of those days that begins with a whine, and continues down hill from there.

So, Evelyn dragged in the refrigerator carton and set it up on its long side in the family room.

Then she crawled in, pulled the flap shut and called to Patty from the inside: "How do you like my new house?"

That's all it took. For most of the day, Patty was in and out of he carton pretending it was a boat, a house, a castle, a cave, and an automobile.

Evelyn cut a couple of windows, at Patty's request, and she joined her inside for lunch.

They had a marvelous day after which the carton went back onto the crawl space.

Now it is held in reserve for special times when Patty and possibly a friend want to go on a pretending spree.

And no matter what they pretend the carton to be—a treehouse, a secret chamber, a disappearing room, or an airplane, Evelyn knows it is also a school room—a learning center where Patty is learning a thousand things about how to be a person. ■

Making Friends

Although three-year-olds can learn many social skills from interacting with parents and siblings, the forming of same-age friendships is an important aspect of growing up.

Same-age friends learn social skills from one another in a unique manner because they can perceive the world from a similar age-related perspective.

One of the ways in which young children learn from one another is by imitation.

For example, if one child has developed a particular skill, he can help his friend develop the same skill. Friendships encourage exploration and learning in a variety of new environments.

Having a close friend can also help a child feel more secure in new situations with other children, such as in a childcare center or park playground.

Because three-year-olds are by nature egocentric, it's not easy for them to perceive the world from another's perspective.

Having a close friend makes it easier to develop perspective-taking skills—and thus become less egocentric—by learning, for example, to share with one another and to take turns.

In the process, children get the rewarding feeling of being better accepted and liked by other children.

Some children make friends easily. If they are extroverts or outgoing by temperament, they quickly learn the social skills needed to make friends.

These social skills might include smiling at others, making, eye contact, showing an interest in others and being willing to

listen to them, as well as learning to share and take turns.

Other children who are shy and slow to warm up have greater difficulty acquiring these social skills, especially if they prefer to play alone most of the time.

Although all children need to eventually develop these skills, it is important for parents not to push too hard. For parents who are themselves outgoing with a large circle of friends, this can be particularly difficult.

A good way for parents to help a shy, introverted child is to invite just one other friendly playmate to their home and then give the children plenty of time and opportunity for their friendship to develop.

For some shy children, playing with either a younger or older child is easier than playing with a same-age playmate.

Playing with a younger child can provide an opportunity to be a leader in the relationship and thereby gain self-confidence.

Playing with an older, friendly playmate can provide a nurturing environment

more similar to the security of being with one's parents or other caring adults.

At three years of age, it doesn't much matter if a child prefers to have only one close friend rather than a whole group of friends.

Friendship social skills can be learned from interacting with just one other playmate.

There is a big difference, however, between having at least one friend and having no friends at all.

When a three-year-old doesn't want to play with any other child, there is a problem which parents need to address.

What parents can do: Here are some suggestions to help a three-year-old child make friends:

• **Become more aware of your child's particular temperament,** whether outgoing, warm and friendly or shy and introverted.

• **Before your child interacts with another playmate, discuss the social skills needed for friendly interaction,** such as the importance of sharing and taking turns.

• **When getting to know a new playmate, a neutral site, such as a park** or playground, will help to prevent squabbles over prized possessions.

• **Before inviting your child's playmate to your home, it's wise to put away your own child's favorite teddy bear or playthings.** If possible, provide duplicates of the same toy so as to avoid conflicts.

continued on next page

continued from front page

• **Avoid games and activities which promote competition rather than cooperation.**

• **If the playmates begin to have a dispute, pay attention to what is happening, but don't immediately rush to intervene**—unless, of course, one child is about to physically hurt the other.

After all, it is from such disputes—unpleasant as they may be—that young children must learn the social skills of compromise and getting along with one another.

• **When playmates begin to show signs of being tired or cranky, it is best to end the interactive playing and provide a quieter activity,** such as listening to a story which you read to them.

• **If your child is consistently rejected by other children, try to determine**

what your child may be doing that irritates others. For example, does he interact with other children in an over-aggressive or hyperactive manner?

Does he know how to enter a game which other children are already playing? Are the other children appropriate playmates?

By determining the reason for rejection, parents are better able to help their child make new friends.

In summary, making friends requires the development of social skills which, like academic and athletic skills, must be learned and repeatedly practiced. Some children acquire these skills easily and rapidly. Others experience greater difficulty.

Parents can help their child develop these social skills more easily when they are sensitive to the child's temperament and personality.

Making friends is still mostly a learning process at this age —and friendships are often short-lived. The time and effort spent in helping a child develop the social skills needed for making friends will ultimately enable the child to lead a richer and happier life. ∎

A Positive Attitude

A positive attitude can lead to better parenting. In life, two people can look at the same glass: while one sees it as "half full" the other sees it as "half empty." It's just a matter of positive versus negative attitude.

An attitude is something we can work on changing. If I perceive that my attitudes on life are more negative than positive, I can deliberately make a greater effort to focus on the positive (versus negative) aspects of each situation.

Here are three good reasons for seeking to develop and maintain a more positive attitude as a parent:

1. My attitude helps to determine how I perceive my child's behavior. For example, if my two-year-old has recently developed the habit of saying "No!"

I can perceive that as either (a) "My child is developing a healthy sense of autonomy and independence" (a positive attitude) or (b) "My kid is becoming a little monster" (a negative attitude)

2. My attitude helps to determine how I will react. If I perceive my child's behavior in a positive manner ("He's learning to develop a sense of autonomy and independence"), I'm more likely to react to his behavior in a positive way.

For example, by showing him more love and affection to reassure him that it's natural and okay for him to want to demonstrate greater independence as he gets older.

On the other hand, if I perceive the same behavior in a negative manner, I'm more likely to respond in a negative way ("You'll get a good spanking from me if you keep saying that!")

3. My attitude will affect how my child will respond. When a parent can consistently exhibit a positive attitude toward a child's behavior, the child will more likely develop a positive attitude toward life.

Giving him the reassurance that he is loved unconditionally will help him to be more in tune with his world and, therefore, behave more positively.

On the contrary, when a child feels threatened and unloved because of a parent's negative attitude, he is more likely to develop negative feelings toward himself, which ultimately will lead to worse misbehavior.

It's important to note, however that having a positive attitude toward a child's behavior ("I think my child is terrific") is not the same as spoiling a child ("My child can do no wrong").

Whereas a spoiled child will eventually exhibit misbehavior increasingly more demanding of parents, the child who is treated by parents with a positive—yet realistic—attitude will more likely develop a similar, more positive outlook on life. ∎

Toilet Learning And Night Dryness

All normal children sooner or later learn how to use the toilet. Bowel control is easier to accomplish than bladder control. It is often established by two years of age.

Bladder control is developed in two stages: first while the child is awake and then when the child is asleep. Girls usually accomplish bladder control while awake by about two years of age, whereas boys are a few months later.

It should be emphasized, however, that bladder control develops at different rates in different children.

About 50 percent of two-year-olds (boys and girls) can stay dry at night, 75 percent of three-year-olds, and about 90 percent of five-year-olds. In other words, bedwetting by a three-year-old is within normal limits.

Bedwetting that occurs past the age of five may be abnormal and should be reported to a physician who can determine if there are physical reasons.

Under no circumstances should a three-year-old be blamed or punished for bedwetting. Heightened anxiety may even increase the likelihood that it will occur again.

Parents should try not to express concern unless the child himself considers his bed-wetting to be a problem.

There are a number of measures that may be taken to decrease the likelihood of bedwetting:

(1) Check on drinking habits before bed-time. This does not mean depriving the child of liquids, but rather seeing that he practices reasonable moderation.

(2) It is important that the child makes a visit to the toilet and tries to completely empty his bladder just before going to bed. Even if he does not think he needs to go, it is wise to establish this practice as a part of bedtime routine.

(3) Some parents have experienced success by taking a sleeping child to the toilet to urinate at the time the parents are getting ready for bed. Some experts believe that this practice simply perpetuates the child releasing the sphincter while still sleeping.

There are a number of other measures, such as medication or an electric alarm apparatus, which may be used for those older children for whom bedwetting continues to be a problem.

Because there are a number of organic causes for bedwetting such as diabetes, kidney disease, or abnormalities of the urinary tract, it is wise to consult a physician if the problem persists. ∎

Receptive and Expressive Language

In trying to understand how a child's language develops, it is important to be aware of the difference between receptive language and expressive language.

Receptive language refers to the ability to understand words that are heard, whereas **expressive** language refers to the ability to use words to speak.

Children's receptive language exceeds their expressive language. In other words, at any age, a child can understand more than she can say.

Here are some characteristics of a three-year-old's **receptive** language.
• Indicates through her activity that she can associate words with one another. For example, she can react appropriately if asked, "May I have a bite of your apple?"

• Knows size differences and can select "small" or "big" cracker when presented with a selection.

• Demonstrates an understanding of most commonly used verbs and adjectives.

• Understands some long and complicated sentences.

• Enjoys stories read from books with pictures and recognizes small details in the pictures.

• Loves a tape or CD player. She may even adjust the sound level, indicating that her hearing is very acute.

• Mimics adult social behavior when asked to show feelings of anger, exasperation, sympathy.

• Identifies geometric forms when asked to point to a square, cross, or circle.

• Comprehends simple cause-and-effect relationships, such as turning a switch when told to turn off the light.

Here are some characteristics of a three-year-old's **expressive** language:

• Refers to herself by using "I" rather than her proper name.

• Employs the pronouns, "I," "me," "you" in speech.

• Says a few nursery rhymes.

• Names at least one color correctly.

• Repeats two or more numbers correctly.

• Tells gender when asked, "Are you a girl or boy?"

• Can give both first and last name upon request.

• Uses three to four word sentences.

• Chatters sensibly to herself as she plays alone.

• Stammers sometimes in her eagerness to talk.

• Displaces inflections such as "He pick it ups," or "I ran homed."

• Mixes up word opposites: hot/cold, open/close, on/off, up/down.

• Asks questions that begin with "what," "why," and "where." ∎

Different Kinds of Attention

Have you had the experience of reading a simple sentence or paragraph and afterwards not having the slightest idea of what you just read?

You looked at all the words but you didn't really focus your attention on them. In other words, your attention was at a low level.

There are different levels of attention. The first level, which may be called *unfocused attention,* is very common in young children.

At this level, although your child may appear to be listening to what you say, her mind is in another world.

She may be just daydreaming or she may be distracted by something that truly interests her such as a large cat outside the window.

She may show some interest in a very simple jigsaw puzzle for a while. But after looking at all the pieces, she quickly becomes disinterested or bored with the task.

The second level may be called *focused impulsive attention.* At this level Youngster will attend to a task but will act in an impulsive manner.

In trying to solve the puzzle, for example, she may pick up one likely-looking piece and repeatedly try to make it fit in a space where it doesn't belong. Or she may blurt out her answer before you have finished asking her a question.

On another occasion she may charge toward her bedroom before you have had time to tell her what you want her to get there. These are all examples of focused impulsive attention.

At the third level Youngster exhibits *active attention.* In working with the puzzle, for example, she will use trial-and-error. If one piece doesn't fit, she will immediately try another. The key to attaining this level is developing the ability to try different solutions to a problem.

The fourth and highest level of attention is *reflective attention.* At this level the child

will give some thought to possible solutions to a problem before taking any action. In solving the puzzle, for example, she would probably examine carefully the shape of the piece that is needed, then look at some similar pieces before choosing the most likely one.

Youngster may operate at different levels of attention at different times of the day, depending on her interest in a task or how tired she may be.

This is not too surprising since adults also may operate at any of the four levels of attention, sometimes daydreaming, sometimes acting impulsively, sometimes using trial-and-error and sometimes being reflective.

Since good attentional skills are important for learning, here are some hints on how to improve your child's attention:

• Select tasks and activities that have a high interest value for your child. She will exhibit the lowest level of attention on tasks that she finds boring or monotonous.

• Be sure that the task is at an appropriate level of difficulty for her. In order to maintain her interest, the task must be somewhat challenging. But if she begins to show signs of frustration or engages in repetitive unproductive behavior, the task is probably too difficult. Either select a less difficult task or offer your help.

• Be sensitive to your child's feelings. A child's level of attention will drop and she

will become frustrated if she is tired or if she has stayed too long with one task.

With young children it is better to arrange for several short periods of attending than to strive for a longer period that exceeds their attention span.

• Act as a role model for the behavior you want in your child. In solving a puzzle, for example, offer some suggestions for possible solutions, if your child is having difficulty.

• Use the "think-aloud" method so that your child will know what you are thinking before you act.

For example: "I'm going to try this piece here because it appears to have the right shape to fit in this space." By using this type of verbal self-instruction you are teaching your child to reflect on the solution rather than using an impulsive or trial-and-error method.

• Encourage your child to attempt to do what you just did, namely, to talk aloud about the solution before taking any action.

Don't try to correct her grammar or pronunciation at this time as this may keep her from talking freely.

• Let your child work at her own pace. It will take her some time to develop the skills for higher levels of attention. As far as possible, resist the temptation to "jump in" with the correct solution.

• Praise your child for effort as well as for success. Above all, don't get angry when she fails. Your anger will only increase the likelihood of failure in the future.

• Make sure to provide at atmosphere conducive to fun as you engage in these activities with your child so that she will develop these important attentional skills in a highly favorable learning environment. ■

Insect Bites and Stings

Insect bites and stings are a part of everyday life, especially when a family lives in or visits a rural, wooded area.

In recent years, as the use of insecticides has decreased, insects have been moving closer and closer to densely populated areas.

Many kinds of insects bite— horseflies, deerflies, sandflies, chiggers, mosquitoes, fleas, bedbugs, and lice.

Other insects, such as bees, yellow jackets, hornets and wasps, sting. Some insects, such as the fire ant, simultaneously bite and sting.

Most insect bites cause discomfort but are not dangerous. Many, particularly those caused by mosquitoes, deerflies, fleas, and chiggers, can be prevented by the use of an insect repellent that can be sprayed or rubbed on the skin.

Two bites that are serious: (1) Some mosquitoes carry the West Nile virus which can cause serious disease. (2) Lyme Disease is an infection transmitted by ticks. Talk with your physician about the warning signs and treatment for both.

Many insect repellents are so mild that they can be used even on a very young baby as long as one takes care to keep them away from eyes, nose and mouth.

One must also take care to keep them away from the hands of children who are prone to suck on their fingers.

Some care should also be taken not to get the repellents on toys or other objects that children might put in their mouths.

Venomous stings (bee, yellow jacket, hornet, wasp) are much more difficult to prevent. They are also more painful and dangerous when they occur.

Children should be warned against going barefoot in clover-loaded grass since stings will likely occur on the feet when the warning is ignored.

Also, eating sweet-smelling foods (oranges, apples, popsicles) in areas where bees are present, will tend to attract them.

Wasps generally do not bother people unless they are disturbed. They particularly like to nest near doors and windows, in summer cottages or garages.

They can be removed only by someone skilled at doing this.

Dangerous spider bites are rare in the United States. They can be prevented by checking the bedroom and basement areas of the home and using insecticides when necessary.

Also, children should be warned against playing on or near wood piles or in old barns since this is where the two significant biting spiders (the black widow and the brown recluse) are likely to be found.

Should a bite occur in these surroundings, and the spider tentatively be identified as black widow (approximately 1/2 inch in length and having light yellow or red markings on its underside) or a brown recluse (approximately the same size but with a dark fiddle-shaped marking on its back) medical help should be sought as soon as possible.

Specific treatments are available for these bites. It is important that they be started as soon as possible after the bite occurs.

Much less dangerous, but still very irritating, are bites by chiggers. These occur most often during the summer months.

They are frequently found after an outing in the woods, particularly after one has been sitting in a grassy or leafy picnic area.

They are more prevalent in isolated, wooded areas than in those that are heavily trafficked.

Good insect repellents will usually prevent chigger bites. But should they occur and cause a great deal of discomfort, antihistamines prescribed by your doctor will help relieve the symptoms.

Scabies is a troublesome itch which is caused by the female itch mite. It spreads from person to person in much the same manner as lice.

Although scabies causes a great deal of itching, it can be treated by specific medicines prescribed by your doctor.

In general, insect bites, regardless of their cause, respond to a few simple remedies: (1) Cool compresses relieve the itching and decrease the area of inflammation;

(2) Antihistamines, orally, or in special lotions or sprays (your doctor can tell you which one to use), will help relieve the symptoms for longer periods of time.

If there is any question about a severe reaction (dizziness, fainting, nausea, fast heart rate, breathing difficulty, itching all over the body, or difficulty with urinating), continue the compresses and take your child to the nearest emergency medical help that is available (doctor, emergency room, nurse, police or fire department).

Once it is known that a child reacts severely to a certain insect bite, emergency medications must be kept on hand. In some cases, your physician may recommend desensitization injections.

Parents need to warn their children that insects, such as bees, do not like to be disturbed, particularly when they are gathering nectar on bright, warm days.

They are especially irritable, and hence more likely to sting, after a shower of rain has washed the nectar from the flowers.

If a child accidentally upsets a nest of insects, it is possible that she may receive numerous stings over her whole body. In this case it is wise to administer an antihistamine, if available, and to place the child in a bath of cool water. Then seek immediate medical assistance.

Bee stings and mosquito bites may become more swollen on the second or third day. But most insect bites begin to disappear within 24 hours. ■

Thumbsucking

"Hey!"

Thumbsucking is a subject of concern to many parents. Infants are born with a natural instinct for sucking.

It is this sucking reflex that enables a baby to obtain nourishment from either the breast or bottle during the first few months of life.

Besides satisfying the baby's physiological needs, sucking also produces feelings of comfort, security and pleasure.

Infants like to suck anything within their reach such as a toy or blanket or—most commonly of all—their thumb or finger.

Sucking usually produces feelings of contentment because of its association with being held and fed. It has been noted that children who regularly suck their thumbs often have a relaxed, serene approach to life.

It has also been noted that thumbsucking is a normal tension-reducing act in young children. When a child is tired or anxious, he is more likely to engage in thumbsucking.

Most children outgrow this practice by the age of three-and-a-half years.

A few persist long past the age of four. They may suck so vigorously and for such a long period that the upper front baby teeth are pushed forward and the lower teeth backward.

Dentists point out that this tilting of the baby teeth will most likely have little or no effect on the permanent teeth unless the thumbsucking persists past the age of four.

Parents who are concerned about the effect of thumbsucking on their child's permanent teeth should discuss this matter with their dentist.

For children over four, dentists will sometimes fit a dental appliance that not only corrects any distortion of the teeth but also serves to discourage thumbsucking.

What about the use of other devices to discourage thumbsucking, such as elbow splints, mittens or bitter-tasting substances?

In general, methods like these have not been effective because as soon as they are discontinued, the thumbsucking begins again.

If the child's thumbsucking occurs at times of anxiety or tiredness, it is more important to try to change these underlying causal factors than to try to terminate the habit.

When the child is old enough to want to stop sucking his thumb, he often does so quite suddenly and spontaneously.

Warm words of encouragement, either from the dentist or from a parent—without any undue pressure—may sometimes speed up the process.

Some parents prefer the use of a pacifier to thumbsucking because children, generally, can more easily give up the pacifier than the thumb.

The age at which children should be encouraged to give up thumbsucking or pacifier varies. Many pediatricians feel it should be before these behaviors become embarrassing to the child or before they begin to harm his teeth, which is usually by age four. ∎

Growing Child®

P. O. Box 2505 • W Lafayette, IN 47996
(800) 927-7289
©Growing Child, Inc.
www.GrowingChild.com

Contributing Authors

Phil Bach, O.D., Ph.D.
Miriam Bender, Ph.D.
Joseph Braga, Ed.D.
Laurie Braga, Ph.D.
George Early, Ph.D.
Carol R. Gestwicki, M.S.
Liam Grimley, Ph.D.
Robert Hannemann, M.D., F.A.A.P.
Sylvia Kottler, M.S.
Bill Peterson, Ph.D.

David was a lonely child, even though he had an older brother and sister and another brother younger. It might seem hard to make the case that a two-and-a-half year old boy in a family of four could be lonely, but David was.

His sister was seven and too busy to bother with him. His older brother was five and a lot more interested in the family baby than in a brother who didn't know how to do many things.

So gradually, David's parents became aware that they had a small boy on their hands who was truly suffering from loneliness. His mother tried to give him extra attention, but with a small baby to tend to, that's pretty difficult.

Both of the older children had a way of commanding their father's attention that often just squeezed David out. So, one day, Dad decided on a special project involving only David and himself. He called it the Mike and Joe board.

All it involved was a two-foot square piece of plywood and about $4.00 worth of hardware. There was a door chain, a window lock, a towel bracket, a hook and eye, and a few other screw-on items. (Other parents might have more ideas of safe items to add.)

Dad would be Mike and David would be Joe. And they would play with that board together, just the two of them. For it wasn't just a toy. It was a reassurance that David, too was special, even as the third among four children. It was a case of a parent showing this child that indeed he was loved, and cared for. ∎

The secret of education lies in respecting the pupil.
Emerson

34 MONTHS

Think of Your Child as a Scientist, Sculptor, Artist

For the child who is almost three years of age, there are many wonderful learning experiences in and around your home.

All you have to do as a parent is be aware of Youngster's curiosity and involve her in some simple and exciting learning activities. We encourage you to be creative in developing your own activities around the home.

To get you started, we offer some suggested ways for your child to assume the roles of scientist, sculptor, and artist!

1. The Scientist. When you take the ice tray out of the freezer, let Youngster see the ice cubes in the tray. If you turn the tray upside down, she will be amazed that the cubes don't fall out.

When you put the ice cubes in a bowl, let her feel one of them in her hand. Let her put a cube in a cup of hot water to watch it dissolve.

When you refill the ice tray with water, let her feel the water before you put the tray back in the freezer to make more ice cubes.

As you and Youngster engage in this activity together, talk with her about what you are doing and about what is happening. (For example, "What happened to the ice cube?")

Obviously she won't understand everything you say. But she is learning new words and new concepts: solid, liquid, ice, freezing, melting.

Ask her some simple questions to test her understanding about what is happening. And be prepared to answer her questions as simply as you can.

2. The Sculptor. Junk modeling can be fun. Start by collecting household junk—paper towel rolls, reels from sticky tape, scraps of material, gift wrap, kitchen foil, paper sacks, ribbons, elastic, candy wrappers, tea bag envelopes, shells, pebbles, and so on.

As Youngster assembles and sorts the junk, ask "Where do you think this came from?" Questions like this encourage your child to organize her ideas and to think creatively.

Obviously she will offer many incorrect and absurd answers. Here's your chance to provide new information without discrediting what she has said: "Well, that's interesting. Do you want to know something else?"

It is also an opportunity to talk about ecology. By collecting junk you are helping to reuse waste rather than discard it.

With some strong glue, cardboard or construction paper and the "treasures" she's accumulated, Youngster is now ready to create some wonderful sculptures which you can display in the kitchen.

3. The Artist. At about age three, Youngster can make a simple drawing of a person.

Don't worry if the drawing is somewhat crude such as a large head with two leg stumps beneath it. Encourage her to talk about what she has drawn.

Sometimes she may just want to scribble to experience the visual effect of her strenuous arm movements. For this purpose a blackboard and chalk are very useful.

As Youngster draws, you can talk about the shapes she makes—"circle," "cross," "square," —or the colors she is using— "red," "green," "blue."

Little children like new words, especially when they can relate the new words directly to what they are doing.

A good learning environment for young children does not require expensive and highly sophisticated equipment.

Everyday household items, especially when used in a creative manner, can be a young child's best learning tools. ■

Animal Bites

Taking care of a pet can teach a child valuable lessons about kindness and responsibility. But, sooner or later, a child must also learn that animals may bite.

Fortunately most animal bites are not serious and can be treated by thoroughly washing the injured area with soap and water and by applying an antibiotic cream or ointment. If the bite wound is deep, cover it with a sterile dressing and bandage. A physician's advice should always be sought if the bite is deep or occurs on any part of the child's head or neck.

Rabies is a major concern for children bitten by animals. It is a fatal disease which is usually transmitted by the saliva of an infected animal. Rabies is extremely rare in pets unless they have been in contact with wild animals.

Children are bitten more often by healthy animals than by infected ones. If your child is bitten by a rodent (rabbit, squirrel, hamster, guinea pig, gerbil, chipmunk, rat, or mouse) it is very unlikely that he will get rabies. In most cases rabies vaccine is not given.

Bites by carnivorous animals (skunks, foxes, coyotes, raccoons, dogs, cats, and bats) are much more dangerous and, in many cases, rabies vaccine is given. An animal that behaves peculiarly or attacks without provocation may have rabies.

Here are some general instructions for handling animal bites.

For the child:

(1) Wash the wound thoroughly with soap and water.

(2) If the wound is extensive or through the full thickness of skin, contact your physician. Suturing animal bites can be done after careful cleansing and trimming of the injured tissue; however, the wound frequently becomes infected.

(3) Check on the child's tetanus immunization status.

For the animal:

(1) Try to capture the animal alive—provided it is safe to do so—and keep it confined for two weeks. An animal that is healthy for at least five days is probably not contagious at the time of the bite or scratch. If it is healthy for two weeks, it can be judged to be non-rabid.

If the animal is killed, save its head or carcass, if possible, because examination can determine if it was rabid at the time of its death. A veterinarian or emergency room personnel can tell you where to find the nearest examining center.

(2) Check on the animal's rabies vaccine if it is a pet and has been seen by a veterinarian. ■

Tick Bites and Disease

Ticks are found in wooded areas and attach themselves to the skin in a painless fashion. Once attached, they suck the blood from the victim and, in some cases, discharge disease-causing organisms into the surrounding tissue and bloodstream.

Most tick bites do not cause much reaction except for minor skin irritation; however, they can be related to two serious generalized illnesses—Rocky Mountain spotted fever and Lyme disease.

Rocky Mountain spotted fever is associated with only a minimal bite reaction but later with a rash, particularly over the knees and elbows, accompanied by a high fever.

It can also involve the brain and spinal cord and can be life-threatening. However, early appropriate antibiotic treatment can prevent these serious complications.

Lyme disease is named for the Connecticut city where it was first reported. It is carried by a small tick and is associated with a severe reaction at the bite site.

The disease itself is characterized by a low grade fever and prolonged feelings of tiredness and aching in the joints and muscles. It too can be successfully treated with antibiotics, especially if they are used early in the illness.

The best way to prevent these diseases is to avoid exposure to ticks. Insect repellents are helpful, but the most effective preventive is protective clothing that covers exposed areas.

A tick can be removed by grasping its head with a tweezer and gently pulling it free from the skin. Or slide a credit card under the tick to the tick's mouth and press upward at the mouth until the tick releases.

Care should be taken not to squeeze the body since this may force additional infecting material into the skin.

If the tick cannot be easily removed, a physician should be consulted. ■

How to Remove a Stinger

In the case of insect stings, if the stinger can be seen and is not too deeply embedded, it may be easily removed.

Gently scrape it loose rather than trying to pull it out. Pinching the stinger between the fingers may force irritating poison from the venom sac into the skin.

Do not attempt to remove the stinger from a honeybee bite since it has a barb at the end which embeds itself into the skin.

The area should be washed well and left alone. ■

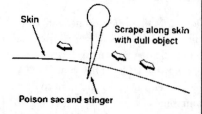

A Tricycle Is a Learning Machine

If you have not bought your child a tricycle yet, it's time you thought about getting one. A tricycle is an excellent tool for good development.

A tricycle helps your child develop some very important skills. As he pedals his tricycle, he learns how to shift from his left side to his right side.

He pushes first with one foot and then with the other. In this way he learns that he has two different sides. Here's why this type of learning is so important:

As teachers and consultants, we frequently deal with school-aged children who experience reading problems. Some of these children have difficulty distinguishing between letters like "b" and "d" or "p" and "q."

The difference between "b" and "d" is, of course, determined by the vertical line being on the left ("b") or the right ("d") side of the letter.

As your child learns to ride his tricycle, he is learning the difference between left and right within his own body.

This is a skill which should help him later in school to distinguish between the letters "b" and "d," "p" and "q."

Don't try to teach him at this stage the difference between the concepts of "left" and "right." This cognitive concept learning will come later.

All he needs right now is the experience of his left foot and right foot as he synchronizes his leg movements.

The tricycle also helps him learn about timing. In order to ride a tricycle well, he must shift from side-to-side at the proper time. He cannot shift at just any old time. He must make the shift at precisely the right time.

Time will also be very important in school learning. To spell correctly he must learn to get the letters in a word in the proper time and spatial sequence.

Some school children who have spelling problems may spell "first" as "frist" or "girl" as "gril." These errors are examples of general problems in organizing time and space.

If Youngster learns to ride his trike smoothly, rhythmically, and efficiently, he is also learning to organize his movements in time. This basic learning should help him with later school learning.

Many parents ask what kind of tricycle they should buy. There are many different varieties on the market so it is wise to shop around in order to find the one that is best for your child.

Three general considerations are important in the selection: (1) your child's safety; (2) your child's learning experiences; and (3) the trike's durability.

Here are some more specific recommendations:

• Choose an upright model—the old-fashioned kind—rather than the plastic "big wheels" type for all of the three reasons listed above.

The upright model is easier for a young child to control and provides him with a clear and unobstructed view of where he's going.

• Select a tricycle that is the correct size for your child right now. Learning to ride a tricycle can be dangerous if the child's feet can just barely reach the pedals.

Some tricycles are manufactured with adjustable seats and handlebars so that your child can safely ride the same tricycle now and, with proper adjustments, at a later age.

• Choose a tricycle with a wide wheel base. Such a tricycle is less likely to tip over if your child suddenly tries to turn a sharp corner.

• Look for a tricycle without spokes. Spokes can cause serious injuries especially to hands and feet. A child's belt or loose clothing may also get caught in the spokes, resulting in an accident.

• Make sure that the handlebars don't turn too freely or too far. Many good tricycles have stops that prevent this from happening.

• The tricycle should be made so that the seat doesn't extend over the back axle.

In this way, if your child ever rides in reverse or is hit from behind, the shock will be absorbed by the trike's frame rather than by the child's back or kidneys.

•Protect your child from injury by making sure he is wearing an approved bicycle helmet that meets the Consumer Product Safety Commission's (CPSC) standards.

Once you have purchased a suitable tricycle, your child will be ready for the fun to begin.

If he doesn't immediately understand how to make the tricycle go, you may push him gently along.

When you push him make sure that his feet are on the pedals so that he will feel his feet moving as the pedals rotate.

Taking his feet off the pedals could result in being hit by a rotating pedal.

It is wise to check your child's tricycle periodically to make sure that it is in good working order. A loose screw or protruding bolt could result in an accident that was easily avoidable.

Teach your child to use the tricycle in the way it was designed to be used. You should not permit your child to try acrobatic stunts such as standing on the pedals or riding with no hands on the handlebars.

You should also discourage your child from "colliding" for fun both for his own safety and for good maintenance of the tricycle.

With a little care and precaution your child can use his tricycle as a wonderful learning machine while enjoying many hours of accident-free, fun-filled riding. ∎

Preschooler's Learning Processes Are Different

For centuries young children were thought of as miniature adults. During the past 100 years, however, more has been learned about the significant differences in the ways in which adults and young children perceive the world than in all previous centuries combined.

Being aware of those differences can enable parents to better understand and stimulate their own child's learning.

Here are six ways in which adults and young children perceive the world differently:

1. While adults lose much of their sense of curiosity, a preschooler is curious about everything in his world.

He wants to know how come he can hear grandmother's voice on the telephone even though she lives over 200 miles away!

Questions seem to be never-ending. What will happen if he mixes the yellow and blue paints? Where does the sun go in the evening? Are those cartoon characters really singing inside the TV set?

Parents can rekindle their own sense of curiosity by telling their child honestly, "I don't know the answer to your question, but we can try to find out the answer together."

Nothing stifles a young child's curiosity as much as a parent's negative rebuke or scolding for asking a question.

On the other hand, the more parents seek to answer questions in a simple and honest manner, the more their child's curiosity and learning will flourish and develop.

2. While adults generally find constant repetition to be boring, preschoolers love repetition and their learning thrives on it.

After reading an enjoyable book, adults are usually ready to begin another one. Not so with a preschooler.

He wants you to read to him "Goodnight Moon"—or whatever his favorite bedtime book may be—tonight, tomorrow night, and the night after, Again and again and again!

Why do young children crave the kind of repetition that can bore adults?

Young children have to deal with so much newness in their daily lives that it's a relief for them to be able at times to experience sameness and predictability.

Amid so many new experiences, it's reassuring that their favorite storybook always has the same predictable ending.

Predictability gives a young child a sense of some control over the events in his life. The more you repeat the same routine in his daily activities, for example, the more at ease he will be.

If you forget some detail in the bedtime routine—such as forgetting to kiss his teddy bear good night—you will promptly be reminded of the proper sequence of events.

Repetition also helps young children deal with feelings of fear or anxiety. For example, your preschooler may ask you to repeat over and over the story of Humpty Dumpty who had a great fall.

Fearing that he may experience a similar consequence if he were to fall, he can

gradually come to terms with his feelings of fear by having you repeat the story in a calm voice—while he is nestled safely and comfortably in your lap.

Repetition also strengthens neuron connections in the brain which are designend to receive, process and transmit information.

3. While adults are clock-watchers, conscious of time, a preschooler has not yet developed a similar sense of time.

There can sometimes be a conflict when parents are focused on the time of day whereas the child is focused on the sequence, but not the timing of events.

For example, if by 3:30 p.m. a preschooler has not yet had his 3 o'clock nap, it's more important to him that you maintain the sequence of reading a story to him before nap time than to be concerned about the time on the clock.

It's best to adjust to his world in which the focus is on sequence rather than time of day.

A good way to avoid hassles when getting ready for a new activity, such as a ride in the car, is to allow twice as much time as you think it will take. In that way, you will feel more relaxed and your child will feel less pressured.

Young children also need a transition period between one activity and another.

Whereas an adult may look at the clock and think, "I must leave immediately," young children need some buffer time between finishing one activity and beginning another.

Before leaving the playground in the park, for example, the parent might announce, "There's time for just three more rides down the slide."

Although a preschooler can't yet tell time, if the parent says, "Just five more minutes," those words will also convey the

continued on page 209

continued from page 208

message that it's time to adjust mentally to the end of one activity and the beginning of another.

It's also a good way to introduce your child gradually to the concept of measuring time.

4. While adults can focus on just one thing over a period of time, preschoolers tend to be multifocused.

While carrying a book for you to read to him, for example, your preschooler may spot a piece of red wool on the floor that attracts his full attention.

He becomes totally absorbed by his new-found interest and will quickly forget what he set out to do.

It's as though one new distraction after another demands his immediate interest and attention.

Because adults don't normally behave in this manner, some parents may find this type of behavior to be very irritating.

They would do well to overcome their initial irritation and use the child's signal of interest as a "teachable moment" during which the child's mind is receptive to new learning—rather than try to impose on the child a rigidly planned schedule of learning activities.

Children learn best when they demonstrate a desire to acquire new knowledge related to what interests them—even when those interests shift from one moment to another.

5. While adults are often more preoccupied with the end product (such as being neatly dressed), preschoolers are more concerned about being involved in and even mastering the process.

Young children have a built-in desire to develop competence. A 12-month-old, for example, may spill half his food on his clothes or on the floor in his determination to get the spoon to his mouth by himself, without any help.

You know—and probably he knows too—that his feeding could be accomplished

much more efficiently if he would just let an adult do all the work for him.

Fortunately his desire to master this skill is more important to him right now than his desire for food.

Throughout their young lives, children continue to develop self-mastery of new skills: brushing teeth, dressing themselves, learning to ride a bike ... and eventually, as teenagers, learning to drive a vehicle.

A child's desire to master self-care skills can be difficult for parents for a number of reasons.

First, it demands a lot of patience on the part of parents. It usually means abandoning one's own standards—such as seeing the child neatly dressed—in the interest of letting him be involved in the process, even though the end result may look far from perfect.

If you tell your child that he is too young to help you, or that he won't do it the right way, he will have missed a very important learning experience.

Another reason that a child's desire to develop self-mastery of new skills may be difficult for some parents is because it makes them feel that their "little baby" is growing up too fast.

They enjoyed taking care of all their child's needs and find it difficult to adjust to a new stage of development.

6. Children learn best when they are involved as active rather than passive learners.

That's why it's important for parents to find ways to involve their child actively in what they are doing.

When preparing dinner, for example, you might invite your preschooler to help you stir whatever ingredients you are mixing. It may make things a little more messy in the kitchen!

Just don't be too surprised to hear him proudly tell someone later that he and

The more parents seek to answer questions in a simple and honest manner, the more their child's curiosity and learning will flourish and develop.

Mom or Daddy were the ones who prepared the dinner.

He will feel so proud of his accomplishment that he will want to help you in other ways as well.

If you are changing his baby sister's diaper, for example, you could ask him to hold the clean diaper for you and hand it to you when you need it.

In that way, you help him become actively involved in this activity rather than being a passive observer who feels excluded from what you are doing.

Children who consistently feel excluded by adults are most likely to exhibit misbehavior problems.

By involving your child in as many of your daily activities—even at the expense of neatness and efficiency—you are not only providing great real-life learning experiences, but you are also helping him develop a positive self-concept. ■

Grandpop?

A child under three isn't very tall. By the same token, the memory of a child under three isn't very long.

Donna is one of those American women who married a man who took her far away from her own home and family. (Obviously Donna realized the implications before saying "I do.")

This means one set of grandparents get to see her children only once in a while. Of course, there is always the telephone. And now people separated by miles can get close together by conversation in a variety of ways—Skype©, and various other computer connections.

But what about children? Especially, very small children?

Donna's oldest son, Rob is almost three. Donna has found that she has to help make his maternal grandparents real for him, because being so far away, he simply can't remember them.

So, what Donna does is to rehearse him before she places a long distance call. Their special names are grandpop and grandmom.

Before any call, Donna shows Rob their pictures, reminds him of things that happened on their last visit and suggests a simple agenda of things that Rob cantalk to them about.

She finds that he can get quite excited about the prospect of the call and when the time comes, he's able to talk to them in a way that is pleasing and informative.

Donna's secret is that she remembers that Rob's memory is no bigger than he is. And it is pretty hard for a toddler to imagine real people from the voices that he hears or from the images he sees.

Anyway, Donna's method delights her parents. And just as important, it helps Rob to understand about people, events, and things that he cannot see.

And that's an extremely important part of his early education. ∎

Teasing

Parents frequently ask how to help their child combat teasing from peers or older youngsters.

Children who engage in a cruel kind of teasing of other children usually come from homes where sarcasm and hostility— sometimes fashioned in joke form—are used constantly.

Most parents are able to control their anger and do not physically harm their child. Yet some parents do not stop to consider that regular teasing sometimes constitutes a form of emotional abuse.

While these parents cannot be accused of physically abusing their child, the effects of emotional abuse may sometimes be more damaging to the child.

Even though some adults engage in gentle teasing with other adults, it is inappropriate to engage in this practice with a preschool child.

The adult may consider it funny or well-intentioned. But the young child has not developed the sophistication needed to handle this practice. Hence it becomes a form of emotional cruelty.

What can parents do to help their child deal with teasing from peers or older youngsters?

Growing Child.

P. O. Box 2505 • W Lafayette, IN 47996
(800) 927-7289
©Growing Child, Inc.
www.GrowingChild.com

Contributing Authors

Phil Bach, O.D., Ph.D.
Miriam Bender, Ph.D.
Joseph Braga, Ed.D.
Laurie Braga, Ph.D.
George Early, Ph.D.
Carol R. Gestwicki, M.S.
Liam Grimley, Ph.D.
Robert Hannemann, M.D., F.A.A.P.
Sylvia Kottler, M.S.
Bill Peterson, Ph.D.

A parent's presence is an effective way to keep older children in line. When trouble appears to be developing, the parent may redirect the play or introduce a new activity.

Children usually take their cues from their parents' behavior. If parents do not appear to be upset themselves, the child will more likely remain calm.

However, if parents become indignant in front of Youngster or retell teasing or bullying incidents, these experiences may become magnified in the child's mind. This tends to reinforce his timidity and fearful feelings.

When parents are overprotective, they intervene to "rescue" their child too soon or too often. This teaches the child that the only defense is the parent's presence. Overprotective parents may inhibit their child's development of self-confidence and positive self-esteem.

It is important for parents to maintain a balance between watchful concern and unnecessary intrusion.

In summary, what can you do to help your child combat teasing and its effects?

(1) Eliminate teasing from your own behavior.

(2) Be present, unobtrusively, when your child is playing with other children.

(3) Let your child deal with problems he is capable of handling without your immediate intervention.

(4) Keep cool and don't become agitated when your child tells you stories about how he was tormented.

Listen to his story, comfort him for a minute and then observe more carefully how the children are playing together.

(5) Avoid discussing the episode with others in Youngster's presence.

(6) Maintain a good sense of humor which is good both for you and for your child. ∎

Growing Child ®

Give a child a little love and you get a good deal back.

Ruskin

Almost Three Years Old

As Youngster approaches her third birthday, it is good to review briefly some of the important changes that have taken place during the past three years.

In general, there has been a gradual shift from a totally dependent baby to a more independent child.

This shift has occurred because of a number of important changes which we will discuss.

These include the effects of her physical growth and development, increased receptive and expressive language, more cognitive abilities, and more varied social experiences.

Because of her physical growth and development, Youngster now enjoys greater mobility, especially around the house and outdoors.

Her newly acquired gross and fine motor skills enable her to enjoy drawing with crayons, or doing projects that involve cutting with scissors and pasting with glue.

Now that she is better able to entertain herself with these and other activities, she is usually easier to take care of and less demanding of a parent's time and attention.

She has also become more skillful in dressing and undressing herself. She can put on or take off socks, shirts, slacks and coats. But she still needs help with buttons, zippers and tying shoelaces.

At mealtimes she can use her own cup or glass and can handle a fork and spoon.

She is also capable of helping with simple chores in the kitchen and yard.

Her efforts don't equal those of an adult, but her active involvement in the world of work is an important part of her developmental growth.

Parents can encourage this involvement, for example, by assigning simple tasks such as: "Please hand me that roll of paper towels", and by praising her efforts.

By now her vocabulary has begun to catch up with her drive to communicate her needs and desires. The use of three- and four-word sentences enables her to express herself more clearly.

She can be very conversational at times, wanting to talk to anyone and everyone. She talks to herself and to her doll, teddy bear, and toys.

In this way she tries out new words and experiments with their meanings.

Her increased cognitive abilities enable her to classify things by function, such as her clothes, books, or toys.

Later will come the ability to classify by size, color, or shape. But she is learning that everything has its own place.

She is more organized in her activities and more orderly in putting away her toys.

She has developed a better understanding of time. Yesterday, today, and tomorrow begin to have meaning. While she will still exhibit impatience with delay in meeting her needs, there is a greater willingness on her part to wait.

She is ready to make simple choices. For example, letting her make some of the decisions about what she will wear today will help her develop decision-making skills.

The time that Youngster spends playing with other children is much more than social interaction—it becomes a key element in her development of new language and cognitive skills.

At first, having to make choices will complicate her world and slow her down. But with practice, she will become more expert at making these choices.

The major breakthroughs in her language and cognitive development that have occurred in the past few months have opened a whole new world of social experiences.

She can now use her imagination to play "house," "shop," "doctor," "nurse," "firefighter," "bus driver," or anything else she chooses.

She will sometimes use these imaginary roles to act out some inner feelings. For example, she might make her doll sit in the corner because she was "naughty" or "misbehaved."

Her games and play will now more often involve interaction with other children.

Whereas one year ago she preferred solitary play, even when she was in the company of other children, she now enjoys playing with others.

She may at times be bossy and demanding as she tries out newly acquired social skills and roles.

Even conflict and disagreement during play are an important part of social

continued on page 212

continued from page 211

Fibs and Obscenities

development. When children disagree about something, they learn that there is another perspective that is different from their own self-centered viewpoint.

The time that Youngster spends playing with other children is much more than social interaction—it becomes a key element in her development of new language and cognitive skills.

When children play with one another, they expand each other's experiences in vocabulary, pretend play, and creative thinking.

As Youngster interacts with other children, she also learns to share. She begins to exhibit altruistic behavior and to show empathy for the feelings of others.

She reaches out to other children. She shows tenderness and compassion especially toward a younger child.

If another child is crying, for example, because her "tower" of blocks just fell down, Youngster probably won't try to rebuild the "tower." She will most likely put her arm around her crying friend's shoulder.

At about this age, children begin to show awareness of their own gender identity and prefer playing with same-sex peers. This is related to their developing cognitive skills of classification and organization which we discussed earlier.

Just as she has learned to classify things by function, such as clothes, books, or toys, so too she has now begun to classify people as either male or female and to observe some of the ways in which males and females differ.

In general, Youngster is happy that she is now able to do so many things on her own. Her demands on her parents become less as she achieves a greater degree of independence in self-care.

She appears to be more sociable and agreeable. She is easier to live with as she learns to achieve a greater sense of balance in her life. ■

About this time most children tell lies or fibs that can be real whoppers! Parents frequently become concerned and wonder what to do.

Most children confuse fantasy and reality. So, before you do anything, we suggest you decide whether the child:

(1) is deliberately creating fantasy,

(2) is telling fibs to avoid possible punishment, or

(3) is simply unable to distinguish between reality and fantasy.

A child is deliberately creating fantasy, for example, when he applies colored chalk to his lips and plays "Mother." Or he may develop an imaginary playmate such as an invisible child or animal.

At this age, a child's intellectual horizons are expanding. As long as you and the child know when it's time to stop, you can enjoy his tall stories. Use language with the child like, "I think that's a good story you're telling me."

Or you can create your own just to see how absurd they may become.

Second, for some children their first lie is often due to a fear of punishment. Parents can sometimes prevent this form of lying if they first ask themselves some questions:

a.) Is it possible that punishments may be so severe as to make the child very nervous?

b.) Did the parents already know the truth about what happened before they questioned their child?

If so, why did they ask their child a question for which they already knew the answer?

In general, it is more effective for parents to confront their child with what they know to be the truth about a situation.

Then they can follow that up with the consequences. These consequences should be moderate so as not to induce more lying.

Third, some children lie because they are consistently unable to distinguish between fantasy and reality.

Those children in this group are frequently unaware that they have told a lie. These children, especially the more severe cases, usually require professional help rather than punishment.

What about the child who more than occasionally fibs?

First, check yourself out to be certain that your own quota of tall tales is low. Children will imitate their parents' behavior.

Next, let the child know that there is a payoff for being truthful. You can do this by immediately rewarding the child for "fessing up" and sparing the punishment.

Youngster's vocabulary by now may include a variety of swear words or obscenities.

When you first notice these words creeping into his comments, first, be aware of your own language.

Second, it is important to be aware that making a big fuss over these words will most likely only increase Youngster's fascination with them.

Third, the most successful treatment is to tell your child quickly and calmly that you don't approve of those words. In this way you communicate your values to your child.

If your child lives in an environment where he constantly hears these words being used by others—playmates or sometimes even their parents—it is important for you to explain that your values are different from those of other people.

Use this opportunity to express your own values to your child. You can say, for example, "In our family, we don't use words like that."

How parents handle a young child's fibs and obscenities can have an important effect on his personality and character. ■

A Start on Telling Time

A preschool child can be given a start toward learning almost anything, as long as the material is presented at his own level.

This does not mean that simple arithmetic or word problems can be learned at this age.

What it means is that every task is made up of a number of simpler tasks. In turn these tasks are composed of still simpler tasks, and so on.

A child can be given a head start if he is allowed to experience those tasks that he can do at his stage of development.

The trick is to break a higher level activity down into its simpler parts. Then let the child do the parts that he is capable of doing, and help him with the parts that he cannot do.

We used this idea in an earlier article, "Dressing As Partnership." This article explained that Youngster could be encouraged to make the simple movements that he could make.

The parent would direct the movements in the right order and continue any movement which Youngster could not complete by himself.

Another example of giving a child a head start is the matter of telling time. We have previously discussed Youngster's developing sense of past, present, and future.

We have suggested fostering his appreciation of time by calling his attention to the order in which different events occur.

The importance of consistency and predictability in his regular daily schedule was also emphasized.

As Youngster's awareness of time grows, time words like "when" begin to appear in his vocabulary, often in the form of questions. Thus he will begin to ask, "When can I play with Ricky?"

To indicate a short period of time, the usual answer to this kind of question is "Pretty soon."

For a longer period of time, it will help to provide a familiar event as a marker such as, "After we eat supper." Youngster will soon learn the meaning of such answers.

In keeping with this idea of introducing an important skill simply and early, there is another answer to Youngster's "when" questions that you can use part of the time.

When Youngster is hungry in the evening and impatient with the speed of the dinner preparations, point to the large hand of the clock and say to him, "We will have dinner when this big hand gets to the bottom (or the top) of the clock."

Point to where the hand will be as you say this. Then make every effort to meet that prediction accurately.

If he is not familiar with the clock, you will have to explain that the hand does move even though it moves too slowly for him to see it.

A kitchen timer is a useful object, however, to help a child preceive the passage of time.

Don't try to teach him hours and minutes. This is difficult even for some kindergartners to understand.

If Youngster asks you what the little hand is for, just tell him that it moves even more slowly than the big hand and he doesn't have to watch it.

We suggest you use only the hour and half-hour positions of the minute hand. Youngster is familiar with top and bottom but will have trouble with the side positions like 3 and 9 o'clock.

Of course, for this method to work, you will have to be no more than an hour away from the predicted event. But that is the longest time Youngster can be expected to check the clock's progress.

You can also use these clock positions for other important happenings. For example, you can indicate the time you

The trick is to break a higher level activity down into its simpler parts. Then let the child do the parts that he is capable of doing — and help him with the parts that he cannot do.

will leave for the store, or show when you will be coming home.

In the same way, the clock can be used to signal the approach of bedtime.

If you suddenly make an announcement about bedtime, Youngster will most likely be upset because your timing appears to him to be arbitrary.

But if you provide a five-minute or 10-minute warning, you are better preparing him for this future event.

He still may not like the final announcement but he has had more time to prepare for it and to adjust to this new reality.

Then when bedtime has arrived, it will seem less abrupt to him and he will feel better about making the change.

Importantly, he will be learning, at his level, the practical activity of telling time. ■

Transactional Analysis

It is not unusual for parents of a preschool child to sometimes feel helpless in dealing with discipline problems.

We may occasionally hear a parent say: "I've tried every form of discipline with my child, from being very nice to being very stern, and nothing seems to work."

When a child's behavior is particularly troublesome, parents often say or do things which they later regret. They don't know what else they could have said or done under the same circumstances.

That's when some knowledge of transactional analysis (called TA for short) can be most helpful.

According to TA, our words and our behaviors can be categorized into three different aspects of our personality. They are the "Parent," the "Adult," and the "Child." These states continue to exist in each of us throughout our whole lives.

Let's consider an example: It's Saturday evening in the Wilson's home. They've worked hard all day preparing for the special friends they have invited for dinner. The guests are due to arrive at any moment.

Suddenly there is a crash in the dining room. Mrs. Wilson rushes in to find her three-year-old daughter, Jane, looking sheepish, getting up off the floor.

Jane, it appears, had climbed on a chair to get a better look at the beautifully festive dinner table. Unfortunately, her foot slipped.

As she fell, she grabbed a corner of the tablecloth. She did not realize that in doing so she would bring all those lovely dishes crashing to the floor.

In that moment, Mrs. Wilson is torn between two extreme emotions: she is very angry with Jane for what she has just done; at the same time, she feels sorry for her daughter who may have hurt herself.

Most parents can probably think of other situations similar to the one we have just described in which they felt torn between the different options of what to say and do. Transactional analysis is a system developed by Dr. Eric Berne to help people deal with such problem situations.

According to Berne, each individual's personality is made up of three parts, which he called *ego states*, namely, the "Parent," the "Adult," and the "Child."

These three ego states have developed by the time a person is two years old. Whenever two people interact, their communication will involve one of the three ego states in one person interacting with one of the three in the other person.

Mrs. Wilson could have reacted in any one of the three ego states by asking her daughter Jane any one of these questions:

• Why did you have to make that mess, Jane? (Mrs. Wilson as "Parent").

• Will you help me, Jane, to clean up this mess? (Mrs. Wilson as "Adult").

• Why does this always happen to me whenever we invite company? (Mrs. Wilson as "Child").

Similarly, Jane could have responded with any one of these statements:

• I shouldn't have climbed on the chair. (Jane as "Parent").

• Mom, I'll help you pick up the pieces. (Jane as "Adult").

• It wasn't my fault that I slipped. (Jane as "Child").

The "Parent" in each person is made up of the "tapes" we have stored of all the parental comments and corrections we have received over the years from those in authority.

Children also have a "Parent" state which imitates what they have observed in their parents.

The "Child" consists of the "tapes" of our experiences in childhood. We can relate to positive feelings in our "Child" state, such as carefree fun on a sunny afternoon.

We can also relate to negative feelings in our "Child" state, such as feeling helpless or like a "no good" person after we have been harshly corrected.

The point of TA is that we don't have to respond to a situation in either our "Parent" state or our "Child" state.

When we think about the situation rationally and objectively, there really is a third option, namely, the "Adult" state.

The "Adult" state is the one in which we gather necessary information before we react. The "Adult" is capable of remaining calm and objective while processing this information in a rational manner.

In our earlier scenario, Mrs. Wilson may have experienced her own "Child" state ("I can't take this any longer") or her "Parent" state ("My daughter Jane deserves a good talking to.").

But if she were able to remain sufficiently calm and rational, her "Adult" state would have been able to function ("Let's all help to get this mess cleaned up before our guests arrive.").

Parents who act in their "Adult" state are more likely to get an "Adult" state response from their child.

For example, Jane's "Adult" state response to her Mom might be to help pick up the dishes on the floor rather than feeling mad at herself (her "Parent" state) or feeling sorry for herself (her "Child" state).

When the child's "Adult" state is given the opportunity to develop—as a result of interaction with the parent's "Adult" state—the child is likely to become a more rational and mature human being.

It should be emphasized, however, that it is not always necessary or appropriate for the parent to act in the "Adult" state.

continued on page 215

continued from page 214

There are occasions when children need correction by the "Parent." An example would be if they disobey the rules of the road. ("You should never run across the road without looking each way.")

Similarly, there are other occasions when the parent's "Child" state is definitely most appropriate. For example, this works when both parent and child are having fun playing a game together.

How then does TA help to foster better parent-child interactions? TA helps by providing a framework in which to analyze and understand parent-child interactions.

On the basis of that analysis and understanding, parents can decide whether the parent-child interaction is appropriate or in need of change.

The methods of TA are particularly suited to the parent who says: "I've tried everything to change my child's behavior, but nothing works for me."

Frequently underlying this statement is the misguided assumption that the "Parent" state is the only state for parents to use in changing a child's behavior.

By changing the questions asked and the statements made by the parent to the child, it is possible to change a "Parent"-to-"Child" interaction into an "Adult"-to-"Adult" interaction, thereby helping to bring out the best in you and in your child.

Parents who wish to know more about transactional analysis can read:

Games People Play by Eric Berne.

TA For Tots by Erie Berne.

I'm OK—You're OK by Thomas A. Harris.

Transactional Analysis by Muriel James.

The Total Handbook of Transactional Analysis by S. Woolams and M. Brown.

■

Teaching Opposites and Associations

Youngster is beginning to understand the concept of opposites. At first he may not understand the relationship, so you may have to spend some time explaining what "opposite" means.

A good way to teach some simple opposites is by means of a picture storybook. Make your own book by clipping from magazines, catalogs, and newspapers those pictures which will help teach the following concepts:

(1) Big/little. An elephant and a mouse. You can even make a rhyme about the elephant as big as a house beside the little gray mouse.

(2) Indoors/outdoors. A picture of children eating at the kitchen table, and another where they are having a picnic on the grass.

(3) Wet/dry. A picture of a child with raincoat, boots, and umbrella walking through a puddle and another of a youngster sitting in front of a warm fire.

(4) Fast/slow. A picture of someone riding a motorcycle and another of someone pushing a baby carriage.

(5) Hard/soft. A picture of two children lying down; one on the hard ground, the other on a soft pillow or mattress.

Eventually you can test Youngster's understanding of opposites by just saying the stimulus word (big, indoors, wet, fast, hard) without showing him any picture and asking him to say the opposite of that word (little, outdoors, dry, slow, soft).

You can use the picture book you made to teach opposites to also teach Youngster about associations.

Start out by placing three pictures in front of him. Now ask an association question. For example, "Which one says meow?"

Youngster must make the association between the sound "meow" and the cat in the picture.

Here are more examples of association questions:

"Which one flies in the air?"

"Which one feels cold?"

"Which one tastes sweet?"

If he has difficulty with the task, you can help him by saying, "Here's one that says meow. It's a cat!"

Put the picture down, and allow Youngster a turn. If he missed one earlier, go back to that one to make sure he has learned it.

Should a wrong choice be made, point out something specific about that card to help him recognize it the next time.

Eventually Youngster will probably want to ask the questions for you to answer as he becomes more familiar with the associations. ■

Compare a big elephant and a little mouse. You can even make a rhyme about the elephant as big as a house beside the little gray mouse.

Improving Listening Skills

In an earlier article, we noted that feeling objects, one at a time, encouraged better concentration and longer attention span than simply looking at several objects all at once.

The principle of considering things one at a time in sequence can also be used in building better listening skills.

Here are three games that can help improve listening skills.

(1) **"I spy."** Pick an object in the room that is visible to Youngster and to you. Describe several of its attributes so that he can guess what it is.

Thus for a chair you might say, "I see something that is made of wood and has a back and four legs. What do I spy?"

Or for scissors, "I see something that is small and shiny and made of metal, and you use it with paper."

The idea is to have Youngster listen to all the clues, remember them and try to put them together.

Be careful about action phrases like "you sit on it" or "you can cut with it," for they may give so big a hint that they detract from the other clues, unless the action phrase also applies to other objects in the room.

Of course, Youngster should get his turn to describe something if he has successfully identified your object.

Naturally his descriptions are apt to be ambiguous and heavily loaded with size and color words ("it's big and red").

But if you choose a "wrong" object that still matches his description, that is part of the educational value of the game, for it shows him that he must be more exact and use words that uniquely describe the object.

(2) **"Which one sounds like mine?"** Save four identical boxes, the kind whose

tops can be closed securely. Place one box in front of yourself and the other three in front of Youngster. Select four pairs of objects small enough to fit into the boxes.

Place one of a pair in your box and the other one of the pair in one of Youngster's boxes. Place a different object in each of the other two of Youngster's boxes. Then close the lids on all the boxes.

Growing Child®

P. O. Box 2505 • W Lafayette, IN 47996
(800) 927-7289
©Growing Child, Inc.
www.GrowingChild.com

Contributing Authors

Phil Bach, O.D., Ph.D.
Miriam Bender, Ph.D.
Joseph Braga, Ed.D.
Laurie Braga, Ph.D.
George Early, Ph.D.
Carol R. Gestwicki, M.S.
Liam Grimley, Ph.D.
Robert Hannemann, M.D., F.A.A.P.
Sylvia Kottler, M.S.
Bill Peterson, Ph.D.

Have him shake your box to hear the sound of the object rattling inside it. After that he should shake each of "his" boxes in turn to try to find the box containing the same object as the one in your box.

Usually each object will have its own unique rattle or thud. It is best to use objects that weigh about the same to eliminate weight clues.

You can change the object in your box four times before you are back to the one you started with.

As in the first game, Youngster must pay close attention and consider each thing in a sequence over a period of time. So concentration is developed as well as listening skills.

(3) **"Whisper game."** Another useful principle in encouraging careful listening—and concentration in general—is to reduce the intensity of the stimulus. You can do this with the "whisper game."

Place in front of Youngster five objects whose names he knows. Then sit behind him and whisper, ever so quietly, the name of one of them.

Ask him to tell you which one you named. Here you can easily vary the difficulty of the game according to the loudness of your whisper and the amount of background noise present.

Youngster will be very anxious to whisper to you, too. That is something he doesn't get much practice in doing during the course of his everyday play!

You can reverse roles so that you have to pick out the object whose name he whispers.

All of these activities can help to improve your child's listening skills. ∎

Growing Child®

> If children developed as they were intended at birth, they would all be pure genuises.
>
> Goethe

Three Years Old

Three years old—magic words which mark the end of babyhood and the beginning of early childhood!

Most parents would like to raise a child who is self-confident, as well as being mature, self-reliant, and socially responsible.

Recent studies have shown that parents who combine loving warmth with clear standards and expectations for their child's behavior are more likely to succeed than parents who are either too strict or too permissive.

By giving your child some work reponsibilities within a loving home environment, you are helping to promote your child's self-confidence.

Where does a child learn self-discipline and responsibility? At home, in what Maria Montessori called "practical life experiences."

At three years of age your child is capable of performing many tasks around the house. Instead of fabricating "busy work" for him, invite him to share in everyday family chores and responsibilities.

He can help set the table and wipe up spills. He can dust furniture, help polish shoes and take clothes out of the dryer.

He can arrange flowers and water them. He can clean floors with a mop or broom.

In the kitchen, he can help prepare food. He can pour cereal and milk in a bowl. He can stir foods that need mixing.

After dinner he can be assigned to dry or sort the flatware.

When you are cleaning the living room give him a cloth moistened with furniture polish. He can help empty wastebaskets.

In the bathroom he can help clean the bathtub and basin. When doing the laundry, he can help sort the clothes.

Be patient with any mistakes he makes. And don't expect perfection the first time he tries to do something.

It won't be long before he exhibits a sense of self-confidence and competency as he masters different skills.

There are many good reasons for involving your child in practical experiences in the home. Learning to pay attention, sorting and counting items, making decisions, and solving problems are all school-readiness skills that are essential for cognitive development.

Most importantly, by working in a loving environment your child learns self-reliance, independence, and self-control, all of which promote greater self-confidence and self-esteem. ■

The Beginning of Early Childhood

Your young learner has made tremendous strides in these first 36 months.

In that period of time she has developed physically, intellectually, emotionally, and socially.

She has learned to walk, run, jump, and throw. She can now take care of many of her own needs.

Having learned the basics of speech and language, she has gained much knowledge.

She has learned to express her feelings and to relate to adults and other children.

At the same time she has been absorbing the customs and values of your home. And she has been learning to adapt to the demands of her environment.

Your young learner has reached this watershed between babyhood and early childhood. So, on the next page of this issue we will review what a "typical" three-year-old child can do.

When we discuss a "typical child," it is important to be aware that if we looked at a large number of three-year-olds, we would find that a majority of them will have achieved or surpassed these skills, while some others will not yet have attained them.

So you will probably find that your child is less advanced in some areas, more advanced in others, and "just typical" in the remainder. ■

Developmental Milestones –Three Years

Language

- Recognizes own name in written form and can identify two or more letters in name.
- Gives information about self when asked, including name, age, and sex.
- Asks questions frequently which begin with "What?" "Who?" and "Where?"
- Knows several simple nursery rhymes, can recite a few, and even sings some on occasion.
- Talks to self, usually about recent events or favorite make-believe characters.
- Carries on a conversation with adults and peers and can be understood even by a stranger.
- Enjoys talking on the telephone to a familiar person.
- Uses grammar in unconventional manner and speech contains some sound substitutions.
- Uses personal pronouns ("I" "me" "mine") as well as some plurals and prepositions.
- Counts by rote up to 10 but has no awareness of quantity beyond two or three.

Gross Motor Development

- Walks smoothly forward, backward, or sideways, some times swinging arms in adult fashion.
- Runs with better control and can now change speed or direction.
- Jumps upward or forward, clearing floor by a few inches.
- Climbs up and down stairs independently by putting both feet on each step. Can climb stairs with alternating feet if someone holds his hand.
- Hops forward on preferred foot two or more times but can stand still on one foot only momentarily.
- Walks on a straight line without falling off line.
- Pedals a tricycle and steers it around corners and obstacles.
- Climbs up the ladder of a slide or other play equipment but may still want a helping hand at the bottom of a high slide.
- Kicks a rolling ball, making contact successfully only about three out of five times.
- Throws a ball in a specific direction with one hand and may step forward onto the foot on the throwing side.
- Catches a large ball with both arms if thrown from less than six feet.

Fine Motor Development

- Holds pencil with fingers in proper position near the point between the first two fingers and thumb.
- Copies at least two simple geometric figures such as a circle or cross.
- Draws a person though the legs may protrude downward directly from the head or the arms may be drawn in place of the ears.
- Paints with a crayon or brush, usually covering a whole page, but the picture may not be named until after completion.
- Cuts paper with scissors but may not yet be able to cut along a straight line.
- Strings beads on a shoelace.
- Completes simple puzzles which have five or six pieces.
- Builds a tower with six or more blocks.
- Opens a door by turning the doorknob.

Self-help Skills

- Can dress and undress self, especially with shirt or coat that opens in front and with pants and underpants—but still needs help with sweaters, small buttons, or other fasteners.
- Washes and dries hands and face.
- Brushes teeth but needs help putting toothpaste on brush.
- Puts shoes on correct feet but needs help with shoelaces.
- Wipes own running nose with a tissue.
- Eats at table with fork and spoon.
- Uses napkin to wipe mouth or hands during mealtime.
- Shows awareness of danger by staying away from hot stove or electrical outlet.
- Shows some awareness of the meaning of money.

Social Relationships

- Starting to have special friends.
- Enjoys having another child at home to play with.
- Learning to take turns in games.
- Learning to share and cooperate, even asking permission to play with a toy being used by another child.
- Says "please" and "thank you" at appropriate times.
- Plays make-believe games with other children.
- Shows greater awareness of people's names.
- Repeats phrases other people have used.
- Demonstrates affection appropriately toward adults and other children.
- Recognizes feelings of others such as joy, sadness, or anger.
- Chooses a favorite television show by operating television controls independently. ∎

These milestones are guidelines only. All children do not develop at the same speed, nor do they spend the same amount of time at each stage of their development. Usually a child is ahead in some areas, behind in others, and "typical" in still other areas. The concept of the "typical" child describes the general characteristics of children at a given age.

Preschool Education Programs

Now that your child is three years old, you may be considering enrolling her in a good preschool education program.

Two wage-earner families are common in our society. So, it is no surprise that in recent years more attention has been devoted to quality preschool education.

Even in families where a parent can be a full-time caregiver, the educational and social benefits of a good preschool program deserve some consideration.

It should be noted, however, that not all preschool programs would be good for your child.

Some programs have such a rigid academic curriculum that they resemble a first or second grade classroom.

Other programs are structured so loosely that they could more correctly be called "play groups."

Somewhere between these two extremes lies the "ideal" preschool education program.

How then does one select a good preschool education program?

There are some general considerations that need to be taken into account such as location, hours of operation, and cost.

There are also some specific aspects—including (1) the program's children, (2) staff, (3) parent participation, (4) facilities, and (5) resources—which need to be evaluated during a visit to the program.

• Children

Do the children in the program appear to be happy?

Do they interact appropriately with one another? Are they encouraged, for example, to learn to take turns?

Are the children encouraged to talk to one another and to the adults in the room?

Are the children engaged in activities that have high interest level as well as social and educational value?

• Staff

Do the adults in charge of the program appear to be warm and friendly? Have they acquired the knowledge needed about preschool education and child development as evidenced by their training and qualifications?

Check for NAEYC accreditation and/or local/state licensing requirements.

Are there at least two adults for every 15 children in the program?

Are the adults aware of the individual needs of each child? Do they vary their expectations accordingly? Do they maintain good records of each child's strengths and weaknesses?

Are staff members acting as role models?

• Parent Participation

Are parents encouraged to participate in the program and to visit their child's classroom in order to observe the various activities?

Are the opinions of parents regularly sought and listened to?

Does the program have a parents' advisory committee?

Are parents well informed about their child's specific strengths and weaknesses?

Is there a parent's handbook with policies on absences, holidays, illness, and accidents?

• Facilities

Is the building safe for children?

Are there smoke detectors and adequate exits in case of fire? Are fire drills conducted periodically?

Is a program in place in case of emergencies?

If food is served, are proper standards of hygiene observed? Are the meals and snacks nutritious?

Is there adequate ventilation in the building?

Is the indoor play area adequate with at least 35-40 square feet of floor space per child?

• Resources

Is there adequate equipment for both outdoor and indoor activities?

Are the outdoor play areas in a safe location? Is the outdoor equipment—swings, slides, climbers—in good condition?

Indoors, is there an adequate supply of hands-on materials—sand, clay, paints, etc.—for the children to engage in creative activities?

Are there other resources available—picture books, blocks, puzzles—for the children to use?

Are songs and music available, along with basic music elements such as bells, tambourines, or rhythm sticks suitable for young people?

In summary, in a good preschool education program, the children are happy, the staff gives attention to planning each day's activities, parents are actively involved, and there are good facilities and resources available.

In an environment where learning is fun, all children are encouraged to develop their own creative abilities. ■

How Three-Year-Olds Think

Sometimes your three-year-old child may behave in ways that you find hard to understand. Such behavior may even upset you.

At times like that it is important to be aware that three-year-olds don't think in the same way adults think.

How then do young children think? A great deal of insight into young children's thinking has been gained by the work of a famous Swiss scientist, Jean Piaget.

He found, for example, that young children are often unable to cooperate with adults and with peers because their thinking is *egocentric*.

This means that they tend to see a situation only from their own point of view. They are not yet capable of seeing it from another's point of view.

Even adults may sometimes have difficulty seeing things from another person's perspective.

As an exercise in perspective taking, write the word "WAS." Now, below that word, write how the word would appear to someone sitting across the table from you.

To see if what you wrote down is correct, just turn the page around to see how the word "WAS" appears when it is upside down!

You can test your child's egocentricity in a number of different ways. For example, one parent asked her three-year-old son: "Do you have a brother?"

He said: "Yes."

"What's his name?" asked his mother.

"Billy," he said.

"Does Billy have a brother?" she asked.

"No."

This three-year-old was simply incapable of seeing the world from Billy's perspective.

Another way to demonstrate egocentricity is to seat Youngster across the table from another child, Jimmy. Use two identical toy animals or pictures. Place one animal in front of Youngster.

Then say, "Jimmy sees the animal from the other side of the table. With this second animal, show me what Jimmy sees."

After he has tried—and failed—you can let him go over to the other side of the table to see what Jimmy actually sees.

Most children of this age will think that the other person will see the same view that they do. They are apparently not yet able to understand that a scene will look different to a person who sees it from a different perspective.

From a social standpoint as well as from an intellectual one, taking another person's point of view is an important skill which Youngster gradually acquires through repeated encounters with other children and adults.

This is one reason why social interaction with other children becomes very important at this age.

When playing a game that involves taking turns in rolling the dice, an egocentric child may show no consideration for another child's point of view.

He wants to continue rolling the dice until he gets a "six" as though he was the only person playing the game.

In attempting to control the behavior of a three-year-old, it is generally useless to explain how his behavior will affect another child's feelings.

Saying to him, "You will hurt Joe's feelings if you don't share your toys" will be ineffective.

But he will understand the personal consequence: "You won't be allowed to visit Joe unless you share your toys with him."

On the other hand, a young child who puts his arm around another child who is crying shows that he is growing out of egocentrism by learning to relate to another person's perspective.

At this stage of development your child is also learning to use and manipulate symbols. Language is an important part of symbolic representation, that is, it is representing an object or event by a symbol.

As a child begins to understand the meaning of words, which are symbols, they begin to take on very concrete or personal characteristics.

The word "tricycle," for example, may refer to "my tricycle which is red" but not to Susie's because it is pink.

Eventually, of course, the child must learn the abstract concept "tricycle" which may be applied to all tricycles irrespective of specific shape, color, or size.

A three-year-old will also demonstrate symbolic thought in play. He can pretend that he is "Mom" or that the large cardboard box is a "house."

Young children often deal with their feelings of anxiety or frustration by engaging in symbolic play.

These symbolic games are important therefore not only for a young child's intellectual development but also for his emotional development.

Another characteristic of a young child's thinking is what Piaget called *transductive reasoning*.

As adults we are familiar with deductive reasoning and inductive reasoning. In deductive reasoning we move from what is general to the specific.

For example, if I know that all Irish setters are red, then if someone promises to give me an Irish setter, I can conclude it will be red.

In inductive reasoning, on the other hand, we move from the specific to what is general. For example, if I note that a Labrador retriever which I have seen is black, I reason inductively that all Labrador retrievers are black.

continued on page 221

continued from page 220

In transductive reasoning, the young child moves from one particular to another particular. Sometimes the conclusion is correct. But often it is not only wrong but also amusing.

Let's consider some examples of transductive reasoning. If Jimmy is accustomed to going to the playground every afternoon, on the day you can't take him to the playground, he is likely to say, "Today didn't have an afternoon."

In other words, for him the concepts of "playground" and "afternoon" are interrelated—you can't have one without the other.

Another example of transductive reasoning is when a three-year-old has noticed that his Daddy wears a certain coat every day he goes to work.

He begins to associate the absence of the coat from the closet with Daddy being at work.

But if Daddy leaves the coat at home one day because the weather is warm, Youngster simply concludes that Daddy cannot be at work. Work and the coat are linked inseparably in his mind.

Transductive reasoning can also lead to animistic reasoning, which is the belief that inanimate objects are alive. If a child hears that the sun will rise tomorrow at six a.m., he will attribute life to the sun.

If asked: "Is the sun alive?" he may answer: "Of course, because it will rise."

Yet another characteristic of a preschooler's thinking is irreversibility. With reversible thinking a person can think about going from one point to another and then return to the starting point.

For example, if I know that 3 + 5 = 8, then with reversible thinking, I will also know that 8 - 5 = 3. A child won't be expected to have this ability until the first grade.

Until they develop reversibility, young children are at a considerable disadvantage with only irreversible thinking.

Consider, for example, the child who rides his tricycle a long way down a sloping street. As he rapidly turns the pedals he is thinking only of the good feelings he enjoys.

He is unable to weigh the consequences in reverse order, namely, that in order to return, he will have to pedal a long way uphill. He can't yet play backward in his head the actions that will be needed to return.

Even after repeating these actions many times, he will still consider it someone else's responsibility—usually Mom's or Dad's—to come get him at the bottom of the hill.

You can check your child's present state of irreversibility using Piaget's classic example with two identical balls of clay.

Let your child see you roll one ball into a long thin shape. Then ask the child if there is more clay in the round piece or in the long thin piece.

Children are usually about seven or eight years of age before they consistently answer this question correctly. To answer the problem correctly a child has to be able to

visualize mentally the long thin strip being rolled back into a ball of clay.

While the errors and fallacies of Youngster's reasoning seem obvious to adults, it is important to be aware that at three years of age, Youngster is not yet capable of such reasoning.

Hence allowances must frequently be made for faulty reasoning—even when it means going to the bottom of the hill to retrieve both him and his tricycle.

This brings us to another point about Youngster's thinking. He does not suddenly change from one form of thinking to another.

The change takes place gradually. It happens first for simple problems, then later for harder problems of the same type.

Thus we can't say that at a certain age Youngster will show one, and only one, kind of thinking.

With problem solving, the kind of thinking Youngster does depends upon the difficulty of the problem.

This in turn is related to several other factors, such as the amount of memory required, the number of items that he must attend to, as well as his general familiarity with the different aspects of the problem.

In discussing egocentricity, for example, we chose a simple situation with toy animals or pictures.

But long after Youngster is able to position the second animal correctly, he will have trouble with a more difficult problem of the same type, like how the word "WAS" would appear from the other side of the table.

Being aware of Youngster's level of development—what he can and cannot do—can help parents to gently inspire him to more advanced levels of thinking.

This awareness, as well as the opportunity to explore and interact with other preschool children are key ingredients of early childhood education. ∎

The Sounds of Music

Now is a good time for parents to give some thought to music's place in their three-year-old's life.

Every child is born with some musical aptitude and abilities which need to be developed. Musical talent is not just something that emerges full-blown at about nine or ten years of age. It is something that needs to be carefully nourished throughout the preschool years.

Young children appear to develop their musical abilities best through casual learning, such as providing musical background for their play activities, rather than through highly structured music lessons.

It is important to remember that, even in later life, most people who learn music don't become professional musicians. But they generally develop a lifelong interest in music that brings a lot of joy into their lives.

Focusing on music in your child's life is not just an investment for future happiness. It pays immediate dividends in the following ways:

• **Play activities.** Children show a natural responsiveness to music—singing, dancing, or listening to nursery rhymes—during their play.

A great benefit of music is that it enhances the learning that takes place in play by providing repetition and heightened interest in the activities.

• **Movement songs.** It is important for later school learning that young children develop good perceptual-motor coordination, for example, connecting what they hear with what they do.

Movement songs help develop coordination, for example, by improving timing, accuracy, and smoothness of muscle movements.

• **Emotional expression.** Children like to create their own music, sometimes in the form of songs with meaningless words

or original sounds. These songs help them to express their inner emotional states. Their own original songs also help them to express their independence, identity, and unique personality.

• **Relaxation and stress reduction.** For centuries parents have used lullabies to sing a child to sleep. Soothing music can also be used at other times to calm a child who experiences stress or who appears tense.

For example, a child who becomes restless and irritable on a long journey may quietly drift into sleep with the sound of soft music.

• **Educational dividends.** Apart from the benefits already listed, music has many other educational dividends. For example, through music many mental disciplines, such as attention, concentration, and memory, are learned and enhanced.

Growing Child. ®

P. O. Box 2505 • W Lafayette, IN 47996
(800) 927-7289
©Growing Child, Inc.
www.GrowingChild.com

Contributing Authors

Phil Bach, O.D., Ph.D.
Miriam Bender, Ph.D.
Joseph Braga, Ed.D.
Laurie Braga, Ph.D.
George Early, Ph.D.
Carol R. Gestwicki, M.S.
Liam Grimley, Ph.D.
Robert Hannemann, M.D., F.A.A.P.
Sylvia Kottler, M.S.
Bill Peterson, Ph.D.

In focusing attention on the place of music in child development, it is important for parents to work within their child's frame of reference rather than impose their own adult requirements.

Most three-year-old children will not respond well to structured music lessons.

Likewise, if a child is upset or tired, it is not a good time to introduce musical movement activities.

By being sensitive to a child's appropriate stage of development and inner emotional state, parents can enjoy much fun with their child while engaged in musical activities.

Children associate music with play and good times and respond with a smile and movement when they hear it. They adore it when adults take an active part in their musical experiences.

Favorable exposure to musical experiences during the early childhood years also helps develop a deeper appreciation of good music in later life. ■